# AGAINST THE DESPOTISM OF FACT

SUNY series, Studies in the Long Nineteenth Century
*Pamela K. Gilbert, editor*

# AGAINST THE DESPOTISM OF FACT

## Modernism, Capitalism, and the Irish Celt



T. J. BOYNTON

Published by State University of New York Press, Albany

Printed in the United States of America



www.sunypress.edu

Library of Congress Cataloging-in-Publication Data

Names: Boynton, T. J., [date] author.
Title: Against the despotism of fact : modernism, capitalism, and the Irish Celt / T. J. Boynton.
Description: Albany : State University of New York Press, 2021. | Series: SUNY series, studies in the long nineteenth century | Includes bibliographical references and index.
Identifiers: LCCN 2020017922 | ISBN 9781438481814 (hardcover) | ISBN 9781438481807 (paperback) | ISBN 9781438481821 (ebook)
Subjects: LCSH: English literature—Irish authors—History and criticism. | Modernism (Literature)—Ireland. | Celts in literature. | Capitalism in literature. | National characteristics, Irish, in literature. | Nationalism and literature—Ireland. | English literature—19th century—History and criticism. | English literature—20th century—History and criticism.
Classification: LCC PR8722.M6 B69 2021 | DDC 820.9/9415—dc23
LC record available at https://lccn.loc.gov/2020017922

10 9 8 7 6 5 4 3 2 1

# CONTENTS

# ACKNOWLEDGMENTS

This book is the product of more than a decade of work, work which began during my time as a student at the University of Illinois, Urbana-Champaign, which continued during my time at DePauw University and Marshall University, and which I have completed at Wichita State University. I would like to thank my former professors, fellow graduate students, my colleagues, and my students for providing stimulating and challenging environments along the way.

More specific thanks must begin with two mentors from my time at Illinois. The first is Joe Valente, whose exemplary scholarship and intellectual vigor have been an inspiration since the moment I first heard him speak. Joe's guidance during the writing of the dissertation out of which this book grew was indispensable. The second is Jed Esty, who has been an equally inspiring example of intellectual and scholarly achievement, and whose tutelage in modernism in particular was formative for me. Both Joe and Jed have continued to provide crucial assistance in bringing this book to fruition during its latter stages.

The other members of my dissertation committee also played valuable roles in the project's conception and development: Jim Hansen, whose guidance in Irish Studies, critical theory, and Beckett helped it take methodological shape; Lauren Goodlad, whose input into the earlier, Victorian reaches of its narrative helped solidify its foundation; and Vicki Mahaffey, whose contributions during my defense provided valuable insight regarding its later, Irish modernist chapters.

More recently, Mark Quigley has provided valuable input into the project. As one of its few additional, non-anonymous readers, his positive response has provided valuable affirmation and encouragement.

I would be remiss if I did not also mention the three key mentors of my undergraduate years at the tiny liberal arts school of Monmouth College in

Illinois: Craig Watson, Mark Willhardt, and Rob Hale. You three helped mold my thinking about literature at a pivotal time, and I continue to look back fondly on our years together.

I must also thank my editors at SUNY Press, Rebecca Colesworthy and, before her, Amanda Lanne-Camilli. Your help in ushering the project through the review and revision process has been pivotal in it reaching its potential.

An earlier version of chapter 1 appeared in *ELH* in 2013, while an earlier version of a portion of chapter 5 appeared in *Éire-Ireland* in 2012. I thank the journals for permission to include those materials here.

Excerpts from the poetry of W.B. Yeats are reprinted with the permission of Simon & Schuster, and the cover image of Jack B. Yeats's "A Word of Advice"/"The Plough and the Earth Spirit"/"The Woodchopper and the Tree Spirit" by George Russell (AE) is reproduced with the permission of the Artists' Right Society.

I dedicate this book to my mom, Sally Faye Boynton (1951–2007), who, in addition to being one professionally, also served as my first English teacher. I also dedicate it to my dad, Tom, and my brother and best friend, Alex.

# Introduction

## *Celticism, Capitalism, and Transnational Modernism*

Sometime around the middle of the nineteenth century, at a fortuitous intersection between the emergence of Victorian anthropology and the escalation of colonial conflict between England and Ireland, begins the career of a unique and remarkably prolific literary figure. At different points of his history, this figure can be found engaging bravely yet haplessly in tribal warfare; sitting rapt in poetic communion with nature; held captive in a London zoo; surveying a prehistoric landscape from a South American tree; suppressing insurrection in colonial India; mediating racial tensions aboard a British merchant ship; serving as a religious idol in an anticolonial Mexican revolution; protesting the influence of popular culture in turn-of-the-century Ireland; modeling the ideal citizen of the twentieth century's first postcolonial state; or deceased, with his decapitated head being worshipped in ritual dance. This is, by any measure, a distinguished record—of service domestic and foreign; military and civilian; rural and urban; real and mythological; political, cultural, and aesthetic; dramatic, poetic, and fictional—and displays a versatility, indeed a virtuosity, difficult to match in the record of modern literature. Yet this figure's achievements have yet to receive full recognition, and where they are noted, they are often denigrated.

More persistently than any of the above labors, this figure may be found performing one special task prior to his retirement sometime around World War II. Beyond his prominent role in buoying aesthetic values in a utilitarian age or in shaping the rising, incipiently global forces of anticolonial struggle, this figure was deployed to combat the harmful effects of modern capitalism. At a time when capital's evolution had begun to issue in the technological forms of the second industrial revolution and the pop-cultural manifestations of the culture industry, this figure became central to a widespread effort to comprehend and combat the perils of these processes. If the variety of this figure's employment during the period from the mid-nineteenth through the mid-twentieth centuries is without peer among his literary contemporaries, the steadfastness of his nearly century-long devotion to gauging and altering the course on which capital had set the world is even more so.

The figure to whom this sketch refers is the Irish Celt. Like many of the ancient deities in which he is thought to have believed, he displays a remarkable shape-changing capacity throughout the extensive archive of British and Irish texts he populates during the nineteenth and twentieth centuries. Across the various guises he assumes in his globetrotting heyday, however, his antagonism to the forces of capital is a constant. This book traces the history of the Irish Celt, reconstructing from his diverse manifestations in British and Irish literature his service to the cause of criticizing capitalism's depredations during the colonial, postcolonial, modern, and postmodern periods. The record of this service is a fascinating study of the Irish Celt's entanglement with some of the most significant civilizational arcs of the modern and contemporary eras, and of his utility for comprehending and criticizing them. In the hands of both British and Irish writers, the Irish Celt served as an unparalleled resource for thinking through the ramifications of imperial/colonial history and the economic forces driving and shaping that history. A study of the astonishing variety of ways in which these writers cultivated this resource thus enables a novel account of some of the most influential works of modern literature in English while also providing a window into some of the most pressing historical problems of the last two centuries.

As indexed in this capsule biography, this book takes the literary history of the Irish Celt as a point of access not only to Irish but also to British literature. Though there is an extensive critical record addressing this figure's role in the former corpus, *Against the Despotism of Fact* is unique by virtue of its simultaneous engagement with his British incarnations. This archipelagic vantage affords both a richer account of the literary history of this unique entity and a novel awareness of the extent to which the two nations were engaged in addressing a common set of problems across the colonial divide. If the Celt has served as a bugbear of postcolonial criticism over the last several decades—as a sort of Trojan horse the embrace of which doomed Ireland to the reproduction of debilitating stereotypes—the transnationality of his career as adduced in the following pages demands a reassessment of this reputation. In particular, the Irish Celt's common appeal to both British and Irish writers as an aesthetic vehicle for the interrogation of capitalism argues for his bearing a critical potential beyond his colonialist limitations.[1]

While respecting the significance of the colonial divide separating the two nations during the period in question, this book attempts to push beyond the postcolonial paradigm that has predominated in studies of their literatures in recent years. Building on work that has begun to delineate new, comparative lines of inquiry into the literary histories of Britain and Ireland, as well as on work in Irish Studies specifically that has emphasized the nation's possession of both colonial and metropolitan characteristics at the turn of the twentieth century, I argue for reframing these literatures as engaged in addressing a common set of concerns in addition to those that divided them.[2] The specific emphasis on capitalist concerns facilitates an awareness of the two nations' transnational connectivity, as, from the late nineteenth century onward, Ireland was increasingly integrated into the domestic British economy, not merely in terms of colonial relations of production and distribution but also in terms of marketing and commodity consumption. In this context, the Celt, who, from his inception in the founding text of British Celticism, Matthew Arnold's *The Study of Celtic Literature*, possessed a marked anticapitalist trait, appears not simply as an instrument of imperial racism by the British or nationalist self-sabotage by the Irish, but as a critical resource for writers of both nations.

This book takes its title from the ethnological definitions of Arnold's *Study*, and it traces the nearly century-long heritage of British and Irish Celticisms to that text's anatomy of the two nations' racial essences. In Arnold's famous description of "the Celtic nature," the Celt's anticapitalist proclivities derive from his "sentimental" biology: "Sentimental—*always ready to react against the despotism of fact* . . . [this term] lets us into the secret of its dangers and of its habitual want of success" (*Study* 84). In contrast to the "essentially Germanic" makeup of "the creeping Saxon," whose knack for "direct practical utility" Arnold credits with "augment[ing] the comforts and conveniences of life . . . Doors that open, windows that shut, locks that turn, razors that shave, coats that wear, watches that go, and a thousand more such good things," the Celt displays a "habitual," allergic resistance to such economic and technological bounty (92–93). This compound binary opposition, equating, oil-and-water-like, Saxonness with capitalist development and Celticness with resistance to it, resides at the root of a largely unacknowledged genealogy of nineteenth- and twentieth-century politics, culture, and aesthetics. By elucidating this genealogy, *Against the Despotism of Fact* offers a fresh perspective on some of the most significant experiments and innovations in modern British and Irish literature.

## CELTICIST THEORY

Most studies of the Celt have tended to marginalize Arnold's taxonomy in keeping with the more general condemnation of his thought, particularly in Irish Studies, as doggedly racist and imperialist. Gregory Castle's *Modernism and the Celtic Revival* places Arnold prominently among a group of anthropological and political thinkers responsible for a series of misrepresentations of the Irish "that invoke a binomial distinction between primitive and civilized" to consolidate British rule, and he stages his recuperation of the cultural politics of the title movement through its "ambivalent" distancing from such images (3). By this account, the Celt of fin-de-siècle Irish nationalism, insofar as he escapes "the charge of complicity" with colonialist categories of thought, does so only by breaking free of such definitions as Arnold's binary propounds (6). Sinéad Garrigan Mattar's *Primitivism, Science, and the Irish Revival* similarly argues for a Revivalist Celt founded not on *The Study* but on the doctrines of continental race science—on "Celtology" rather than Celticism.[3] Such work in Irish Studies has extended the theoretical models for understanding the challenges of identity formation during and after decolonization contained in such texts as Franz Fanon's *The Wretched of the Earth* and Partha Chatterjee's *Nationalist Thought and the Colonial World*, which argue, in the words of the latter, that "There is . . . an inherent contradictoriness in nationalist thinking . . . whose representational structure corresponds to the very structure of power [it] seeks to repudiate" (38). Such postcolonial conventional wisdom informs efforts to reposition the Celt of Irish nationalism away from the "representational structure" of Arnold's colonialism.[4]

This book seeks to restore Arnoldian concepts to a place of centrality in studies of the Celt without losing the crucial gains made by such accounts. What follows should not by any means be taken as an endorsement of Arnold's theories, which in many ways deserve the condemnation they have received in recent years for their racism, essentialism, and retrograde political legacy. Nor does this book claim that the Celticisms that followed in his wake for the ensuing century—British or Irish—rigidly or slavishly adhere to the terms of *The Study*. Rather, I contend that Arnold's Saxon-Celt binary demarcates an intellectual territory in which an extensive and diverse group of thinkers, political activists, and writers on both sides of the Anglo-Irish divide found it attractive and productive to work over the next century. I further contend that, in spite of his racial and political baggage, the Celt who inhabited this territory, with his unique proclivity for resisting capitalism, played a leading role in some of the most sophisticated and savvy efforts to interrogate and challenge its forms at an early moment of their global ascendancy. Though I will have frequent occasion to differentiate the Celticisms that compose the discourse's subsequent history from the more insidious aspects of Arnold's founding typology, the figures and texts I address remain committed throughout to the notion that the Celt bears a unique utility for efforts to gauge and navigate the challenges of a globalizing capitalist modernity. As I will show in the book's latter half, even the Irish nationalist movement of the fin de siècle, while necessarily resistant to some of the Celt's features, itself expressed such a commitment and would owe many of its signal achievements to the image of the Celt as an antagonist of capital.

To a certain extent, then, my reading of the Celt, which is committed to recovering a critical potential beyond its "complicitious" dimension, constitutes what Gayatri Spivak would call an "ab-use" of Arnold's ethnological definitions: a deployment of his concepts that "moves away" from his colonialist intentions and reconfigures them "from below"—that is, from the point of view of Irish subaltern resistance.[5] However, the particular Celticist inheritance traced here also argues for a materialist complication of postcolonial accounts. The theoretical bite of the classic three-stage, Fanonian model of decolonization depends upon the initially negative or instrumental definition of the subordinate term in the colonial binary opposition. That is to say, the progression from a first, imitative or assimilative stage of subaltern identity formation to a second, repudiative stage falls prey to what Fanon calls "the pitfalls of national consciousness" because the original formulations of colonial discourse are inherently disadvantageous and disabling to the colonized. To embrace views of the colonized as politically incompetent or unruly or as economically ineffectual seems irresistibly to "surrender to the stereotype" and thus to hamstring colonial nationalism, rendering it irreparably disadvantaged in the games of modern state formation and economic development. Thus, what is needed is indeed a Fanonian, dialectical alternative to imitative assimilation or its reactionary inverse, a "revolutionary," self-determined modality capable of fully independent identity formation.[6] If, however, the original definition of the colonized is itself already part of an effort to challenge the civilizational norms of the colonizer—if, that is, the erstwhile colonialist theorizer of race identifies in the subaltern figure a resource for criticizing hegemonic norms—then it would seem the decolonizing and postcolonial embrace of such a definition need not entirely disable efforts to throw off those same norms. In such a circumstance, the attractiveness of a stereotype may inhere not in an infantile, knee-jerk embrace of whatever traits or behaviors be opposed to "civilized" standards, but in the specificity of a trait configured in a dynamic, critical relationship to those standards.

In what follows, I argue that the anticapitalism of the Celt bears such a critical potential, and that an array of British and Irish authors seized on this potential to devise aesthetic critiques of a modernity defined by British capitalism. Both the Irish nationalist moment usually emphasized in accounts of the

Celt and the contemporaneous British moment evince a widespread embrace of the stereotype of Celtic anticapitalism, and even where this embrace is not complicated by postcolonial suspicion, it issues in aesthetic, cultural, and political projects that interrogate and offer sophisticated alternatives to both British imperialism and capitalism. Such projects affirm the critical potential residing in the anticapitalism of the Arnoldian Celt, effectuating a sort of bypass between the second and third stages of Fanon's dialectic. Devised by Arnold as an imaginative lever against an overly capitalist British civilization, the Celt would not only inspire and serve as the model for metropolitan self-revision in the decades subsequent to his coinage; he would also be exported to the colonial nation whose subjection was one of his inbuilt purposes, and in that context his anticapitalist talents would instead facilitate anticolonial resistance.

This argument accords with a materialist rejoinder to Fanonian accounts of decolonization mounted in recent years by theorists like Neil Lazarus and Laura Chrisman, who have argued, in the words of the latter, that to view the adoption of colonialist definitions as always and everywhere disabling "is to deny the capacity of formerly colonized peoples to transform structures of thought and governance" (185).[7] As we shall see, the Irish nationalist movement of the fin de siècle would coopt the basic terms of Arnold's Celticism, and it would succeed in articulating a liberatory decolonizing vision not despite but, in many ways, through that cooptation. Beyond the mere demonstrable fact of this "transformed" or ab-usive deployment of Arnoldian ideas, however, what enables such a deployment to effectuate a sort of bypass of Fanon's second and third stages is the common capitalist civilization shared by British metropole and Irish colony during the historical moment on which this book is centered. Earlier than any other colony in the British Empire, Ireland, by virtue of its domestic proximity to the metropole, became encircled within the expanding domains of modern European capital. Its situation at the turn of the twentieth century may thus be read as presaging the fully global dimensions of such expansion that would later extend to other British colonies in Africa, South Asia, and the Caribbean.[8] In some ways, Ireland's early entry into economic modernity reflects a sort of historical short-circuit between what were for other territories the temporally distant obstacles of colonialism and advanced capitalism—the latter designating not merely market dependency or an international system of resource extraction and distribution, but phenomena of mass marketing and commodity consumption. As a result of its nationalism at the turn of the century thus being addressed not only toward imperial domination but also toward a highly advanced, metropolitan capitalist hegemony, the Celt's appeal resided not simply in his potential to serve as a vehicle of identity contrast with the Saxon invader, but in his original coinage as a tool of capitalist critique. This inbuilt resistance to capital, in the unique set of Irish circumstances Joseph Valente has dubbed "metrocolonial," could be more beneficially, though not unproblematically, adopted than other stereotypes devised as an imperial wedge, because the nationalist agenda confronted there the same socioeconomic problems as Arnold himself.[9]

Much of this book offers an attempt to reckon with the implications of Ireland's colonially proleptic incorporation into the more advanced dimensions of capitalist modernity. In Ireland at the turn of the century, the decolonization process was thus complicated by the penetration of the forms of modern capitalism in ways that presage challenges only faced toward midcentury by other colonial nations. In an under-remarked passage in *The Wretched of the Earth*, Fanon, from such a mid-century vantage, addresses the additional challenge posed to postcolonial self-authorization by the dissemination of European commodities:

> Normally, there is a certain homogeneity between the mental and material level of the members of any given society and the pleasures which that society creates for itself. But in underdeveloped countries, young people have at their disposition leisure occupations designed for the youth of capitalist countries: detective novels, penny-in-the-slot machines, sexy photographs, pornographic literature, films banned to those under sixteen, and above all alcohol. In the West, the family circle, the effects of education, and the relatively high standard of living of the working classes provide a more or less efficient protection against the harmful action of these pastimes. But in an African country, where mental development is uneven, where the violent collision of two worlds has considerably shaken old traditions and thrown the universe of the perceptions out of focus, the impressionability and sensibility of the young African are at the mercy of various assaults made upon them by the very nature of Western culture. (195–96)

Though Fanon leaves this line of inquiry relatively undeveloped alongside the colonial identity dynamics that are his main concern, it bears profound implications for the Irish context of half a century earlier, as well as for the theorization of the intersection of empire and capital more generally. Experiencing through the collocation of the two influences a sort of "mental uneven development," an epistemological mismatch between the cultural products of the metropole and the economic and educational infrastructures of the colony, colonial youth at the moment of decolonization are held mentally in thrall by the pop-cultural forms of European capital. Their perceptions and their *self-perceptions* must thus overcome not only the limitations imposed by colonialist structures of thought, but those imposed by capitalist reification.

To students of the fin-de-siècle Irish Revival, Fanon's diagnosis of the dissemination of metropolitan popular culture as an exacerbative barrier to anticolonial resistance should ring immediate bells, for it also arises in many canonical tracts of Revivalist nationalism. Witness, for example, the account offered by Douglas Hyde's seminal screed against British cultural hegemony or "West Britonism," "The Necessity for De-Anglicizing Ireland":

> We must set our face sternly against penny dreadfuls, shilling shockers, and . . . the garbage of vulgar English weeklies like *Bow Bells* and *The Police Intelligence*. . . . We must strive to cultivate everything that is most racial, most smacking of the soil, most Gaelic, most Irish, because . . . this island *is* and will *ever* remain Celtic to the core. . . . On racial lines, then, we shall best develop, following the bent of our own nature; and, in order to do this, we must create a strong feeling against West-Britonism, for it . . . will overwhelm us like a flood, and we shall find ourselves toiling painfully behind the English . . . following the same fashions, only six months behind . . . reading the same books, only months behind . . . taking up the same fads, after they have become stale there, following them in our dress, literature, music, games, and ideas. . . . We will become, what, I fear, we are largely at present, a nation of imitators. (159–60)

As in the Algeria of the 1950s, so in the Ireland of the 1890s, where, by imperial proximity, the shadow of capital applies additional pressure to the politics of culture beyond the obstacle of state oppression. Where Fanon worries over slot machines, detective fiction, pornography, film, and alcohol, Hyde calls his listeners' attention to sensational fiction, tabloid reporting, fashion, popular music, and games. Just as Fanon does in his description of the disturbance of Africa's "mental development" by such commodities, which have "thrown the universe of the perceptions out of focus," so Hyde's litanies continue to light upon concern over the nation's "ideas" not being developed along independent lines. In such circumstances, the challenges of colonial identity formation do not stop at political resistance or racial self-definition, but are compounded by the suffusion of the mind of the colonized by the pop-cultural forms of capital. Different states of infrastructural development aside, this homogenization of the *consumer dimensions* of the imperial economy threatens to smother colonial resistance in its infancy by molding the perceptions of the colonized according to metropolitan norms.[10]

It is just this compound problematic that the Irish case addressed in this study presents, and it is toward this problematic that, in the aesthetic projects of a diverse group of British and Irish writers, the Celt's anticapitalist propensities bare their critical teeth. Already, in Hyde's dual commitment to a model of decolonization that extricates Ireland from British consumer products and to a postcolonial identity "Celtic to the core," we gain a glimpse into the manner in which Arnoldian concepts, in the colonially divided but economically merged Anglo-Irish situation of the late nineteenth and early twentieth centuries, could mobilize a liberatory vision despite their colonialist coinage. In response to the particular problematic outlined here via Hyde and Fanon, that of the mental domination of the colonized by the reifying tendencies of capital, Celticism evinces a counterhegemonic utility slighted in prior accounts, one that generates a host of insights regarding the challenges posed by the insidious imbrication of empire and popular culture. This study will argue that Celticism became a powerful discourse for diagnosing and resisting the manner in which, at the moment of decolonization, the reification of mental perceptions and cultural values produced by such products as Hyde and Fanon list threatens to contribute to the reproduction of imperial hegemony and, where decolonization succeeds, to continue to mold postcolonial minds according to imperial and capitalist priorities.

Through its critical responsiveness to such economic phenomena, Celticism in fact encompasses a series of cultural concerns typically considered alien to both metropolitan and colonial history circa 1900. Namely, in the trajectory between Hyde's 1890s Ireland and Fanon's 1950s Africa, we witness a major segment of the route traveled by European capital's pop-cultural products during the process of economic globalization. This circuit places turn-of-the-century Ireland at an early stage of the connective processes in which our contemporary world is so extensively entangled, and it locates Ireland during the period of this study in an oddly anachronistic mode of cultural experience more often associated with theories of *post*modernity. Both passages above may be read as linking postcolonial and Marxist or neo-Marxist theoretical models like those contained in Theodor Adorno and Max Horkheimer's *Dialectic of Enlightenment* and in other texts such as Jean Baudrillard's *Simulacra and Simulation* and Guy Debord's *Society of the Spectacle*. This book will argue that the more sophisticated of the Celticisms that emerged in Arnold's wake mount a prescient critique of the entanglement of colonialism, decolonization, and postcoloniality with an incipient form of postmodern cultural reification. It will suggest that the especially refined form of Celticism advanced by Irish writers such as W.B. Yeats, J.M. Synge, and James Stephens in the early twentieth century positions the Celt as a sort of reification detector—an instrument for identifying and resisting the culture industry's insidious colonial effects. Celticism, in this context, constitutes an early and especially revealing chapter in the larger story of the global spread of postmodern cultural forms and their complication of the legacies of empire.[11]

What enables the Celt to serve as such an instrument is the particular aesthetic traits Arnold and his successors attribute to him alongside his talent for economic resistance. *The Study* in fact links these two characteristics directly in a binary opposition that is foundational to Celticism's subsequent history. As he advocates for a greater appreciation of the contributions of the junior, Celtic component of the predominantly Saxon modality he calls "the composite English genius," Arnold assigns an inverse proportionality to the Celt's material and aesthetic capacities: "Style is the most striking quality of [his] poetry. Celtic poetry seems to make up to itself for being unable to master the world . . . by throwing all its force into style, by bending language . . . to its will, and expressing the ideas it has with an unsurpassable intensity, elevation, and effect" (63). The Celt's sentimentality, if an economic and political disadvantage, bestows an equal aesthetic advantage, generating a "Titanism in poetry" that informs not just Irish or Welsh but the best English literature (67). Arnold traces this aesthetic potency to "the Celt's quick feeling," "his indomitable personality," and "his sensibility and nervous exaltation," which together form a sort of biological wellspring of responsiveness to what he calls "the magic of nature"—"her weird power and fairy charm" (70–71). This potent capacity, Arnold hopes, will "free" the English "from hardness and Philistinism," an intellectual stagnation that he elsewhere defines as the baleful flipside to the Saxon knack for "direct practical utility" (78).

This compound opposition between Saxon and Celt, capital and the aesthetic constitutes the major through-line of nearly a century of British and Irish experiments in politics, culture, and literature to follow. Throughout this heritage, it is the conception of the Celt's compound biological repulsion of capital and aesthetic attunement to nature's "Titanism" that enables him to serve as a sort of reification detector. The opposition of a passional, "magical" aesthetic to the forms of capital outfits the Celt with a preternatural sensitivity to the impingements of the latter on the human organism. The Celt, in this sense, is not simply a critical resource for interrogating capital's transformation of human consciousness, but a fully *negative-dialectical* one. His knack for both apprehending and embodying nature's primordiality outfits him with a heightened awareness of capital's ontological encroachments, and his "quick feeling" in turn furnishes an aesthetic "style" that throws such encroachments into relief. A passage from Adorno's *Aesthetic Theory* on the critical utility of the sublime helps elucidate this potential. Adorno's description of this utility emerges from a dense critique of the limitations of the Kantian sublime:

> By its transplantation into art the Kantian definition of the sublime is driven beyond its boundaries. According to this definition, spirit, in its empirical powerlessness vis-à-vis nature, experiences its intelligible essence as one that is superior to nature. However, given that the sublime is supposed to be felt in the face of nature, the theory of subjective constitution implies that nature itself is sublime; self-reflection in the face of its sublimity anticipates something of a reconciliation with nature. Nature, no longer oppressed by spirit, frees itself from . . . subjective sovereignty. Such emancipation would be a return of nature, and it—the counterimage of mere existence—is the sublime. Through the traits of domination evident in its dimensions of power and magnitude, the sublime speaks against domination. . . . The feeling of the sublime does not correspond immediately with what appears; towering mountains are eloquent not as what crushes overwhelmingly but as images of a space liberated from fetters and strictures, a liberation in which it is possible to participate. The legacy of the sublime is unassuaged negativity, as stark and illusionless as once promised by the semblance of the sublime. (196–99)

Adorno here reverses Kant's confinement of the sublime within the phenomenal sovereignty of the subject by emphasizing nature's excess of this rationalizing maneuver, and he goes on to locate a critical potential in specifically aesthetic representations of this excess.[12] "Self-reflection in the face of nature," representation of the self in the midst of nature's sublimity, gives the slip to the Kantian sublation of the latter, releasing its potential to serve as the "counterimage of existence," the latter being defined as suffused with the "domination" of capitalist modernity.[13] Adorno's dialectical rumination avoids the commonsense equation of sublime effects with those of such domination, insisting that "the feeling of the sublime does not correspond immediately with what appears." Rather, domination inheres in the Kantian effort to "subject" the sublime to rational representation or apprehension, and thus, preserving its disturbing power from such subjection inspires "images of a space limited from fetters and strictures." A properly sublime aesthetic is in this sense a "negative" resource bodying forth a view of "a liberation in which it is possible to participate."[14]

Adorno's terms are remarkably close to Arnold's: just as Arnold positions Celtic style as a Titanic representation of nature's "weird power," and just as he opposes this aesthetic capacity as a resource for "freeing" the English from modernity's "hardness and Philistinism," so Adorno defines sublime aesthetics as a spur toward resisting modernity's rationalizing and dominatory effects. It is in this manner that a Celticist aesthetics conceived on Arnoldian lines can serve as a negative, sublime "counterimage" of capitalist modernity.[15] This positioning of the Celt as the biological bearer of a Titanic, magical "style" capable of both registering capital's ontological depredations and helping envision alternative social modalities bears the seeds for a host of experiments by British and Irish writers over the next century. Indeed, I will claim that the radical aesthetic visions to which Arnold's seminal formulations gave rise locate Celticism at the root of a significant body of modernist formal innovations.

## CELTICIST MODERNISMS

In addition to the Celt's affinities with the Adornoan sublime, the binary of Celt and capital bears affinities with another binary opposition critics have perennially found central to modernist aesthetics, Friedrich Nietzsche's opposition between the Dionysian and the Apollonian in *The Birth of Tragedy*.[16] Invoking this binary and defining the aesthetic capacity of the Celt as racially ingrained brings *Against the Despotism of Fact* into the orbit of critical discussions of modernism and race that have emerged in recent decades. Many of these discussions have proceeded under the "primitivism" paradigm, which has traced the debt of Euro-American modernism to the nineteenth-century pseudosciences of anthropology and ethnology and has chronicled the widespread modernist effort to embrace "primitive" over "civilized" values, social institutions, and aesthetic forms. While recent studies such as Urmila Seshagiri's *Race and the Modernist Imagination* and the edited volume *Modernism and Race* (Len Platt) have made some progress in pushing beyond the binary terms of this schema, the relative scarcity of such efforts may be taken as affirmation of modernism's deep indebtedness to the Victorian racial episteme.[17] Given its Arnoldian origins, Celticism necessarily shares this debt, and, through its central distinction between Saxon and Celt, it often functions as a primitivist aesthetic discourse.[18] The Celticist modernisms traced in what follows suggest, however, that the study of modernism and race cannot stop at simple condemnations of racism or essentialism but must continue to probe the agendas that modernists used the languages of race to pursue. I am in sympathy with Richard Begam and Michael Valdez Moses when they remark, in the introduction to the edited volume *Modernism and Colonialism*, that recent criticism "has sometimes pushed modernism too far . . . treating it as indistinguishable from colonialism," and I would extend this assessment to the modernist reliance on Victorian race theory (6). Particularly in the case of the Celt's opposition to the global march of capital—deriving partly from the anticapitalist bent of Arnold's original definitions and partly from the sheer creativity of the aesthetic visions to which Celticism gave rise—I argue for scaling back the tendency to view primitivism as inevitably baleful.[19]

This is not to say, however, that the modernist Celticisms traced here rigidly adhere to the script laid down by Arnold, or even that they all evince a primitivist aesthetic more generally. A number of the authors addressed in subsequent chapters do rely fairly directly on Arnold's taxonomy, and many of them do, indeed, pursue its exfoliation toward primitivist visions. Often, however, in the hands of modernist writers whose aesthetic projects conduct searching examinations of the prevailing norms and tendencies of British modernity, Celticist aesthetics leads to outcomes that deviate from the Victorian anthropological script and contribute to what Seshagiri calls "the erosion of Victorian-era racial codes" (9). Beyond such expansions of the aesthetic and ideological ambit of original Celticism, it is the particular negative, critical capacity of the discourse relative to the civilizational forms of capital that drives modernist innovation. Even in texts that deviate from Arnold's definitions to imagine more capacious and dynamic notions of Irishness, the Celt's positioning as a uniquely sensitive instrument for registering and resisting capitalism's pressures proves pivotal. Especially in the case of what I will argue—along with Castle but in contrast to a number of other critics—is the modernism of the Irish Literary Revival, in the hands of writers such as William Butler Yeats and John Millington Synge, the Celt's aptitude for capitalist critique underwrites aesthetic visions whose innovations derive from the effort to gauge, comprehend, and resist the effects of British capital in its productive, distributive, and, especially, pop-cultural dimensions.[20]

This last area of Celticist modernisms' critical stance toward capital—popular culture—draws the readings to follow into another prominent context in recent modernist studies in addition to that of race. In the wake of Michael North's pathbreaking *Reading 1922*, there has been a marked shift toward recognition of the pop-cultural affiliations of modernist aesthetics. North's bold relocation of Anglo-American modernism "across the great divide" previously viewed as separating modernist works and mass- or pop-cultural artifacts and media forged a new paradigm that has since driven much important work in the so-called New Modernist Studies. The edited volume *Bad Modernisms* (Walkowitz and Mao), North's own subsequent *Camera Works* and *Machine-Age Comedy*, and Enda Duffy's *The Speed Handbook*, among numerous other studies, have fleshed out and expanded this paradigm in recent years, resulting in a reconfigured image of modernism's relationship to "pulp" literature, photography, advertising, film, the automobile, and innumerable other forms of early-twentieth-century popular expression.[21] *Against the Despotism of Fact* builds on such work by reading Celticist aesthetics as a medium through which a number of prominent modernists interrogated pop-cultural forms such as advertising, fashion, the music hall, tabloid reporting, and film. Especially in its Irish half, it shows that Celticism's anticapitalist utility served as an imaginative resource for early modernist writers such as Yeats, Synge, and James Stephens seeking to stem the tide of cultural reification emanating from the British metropole, as well as for later modernists such as Joyce, the late Yeats, Flann O'Brien, and Samuel Beckett, who instead willingly (sometimes exuberantly) submitted their work to capital's suffusion of popular perceptions. Throughout such aesthetic negotiations with capital's pop-cultural dimensions, the Celt's special sensitivity to reification appears again and again.

Earlier, I claimed that the Celt's entanglement with capital in the metrocolonial context of fin-de-siècle Ireland places him in contact with an incipient form of the postmodernity that has since engulfed much of the remainder of the globe. The location of the Celticist modernisms traced here at an early stage of this globalization process also places him in at least one further context within the new modernist studies, one that the title of this study invokes directly and that the foregoing emphasis on theoretical considerations of Irishness should not be read to belie: transnationalism. Both Irish modernist writers situated at the cutting edge of such economic processes and British ones attuned to their portents would call upon the Celt's unique talents as a means of confronting them. Their parallel and, in some cases, explicitly allied efforts render Celticism a fully transnational discourse—one capable of serving the cultural and aesthetic purposes of thinkers and writers across the divide (equally great) separating metropole and colony. The various Celticisms they devised express a larger, archipelagic sensibility that anticipates later global commonalities like those indexed in the passage from Fanon above.[22]

The distinctive combination of race theory, capitalist critique, and aesthetic experimentation that is the signature of Celticist modernisms also bears a distinctive gender dimension. Most notably, Celticism seems to have held particular appeal for *male* writers. This fact is most readily explicable as an outgrowth of Arnold's own gendering of the Celt: "the sensibility of the Celtic nature, its nervous exaltation, have something feminine in them, and the Celt is thus peculiarly disposed to feel the spell of the feminine idiosyncrasy" (46). Building upon the French ethnologist Ernest Renan's definition of the Celts as an "essentially feminine race," Arnold's formulations locate the Celt's "sentimental" capacity beyond the normative qualities of capitalist modernity. In this sense, later Celticists exfoliating this capacity may be viewed as exemplars of what Rita Felski, in *The Gender of Modernity*, calls "the feminized male": writers who, in order to elude an overly rigid modern regime often coded as male by the Victorian logic of the "separate spheres," embraced qualities conceived as female as an oppositional strategy. The modernist embrace of the Arnoldian Celt—himself, as the quotations above illustrate, a sort of feminized male—is thus a gendered as well as racialized strategy for antagonizing the reifying tendencies of capitalist rationalization.[23] It is important to note, however, that where Felski's gender-switching male modernists are often ironic or parodic in their dalliances with femininity, especially in the hands of Irish writers pursuing an essentialist rationale for decolonization, Celticist modernisms' gender commitments are correspondingly earnest. Across the imperial divide, conversely, with writers such as Doyle, Kipling, and Conrad whose Irish investments were rather different, we shall indeed encounter versions of Celticism that handle its primitive and feminine components through a layer of ironic distance.

This is not to suggest that women did not participate in Celticism. Particularly in Revivalist Ireland, a number of prominent women such as Lady Augusta Gregory, Alice Milligan, and Maud Gonne full-throatedly embraced Celticist anticapitalism as a key component of their nationalist agendas. Such efforts will come to the fore of this study in chapters 4 and 5, where attention will turn, respectively, to the Revival's particular iteration of Celticism and the efforts of its modernist participants to reform the popular-cultural predilections of the young, female Irish consumer. As chapter 4 will address, however, Revivalist literature shows a marked split between literary work that aspired to practical, popular contributions to decolonization—works that Yeats would dismissively dub "propagandist"—and works that envisioned successful decolonization as inseparable from formal challenges to prevailing, colonial norms. Whereas in the case of British modernism the paucity of female Celticists is explicable mainly through the lack of a deep investment in matters Irish by prominent figures such as Virginia Woolf, Mina Loy, Mary Butts, and Dorothy Richardson, in the case of Ireland, it is the commitment of writers like Gregory, Milligan, and others such as Katherine Tynan to more popular and accessible literary forms that best explains the scarcity of female Celticist modernisms. As chapter 5 will suggest, if this commitment tended not to issue in the more avant-garde challenges to capitalist reification of which Celticism would prove capable, the judgment that more traditional styles and genres were better suited to galvanizing the Irish public would prove a sound one.[24]

## CELTICIST MODERNITIES

Much of the best work being done in transnational modernist studies heeds warnings laid down by postcolonial theorists that the "transnational turn," if not nuanced in relation to the uneven history and legacies of Western colonialism/imperialism, threatens to proffer a shallow and insufficiently differentiated understanding of contemporary experience.[25] Books such as Rebecca Walkowicz's *Cosmopolitan Style*, Matthew Hart's *Nations of Nothing but Poetry*, Peter Kalliney's *Commonwealth of Letters*, Jed Esty's *Unseasonable Youth*, and Susan Stanford Friedman's *Planetary Modernisms* have thus, in the words of the editors of the influential volume *Postcolonial Studies and Beyond* (Loomba et al.), usefully deployed "postcolonial studies as a critical strain posed within and against, as well as antecedent to, dominant notions of globalization" (8).[26] What is needed to register the complexities of the transition of territories like Ireland to a larger global economic order is a method that remains sensitive to the legacies of colonial subalternity and underdevelopment while also attending to the ways in which postcolonial nations now share an economic modernity and cultural postmodernity with both other former colonies and the erstwhile metropolitan core. This study tries to achieve such an account by addressing the distinct experiences bred by the two nations' colonial differentiation while at the same time suggesting that their economic entanglement circa 1900 bears the seeds of larger, global commonalities.

The dual or split attention of transnational modernist studies of course stems from a much larger intellectual project underway in recent years devoted to leavening universal narratives like that of "globalization theory" with particularizing approaches devoted to conceptualizing states of indigeneity and subalternity: that of alternative modernities. This theoretical paradigm has guided much work both in postcolonial studies "and beyond" in recent years, and has expanded the notion of modernity to reflect adaptive, indigenizing inflections of its otherwise-Eurocentric narrative trajectory by formerly colonized peoples throughout the globe. As outlined in Dilip Gaonkar's seminal brief for the concept, such "alternatives" have been defined as emerging through complicated "cultural" modifications to the "societal" pressures placed on colonial and postcolonial territories through imperial and capitalist development. Against the "convergence" produced by such material impositions are situated "divergences" facilitative of "creative adaptations" of modernity's master narratives (18). It is noteworthy, relative to this study's reassessment of Matthew Arnold, that the notion of "culture" as a critical, interrogative resource pitted against "societal" modernization centrally informs such alternatives for Gaonkar. More importantly than this Enlightenment-based definition, however, Gaonkar also deploys the later conception of culture not as an agency for criticizing modernity's trajectories, but as a term for the "whole way of life" of a particular people—in the formulation of another text devoted to envisioning "cultural" alternatives to "societal" limitations, Raymond Williams's *Culture and Society*. Gaonkar in fact protests against the notion that the Arnoldian concept is solely responsible for driving such alternatives when he describes that "cultural modernity" does not "inevitably take the form of an adversary culture that privileges the individual's need for self-expression and self-realization over the claims of the community" (16). Alternatives to modernity's trajectory may thus emerge both through an Arnoldian conception of culture as—again in Williams's terms—"an abstraction" denoting "the practical separation of certain moral and intellectual activities from the driven impetus of a new kind of society," activities that come to serve "as a court of human appeal, to be set over the processes of practical social judgment and yet to offer itself as a mitigating and rallying alternative," and through the notion of culture "as an absolute," as "a mode of interpreting all our common experience" (*Culture and Society* xviii). This second imperative of Gaonkar's program, which locates in "the claims of the community" and its "whole way of life" a divergent shunting of modernization's narrative of convergence, has proved especially central to work in alternative modernities.[27]

*Against the Despotism of Fact* necessarily bears a complicated relationship with the alternative modernities paradigm through its claim that both British and Irish Celticisms, while distinct through their metropolitan and colonial vantages, together propound a critical perspective on the global telos of capital. In what follows, I indeed note the ways in which Irish writers deviate from their British counterparts through their greater intimacy with "the claims of the community" of the Irish, but I suggest that beyond such differences British and Irish Celticisms, especially the modernist Celticisms emanating from these two metrocolonial counterparts, in many ways express a common alternative vision. I read Celticism in both its economic and aesthetic dimensions as the critical resource for an alternative modernity in both "cultural" senses: as an "adversary," "moral and intellectual" discourse pitted against the excesses of British imperial and capitalist development, and as an "absolute" whose contents—especially for Irish Celticists but also for British ones—derive from the conception of Irishness as a "whole way of life." The readings to follow thus trace how the discourse's transnationality embodies what Gaonkar describes as "the elusive and fragmentary band of similarities that surface unexpectedly on the axis of divergence," with the exception that in this case, such similarities connect not two colonized communities (on the model of "minor transnationalisms") but the colonized community and the metropolitan one (23).[28]

Many proponents of alternative modernities theory would find dubious, if not outright objectionable, my suggestion that such similarities span the colonial divide between England and Ireland and my further suggestion that these similarities derive from the very economic development processes the theory arose as a mode of questioning. The question of whether colonial and postcolonial histories either conform to the teleological explanatory model of modernization theory and the dialectical-materialist model of Marxist historiography or confound such models of course undergirds the claims of alternative modernities proponents, as well as those of transnational and global modernisms. The so-called "difference versus development" debate has raged for decades between postcolonial and Marxist proponents, and has recently been reenergized by the acrimonious reception of Vivek Chibber's broadside on Subaltern Studies, *Postcolonial Theory and the Specter of Capital*.[29] Subaltern Studies theorists themselves, however, against the more reductive tendencies of Chibber's account, often avow the need to recognize capital's structuring influence and even embrace the potential benefits of economic and infrastructural development as a handmaiden to postcolonial agency. Dipesh Chakrabarty's influential conception of the "two histories of capital" in *Provincializing Europe* highlights these aspects by stressing the imperative of allowing "both the universal history of capital and the politics of human belonging . . . to interrupt each other's narrative" (70), while Spivak's advocacy for "aesthetic education in the era of globalization" depends directly on the development of postcolonial "societal" infrastructures for its practical effectuation (Spivak, *Aesthetic* 4).[30] Jed Esty's formulation "one world system, many modernities," offered as a "working compromise" between the notion of incommensurable, global cultural difference and the Marxist view of a world structured by the universality of capital, aptly renders the kind of mixed methodology required for respecting both claims—and indeed for comprehending the contemporary world in both its unity and diversity (200–201).[31]

The critical narrative of modernity offered in the following pages takes its methodological cue from such studies by situating Celticism as an alternative modality resistant to capital's teleology but at the same time responsive to that teleology's material force. I will argue that the history of the Celt reaches its logical and practical conclusion in decolonizing Irish visions and postcolonial Irish projects devoted to imagining and enacting an alternative economic development in tune with the Irish Celt's anticapitalist vitality. Ultimately, however, I will argue that this history provides evidence for the view that capitalism tends to subsume not only precapitalist cultural formations but also efforts to forge civilizational alternatives amid capital's global shadow. I show that for a number of complex reasons, a viable Irish alternative capable of evading capital's depredations and fulfilling Celticism's potential never successfully took shape. The project begun by Arnold terminates in the early years of the postcolonial Irish state, whose stultifying cultural and economic vision rings the death knell of the discourse's alternative potential. In the wake of the full-throated Irish embrace of capital undertaken in the 1950s and, more recently, in the 1990s during the financial boom of the Celtic Tiger, the nation has now long since capitulated to the capitalist world system and abandoned that portion of its self-conception that viewed capital as a threat to the national identity just as grave as British domination.[32] This study is thus just as much an archeology (in the non-Foucaultian sense) of the alternative modernity it depicts as it is a genealogy. In the retrospective vantage afforded by this genealogy, the Irish Celt appears, in ironic fulfillment of his sublime, Nietzschean potential, as the tragic hero of a major chapter in the history of capital's global ascendancy.

This book consists of two parts, each devoted to one half of the transnational narrative of Celticism outlined here. Given the discourse's British origins, the first half traces its efflorescence within the metro- portion of the metrocolonial archipelago. Chapter 1 extends and augments the analysis of Arnold's *Study* offered above and consolidates my reading of his Celticism as a radical anticapitalist and aesthetic discourse. I set Arnold's Celt alongside both his own critique of the "machinery" of capitalism in *Culture and Anarchy* and contemporaneous critiques by thinkers like Karl Marx, arguing, first, that Arnold positions the Celt as a "mitigating and rallying alternative" to modernity's depredations similar to but more radical than that of culture, and, second, that his ethnological account identifies in the Celt the same propensities Marx identified in communism. Arnold's definition of capitalism as an inherently Saxon modality racially repulsive to the Celt sets the terms for the colonial, economic, and aesthetic binaries that mark Celticism—and the literary, cultural, and political programs it inspired—for the duration of its history. The chapter concludes by comparing the aesthetic capacities with which Arnold imbues the Celt to those described as "Dionysian" by Nietzsche, arguing that these pave the way for the figure's later deployment in British and Irish primitivist modernisms.

Chapter 2 focuses on premodernist Celticist aesthetics by British writers such as Arthur Conan Doyle and Rudyard Kipling. It lays the foundation for discussion of their work by conducting the first of two major historical supplementations of Arnold's theories, both of which are designed to ground the Celticisms that succeed his in a larger set of considerations derived from the material realities of Irishness at the turn of the century. This first supplementation argues that because the Irish in the late nineteenth century were in several respects both metropolitan and colonial subjects, and because British popular-cultural characterizations defined them as both racially white and non-white, they came to be viewed as a hybrid racial group possessed of both civilized and primitive tendencies. This mix of attributes led imperialist writers like Doyle and Kipling to view the Irish as a uniquely advantageous imaginative resource. I argue that imperial-romantic fictions such as *The Hound of the Baskervilles* and *Kim* seize on this putative hybridity to devise Irish protagonists who utilize primitive commonalities to infiltrate resistant native populations in such locales as Ireland and India and subjugate them to the imperial authorities. The "civilized" features of these hybrid protagonists thus serve as the medium for the global consolidation of empire and capital in these pre-modernist texts, whose aesthetic forms likewise disclose a rational epistemology reflective of hegemonic priorities.

Chapter 3 argues the reverse of the second: that, in the hands of modernist British writers such as Conrad and D.H. Lawrence, the hybridity of the Irish Celt becomes the means for destabilizing imperial and capitalist values. The same racial flexibility that outfitted imperialists like Doyle and Kipling with the tools to undermine native resistance provides such writers with the tools to undermine British hegemony through the cultivation of racial primitivity. Where imperial-romantic Celticists devise straightforward, realistic adventure tales that embody imperialist fantasy, in keeping with their agenda of destabilizing the hegemonic forms of the metropole, Conrad's *The Nigger of the "Narcissus"* and Lawrence's *The Plumed Serpent* instead fashion difficult, "magical," and avant-garde aesthetic forms as the vehicles for countercultural visions. Just as in imperial romance the Celt's metropolitan traits provide for his contribution to the imperial civilizing mission, so in modernism his colonial traits, in particular that of Arnoldian "sentimentality," facilitate imperially subversive aesthetic, political, and economic visions.

Chapter 4 offers a second major historical supplementation of the Celticist heritage by chronicling the deployment of Celticist ideals in the Irish Revival. This first Irish chapter corresponds to both the discussion of Arnold in chapter 1 and the historical survey at the beginning of chapter 2, and seeks to elucidate the Irish discourse of Celticism as those sections did the British. It begins by tracing the vast body of nationalist writing that defined Irishness as resistant to Saxon modernity, arguing that it shows the emergence of a dispute between different ideological versions of Celticism—that of popular, Catholic nationalism and that of the "Literary Revival"—over the proper methods for overthrowing British capital. It outlines three components to what I call Revivalist anticapitalism—a general critique of the civilizational forms of capital, a specific critique of the commodity form, and a practical effort to "Celticize" the Irish economy—and argues that the divergent perspectives of Catholic nationalists such as D.P. Moran and Arthur Griffith and Literary Revivalists such as W.B. Yeats, Edward Martyn, and J.M. Synge drove a hegemonic war of position over the postcolonial state's projected form. I claim that while the Literary Revival's Celticism offered a more radical capitalist critique, it was popular Celticism that ultimately and deleteriously won the day, thus hemming nationalist anticapitalism into a repressive and chauvinistic ideological box and disabling later cultural and economic efforts after independence.

Chapter 5 is devoted to the literature of the Revival and its contribution to the project of anticapitalist decolonization. It argues that Revivalist works by Yeats, Synge, and James Stephens devise modernist aesthetic innovations as vehicles for the Celticist critique of British capital, and it highlights the central place that specific nationalist concerns over the Anglicization of the young, Irish female consumer played in these efforts. I read Yeats's *The Land of Heart's Desire* as fulfilling the anticapitalist potential of a "sublime" Celticist primitivism conceived on Adornoan and Nietzschean lines, and I read Synge's *The Playboy of the Western World* and Stephens's *The Charwoman's Daughter* as utilizing the Celt's sentimental sensitivity to reification as the basis for critiques of the British culture industry. I argue that these critiques, by attempting to prevent the reification of Irish identity in general and that of Irish females in particular, anticipate the postmodern insights of theorists such as Guy Debord and Jean Baudrillard and thus locate the Revival at an early stage of the global spread of capitalist pop culture. Synge and Stephens combat a phenomenon I call "the colonial spectacle," whereby the consumption of capitalist media compounds the challenges to decolonization by reifying the thralldom of the colonized to imperial norms.

Chapter 6 places a group of Irish writers traditionally viewed as simply modernist—James Joyce, Yeats, and Flann O'Brien—instead, along with Samuel Beckett, in the period of late modernism by virtue of their critical deflation of the anticolonial, anticapitalist aesthetics addressed in chapter 5. These writers devise a modernism that, while engaging the same racial, socio-political, and economic terms as the Literary Revival, instead inverts the triumphal nationalism of those works to stage the historical failure and collapse of the Irish Celticist project. The concept of the colonial spectacle proves even more central to these texts than to those of the Revival, with the crucial difference that here, the emphasis falls on the nation's engulfment by this reifying technology and the consequent perpetuation of the political and economic modes of the colonial era. Offering, variously, lamentations and lampoons of the process by which postcolonial Ireland betrayed its anti-capitalist ideals and recrudesced toward the very "Saxon" norms that inspired them, Irish late modernism in such texts as *Ulysses, The Death of Cuchulain, At Swim-Two-Birds*, and *Murphy* illustrates the ultimate failure of the Celt's century-long campaign against capitalist modernity.

# PART I

# British Celticism

CHAPTER 1

# Matthew Arnold, the Ontology of English Capitalism, and the Rebirth of Celtic Tragedy

The above introduction has already begun to indicate the centrality of Matthew Arnold to the genealogy of Celticism as an anticapitalist, aesthetic discourse. The current chapter will build on the claims made thus far through a more detailed reading of Arnold's race-minded texts of the mid-1860s, *Culture and Anarchy* and *The Study of Celtic Literature*, with an eye to their economic and aesthetic dimensions. Comprehending how these texts situate Arnold's Celt and the Celticist heritage to follow requires grounding his race theories in the larger anthropological milieu in which he wrote. Working from a set of "scientific" assumptions that encoded cultural tendencies as manifestations of biology, Arnold's criticism would help shape a broad array of political, economic, and aesthetic notions central to subsequent Anglo-Irish history, chief among them the notion of an inherently capitalist, Saxon England in need of supplementation by an inherently aesthetic Celticness. Arnold's project of culture expresses what we might call a *creative-determinist* vision for the recalibration of an overly capitalistic Englishness, and through the recovery of its racial nuances we shall be better positioned to track the long unfolding of the agon of Celt and capital even where its underlying sociohistorical terms are less explicit, as well as to begin to grasp the manner in which Celticism would come to offer an alternative to capitalist modernity's homogenizing drive.

## *CULTURE AND ANARCHY*: TEUTONIC DISCOURSE AND "THE MANUFACTURE OF PHILISTINES"

Pinpointing the racial assumptions of Arnold's criticism is difficult, especially in *Culture and Anarchy*. Beginning with the pathbreaking claims of Robert

J.C. Young's *Colonial Desire* (1995), ethnologically minded critics have typically taken Arnold's comments on the "Hellenic" and "Hebraic" affiliations of the English as fully encapsulating his racialization of the nation's history.[1] The impression that *Culture and Anarchy* defines Englishness as inherently Hellenic derives from the following passage, from the chapter that names these two groups in its title: "Science has now made visible to everybody the great and pregnant elements of difference which lie in race, and in how signal a manner they make the genius and history of an Indo-European people vary from those of a Semitic people. Hellenism is of Indo-European growth, Hebraism is of Semitic growth; and we English, a nation of Indo-European stock, seem to belong naturally to the movement of Hellenism" (135–36). It would seem a fairly straightforward conclusion that Arnold defines the English as Indo-European, and therefore linked biologically to the Greek civilization he admires for its "spontaneity of consciousness," in contrast to the "strictness of conscience" that defines the opposed tendency of Hebraism (128). While noting that Arnold is sometimes inconsistent in the attributes he ascribes to the national biology, ethnological readers have understandably tended to view Arnold's idea of Englishness as strictly Hellenic.[2]

But Arnold's conflation of English and Greek, while prominent in the text, is hard to square with comments that arise elsewhere in *Culture and Anarchy*. Specifically, in "Barbarians, Philistines, Populace," Arnold points repeatedly to what he calls "the want of flexibility of our race" as a source of its Hebraic tendencies (123). How can readers make sense of this comment, which seems to run directly counter to the Hellenic "gift" of the English for "imaginatively acknowledging the multiform aspects of the problem of life" (136)? Vincent Pecora's hypothesis that Hebraism is both an external influence—a religious import that stunts the natural English tendency toward Hellenic creative consciousness—and also the outcropping of a latent English racial element is suggestive but lacks a discursive frame by which to define this mysterious, Hebraic gene (Pecora 376).

Part of the confusion that arises in the attempt to parse Arnold's ethnological definitions derives from the fact that, in terms of its compositional history, *Culture and Anarchy* consists of a patchwork of separately written essays, and therefore cannot quite be read as the unified expression of a single set of ideas. Given this partial dispersal of intent across the book's six chapters, it is not so surprising that Arnold would shuttle between seemingly disparate claims.[3] I would suggest, however, that there is an unregistered coherence to the text's racial maneuverings, a coherence that derives from its persistent evocation of the contemporary discourse of Teutonism. Only by attending to the operations of this discourse can the reader identify the racial underpinnings of Arnold's key concepts, culture and "machinery," and only through such a modified assessment can the reader then locate Arnold amid the broader Victorian concerns to which his work responds. Because his reliance on this discourse spans both *Culture and Anarchy* and *The Study*, explicating the Teutonic dimension of the former text will prepare the way for consideration of the latter, where Arnold's ethnological gaze expands beyond Britain to take in the entire United Kingdom.

Peter Mandler, along with others such as L.P. Curtis Jr. and George Stocking, has argued that the dominant English racial ideology at mid-century was Teutonism, a doctrine that traced the nation's heritage to barbarian communities in northern Europe. Citing among other sources John Mitchell Kemble's *The Saxons in England* (1849), Mandler lists several central tenets of Teutonic discourse, foremost among them "individual liberty" (53). The "spirit of independence" discovered by Kemble in the "misty forests" of ancient Germany grew into what Mandler terms an "autostereotype" of English racial thought, producing a full-blown "Teutonic Zeitgeist" by the time of Arnold's writing (53–54, 96). Mandler notes that Arnold himself coined the pejorative phrase "Teutomania" to describe the racial-nationalist fanaticism of his father Thomas, and states that during the 1860s public credence in this autostereotype was at its height (88–89). It should not surprise us, therefore, to find this discourse surfacing in *Culture and Anarchy*, the constituent essays of which Arnold penned around 1867.[4] In addition to individual liberty, Mandler enumerates other elements of the Teutonic myth such as "orderliness" and "domesticity" to illustrate the extent to which it served to valorize contemporary middle-class norms. Beyond these attributes, however, Mandler lists another characteristic, one with even more direct bearing on *Culture and Anarchy*: "industry." In Mandler's account, the English came to believe their stock "combined industry and independence, which combination was responsible not only for the unique accumulation of material goods in Britain but also for their achievements in innovation and enterprise" (56). Thus Teutonism took on an economic dimension in addition to its primary, political one, with the result that *capitalism itself* came to be viewed as an outgrowth of a preeminently English racial capacity.

Through this discourse, then, the motive forces of British modernization, from rationalization to democratization and capitalist production, became outward and visible signs of an inner and hidden racial essence. Within the prevailing zeitgeist, the English were the paradigmatic rational, liberal, enterprising members of human family. Given that, as Ellen Meiksens Wood documents in *Empire of Capital*, England was the first nation to implement the capitalist mode of production—that is, the organization of life according to market dependency and the competitive production of surplus value—it is perhaps fitting that Teutonism would specifically define the protagonist of classical political economy, the *homo economicus*, as an Englishman.[5] The tenets of Teutonism conform neatly to the definition of this prototype human as a self-interested pleasure-seeker accepting regulations only in order to minimize the pain of competitive acquisition. The autostereotype of the Teuton, with his hatred of restraint and inclination toward productive labor, can thus be understood as a post facto racialization of British political-economic doctrine—indeed, as a post facto racialization of the motive forces of British civilization. This racialization reified modernizing social tendencies, encoding them as intrinsic qualities of an essential Englishness.

Each of *Culture and Anarchy*'s bêtes noires falls within the purview of Teutonism. Arnold traces the flaws in the national character, from "doing as one likes" to vulgar materialism and religious dogmatism, to Germany's misty forests, from whose inhabitants the British aristocracy are directly descended:

> The Barbarians . . . who reinvigorated and renewed our worn-out Europe, have, as is well known, eminent merits; and in this country, where we are for the most part sprung from the Barbarians, we have never had the prejudice against them which prevails among the races of the Latin origin. The Barbarians brought with them that staunch individualism . . . and that passion for doing as one likes, for the assertion of personal liberty, which appears . . . the central idea of English life. . . . The stronghold and natural seat of this passion was in the nobles of whom our aristocratic class are the inheritors; and this class, accordingly, have signally manifested it, and have done much by their example to recommend it to the body of the nation, who already, indeed, had it in their blood. (105)

Thus the first component of what Arnold dubs "machinery," the master metaphor for those "stiff-necked," Philistine institutions that resist the pursuit of culture, is encoded as Teutonic. The "Barbarian" class, the aristocracy, secures England's political link to its Germanic ancestors, and by imbuing the early nation with a libertarian proclivity for "doing as one likes," they ensure the continued influence of this attribute on its other classes, the "Philistine" middle classes and the lower-class "Populace" who "already, indeed, had it in their blood" by genealogical descent.

The second component of British "machinery," "wealth," maps equally well onto the Teutonic autostereotype, with its emphasis on industry and enterprise. "The commonest of common-places tells us how men are always apt to regard wealth as a precious end in itself; and certainly they have never been so apt thus to regard it as they are in England at the present time," Arnold laments in "Sweetness and Light," and the duration of *Culture and Anarchy* is anxiously preoccupied with challenging the consensus that "our greatness and welfare are proved by our being so very rich" (65). Arnold conjoins this second, economic aspect of "machinery" to the first, political one in numerous passages, but perhaps the neatest encapsulation of their symbiosis occurs not in *Culture and Anarchy* but in the earlier essay "The Function of Criticism at the Present Time" (1864). There, in the midst of a passage praising the British Constitution, Arnold suddenly levels an indictment against this patchwork entity, which, if it "looks like a magnificent organ of progress and virtue" when "seen from the practical side," if viewed "from the speculative side," instead appears "a colossal machine for the manufacture of Philistines" (42). Arnold links economics with politics in a direct causal chain: the idolatry of wealth that is perhaps Britain's foremost cultural shortcoming is an outgrowth of the Constitution, which has enshrined the Barbarian urge toward bull-headed individualism. If the Constitution is the product of Teutonic individualism, and if, in turn, it functions as a "colossal machine for the manufacture of Philistines," there is then some element of "doing as one likes" that contributes directly to this vulgar, materialist trend. Arnold's metaphor here makes the case quite blatantly: it is as if the Constitution is a massive factory churning out Philistines as its finished products.

Arnold's political-economic assumptions here come to light, as does their foundation in Teutonic discourse. The British state represents the embodiment of primitive Barbarian liberty, and thus reinforces the middle classes in this behavioral tendency that is also their own racial property. This libertarian politics gives the equally racially ingrained productive and acquisitive impulses of the Teutonic *homo economicus* free rein. Philistinism, the "stiff-necked" resistance to cultural progress, is the compound product of this nefarious coalescence of domains. The Philistine's "natural taste for bathos," his vulgar materialist deflation of the nation's lofty aspirations, is a degenerative racial force that the laissez-faire Victorian state aids and abets, when it should instead be occupied with mitigating its harmful effects the better to install "right reason" in the population (*Culture* 118, 91). Arnold thus calls for a more interventionist state management of British society to stem the tide of "anarchy," a disintegrative social principle whose Teutonic basis we are now in a position to identify.

Once Teutonic individualism and materialism are identified as obstacles, the path for putting culture into practice to foster a "national glow of life and thought" becomes clear (79). However, as Amanda Anderson notes apropos of Arnold, race theory at midcentury could be a stultifying force in that it carried the baggage of a certain racial determinism and therefore placed firm boundaries on human potential (Anderson 104–106). Thus, Arnold's evocation of Teutonism places him in a rhetorical and ideological bind. How could he promote his "great social idea" to a people so strongly anchored to a Teutonic foundation? If his readers bear these tendencies in their very blood, any effort to transform them into more imaginative, right-reasoning subjects would seem doomed a priori. By accepting the anthropological premise that civilization manifests biology in his diagnosis of Teutonic "machinery" as the British national malady, Arnold confines his search for a cure to this same biological register. If race is the prime mover of history, then his efforts to alter its course must also obtain a racial sanction.

Arnold's solution for extricating Englishness from "machinery" arrives in the taxonomy of Hebraism and Hellenism, and it is the precise function of this belated ethnological reorientation to give the slip to the stultifying dictates of Teutonism. In that the chapters of *Culture and Anarchy* were originally separate essays, the cohesion of its six sections must, occasionally, break down. This proves particularly to be the case in "Hebraism and Hellenism," where Arnold significantly revises his anatomy of Englishness. He supplies transitional language between chapters to make this sleight of hand nearly imperceptible, concluding the foregoing essay, "Barbarians, Philistines, Populace," which grounds "machinery" firmly in Teutonic biology, by proposing to revise its ethnological picture: "But now let us try to go a little deeper, and to find, beneath our actual habits and practice, the very ground and cause out of which they spring" (125). Taking up this "deeper" question at the outset of the subsequent essay, Arnold seems again to verge on confining Englishness to the Teutonic arena of material development, stating, "This fundamental ground is our preference for doing over thinking. Now this preference is a main element in our nature" (126). The proclivity for "doing" continues to "ground" English "nature" at the expense of "thinking"—of culture—in seeming conformity to the "stiff-necked" Teutonic autostereotype. However, Arnold displays a newfound caginess: if the Philistine preference for doing over thinking is a main element of Englishness, it is merely *a* main element, merely one trait among others, however prominent.

The duration of "Hebraism and Hellenism" follows through on this equivocation to achieve ideological cohesion. The "sleight of hand" to which I refer operates as follows. First, Arnold redefines the racial filiations of "machinery" as Hebraic instead of Teutonic, a blunt but unavoidable first step toward escaping the bind of Teutonic determinism. Second, he explains the presence of this Hebraic tendency as the byproduct of Puritanism, the religious heir to Judaism, thereby enabling him to reclassify it as an unnatural importation. Third, having rezoned "machinery" as biologically Hebrew, Arnold redefines Englishness as inherently Hellenic via a generalized Indo-European ethnicity. The following passage, describing the dialectical alternation of these agencies in British history, displays these strategies in sequence:

> Puritanism . . . was originally a reaction . . . of Hebraism against Hellenism; and it powerfully manifested itself . . . in a people with . . . a Hebraising turn, with a signal affinity for the bent which was the master-bent of Hebrew life. Eminently Indo-European by its *humour*, by the power it shows . . . of imaginatively acknowledging the multiform aspects of the problem of life . . . our race has yet . . . in matters of practical life and moral conduct, a strong share of the assuredness, the tenacity, of the Hebrews. . . . [Thus] the main impulse of a great part, and that the strongest part, of our nation, has been towards strictness of conscience. [We] have made the secondary [force] the principal at the wrong moment. . . . This contravention of the natural order has produced . . . confusion and false movement . . . and we want a clue to some sound order and authority. This we can get only by going back upon the actual instincts and forces which rule our life, seeing them as they really are, connecting them with other instincts and forces, and enlarging our whole view and rule of life. (136–37)

This is a remarkable example of the tortuousness of Arnold's ethnology. Initially Puritanism, though a Hebrew import, meets in England a native element already given to a "Hebraizing turn." Because it manifests in "practical life" and resists Hellenic "spontaneity of consciousness," this native Hebraic element is surely Teutonic in derivation. As the passage proceeds, however, Arnold minimizes this Teutonic determinism: what begins as a "signal affinity" for the Hebrew "master-bent" becomes only a "share" of it, a "secondary" "impulse" that is finally classed as a "contravention of the natural order," which order must then favor the antithetical agency of Hellenism. What begins as a Teutonic Englishness ends with Hellenism, instead, as its "signal affinity." The passage thus enacts what it prescribes, "going back upon the actual instincts and forces" seemingly ruling British life—Teutonic ones—"seeing them as they really are"—as Hebraic—displacing them with "other instincts and forces" of Hellenic "bent," and thereby "enlarging our whole view and rule of life"—itself a quintessentially Hellenic project. The national attainment of culture, of "sweetness and light," will merely mean the restoration of a bygone racial homeostasis. In this profoundly strained passage, the reader witnesses each of the successive maneuvers by which Arnold writes his way free of the bind of Teutonic determinism.

## CULTURE AND THE ONTOLOGICAL CRITIQUE OF CAPITALISM

To begin defining the larger significance of this racial picture, we must step back and consider the real historical coordinates of Arnold's cultural program, the underlying referents to which his ethnological terms correspond. The transformation for which Arnold advocates in his revision of Teutonism concerns the historical structures of which this discourse was the ethnological crystallization. The "machinery" he savages is, in effect, a metaphor for the motive forces of British development, central among which is the economic. Indeed, I would suggest that a major part of what Arnold calls "machinery" is what we would call capitalist reification, and that the Philistine norms he reviles index the narrowing of human existence in the mid-nineteenth century to primarily economic or, in Marxist terminology, "instrumental" imperatives. "Machinery" is a figural attempt to describe the rigidity of British capitalist modernization and the ontological pressures attending this radically transformative process.

Marx himself mounts his early critique of political economy on precisely this ontological plane, where humanity's rich species potential becomes subjected to the "estrangement" of capitalist labor. In the *Economic and Philosophical Manuscripts of 1844*, Marx models what we might call the ontological critique of the capitalist mode of production, a critique that, in my view, *Culture and Anarchy* also advances:

> Political economy, the science of *wealth*, is therefore simultaneously the science of denial, of want, of *thrift*, of *saving*. . . . This science of marvelous industry is simultaneously the science of *asceticism*, and its true ideal is the *ascetic* but *extortionate* miser and the *ascetic* but *productive* slave. . . . Thus political economy . . . is a true moral science, the most moral of all the sciences. Self-denial, the denial of life and of all human needs, is its cardinal doctrine. The less you eat, drink and read . . . the less you

> think, love, theorize, sing, paint, fence, etc., the more you *save*—the *greater* becomes your treasure . . . your *capital.* The less you *are,* the more you *have*; the less you express your own life, the greater is your *alienated* life—the greater is the store of your estranged being. (95–96)

Marx bases his evisceration of both the "science of wealth" and the processes it glorifies on the grounds of their "denial of life and of all human needs." The dual result of humanity's subjection to this regime, governed by what we might call *a repressive-productive dynamic*—whereby the denial of certain activities and impulses enables the intensified pursuit of others better fitted to capitalist production—is the increase of capital and the impoverishment of human species being. Just as political economy codifies philosophically this central capitalist principle, so Teutonism encodes it ethnologically, so that Arnold, by opposing its historical trajectory, communicates an encrypted critique of an emergent capitalist instrumentality.

Ironically, the transformation of Teuton into Hebrew, though the product of ethnological convenience, enables Arnold to identify the forces driving British capitalism yet more accurately. The figure of the Hebrew conjoins the domains of economics and *religion* in a manner that presages the work of one of Marx's most influential followers, Max Weber. Just as Weber reads early capitalism as founded on the Calvinist Protestant Ethic, the "ascetic" morality of which fosters precisely the repressive-productive dynamic I have described, so Arnold links the third component of "machinery," religious dogmatism, with Britain's economic achievements:

> The whole middle class have a conception of things—a conception which makes us call them Philistines . . . [in which] the main concerns of life [are] limited to these two: the concern for making money, and the concern for saving our souls! And how entirely does the narrow and mechanical conception of our secular business proceed from a narrow and mechanical conception of our religious business! What havoc do the united conceptions make of our lives! It is because the second-named of these two master-concerns presents to us the one thing needful in so fixed, narrow, and mechanical a way, that so ignoble a fellow master-concern to it as the first-named becomes possible; and, having been once admitted, takes the same rigid and absolute character as the other. (*Culture* 147)

English "industry" is the offspring of Puritan morality, the "narrow" observance of which trains the British middle classes for the repressive dynamics of capitalist production. What Weber calls the *summum bonum* or greatest good of his ethic, the accumulation of wealth, is the same *unum necessarium* or "one thing needful" that Arnold defines as the linchpin of "machinery" (Weber 53). "For no people," Arnold argues, "has the command to *resist the devil, to overcome the wicked one* . . . had such a pressing force and reality. And we have had our reward . . . in the great worldly prosperity which our obedience to this command has brought us" (68). Hebraic "strictness of conscience" instills a repressive moral imperative propitious to capital, and through the "mechanical" observance of this religious-economic code the British have been—again in Arnold's words—"*baptized into a death*," into an ontological state governed by Marx's "denial of life and of all human needs" (32).

When Arnold complains that the Philistines' "idea of human perfection is narrow and inadequate" (70), and when he states that Culture "consists in becoming something rather than in having something, in an inward condition of the mind and spirit, not in an outward set of circumstances," he is advancing the same ontological critique as Marx and Weber, which views the "asceticism" of British capitalism as desiccating humanity's species potential (62). His recurring metaphor for the reified state of British capitalist modernity, "machinery," perfectly renders in figural form what one of Marx's recent interlocutors calls "social domination," that is, the overwhelming of the human subject by the agglomerated, exploitative apparatuses of capital.[6] When Arnold bemoans in "The Function of Criticism at the Present Time" that the contemporary British moment is an "epoch of concentration" or narrowness, he is describing the ontological trajectory of capitalist modernization, and by promoting a regenerative, Hellenic "epoch of expansion," he attempts to counteract that trajectory's insidious effects (33–36).

## CAPITALISM AND CELTICISM

We can now incorporate the broader considerations raised by Arnold's other mid-1860s ethnological text, *The Study of Celtic Literature*, and can buttress the claims advanced above regarding prevailing critical views of his definition of Irishness. As summarized in this study's introduction, through the postcolonial reappraisal of his work mounted in recent years by Irish Studies critics, Arnold's race theories have been depicted as a sort of Trojan horse by which, under the guise of celebrating the racial talents of the Celt, he sought to shore up Anglo-Irish colonial rule through the pseudoscientific codification of an imperially instrumental definition of Irishness.[7] Beneath its imperially instrumental political function, however, through its extension of the capitalist critique propounded by *Culture and Anarchy*, *The Study* comes to bear radical implications.[8]

Once we have noticed how *Culture and Anarchy*'s ethnological maneuverings cluster around the problem of "machinery," and once we have recognized the fully ontological import of this condition for Arnold, we will have already made progress toward pinpointing the concerns of *The Study*. Much more openly than *Culture and Anarchy*, *The Study* defines capitalist modernity as a Teutonic state of affairs. What is a veiled, mainly implicit equivalence between modernization and Teutonic capacities in the later text proves an overt and explicit equation in its predecessor within the Arnold oeuvre. The following passage, in which Arnold distinguishes the compound English "humour," defined as "energy with honesty," from the purer, Teutonic humor of the German, demonstrates this link:

> Take away some of the energy which comes to us . . . in part from Celtic and Roman sources . . . and you have the Germanic genius: *steadiness with honesty* . . . the danger for a national spirit thus composed is the humdrum, the plain and ugly, the ignoble . . . the excellence of a national spirit thus composed is freedom from whim . . . [and] patient fidelity to Nature,—in a word, *science*. . . . The universal dead-level of plainness . . . the lack of all beauty and distinction . . . the slowness and clumsiness of the language . . . this is the weak side; the industry, the well-doing, the patient steady elaboration of things, the idea of science . . . this is the strong side . . . through this side of her genius, Germany has obtained excellent results, and is destined . . . to an immense development. (82)

Here, both sides of the coin of modernization, positive and negative, are classed as Teutonic. The German "steadiness with honesty" is a boon insofar as it enables the advance of "industry," "science," and the overall "development" of material civilization, but it is a bane insofar as it also makes Germanic peoples "humdrum," "ugly," and "ignoble" in the cultural realm. If Teutonic discourse provides for a "patient steady elaboration of things," both epistemologically and materially, in Germany and England, it also explains the "lack of all beauty and distinction" in Saxon nations. Teutonism drives Arnold to link modernization with its social byproduct, a "humdrum" tendency toward "ugliness" and "ignobility" easily recognizable as Philistinism, as dual manifestations of the Anglo-Saxon racial blueprint. Capitalism would seem, again, inescapably Teutonic and, for the Teuton, inescapable.

Already, however, the above passage begins to provide a glimpse of the ethnological strategy that Arnold will deploy in *The Study* to elude Teutonic racial determinism. In *Culture and Anarchy*, the transposition of Teutonic discourse into the Hellenic/Hebraic binary rather heavy-handedly accomplishes this purpose, but here we must search for the key to Arnold's maneuverings in the mixed character of Englishness, the element that makes its humor "energy with honesty" instead of simply "steadiness with honesty." Already, Arnold mentions "Celtic and Roman" sources as supplying the "energy" that leavens Teutonic steadiness and complicates the predominantly Germanic makeup of the English, but it is the former of these, the Celtic, that Arnold most persistently emphasizes as supplementing that dominant component with an alternative tendency. The precise nature of that alternative tendency becomes evident in the later passage mentioned briefly in this book's introduction, which I quote more fully here:

> Out of the steady humdrum habit of the creeping Saxon . . . has come . . . Philistinism, that plant of essentially Germanic growth. . . . This steady-going habit leads, at last . . . up to science . . . the comprehension and interpretation of the world. With us in Great Britain . . . it does not seem to lead so far as . . . in Germany, where the habit is more unmixed. . . . Here with us it seems . . . to meet with a conflicting force . . . but before reaching this point what conquests it has won! And all the more, perhaps, for stopping short at this point, for spending its exertions within a bounded field, the field of plain sense, of direct practical utility. How it has augmented the comforts and conveniences of life for us! Doors that open, windows that shut, locks that turn, razors that shave, coats that wear, watches that go, and a thousand more such good things, are the invention of the Philistines. Here, then . . . are two very unlike elements to commingle; the steady-going Saxon temperament and the sentimental Celtic temperament. (92–93)

In this dense description, several things become clear. First, Philistinism, connected in more detail here than anywhere in *Culture and Anarchy* with the domain of capitalist development and middle-class materialism, the domain of "direct practical utility" and "comforts and conveniences," is an "essentially Germanic" modality, cropping up everywhere Teutonic peoples hold sway. Second, Philistinism is not the endpoint of the development immanent in Teutonic biology; rather, that endpoint is "science," "the comprehension and interpretation of the world," the very definition of the rational "light" by which Arnold defines culture. Finally, the counterinfluence in English biology preventing its consummation of its Germanic destiny is the "commingling" of Teutonic stock and its "steady-going" temperament with the "sentimental," Celtic one native to the British Isles. In other words, Arnold simultaneously seems to define Philistinism as the product of a Germanic racial tendency toward material development and as the product of a counteracting or dilution of this tendency by a "Celtic vein" "running through" the English (73–75). This leads the reader to assume that the ancient Celtic infusion of blood into England's Anglo-Saxon invader population may bear part of the responsibility for the Philistine rut into which their mid-Victorian descendants have fallen.

However, the additional concern taken up by the earlier text, that of the Celt's aesthetic talents, significantly complicates the portrait culled from *Culture and Anarchy*. To understand the service rendered Arnold by the Celt, we must first understand the Celt's place in contemporary British ethnology. Numerous critics and historians have excavated the multitude of characteristics attributed by the British to their Irish colonial subordinates during the mid-nineteenth century. Just as Teutonism valorized British civilization, so the corresponding discourse of Celticism helped justify the Anglo-Irish colonial enterprise by defining atavistic qualities like irrationality, violence, and economic incompetence as inherently Irish. As Thomas Boylan and Timothy Foley document in *Political Economy and Colonial Ireland*, this last aspect of Irish difference, economic incompetence, became perhaps the most potent criterion of legitimation for British rule. In their account, by the time of *The Study*, Irishness had come to signify an economic recalcitrance so stubborn as to trouble the lofty pretensions of political economy itself, ultimately precipitating a relativization of its laws as specifically *English* in derivation and applicability rather than universal (159–60).

Terry Eagleton and Mary Poovey have also documented the process by which Irishness became synonymous with economic ineptitude during the mid-Victorian period. Eagleton views the Great Famine as a watershed in this process, while Poovey highlights the perceived economic threat of Irish immigration in her account of British social reformer James Phillips Kay. "The Irish," in Kay's words, through the "contagious example" of their "barbarous disregard of forethought and economy, . . . have taught the laboring classes of this country a pernicious lesson," one with dire, depressive consequences for the nation's productivity (qtd. in Poovey, *Making* 63–64). Irish immigrants, in his portrait, are the bearers of a congenital, and catching, "pauperism." Kay deploys the same economic keyword as does George Stocking in his discussion of the *homo economicus* in *Victorian Anthropology*: "forethought." The "respectable middle-class man" of the mid-Victorian period, according to Stocking, observed "a prudent self-denying industry" that distinguished him from those races or classes "who had not achieved respectability," opting instead for "present self-indulgence" (216–17). In the terms of John Stuart Mill by which Mandler defines *Teutonic* "industry," the Irish prove incapable of sacrificing "present exertion for a distant object," instead succumbing to base, instinctual impulses (Mandler 56). As political economy promotes the exponential increase of the nation's wealth, the presence of the Irish, a "debilitated race" Kay calls "dissipators of capital," cannot be suffered (qtd. in Poovey, *Making* 69).[9]

From Kay's study of 1832 through the Famine of the 1840s and British political economy in the 1860s, there emerges a widespread tendency to identify Irishness as an anti-economic agency threatening to counteract Britain's development. If capitalist modernity is preeminently a Teutonic state of affairs, the Celtic component of the Anglo-Irish binary is intrinsically anticapitalist. This context undergirds Arnold's definition of the Celt's "humour" as "sentimental," and makes fully legible Arnold's view of the Celtic element in the English "composite." The penchant for sentimentality, a powerful sensitivity to external stimuli, defines the Celt as a primarily emotive rather than rational being. "An essentially feminine race," the Celt lacks the practical *male* capacity for "high success" in the world of "fact."[10] The Celt's "habitual want" of economic achievement derives from a congenital inability to subordinate the body's drives to capitalism's repressive-productive dynamic, which demands "balance, measure and patience"—in a word, "forethought." It is not, then, that Philistinism is a byproduct of an English Celticness, as it earlier seemed, but rather that the anticapitalist, Celtic trait stalls Teutonic industry at a "weak" point along its own developmental trajectory.

At this same point, however, the Celt's aesthetic potency can be made to compensate for his material impediments. While lacking the "industry, the well-doing, the patient steady elaboration of things" that is the "strong side" of Teutonic peoples and spurs them toward their "immense development" (82), the Celt possesses the "sweet" resources needed to prevent "the steady humdrum habit of the creeping Saxon" (92), the "lack of all beauty and distinction" that is his "weak side" (82), from further fertilizing "Philistinism," that "plant of essentially Germanic growth" (92). The purpose of Arnold's "commingling" of these "very unlike elements . . . the steady-going Saxon temperament and the sentimental Celtic temperament," is thus not simply to naturalize as a biological *fait accompli* Ireland's Union with Britain, but to stimulate the reform of Philistinism by alternative means (93). The "sweetness" that will enable such reform is at work in the best English poetry, furnishing "its turn for style, its turn for melancholy, and its turn for natural magic, for catching and rendering the charm of nature in a wonderfully near and vivid way" (113). The Celt's immersion in the state of nature provides for a "vivid" ability to render its "charm," a visceral intensity of utterance that manifests formally the sentimental capacity of this "poetical race" (115). The Celt's low evolutionary standing, while rendering him unfit for political and economic equality, generates an aesthetic capacity with the "magical" ability to repair the machinery of Teutonism.

Arnold thus places sentimentality at the heart of his "ideal genius" (89). He stops short, however, of advocating an undiluted Celticism, insisting that the Celt's "natural magic" must be "mastered" to achieve its potential (90). It is here, with the notion of a mastering of the Celt's aesthetic gifts, that we must differentiate the Celt of *The Study* from the Hellene of *Culture and Anarchy*. Arnold indeed describes both racial entities as providing a "sweet," expansive counterinfluence to the "narrow" ontology of Teutonic "machinery," but he draws several pivotal distinctions between the two that flesh out the architectonics of his ethnology across the 1860s oeuvre.[11] What Arnold seeks is a way to take advantage of the Celt's potential to infuse "sweetness" and to avoid falling prey to his putative practical deficiencies. The Celtic component of the "ideal genius," the perceptual hypersensitivity known as sentimentality, is a "beautiful and admirable force," but it must be bridled in order to correct the Celt's insufficiently "successful activity" (90). It is just this capacity for mastery, a supplementary "law of measure, of harmony, presiding over the whole" of "composite" Englishness (89), Teutonic and Celtic, that Arnold locates in Hellenism: "The Greek has the same perceptive, emotional temperament as the Celt; but he adds to this temperament the sense of *measure*; hence his admirable success in the plastic arts, in which the Celtic genius, with its chafing against the despotism of fact, its perceptual straining after mere emotion, has accomplished nothing" (86). The Hellenic genius supplies what the Celtic lacks, the "sense of measure" needed to channel "mere" emotive and perceptual powers toward artistic achievement. The Hellene possesses a raw aesthetic talent to match the Celt's, but his cultivation of that talent better heeds and conforms to "the despotism of fact."

What emerges, then, is a tripartite schema involving three distinct entities—the Teuton, the Celt, and the Hellene—each possessing a different proportion of aesthetic and material abilities. Crucially, for the larger purposes of this book, Arnold goes on to crystallize this schema by distinguishing the three according to their distinct *representational* propensities. "The Celt's quick feeling" he credits with lending "his poetry style," while "his sensibility and nervous exaltation gave it . . . the gift of rendering with wonderful felicity the magical charm of nature" (132). This "magical" quality is not to be confused with "the beauty of nature,—that the Greeks and Latins had; not merely an honest smack of the soil, a faithful realism—that the Germans had," but shows a preternatural attunement to "the intimate life of nature, her weird power and fairy charm" (132–33). Arnold thus defines the differences between the talents of Celt, Hellene, and Saxon against the common backdrop of nature, and describes their relationship to this referent as consisting respectively of "magic," "beauty," and "a faithful realism." The Celt offers a "weird power and fairy charm" in his rendering of nature that is directly opposed to the tame realism of the "humdrum" Saxon, and between these two extremes resides Hellenic art, retaining some of nature's raw power but muting it with an element of control and specular distance. The Hellene inhabits an ideal middle ground between Teutonic and Celtic aesthetics.

The mid-century anthropological discourse on which Arnold draws distinguished between "primitive" and "civilized" races in several interdependent registers. Thus far I have emphasized the economic and have shown how this discourse constructed the Teutonic/Celtic opposition according to the putative bent for or against "industry," the behavioral engine of capitalist development. It is essential to stress, however, that this economic opposition rested on a parallel, *epistemological* one, such that Teutonic "success" was thought to arise from a proclivity for rationality, while the Celt's lack of success was thought to arise from "magical" or "homeopathic" mental habits.[12] Probing the consequences of anthropological distinctions for the aesthetic theorization of the Victorian period, this anatomy becomes pivotal. The rational/magical dichotomy devised to naturalize colonial difference and legitimate British rule also delimited the aesthetic practices to which the Empire's constituents, "civilized" and "primitive," could be expected to tend. Given that capitalist modernization distanced the "civilized" British from nature, it is logical for Arnold to define Teutonic aesthetics as muffling nature's uncanny power almost beyond recognition. Moreover, because Teutonic modernity rests on a rational representational regime, one that Arnold simply dubs "science," he defines this aesthetic as a *realist* one. Conversely, because the "primitive" Celt resides outside capital in original nature, it is logical that his aesthetic renders its "weird power and fairy charm" in a comparatively direct manner. Because Celtic epistemology is sentimental, consisting of a preternaturally sensitive relation to its objects, Arnold can only define the Celt's aesthetic as *magical*.

Arnold's maneuvering between the economic and aesthetic registers via the epistemological one linking them reveals the full picture of his ethnological thought. He reviles Philistinism as a degenerated developmental state in which the British have been reduced to machine-like automata, deficient in both light and sweetness. His politics demand that he define the talent for "light" as Teutonic, because only an equivalence between rational epistemology, capitalist development, and Anglo-Saxonness can naturalize the British as imperial masters of the universe. But reason and capitalism cannot overcome the deficit entailed in Teutonic "machinery," because both require the repression of energies that must be expressed to achieve the utopian ontology of culture. Thus, to transform Teutonic *reason simple* into the Hellenic *right reason* that defines "perfection," a counteragent to Philistine ontological alienation, "sweetness," must be sought in a racial elsewhere, in the makeup of a figure residing outside modernity, the Celt. So as not to interfere with the material domain, this counteragency is confined to the aesthetic, a marginal location from which the Celt can exert his "sweet" influence without disturbing Anglo-Irish power relations.

*The Study* is a deeply conflicted text, but it is a legible one. Arnold finds the Celt's evolutionarily vestigial being a wellspring of energies capable of repairing the ontological damage wrought by capital, but he cannot bring himself to embrace the political correlative of this radical gesture. Ultimately, his definition of the Celt as materially hapless spills over into his aesthetic prescriptions as well, with the result that his ideal aesthetic cannot remain strictly Celtic. It thus becomes Hellenic, in direct prefiguration of *Culture and Anarchy*. The term by which Arnold defines the Hellene's paradigmatic Indo-European epistemology in *The Study*, "imaginative reason," neatly encapsulates his desire to fuse magic and rationality, instinctual fulfillment and material development, "sweetness and light" (125). *Imaginative reason*: this compact phrase combines the Celt's visionary talents with the Saxon's rational, "realist" perceptions in an ideal formula. By emulating this hybrid figure, the English can better farm their own "mixed" biology and "use the German faithfulness to Nature to give us science . . . [and] use the Celtic quickness of perception to give us delicacy, and to free us from hardness and Philistinism" (147). The Hellene, fusing Teutonic "measure" and Celtic "sentiment," becomes the racial paragon of Arnoldian culture, resolving the tension between his political subordination of the Celt and his celebration of his aesthetic talents. Just as *Culture and Anarchy* will utilize ethnological encoding to provide for the repair of Teutonic "machinery," so *The Study* performs a slightly different encoding, one complicated by the political demands of Anglo-Irish colonialism, toward this same end.

## THE (ABORTIVE) REBIRTH OF CELTIC TRAGEDY

Arnold's Celticism provides a striking case study in the contradictions of his mid-Victorian moment. At the purely instrumental level, the ethnological view of the Celt as unfit for self-government functioned to legitimate British colonial rule, while in the economic domain, the definition of the Celt as incapable of "industry" and "forethought" enabled Arnold to naturalize capitalist modernity as a biologically English state of affairs. Beyond these instrumental functions, however, Arnold's Celticism must be understood as motivated by an urge for the return of repressed energies, for an alternative ontology of which the British were deprived by the rigid, mortifying demands of Victorian respectability, among which, as I have argued, the repressive-productive dynamic of capital is foundational. In the words of *The Study*, the utopian Britain that lies beyond the reified ontology of machinery "can only be reached by studying things that are outside of ourselves" (151–52).

If pushed a bit further, Arnold's ethnological project would entail the prescription of a primitivist aesthetic program for the recalibration of this ontology. *The Study* is thus an exemplary instance of the long history, dating from the early modern period in the seventeenth century, of the effort to heal modernity's wounds via the aesthetic that Eagleton, John Guillory, and others have copiously documented.[13] Indeed, Arnold's ideas come remarkably close to those of the text that many critics read as inaugurating the program of modernist primitivism toward just this utopian goal, Nietzsche's *The Birth of Tragedy*. Just as Nietzsche anatomizes the history of aesthetics as a dialectical alternation between rational/logical and instinctual/passional poles, bemoaning the ontological state of late-nineteenth-century Europe as overly "Apollonian" and insufficiently "Dionysian," as what he calls an "Alexandrian" age, and therefore urges the rebirth of the Attic tragic form in which the two capacities were better proportioned, so Arnold divides aesthetics into the rational and instinctual poles of Teuton and Celt and urges their Hellenic union as a dialectical path beyond that same rationalist, repressive, European modernity in its particularly intense British form.

In the end, however, Arnold stops short of advocating the kind of radical reversal Nietzsche embraces, in which the primitive, Dionysian experience would be primary and the civilized, Apollonian one merely its adjunct. In accord with his material commitments, Arnold's Hellenic ideal in fact inverts this binary arrangement to subordinate Celtic aesthetic powers to Teutonic rational control, thereby robbing "culture" of most of its radical potential. As we shall see in subsequent chapters, where Nietzsche's plan for the rebirth of

Attic tragedy would result in an avant-garde program of modernist primitivism, Arnold's plan for a rebirth of Celtic tragedy, while bearing the same motives and using the same terms, would instead yield a mere *romantic* primitivism, an aesthetic mode with comparatively conservative implications.

Nonetheless, subsequent chapters will argue that beneath the compromised form Arnold's theories finally assume, they would go on to serve as both a potent anticapitalist resource in themselves and a remarkably prescient diagnosis of the terms—racial, colonial, economic, aesthetic—in which much of Anglo-Irish history would play out. The dual codification of capital as an ontologically predatory, biologically English agency and of the aesthetic as an ontologically restorative, biologically Celtic one controls a remarkable amount of territory over the next century, and if Arnold could not bring himself to embrace the radical potential he glimpsed in Celticism, other writers, both British and Irish, would develop that potential to produce some of that century's most remarkable anticapitalist theories and aesthetic visions.

CHAPTER 2

# The Uses of Irishness, I

## *British Imperial-Romantic Celticism*

Arnold's criticism of the late 1860s represents a breakthrough in the history of British aesthetics whereby the tenets of Victorian anthropology begin to shape literary visions of both British society itself and its larger imperial vistas. Arnold's program for alleviating the ontological damage of capitalist modernity through the increased cultivation of the sentimental, Celtic component of the "composite English genius" transfers the assumptions of mid-century race science into social criticism and aesthetic theory, both of which would henceforth be increasingly couched in racial terminology. As this chapter and the next will show, this maneuver sits at the root of a long history of literary responses to British domestic and imperial concerns that is defined by the dialectical interplay of Arnold's central binaries, Teuton/Celt and capital/aesthetics.

This minor tradition of British Celticism manifests in two distinct phases in British fiction from the fin de siècle to about 1930, phases distinguished by the linked aesthetic and political agendas of the authors representing them. The first, which I will designate the *imperial-romantic* phase, preoccupies the present chapter and is embodied in two authors whose careers span the late nineteenth and early twentieth centuries, Sir Arthur Conan Doyle and Rudyard Kipling. Key works by both writers follow in Arnold's footsteps to envision Anglo-Celtic hybridity as a medium for resolving the problems of late-Victorian British imperialism. Working from the same anthropological assumptions as Arnold and thus led, like him, to invent what I have called creative-determinist solutions to the Empire's racial, political, and economic tensions, Doyle and Kipling deploy Anglo-Celtic hybridity as an imaginative suture for binding together the putatively incompatible identities of colonizer and colonized, and thus for shoring up British hegemony amid a threateningly different and resistant colonial world.

Because this chapter offers the first part of a two-part argument about the history of British Celticism, a few words in preview of the next are needed here. Where the first, imperial-romantic phase of British Celticism deploys Anglo-Celtic hybridity as a tool for consolidating British political and economic hegemony, its second, which I will simply designate the *modernist* phase, pursues an inverse agenda. Where Doyle and Kipling duplicate the pattern observed in Arnold, in which the Celt's progressive potential is stunted by a conservative, Teutonic or Saxon ideological vision, modernist British authors such as Joseph Conrad and D.H. Lawrence instead seek to cultivate this potential. If Doyle and Kipling deploy the Celt as an adhesive binding together the Empire's "civilized" and "primitive" peoples, Conrad and Lawrence, conversely, deploy him to tear down the imperial hierarchy and forge an alternative ontology for both the metropolitan and the colonial subjects of British modernity.

While the work of these modernist writers pursues a very different agenda than that of imperial romance, both phases of the British Celticist tradition continue to rely on the Victorian anthropological assumptions whose problematic implications we have begun to trace via Arnold. British Celticism after Arnold, however, is not merely a theoretical or academic enterprise but also derives, to recall the terminology of this book's introduction, from prevailing views of the "whole way of life" of the Celtic people with which the British were most preoccupied. This chapter's first section is thus devoted to a more properly historical account of late-nineteenth-century Irishness as a complement to the more abstract musings of *The Study*. It aims to establish the ways in which Irish identity at the moment of imperial romance was already, in practice, a hybrid of metropolitan and colonial elements and could thus serve as a real example of the "composite," Anglo-Celtic possibilities Arnold envisioned. The unique aesthetic visions that define British Celticism after him derive both from his theory of Celtic sentimentality and from the hybrid attributes that characterized Irishness at the turn of the century.

## "WHITE CHIMPANZEES": LATE-VICTORIAN IRISHNESS

As touched upon in this study's introduction, recent research in Irish Studies has shown that Irish history presents an "anomalous" case in the annals of British colonialism.[1] In several historical registers, Irish experience under British rule cannot strictly be labeled either colonial or metropolitan. The analytical binaries of postcolonial theory are only partially suited to illuminating Irish history, which, while displaying some features that are ineluctably colonial and link Ireland with other colonial territories within the British Empire, displays others that seem to correspond to the experience of the colonizer. This research has generated new critical terminology such as "domestic colony," "metropolitan colony," "semi-colonial," as well as the term favored by this study, "metrocolonial," designed to capture the liminal, hybrid quality of Ireland's position. Where the canonical texts of postcolonial studies, from Alberto Memmi's *The Colonizer and the Colonized* to Franz Fanon's *Black Skin, White Masks* and *The Wretched of the Earth* and Homi Bhabha's *The Location of Culture*, conceive of colonialism as a binary phenomenon, the Anglo-Irish case blurs such oppositions and demands distinct conceptual tools.

At least five aspects of Irish history underscore the hybridity or liminality of its imperial situation. The first provides a concise means of outlining Ireland's more general divergence from standard postcolonial concepts. As Joe Cleary has shown, Irish society under British rule consisted of at least three different strata, while other British colonial contexts typically consisted of two. Cleary's analysis adapts a taxonomy devised by American sociologist George Fredrickson that groups European colonies from the seventeenth century onward into four categories: "administrative colonies," "plantation colonies," "mixed settlement colonies," and "pure settlement colonies" (Cleary, "Misplaced Ideas" 110). The vast majority of British colonies during the ensuing period were "administrative" ones, which "aimed at military, economic, and administrative control of a politically strategic region and were never settled by Europeans on a mass scale" (110). An example of this type of colony would be the one that serves as the foundation of many canonical texts in postcolonial studies: India, where the British presence was fairly minuscule alongside the native population it "administered." By these criteria, Britain's African and Caribbean colonies would also qualify as administrative. This observation illuminates the reason for postcolonial theory's binary analytical tendencies: its foundational figures built their work mainly on administrative premises, which present a neat division between colonizing and colonized groups. In contrast, Cleary argues, Ireland was an instance of "mixed settlement" colonialism, in which a colonial settler class came to function as a "buffer" between the native and imperial groups. Thus did the English settlers of the sixteenth century transform, after centuries of residence, into a liminal group with both Celtic and Saxon allegiances and mores: the "Anglo-Irish." Irish mixed-settlement colonialism presents a tripartite rather than a binary social hierarchy.

In addition to this social hybridity, Ireland was also "mixed" in terms of its role in the broader Empire. While Britain's political, economic, and military domination of the island affirms its status as a colony, the mobility of the Irish within the Empire's broader structures reflects a status superiority over their "administrative" counterparts.[2] As Keith Jeffery has argued, while colonized at home, the Irish, through their role in the British military, functioned as colonizers abroad, such that on average, to cite one example, 45 percent of the British army in the Indian province of Bengal was Irish from 1825 to 1850 (94). Along the same lines, Kevin Kenny notes that during the "Sepoy Mutiny" of 1857, half of the 14,000 soldiers of the East India Company, "and perhaps 40 per cent of the 26,000 regular British troops in India, were Irish," thus placing them in the contradictory position of suppressing anticolonial insurrection at the same time as advocating for the end of domestic British rule through repeal of the Act of Union (104–105). Alvin Jackson describes the contradictory position of the Irish in the Empire succinctly: "For Ireland, therefore, the Empire was simultaneously a chain and a key: it was a source both of constraint and of liberation" (136). Straitjacketed at home, the Irish enjoyed a freedom and authority abroad akin to that of their rulers. Again, where "administrative" experience was either/or, Ireland's "mixed" condition was neither/nor.

A third, more nebulous category of Irish hybridity is that of culture (in the non-Arnoldian sense). While its colonial status determined that Ireland remained partly distinct from Britain, its geographical proximity drew it into the sphere of domestic British society. In addition to the English heritage of the Anglo-Irish, the Act of Union, by dissolving many of the two islands' political and economic boundaries, precipitated a long process of cultural assimilation during the nineteenth century, one accelerated by the annulment of the Penal Laws in 1829. Particularly in the southeastern "Pale" region around Dublin, Irish culture gradually adopted metropolitan mores and institutions. The persistence of the colonial hierarchy determined, however, that Irish culture resided in a liminal state homologous to its "mixed" social makeup and imperial position. As described in F.S.L. Lyons's *Culture and Anarchy in Ireland*, the Irish, both like and unlike the British, presented the British with "a problem which seemed familiar but was in fact outside the normal range of English experience"; a perplexing compound of similarity and difference, Irish culture "helps to explain the fluctuations of policy from indifference to reform to coercion, and back again to indifference" by the British throughout the nineteenth century (13).

The final two aspects of Ireland's hybridity have received less attention than those outlined thus far, and it is with these two aspects that the remainder of this chapter—and the duration of this study—is most concerned. The first is economic. Here, Ireland again displays elements that align with both terms of the colonial binary. The plantation of the island began the economic subordination of the Gaelic Irish to the imperial representatives who would become the Anglo-Irish landlord class. Throughout the seventeenth, eighteenth, and nineteenth centuries, natives were then economically subordinated to the metropole through agricultural labor. In contrast to this politically, socially, and often militarily enforced exploitation, however, especially in the later nineteenth century, Irish society achieved a state of parity in several respects with the British. Particularly in places like Belfast and Dublin, Ireland's economic lifeworld was in many ways identical to Britain's. Especially in the domain of *consumption*, Irish subjects, as a valuable demographic for British commodities, grew increasingly indistinguishable from their imperial counterparts. Many of the same attractions available to the British were also available to the urban Irish, and the burgeoning British advertising industry of the late nineteenth century addressed Irish and British subjects in an identical manner. Thus, while the Irish experienced economic subordination comparable to other colonized peoples, they also found themselves incorporated and *interpellated* as equals of the British to an extent unimaginable elsewhere.

In subsequent chapters I will probe more deeply the implications of Ireland's economic hybridity. This chapter, however, is more directly concerned to elaborate the significance of another category of Irish hybridity, namely race. The racial definition of the Irish in the latter half of the nineteenth century, a key component of which we have already glimpsed through *The Study of Celtic Literature*, crystallized the political, social, cultural, imperial, and economic aspects of its colonial makeup. Not surprisingly, given Victorian anthropology's penchant for essentializing such features, the British racial definition of the Irish displays a "mixed" character parallel to its material liminality. It is crucial to note the obverse of the epistemological phenomenon by which racial theory indexes material forces, however, namely that racial negotiations such as Arnold and his Celticist successors undertook inevitably bore corresponding, material implications. Though this chapter is most explicitly concerned with visions of Anglo-Celtic racial hybridity, then, it reads each such vision as a coded response to material concerns, in particular those associated with British imperialism and British capital.

My reading of Irish racial hybridity is centrally indebted to the work of L.P. Curtis, Jr., whose *Apes and Angels* remains an invaluable resource regarding nineteenth-century British perceptions of the Irish. Curtis famously argues that popular depictions of the Irish in "comic weeklies" such as *Punch* responded to

Irish nationalist agitations such as the Fenian disturbances of the late 1860s and the Land Wars of the 1880s. Curtis's survey of the work of artists like George Cruikshank and John Tenniel establishes that at such moments British weeklies sought to "simianize" the Irish and define them as evolutionarily retrograde. The stock depiction of the Fenian dynamiter as a "hybrid ape-man" or "Celtic Caliban" defined the Irish as racially mixed in a manner corresponding to their broader colonial liminality. If the Irish were both metropolitan and colonial, colonizers and colonized, economically exploited and hailed as equals, and if their culture was both Anglicized and Gaelic/Celtic, it is logical that Irishness would sit midway on the scale of British racial classifications, between the civilized British and the putatively primitive colonial peoples of India, Africa, and the Caribbean.

As a result of these overdetermining factors, the British would define the Irish as racially liminal—as a race of "white negroes," in the popular media surveyed by Curtis.[3] As their threat to the Empire mounted, the Irish were thus subjected to an *evolutionary demotion* of sorts. Their violent behavior inspired the British to revoke their "white" credentials and to recodify them as the evolutionary kin of the "black" peoples residing in fully colonized sites throughout the globe. In one of the more famous instances of the racial blackening of the Irish during the late nineteenth century, the British clergyman and author Charles Kingsley wrote to his wife, Francis, during a fishing expedition to Ireland of being "haunted by the white chimpanzees" he encountered there (Kingsley 236). Kingsley's racial anxiety takes rhetorical shape in the categorization of the Irish as a class of "hybrid ape-men" whose simultaneous similarity to and difference from him renders them unfit for inclusion in either the human or the animal kingdom.

Such characterizations became increasingly popular during the late Victorian period, to the remarkable extent that in 1892 the administrators of the London Zoo christened a newly arrived African chimpanzee "Paddy," after the nickname of the Fenian caricatures of the comic weeklies (Curtis, *Apes* 101). The overtly evolutionary argument of such prejudice was that the Irish, through cultural difference and political resistance, shared a kinship with the primitive, black races of the empire that rendered suspect their membership among the white races at the top of the great chain of Darwinian being. The texts analyzed by Curtis, such as the 1881 *Punch* cartoon "Time's Waxworks"—in which "Father Time," acting as the curator of a sort of evolutionary wax museum, introduces Punch to a simianized Fenian who is displayed alongside a Zulu warrior, complete with "savage" regalia, and an Indian Maharaja—emphatically assert this evolutionary demotion. Ireland's status as the most pressing problem in Father Time's "chamber of horrors" equates its subjects with the "black" races of India and Africa that Victorian ethnology defined as animalistically primitive.

It is not difficult to find instances of the simianization or Africanization of the Irish within the texts of Victorian ethnology proper. *The Races of Britain*, an 1885 study by John Beddoe, ex-president of the London Anthropological Society, subscribes to the trend in a number of striking ways, including through the oft-remarked, pseudo-scientific taxonomy he calls "the index of nigrescence," which catalogued the range of skin color in the British Isles. In Beddoe's statistical tables, it is Ireland that demonstrates the greatest degree of "nigrescence." Affirming the dependence of Victorian race theory on elements of material culture, Beddoe lists the lowest "nigrescence" in Ireland as occurring in Dublin, the epicenter of Anglicization, and the highest as occurring in Galway, in the farthest reaches of Ireland's indigenous "Gaeltacht." While Dublin's inhabitants manifest an "index" of only 14, those of Galway show an astonishing 89.5. In keeping with Curtis's findings, Beddoe utilizes the craniological criterion of "prognathism," the ape-like elongation of human facial features, as a gauge of overall "nigrescence," and concludes regarding this feature, "most of its lineaments are such as lead us to think of Africa as its possible birthplace; and it may be well, provisionally, to call it Africanoid" (11).[4]

The profound degree to which the simianization and Africanization of the Irish shaped the British *episteme* is evident even in the mindset of perhaps Ireland's greatest British political advocate, Prime Minister William Ewart Gladstone. Gladstone's support for Irish Home Rule split the British Liberal party asunder in the elections of 1886, as its dissenting wing sided with the conservative Tory minority against Gladstone's Bill, in turn ousting him as PM. Later the same year, Gladstone published a pamphlet titled *The Irish Question* intended to vindicate his failed advocacy. In spite of his ministry's defeat, Gladstone claims a general liberality for the British view of Ireland that distinguishes current political and popular perceptions from the preceding era of Irish Africanization, in which "the proposal of self-government for Ireland [was] compared with the proposal of self-government for the Hottentots," the "negroid" peoples of southern Africa so often invoked as the epitome of ape-like "savagery" (18–19). Gladstone thus positions himself against a now-hegemonic Celtic-African equivalency propagated by print institutions like *Punch*, academic institutions like the Victorian Anthropological Society, and popular entertainment venues like the London Zoo during the 1860s, '70s, and '80s.

All told, the campaign to blacken and simianize the Irish Celt proves symptomatic of the problematic status of Ireland in general, the hybrid mix of familiarity and foreignness that left Charles Kingsley "haunted" by his travels there. If the whiteness of the Irish came into question, however, there was never any question of its complete erasure. Ireland's cultural commonalities with Britain, its dynamic role in the British empire, the permeability of boundaries between the two nations and their basic similarity of pigment, all determined that Anglo-Irish colonialism would continue to occupy a middle ground between civilized, metropolitan status and primitive, colonial status. The sheer volume of the texts and media devoted to distancing the Irish racially testifies to their being too close for comfort to their British rulers. Phrases like "white negro" and "white chimpanzee" are fitting encapsulations of this mixed colonial condition, and they suggest that the net effect of this cultural campaign was to affirm Irish similarity *and* difference.

This chapter represents an attempt to gauge the ramifications of the hybrid racial status to which the Irish were relegated as a result of their ambivalent position in the Empire. One further quotation from Curtis helps outline the particular aspect of this racial liminality with which my analysis of British fiction is most concerned. Curtis describes how Irishness, as interstitial racial entity, could palliate British anxieties in the discomfiting, newly Darwinian era of the latter nineteenth century: "There are clues in both Victorian literature and caricature which indicate that those who were most disturbed by the prospect of being cousin to apes and monkeys derived some temporary relief by treating the Irish . . . as a buffer or evolutionary *cordon sanitaire* between themselves and anthropoid apes" (103). If the view of Irishness as a sort of evolutionary halfway house between "Negroid" savagery and white, Saxon civilization derived from Ireland's real social, cultural, political, economic, and imperial characteristics, it also brought the ancillary benefit of providing a psychic "buffer or evolutionary *cordon sanitaire*" between the British and the primordial origins with which Darwin's *epistemic* shift linked them, and which they took "negroid" peoples to approximate.

The function of Irishness as an *imperial mediator* between the British and the so-called primitives of Africa, India, and the Caribbean finds expression in the work of the authors addressed below. These British writers follow in the footprints of Arnold's *Study*, where racial amalgamation between the English and Irish becomes a strategy for resolving Anglo-Irish tensions in the late 1860s. While Arnold defines the Celt in nearly wholesale primitive terms and positions Anglo-Celtic hybridity as a means for binding Irishness to an antithetical, Teutonic Englishness, these authors recognize what the career of the "Celtic Caliban" clearly affirms: that Irishness was itself a kind of Anglo-Celtic hybridity already. In its imperial-romantic phase, British

Celticist fiction takes advantage of this hybridity to pursue in a fully global, imperial domain the fantasy Arnold pursues in the British Isles, namely to secure British hegemony by fusing metropole and colony in a single entity. In its subsequent, modernist phase, British Celticist fiction also relies on a hybrid conception of Irishness as a mediating resource for the exploration and management of the imperial interface, but it does so with the antithetical purpose of short-circuiting British hegemony through an embrace of the "other" ontologies of the colonized. With these considerations in place and with the "sentimental" features of Arnold's Celt still in mind, we can assess the Celticist filiations of one of the fin de siècle's most popular imperial romances, Sir Arthur Conan Doyle's *The Hound of the Baskervilles.*

## CELTICISM AND IRISH NATIONALISM IN *THE HOUND OF THE BASKERVILLES*

At the beginning of Doyle's 1903 story "The Adventure of the Empty House," the opening tale of *The Return of Sherlock Holmes,* Watson collides unexpectedly in London with a disguised Holmes, supposedly killed by his arch-nemesis Moriarty a decade prior, knocking loose from his apparently resurrected friend's arms a large bundle of books, for only one of which does Watson note the title: "The Origin of Tree Worship" (451). This fictional tome alludes to one of the canonical texts of Victorian anthropology, J.G. Frazer's *The Golden Bough,* one of whose chapters is titled "The Worship of Trees." By invoking Frazer's *summa anthropologica,* Doyle affirms a longstanding subtext of the Holmes oeuvre, namely its use of anthropology as a framework for comprehending the social threat of late-Victorian criminality. The disciplinary affiliations of "The Adventure of the Empty House" avow openly what earlier stories assume silently—that normative Victorian society represents an ideal evolutionary state requiring protection from criminal hordes whose animalistic, subversive designs threaten to reverse the nation's developmental trajectory.

This threat is encapsulated in the term by which Stephen Arata focuses his exploration of the sub-discipline of criminal anthropology as promulgated by figures like Max Nordau and Cesare Lombroso, "degeneration." In this tale of the second coming of late-Victorian Britain's preeminent fictional social guardian, Doyle defines Holmes as a sort of civilizational immune system, preserving the social body from the pathogen of degenerate criminality. As Arata demonstrates, popular perceptions of crime after Darwin became colored by evolutionary assumptions that linked the criminal with other British foils such as the colonial savage or primitive and his cousin, what Curtis calls the "anthropoid ape." By couching the Holmes oeuvre in this discourse, Doyle defines the detective's goal as the maintenance of a kind of anthropological legality, an evolutionary threshold beyond which British society must not regress. This generic modulation impels intensive engagement with Britain's ethnological others, primitive agents that must be cordoned off from the middle classes to preserve their ontological homeostasis.[5]

The text whose popular success in 1902 seems to have provided the commercial inspiration for Holmes's later resurrection, *The Hound of the Baskervilles*, demonstrates a remarkably open engagement with anthropological themes. The depth of this engagement has even led some critics to argue that the ideological allegiances of the novel lie more with the evolutionarily primitive, criminal forces confronted by the sleuth than with the civilized, metropolitan order whose greatest protector he has the reputation of being.[6] Such readings, however, tend to elide the difference between the novel's content and its form. However magnetic its primitive moments, the story ultimately resolves any ambivalence toward metropolitan values through its hyper-rational final chapter, "A Retrospection," which recasts the novel in the form of a strict chronological and causal chain. Given that throughout his adult life, Doyle consistently affirmed his imperial loyalties not only in general (as he had just done just prior to the publication of *The Hound* in two tracts vindicating British conduct in the Boer War) but in the Anglo-Irish context specifically, it is no surprise that the novel finally re-contains the subversive forces engaged by its primitive and gothic narrative elements.[7]

My reading of *The Hound* aligns with that offered by the first major study of Doyle's imperial engagements, Catherine Wynne's *Colonial Conan Doyle*, in that I too view the threat of Irish nationalism as the central subtext of the novel's primitive themes. Contrary to Wynne's account of Doyle as a closet nationalist sympathizer, however, the assessment I offer here conforms more closely to the ideological priorities toward which its author's biography so emphatically gestures.[8] Far from expressing a latent desire to throw off British civilization, *The Hound* demonstrates a thorough opposition to Irish nationalism and a thorough commitment to the globalization of British norms. It is, in fact, *through* the very primitive, Celtic elements critics like Wynne read as counter-hegemonic that Doyle effectuates the symbolic maintenance of British hegemony. Doyle figures Irish Celtic primitivity as the vehicle by which colonial resistance to British authority can be ferreted out and suppressed. In so doing, he shapes *The Hound* into a prime specimen of imperial-romantic Celticism.

As the novel begins, Holmes has been hired by a Dr. Mortimer to investigate the recent, sudden death of his friend, Sir Charles Baskerville. Mortimer begins acquainting Holmes with the case by providing him the manuscript of an "old-world narrative" of "a certain legend which runs in the Baskerville family," the salient details of which are as follows: "in the time of the Great Rebellion," Lord Hugo Baskerville, "a most wild, profane, and godless man," "came to love . . . the daughter of a yeoman who held lands near the Baskerville estate," but, finding his overtures rebuffed by the "young maiden . . . discreet and of good repute," in the throes of a "dark passion" Hugo "stole down upon the farm and carried off the maiden," who became his captive; during one of Hugo's bouts of drunkenness, the "maiden" slipped away; upon discovering her escape, Hugo vowed "that he would that very night render his body and soul to the Powers of Evil if he might but overtake the wench"; after a frenzied chase "the unhappy maid" collapsed, "dead of fear and fatigue," shortly to be followed by Sir Hugo himself, above whose mutilated corpse his retainers found "a foul thing, a great, black-beast, shaped like a hound, yet larger than any hound that ever mortal eye has rested upon," a monster which "is said to have plagued the family so sorely ever since" (581–83). Balking at the implication that this fantastic story might illuminate Sir Charles's death, Holmes scoffs that it could only hold interest to "a collector of fairy tales" (583).

Although Doyle's source for this "old-world narrative" was a British folktale, his adaptation of the legend reflects concerns that are more properly Irish.[9] The novel first foregrounds its Irish orientation when Watson and Mortimer travel with Sir Charles's heir, Sir Henry, to the ancestral home in Devonshire, on a reconnaissance mission for Holmes, who has supposedly been detained in London by other casework. Mortimer, whose credentials as an anthropologist are affirmed, according to the biography Watson reads from a British "Medical Directory," by his having won "the Jackson prize for Comparative Pathology" for essays such as "Some Freaks of Atavism" and "Do We Progress?," provides a running ethnological commentary on Sir Henry as they approach their destination. He observes to Watson, "a glance at our friend here reveals the rounded head of the Celt, which carries inside it the Celtic enthusiasm and power of attachment. Poor Sir Charles's head was of a very rare type, half Gaelic, half Ivernian" (613). The Baskerville line is Celtic, a blend of Gaelic and "Ivernian," Hibernian or Irish, stock. Watson's description of Sir Henry's reaction to the Devon landscape surrounding Baskerville Hall corroborates Mortimer's identification. "Young Baskerville," he reports, "stared eagerly out of the window and cried aloud with delight as he recognized the familiar features of the Devon scenery . . . like some fantastic landscape in a dream.

Baskerville sat for a long time, his eyes fixed upon it . . . this first sight of that strange spot where men of his blood had held sway so long and left their mark so deep" (613–14). Sir Henry displays a biological attunement to the "fantastic" landscape of Devonshire, a "power of attachment" whose primitive "enthusiasm" Watson reads as a manifestation of the "blood" that, by virtue of his shared ancestry with Sir Charles, is not merely Celtic but also Irish.

The racial orientation of the Baskervilles helps elucidate the allegorical significance of the family legend. The "old-world" story of the hound serves as a parable of the injustices of colonial rule. Though his kidnapping of the "maiden" presents Hugo's crime as a sexual one, her identity as the daughter of a yeoman residing near the Baskerville estate renders this sexual expropriation as a thinly veiled transcoding of the economic violence of colonial primitive accumulation. The maiden provides a late example of one of the perennial themes of British literature during the era in which the "Great Rebellion" of the "legend" occurred, namely the so-called "woman-as-land metaphor," used by Restoration writers like Aphra Behn to anthropomorphize the territorial concerns attending first-wave European imperialism in the "New World." Translating the family's "legend" via this trope, Sir Hugo's forcible sexual arrogation of the peasant "maiden" encodes the broader economic injustices of imperial conquest. The spectral hound that plagues the succeeding generations of Baskervilles thus functions as an agent of symbolic justice, wreaking karmic vengeance for Sir Hugo's expropriative violence.[10]

If this would seem to place the novel on an anti-imperialist path, Doyle quickly supplements Mortimer's legend with information that spins its allegiances dramatically. A newspaper report on Sir Charles's death depicts him as the antithesis of Sir Hugo:

> The recent and sudden death of Sir Charles Baskerville, whose name has been mentioned as the probable Liberal candidate for Mid-Devon . . . has cast a gloom over the county. Though Sir Charles had resided at Baskerville Hall for a comparatively short period his amiability of character and extreme generosity had won the affection and respect of all. . . . In these days of *nouveaux riches* it is refreshing to find a case where the scion of an old country family which has fallen upon evil times is able to make his own fortune and to bring it back with him to restore the fallen grandeur of his line. . . . It is two years since he took up residence . . . it is common talk how large were those schemes of reconstruction and improvement which have been interrupted by his death. (583)

Sir Charles's treatment of the neighboring tenants sets him apart from his ancestor's tyrannical landlordism. While the report describes that he accumulated his fortune in "South African speculation," affirming his own credentials as a colonial exploiter, it is clear that Doyle intends to distance him from the symbolic implications of the hound legend within the sphere of his domestic authority (583). Sir Charles's benevolent "schemes of reconstruction and improvement" contrast starkly with the sexual-economic rapine of Sir Hugo, promising to redress the "fallen grandeur" of the Baskerville line.

This turn, however, complicates the symbolic function of the hound in that it preys indifferently upon a benevolent aristocrat, the very model of *noblesse oblige*, and his malevolent predecessor. The novel goes on to resolve this inconsistency by revealing that Sir Charles's murder is not in fact the product of supernatural vengeance, but of a very human set of motivations. The logical contradiction between the hound's allegorical function and his present-day reign of terror against a comparatively just landlord paves the way for Holmes's apprehension of Stapleton, a distant Baskerville relative who orchestrated Sir Charles's death and who attempts to arrange Sir Henry's to secure his own inheritance of the estate. Stapleton, the story reveals, has taken advantage of the family legacy to create his own "spectral" hound, covering a large mastiff in phosphorus in order to shock his cousins' notoriously hypersensitive Baskerville constitution into cardiac arrest. What begins as a parable of colonial economic injustice ends, it would seem, as a garden-variety tale of British criminality.

As Franco Moretti has noted of detective fiction with particular reference to Doyle, its *modus operandi* is to obliterate memories of past violence and affirm the bourgeois legalities of the present. Moretti's insight regarding one of the genre's perennial bogeys, the social-climbing "upstart," has direct relevance here: "the specter of primitive accumulation materializes through him: capital as theft, and even as murder. By catching him, the detective annihilates a memory painful to his philistine audience: the original sin of nineteenth-century 'legality' . . . its infected roots in the past must be eradicated" (140). The narrative function of Stapleton, the "upstart," would-be usurper of the Baskerville fortune, is then to serve as the scapegoat for its original violence. The "specter of primitive accumulation," the hound itself, provides an uncomfortable reminder of the origins of the British colonial order, and it must be purged for Holmes, and Doyle through him, to reify contemporary British colonial capitalism. The novel thus enacts fairly neatly the strategy of containment whereby subversive primitive and colonial forces ultimately buttress a hegemonic ideological agenda.

In fact, through the machinations of "Stapleton," the novel comes to embody a rather different historical allegory, one with colonial implications diametrically opposed to those of the Baskerville legend. The closest parallel in recent British colonial history for Stapleton's "upstart" campaign is the Anglo-Irish Land Wars of the late 1870s and early '80s. Given the novel's generally Celtic and partly Irish orientation, and given its evocation of the economic violence of British colonialism, Stapleton's activities cannot but resonate with this context. Having affirmed Sir Charles's benevolence as a landlord, thereby annihilating the painful memory of "capital as theft, and even as murder," Doyle figures Stapleton's schemes as a sort of colonial insurrection, thus converting the hound from a symbol of colonial injustice to one of colonial rebellion.

In this regard, Stapleton's plot closely resembles the nationalist campaigns of the Fenian Brotherhood and the Irish National Land League. Like Stapleton's subversive activities, those of the Fenians and Land Leaguers during the late 1870s and early '80s took shape in a framework of protest against colonial economic injustice, and also like his, their activities sometimes included assassination, both of Anglo-Irish landlords such as Lord Sydney Leitrim, ambushed outside his "big house" in county Donegal in 1878, and of prominent colonial officials like Lord Frederick Cavendish and T.H. Burke, the chief secretary and undersecretary of the British administration, who were stabbed to death in Phoenix Park in Dublin in May of 1882. Finding their peaceable petitions for "the three Fs"—fixity of tenure, freedom of sale, and fairness of rents—unsuccessful, these militant organizations took matters into their own hands, eventually persuading British parliament to pass a conciliatory Land Bill in 1882 that provided for tenant buyouts of Irish landlords and paved the way for the demise of the Protestant Ascendancy.[11]

The case of Lord Leitrim is particularly revealing with regard to the hound legend's implications. One of the most hated landlords of nineteenth-century Ireland, Leitrim earned his notoriety not only through practices of rack-renting and summary eviction, but through rumored sexual mistreatment of his female tenants. Though it is impossible to be certain that Doyle's adaptation of the original folktale alludes directly to Lord Leitrim, the parallels are striking. The symbolic significance of the original Baskerville legend hews so closely to the events surrounding this landlord's demise as to render them almost indistinguishable. Doyle introduces this allegory of colonial tyranny, however, only to invoke the Anglo-Irish context generally, rather than to endorse the anticolonial implications of the Leitrim case or other, similar episodes. While the contemporary hound also assassinates a landlord in Sir Charles, his benevolent treatment of his tenants spins his assassination as an act of *in*justice. Papering over the original and ongoing violence of British colonialism, Doyle, through Stapleton, fixes the blame for its turbulence on physical-force Irish nationalism. The symbolic function of the foiling of Stapleton's plot is then to suppress an act of colonial insurrection and shore up the legitimacy of the threatened Anglo-Irish landlord class.[12]

This symbolic undercarriage corresponds to the position taken during the Land War by one eminent British commentator on matters Irish, namely Matthew Arnold. Returning to the subject for the first time since his mid-sixties lectures on Celtic literature, in whose background the percussion of Fenian dynamite was clearly audible, Arnold wrote a series of "Irish Essays" on the eve of the 1882 Land Bill's passage, the first of which, titled "The Incompatibles," presents an assessment of "physical force" Irish nationalism remarkably similar to the symbolic import of the hound legend. As if driven by current events to compromise his unflinching legitimation of British rule, Arnold is now willing to grant the charge that "England holds Ireland . . . by means of conquest and confiscation," though he points out that "almost all countries have undergone conquest and confiscation; and almost all property, if we go far back enough, has its source in these violent proceedings" (8). Arnold's analysis of the nationalist disturbance rests on his impression that the native Irish have never "prescribed" to the British colonial, capitalist order. In an ideal scenario, in Arnold's view, after the violent imposition of imperial power people "go about their daily business, gradually things settle down, there is well-being and tolerable justice, prescription arises, and nobody talks about conquest or confiscation any more" (9). Turning to the specifics of the Anglo-Irish case, however, Arnold laments, "In Ireland [this] did not happen. . . . The angry moment of conquest and confiscation, the ardour of revolt against them, have continued . . . to irritate and inflame men's minds . . . the present relations between landlord and tenant in Ireland offer only too much proof of it" (9). Arnold argues that British rule in Ireland has consisted of "a system for enabling the grantees of confiscation to hold Ireland without blending with the natives or reconciling them," and he urges that "healing measures" be taken in order to move past the violent origins subsequent history has continually revived (17). He even offers a specific policy suggestion: "what is most needed, in dealing with the land in Ireland, is to redress our injustice, and to make the Irish see that we are doing so . . . the most effective way, surely, to do this is . . . to execute justice on bad landlords" (23).

A reader of *The Hound* with an awareness of recent Anglo-Irish history and a familiarity with Arnold's account of the two nations' "incompatibility" is almost led to wonder whether Doyle lifted his plot from Arnold directly.

Doyle adapts the Devon folktale of the hound to allegorize the original violence of colonial conquest. Just as Arnold seeks to transcend the violence and injustice built into the foundation of the Anglo-Irish colonial order, so Doyle arranges the novel to legitimize the Baskerville line as a philanthropic institution. The original hound, whose function is precisely to "execute justice on bad landlords," returns to perform the opposite function in the novel's present, the early 1890s, namely to embody a subversive threat to a now-benevolent landlordism. The shift between the hound's opposed symbolic roles in the past and the present, and the broader shift between an anticolonial and a pro-colonial set of implications, serve to secure the fictional achievement of Arnoldian "prescription."[13]

Something more, however, than use of an Irish historical context is necessary to define the novel as an example of British Celticism. If, as I have argued, *The Hound* represents the fictional enactment of Arnoldian race theory, Celtic aesthetic modalities should somehow prove instrumental to accomplishing its macro-political designs. In the passage already quoted above in which Dr. Mortimer describes Sir Charles's "Celtic enthusiasm and power of attachment," Doyle indicates a familiarity with Arnold's definition of Celtic "sentiment" as emotionally passionate and perceptually sensitive. Such susceptibilities in turn inform Sir Charles's death by cardiac arrest in response to Stapleton's sham monster. Where the Celtic racial substratum of the novel surfaces most markedly, however, is in the investigative methodology of Sherlock Holmes himself. Holmes, in fact, proves a specimen of Anglo-Celtic hybridity as imagined by Arnold and as inhabited experientially by Irish subjects during the late nineteenth century, and in his approach to the Baskerville case, he demonstrates the deployment of primitive, Celtic epistemological resources for colonially hegemonic ends.[14]

In the classificatory system devised by James Frazer's *Golden Bough*—to which, as we have seen, the Doyle oeuvre directly alludes—Holmes's investigative methodology would be considered a fully *magical* practice. Frazer, famously, divides humanity's epistemological evolution into three developmental phases—magic, religion, and science—and defines the progress of the species by its ascent from the first, most primitive phase to the last, most civilized one. Holmes's investigative techniques are best described as a kind of "sympathetic magic," in Frazer's terms, an especially primitive practice that corresponds perfectly with the Celt's epistemology as defined by Arnold. Frazer divides sympathetic magic into two subvarieties, "homeopathic" and "contagious" magic, and summarizes their common characteristic as follows:

> Both trains of thought . . . may conveniently be apprehended under the general name of Sympathetic Magic, since both assume that *things act on each other at a distance through a secret sympathy*, the impulse being transmitted from one to the other by means of what we may conceive as a kind of invisible ether, not unlike that which is postulated by modern science for a precisely similar purpose, namely, to explain how things can physically affect each other through a space which appears to be empty. (14, emphasis added)

Frazer's anatomy describes a sort of *manipulative mimesis* whereby, obeying the law of "like produces like," "things act on each other at a distance through a secret sympathy" (13). The "sympathetic magician" performs imitative gestures and incantations that enable him to control distant objects or forces by mimicking their makeup and activity. This, I would argue, is the anthropological theory that informs Holmes's investigative methods in *The Hound*.

In one early scene, Holmes performs a markedly "magical" act of preparation for his later, more direct investigation of the case in Devonshire, one that demonstrates its "sympathetic" character unmistakably. Returning from his "club" to 221B Baker Street, Watson finds his and Holmes's lodgings altered radically: "the room was so filled with smoke that the light of the lamp upon the table was blurred by it . . . the acrid fumes of strong, coarse tobacco . . . took me by the throat and set me coughing" (592). After Watson ventilates the "poisonous atmosphere" generated by Holmes's pipe, the latter explains that in Watson's absence he has in fact "been to Devonshire," a physically impossible feat given that absence's brevity (592–93). Watson concludes that he must then have traveled "in spirit," to which Holmes replies: "Exactly. My body has remained in this armchair and has, I regret to observe, consumed in my absence two large pots of coffee and an incredible amount of tobacco. After you left I sent down to Stamford's for the Ordnance map of this portion of the moor, and my spirit has hovered over it all day" (593). This passage figures Holmes's methods as a kind of "sympathetic magic." To align his mind with the rural crime scene, Holmes transports his spirit to Devonshire through the "invisible ether" between them with the aid of a mimetic representation, the Ordnance map. Through it, Holmes gains an impossibly "sympathetic" access to the distant region, in effect teleporting there. Holmes affirms the sympathetic-magical orientation of his epistemology when he apologizes to Watson for the room's condition: "it is a singular thing, but I find that a concentrated atmosphere helps a concentration of thought" (593). For Holmes, as with Frazer's "savage," like produces like. His methods display a double "sympathy": first between his mind and the room's atmosphere, the former of which gains in concentration in proportion to that of the latter, and second, between his newly "concentrated" mind and the distant moor, with which he is now familiar to a degree only possible through some super-rational means.

Later developments elaborate the specifically Celtic affiliations of this "magical" theme. With Holmes still supposedly delayed in London, Watson compiles several reports to keep him abreast of the case's development, in one of which he describes one of the peculiar features of the Devon landscape. "When you are once out upon its bosom," he conveys, "you have left all traces of modern England behind you, but . . . you are conscious everywhere of the homes and work of a prehistoric people" (629). Watson finds it curious "that they should have lived so thickly on what must have been unfruitful soil," and accordingly speculates, "I am no antiquarian, but I could imagine that they were some unwarlike and harried race who were forced to accept that which none other would occupy" (629). Watson's conjectures evoke the epigraph of Arnold's *Study*: "they went forth to the war, but they always fell" (1). Unsuited to the conflict of a barbaric age, Arnold's Celts were similarly "harried" and "forced to accept" a fate "which none other would occupy." Having already identified the Celtic and Irish elements of the novel's setting and contemporary inhabitants, Watson's musings serve to clinch this Celtic racial theme as the novel's predominant anthropological strand.

It is significant, then, that Holmes, who has been residing on the moor in secret, displays a remarkable affinity for it. Before Holmes reveals himself, Watson unknowingly catches sight of him during a nighttime expedition with Sir Henry to apprehend Selden, an escaped criminal whom Mrs. Barrymore, a member of the Baskerville Hall staff, has been supplying with clothes and food:

> The moon was low upon the right, and the jagged pinnacle of a granite tor stood up against the lower curve of its silver disc. There, outlined as black as an ebony statue on that shining background, I saw the figure of a man upon the tor. . . . As far as I could judge, the figure was that of a tall, thin man. He stood with his legs a little separated, his arms folded, his head bowed, as if he were brooding over that enormous wilderness of peat and granite which lay before him. He might have been the very spirit of that terrible place. (645)

Appearing as "the very spirit of that terrible place," Celtic Devonshire, Holmes demonstrates a preternatural affinity for its "dreamlike" environs.

Later, when Watson finally discovers the identity of "the man upon the tor," he learns that Holmes has been residing in one of the abandoned stone domiciles of the ancient Celts. Holmes, it seems, further cultivates "sympathy" with the Celtic setting by directly inhabiting its indigenous architecture.

The net weight of these examples is to tie Holmes's "magical" methods firmly to the novel's Celtic context. Mortimer specifies the key characteristics of Arnoldian "sentiment," "enthusiasm" and a "power of attachment," as pronounced in his deceased friend, Sir Charles, and Sir Henry's responsiveness to the Devon "scenery" reflects his own possession of these characteristics. Holmes's success in the case relies on this same "power of attachment," the perceptual hypersensitivity which, for Arnold, renders Celtic aesthetics a kind of "magic" capable of conveying the "weird power and fairy charm" of nature with unparalleled directness and fidelity. Holmes's methodology consists, in effect, of a magical perceptual affinity for the "weird" features of this Celtic region, a sympathetic epistemology capable of perfect alignment with its nebulous essence. Through Watson's descriptions of Holmes's methods, furthermore, Doyle renders such passages exercises in Celticist *aesthetics*. At these moments, however briefly, the novel's representational texture merges, like producing like, with the movements of Holmes's sympathetic epistemology. Celtic mental and aesthetic resources prove indispensable not only to Holmes's investigative techniques but also to Doyle's authorial agenda.

*The Hound* is indeed an exercise in the symbolic legitimation of British colonialism in Ireland. To achieve this legitimation, however, Doyle infuses its narrative with a Celtic element, as if Celtic resources are needed to negotiate the Anglo-Irish colonial interface, to suppress its conflicts and ratify British "prescription." British epistemology thus appears insufficient to the maintenance of imperial rule in a context striated by ethnological difference. Holmes adopts the very racial characteristics of which Doyle would seem to desire the eradication, rendering his detective labors, and the novel's overall form, contradictorily primitive despite their civilized socio-political priorities. The novel symbolically accomplishes the elimination of Irish resistance to British rule, but Irish difference persists in the novel's aesthetic structure by virtue of Holmes's magical methods. Doyle finds, seemingly, that it is only by inhabiting a Celtic modality that the threat of Celtic difference can be effectively engaged and eradicated, thereby leaving the means of his imperialist project at cross purposes with its ends.

The novel thus displays a conspicuous hybridity at the level of character and at the level of narrative form. Indeed, *The Hound* presents this hybridity not simply as an aesthetic or methodological resource for the suppression of colonial resistance, but as a biological necessity for the prosecution of this counterrevolutionary agenda. The ethnological theme introduced by Dr. Mortimer's anthropological commentary rests on a markedly determinist set of racial assumptions. Sir Henry's Celtic constitution leads inevitably to "sentimental" displays of passion and "attachment," just as Sir Charles's "sentimental" proclivities played a primary causal role in his untimely demise. Like Arnold before him, Doyle thus positions Celtic affinities as outgrowths of biology. Such determinist assumptions raise, and immediately suggest an answer to, the question of how Holmes himself could attain such a facility with the Celt's "magical" abilities. It would seem that Holmes, to inhabit such modalities, would need to bear a Celtic element in his own makeup. The reader is provided the basis for such a conclusion in the very first chapter, when Dr. Mortimer subjects Holmes to craniological analysis: "You interest me very much, Mr. Holmes. I had hardly expected to see so dolichocephalic a skull or such well-marked supra-orbital development. . . . A cast of your skull, sir, until the original is available, would be an ornament to any anthropological museum" (578–79). Mortimer, though dexterous in distinguishing "the skull of a negro from that of an Esquimau," in expounding "the comparative anatomy of the Bushman and the Hottentot," and in tracing the Celtic descent of the Baskervilles, is stumped by the specimen of Sherlock Holmes (597, 586). There is no position for his anomalous physiognomy on Mortimer's anthropological bugboard.

Doyle thus suggests that Holmes's unique investigative talents derive from a unique biology. Nowhere does Mortimer specify the racial affiliations betokened by Holmes's cranial topography, and the reader is thus left to devise some means of inferring them from Holmes's activities, using the determinist principle operative elsewhere as a guide. According to this principle, we may already deduce that part of Holmes's biology must be Celtic, given the sympathetic magic and sentimental characteristics of his methodology and his deep affinity with the landscape of Devonshire. While reliant on Celtic modalities, however, Holmes's methods are also unmistakably rational, and it is toward civilized rather than primitive ends that his casework moves. In the scene depicting Holmes's magical preliminary investigations, Holmes accomplishes his sympathetic vision of its layout with the aid of a preeminently rational tool, the "Ordnance map." Holmes's Celtic epistemology requires some sort of rational catalyst in order to transmit this vision through the "ether" between London and Devonshire. As Stiofán Ó Cadhla documents in *Civilizing Ireland*, "ordnance maps" were devised by the British to aid the Irish imperial administration during the mid-nineteenth-century period that saw the initial stirrings of the Fenian and Land League campaigns of the 1860s,

'70s and '80s. Holmes's reliance on such a map signals the novel's counter-revolutionary agenda, even as his manner of using it bespeaks a reliance on the very Irish racial difference that agenda would erase. His methods, finally, subordinate magical to rational epistemological priorities, as it is only the latter which can fulfill the imperial spread of British civilization desired by his creator. Through Holmes, Celtic sentimentality becomes the instrument of a sort of Foucauldian imperial panopticism.[15]

Holmes himself coins a formula for the hybrid epistemology required for the sequential engagement and eradication of colonial difference when he refers to his methodology as "the scientific use of the imagination" (598). This formula provides the best available means of deducing from his actions and talents Holmes's racial constitution. In addition to his Celtic features, which supply Holmes with his magically adept imagination, Holmes must also possess features that inform his scientific analyses. We have, in fact, already witnessed the operations of such features in the previous chapter of this study, where Arnold's anatomy of Celt and Teuton hinges on the binary opposition between respectively magical and rational or scientific epistemologies. By infusing Holmes with a scientific bent to match his "magical" talents, Doyle implicitly defines his biology as a "comingling" of Celtic and Teutonic features. Holmes may be read, in short, an Anglo-Celtic hybrid, an adept whose imperial practices manifest the flexible racial compound Arnold dubs "the composite English genius." Just as Arnold envisions a hybrid Englishness whose inner hierarchy models his ideal United Kingdom, so Holmes contains both Celtic and Teutonic elements arranged in imperialist proportions. Subordinating the former to the latter, Holmes puts the Celt's imagination to Teutonic, scientific use. Holmes's phrase replicates perfectly the ideal epistemology of Arnold's racial paragon, the anthropological figure who seamlessly blends Celtic and Saxon abilities, the Hellene: *imaginative reason*. Holmes, in this light, appears an exact fictional embodiment of Arnold's theories, just as *The Hound* as a whole does relative to the fantasy of "prescription." It would seem that Doyle can only envision the kind of imperial agent required to achieve such prescription as an Anglo-Celtic hybrid whose biological proportions parallel the racial and political hierarchies of the United Kingdom.

## THE CELT AS COLONIAL AGENT IN *KIM*

In his depiction of Anglo-Celtic hybridity as integral to the British imperialist agenda at the fin de siècle, Doyle was not alone. Rudyard Kipling's *Kim* likewise figures such hybridity as an indispensable resource for the maintenance of British rule. An examination of *Kim*'s Irish elements not only enables a reassessment of the significance of the canonical text but also extends the examination of Anglo-Celtic dynamics in an illuminating new direction. Namely, in addition to replicating the same fundamental racial, political, and aesthetic concerns presented by Arnold and Doyle—concerns mostly limited to the "domestic colonialism" of Ireland—*Kim* demonstrates the application of Celticist theories and Anglo-Celtic hybridity in a full-fledged imperial context. Where Arnold's criticism and Doyle's *Hound* pursue the implications of the Anglo-Celt within his own native setting, Kipling envisions the deployment of Anglo-Celtic resources within an imperial possession, India, that is more properly representative, as an "administrative colony," of the governmental and logistical challenges of the Empire at large.[16]

In recent years, numerous critics have attempted to unlock the mystery of why Kipling would make his protagonist Irish. Most, however, have limited their readings of Kim's Irishness to political considerations, so that, in the most common scenario, Kim's transformation from faux Indian native to British imperialist *par excellence* models the imperial assimilation of two recalcitrant colonial populations, the Irish and the Indian, simultaneously. Through Kim, in this reading, Kipling is able to kill two birds with one imperialist stone, resolving at a single stroke two of the Empire's most vexing administrative problems.[17] Drawing on a broader movement among historians and literary critics to place Ireland and India in comparative relationship, this critical approach has helped elucidate the novel's pan-colonial agenda.[18] However, the comparative methodology on which this reading relies inevitably elides the differences between the two imperial possessions. The uniquely mixed character of Ireland's role in the Empire thus evaporates, blinding readers to a crucial area of the novel's complexity. To map in full its racial, colonial, and aesthetic concerns, knowledge of *both* the commonalities *and* the differences between India and Ireland is essential.

Among the smaller selection of readings that heed the specificities of Irishness, the hybrid features of Irishness are properly identified as driving Kim's remarkably adept negotiation of the hierarchy of British India. Here, Kim assumes his rightful place as the fictional counterpart of those real Irish who composed 48 percent of the British army in Bengal from 1825 to 1850, who composed 15 percent of the Indian Civil Service in the 1880s, who served as two Viceroys from 1884 to 1894, who served as governors of seven of India's eight administrative provinces in the 1890s, and who helped suppress Indian nationalist resistance throughout the period from the Sepoy Mutiny of 1857 to the Amritsar Massacre of 1919.[19] If, however, such readings succeed in attending to the historicity of Irishness, the critical record shows little consideration of the ethnological definition of the Irish in the work of Arnold and Victorian culture more broadly. A reading of Kim's Irishness that fails to attend to both factors, sociohistorical and ethnological, is incompletely equipped to track its significance. Indeed, in that the ethnological definition of the Celt is more closely related to the aesthetic than sociohistorical Irishness, attention to the former is crucial to assessing the novel's form.[20]

Kipling provides clear indications that Kim's Irishness is ethnologically based. The novel telegraphs its anthropological allegiances, as well as the discipline's implication in imperial power. The British Secret Service into whose ranks Kim is drafted pursues its agenda under the guise of "The Ethnological Survey," and its head, Colonel Creighton, values his avocation as a field researcher for the British Royal Society as much as his political work. Kim's ascendancy to a privileged position in the Survey/Service is repeatedly tied to this "scientific" frame. Though the novel features no expert in craniology to match Dr. Mortimer of *The Hound*, a comment on Kim's cranial features by Father Victor, the Catholic chaplain of the Irish Regiment whose arrival is foretold by the talismanic "prophecy" Kim inherits from his father, recalls the terms of Mortimer's diagnosis of the heritage of Sir Henry Baskerville. Just before Creighton's intervention shunts Kim's *Bildung* onto the path of Anglicization, Victor, finding Kim's self-possession amid his rapidly changing circumstances intriguing, tells him, "I'd give a month's pay to find what's goin' on in that little round head of yours" (153). Victor's brief description alludes to the same anthropological criterion by which Dr. Mortimer marks Sir Henry's racial filiations: "the rounded head of the Celt," which, in Doyle's characterization, houses the "enthusiasm and power of attachment" of Arnoldian sentimentality. This reputed Celtic feature, first asserted by the French anthropologist M. Paul Broca, whom George Stocking calls "the founder of modern physical anthropology," in two texts of the early 1860s, *Sur l'ethnologie de la France* (1860) and *Sur les Celtes* (1864), would go on to inform British texts like Beddoe's *Races of Britain* (with its "index of nigrescence") and would become a sort of conventional craniological wisdom regarding Celtic peoples by the end of the century (Stocking, *Race* 56). Father Victor's seemingly offhand reference to the shape of Kim's skull is, in fact, a sort of pseudo-scientific wink by Kipling signaling his protagonist's conformity to the "round-headed" or "brachycephalic" stereotype of the Celt. Kim is not simply an Irish character but also, crucially, a Celtic one.[21]

Celtic traits provide part of the basis for Kim's preternatural adaptivity to native India, securing a fully biological connection with its "primitive" setting to supplement his Irish liminality. Before his schooling at St. Xavier's and his initiation into the "Great Game" of Anglo-Russian imperial competition, Kipling straightforwardly depicts Kim's epistemology as a kind of sympathetic magic. Kim's first encounter with Lurgan Sahib, the master of espionage through whose tutelage all agents of the "Game" must pass, illustrates this theme: "A black-bearded man, with a green shade over his eyes, sat at a table, and, one by one, with short, white hands, picked up globules of light from a tray before him, threaded them on a glancing silken string, and hummed to himself the while" (197). Kim's inability to parse rationally the visual data presented by Lurgan's necklace of pearls renders his perspective entirely imitative or sympathetic, and his keen sensitivity to the illusion invokes the sentiment of Arnold's Celt. Kipling's description of Kim's fitful first night at Lurgan's house further attests to this "magical" epistemology, as he is repeatedly awakened by a "trumpet box" that emits "a string of the most elaborate abuse that even Kim had ever heard, in a high uninterested voice," which he proceeds to attack and silence under the belief that it carries "a devil inside" (198–99). Kim can only interpret the principle behind the phonograph as a kind of *animism*, whereby its mechanical structure is inhabited by a controlling spirit. Kim's initial epistemology belongs to the primitive anthropological domain, where evolutionarily unsophisticated peoples relate to the world through magical interpretive protocols.

The famous scene in which Lurgan coaxes Kim's perceptions into "civilized" channels further demonstrates the presence of the Celtic element in his makeup. As the final test of his training, Lurgan again disorients Kim through the illusory manipulation of light, this time reflected on the surface of a jar of water. "Fifteen feet off" from Kim, Lurgan "laid one hand on the jar," and "next instant, it stood at Kim's elbow," causing Kim to exclaim, "'That is magic!'" (201–2). Lurgan then intensifies the "magical" test by trying to hypnotize Kim into accepting further distortions of physical reality through the jar's seeming self-reconstitution:

> Lurgan Sahib laid one hand gently on the nape of his neck, stroked it twice or thrice, and whispered: 'Look! It shall come together again, piece by piece.' . . . To save his life, Kim could not have turned his head. The light touch held him as in a vice, and his blood tingled pleasantly through him. There was one large piece where there had been three, and above them in shadowy outline of the entire vessel. He could see the veranda through it, but it was thickening and darkening with each beat of his pulse. Yet the jar . . . had been smashed before his eyes. . . .

> So far Kim had been thinking in Hindi, but a tremor came on him, and with an effort like that of a swimmer before sharks, who hurls himself half out of the water, his mind leaped up from a darkness that was swallowing it and took refuge in—the multiplication table in English! . . . the jar had been smashed—yess [*sic*], smashed—not the native word, he would not think of that—but smashed—into fifty pieces, and twice three was six, and thrice three was nine, and four times three was twelve. He clung desperately to the repetition. The shadow-outline of the jar cleared like a mist after rubbing eyes. (201–202)

A better illustration of Kim's transition from an epistemology of sympathetic magic to one of "science" would be difficult to devise. Kim initially accepts the impossibility with which his perceptions are confronted, but is seized with a "tremor" that leads him to seek "refuge" in that bulwark of British rationality, "the multiplication table in English." Following this seizure-like shift, he efficiently masters the data before him by mathematical tally, and the "mist" of primitive epistemology "clears" from his eyes.

Kipling is careful to specify Kim's blood, which "tingle[s] pleasantly" in sympathetic acceptance of the jar's apparent reassembly, as the source of his response. By doing so he gestures toward a specifically Celtic epistemological affinity with Lurgan's "magic." It is Celtic proclivities that render Kim susceptible to being "swallowed" in mental "darkness." The description of primitive epistemology as an absence of light is doubly significant, in that throughout the novel, whenever Kim's British handlers observe him becoming too fully native, they fear that he is "leagued with all the Powers of Darkness," in the words of Father Victor (135). "Darkness," in addition to its religious meaning, is both an epistemological state and a racial one, and there is a palpable risk that the Celtic Kim, through his "primitive" evolutionary affinity with India, will somehow be absorbed into its "dark" population irretrievably. The Muslim horse dealer and spy Mahbub Ali goes so far as to describe Kim's dexterity in terms that may draw on the caricature of the Irish as "white chimpanzees." "A monkey does not fall among trees," he tells Creighton to quell his anxieties when the newly discovered Kim has vanished into the populace of Lucknow (176). Kipling seemingly draws on the popular mythology of the Irish as "anthropoid apes" to throw Kim's colonial adaptivity into ethnological relief. As a "Celtic Caliban" or "white negro," Kim is perfectly positioned to blend with native India, and this racial commonality underwrites Creighton's keen interest in his imperial potential.

Creighton's eagerness to draft Kim into the British Secret Service, however, depends not merely on the "nigrescent" associations of Irishness but also on its white ones. It is the combination of the two components of Irishness, white and "negro," that enables Kim to become "the first that ever saved himself" from Lurgan Sahib's epistemological darkness (203). Later in his training, Kipling contrasts Kim's facility with the final, most crucial resource of operatives in the Great Game, disguise, with the fumbling attempts of Lurgan's other, native pupil, thus affirming Kim's Irishness as the source of his unique talent: "The Hindu child played this game clumsily. That little mind . . . could not temper itself to enter into another's soul; but a demon in Kim woke up and sang with joy as he put on the changing dresses, and changing speech and gesture therewith" (207). It is as if the "Hindu child" is present merely to underscore the unparalleled utility of Irishness to imperial service. The changeability of Kim's identity is so pronounced that he can "enter into another's soul," as if a "demon" taking possession of it. The "magical" register of this description reinforces the novel's "primitive" epistemological theme, enlisting Celtic sentimentality as the very medium through which Kim's Irish liminality takes effect. Like the Irish "*pukka* devils" whose coming was foretold by his father's "prophecy," Kim is a kind of devil or "imp," as his mentor, Teshoo Lama, repeatedly calls him, adapting his being to both sides of the Anglo-Indian interface. As Kim tells the Lama, and as his success in the "Game" testifies, he "can change swiftly" (139).

Kim's changeability and its utility to navigating the primitive environs of British India are fascinatingly indexed in the series of terra cotta, bas-relief illustrations created by Kipling's father, John Lockwood Kipling, to adorn the first edition of the novel, published by Doubleday in 1901.[22] In one such image, titled simply "Kim and the Lama," the title character bears a remarkable facial resemblance to his native mentor. Here, despite the racial gulf that separates them as Irish and Tibetan subjects, respectively, Kim seems to display the same genetic feature that most prominently marks his mentor's Asianness: epicanthic eye folds. Though part of the effect may derive from Kim's facility with disguise—his avatars ranging from Muslim to "low caste Hindu" to Sahib to Buddhist "chela"—this depiction corresponds to a widespread emphasis throughout the novel on Kim's "Asiatic" or "Oriental" affinities. "Very few white people, but many Asiatics" display Kim's capacity for "throwing themselves into a mazement . . . letting the mind go free upon speculation as to what is called personal identity" (233). Given this theme and the image's remarkable convergence of traits, we must entertain the inference that Kipling perhaps directed his father's illustrative work to punctuate his protagonist's preternatural racial adaptability to the "darkness" of native India.[23]

Kim's Irishness is thus complexly overdetermined by both ethnological and sociohistorical factors. His adaptability to the "mazement" and "darkness" of India results doubly from his primitive, Celtic epistemology, the sympathetic magic of which draws him into its putative evolutionary backwardness, and from the "negro" half of his colonially hybrid Irishness. Likewise, Kim's facility with disguise itself figures as a kind of sympathetic magic, through which he is able to bring his being into mimetic conformity with that of native Indian and "sahib" alike. Where the biology of native Indian subjects like Lurgan Sahib's "Hindu boy," though also primitive and "magical" in epistemological orientation, confronts an internal limit to its adaptability, Kim's Irish biology, a hybrid compound of "black" and "white" elements, is saddled with no such limitation, and thus enables him to exploit his extraordinary capacity for "attachment" to its fullest. Kim's fluidity, in other words, derives simultaneously from a Celtic epistemology defined in Arnoldian terms and from a sociohistorical Irishness situated on the boundary between British colonizer and Indian colonized.

It is worth noting here the extent to which Kim's identity converges with that of his contemporary, Sherlock Holmes. Like Holmes, Kim presents an example of Anglo-Celtic hybridity, and like Holmes—and Arnold's composite English genius before him—Kim models in his own biology the composition of the British imperial hierarchy by subordinating his primitive to his civilized aspect. Of the many parallels between Holmes and Kim, it is perhaps their relationship to *cartography* that is most striking and that best indexes their common origins in the tenets of Victorian anthropology. As we saw above, Holmes, prior to journeying to Devonshire, uses Celtic magic to inhabit it through a British "Ordnance map," thereby modeling the deployment of primitive means toward civilized ends. Kim's own mapmaking activities for the "Ethnological Survey" manifest an identical configuration. Creighton's description to Kim of the mental habits required of a successful "chain man" presents imperial cartography as a labor for which his Celtic epistemology will be ideally suited: "thou must learn how to make pictures of roads and mountains and rivers—to carry these pictures in thine eye till a suitable time comes to set them upon paper" (166). No ethnological figure could be better equipped for this task than the Celt, whose sentimental talents enable him to apprehend nature's sublime immensity in all its "weird power and fairy charm."

The novel's aesthetic manifests an identical division of labor between primitive and civilized elements. Through free indirect discourse, in scenes like those quoted above the novel presents external events from Kim's own internal perspective. As a consequence of this strategy, during those moments where Kim inhabits a magical epistemology, the novel itself comes temporarily to inhabit a primitive modality. We have witnessed several examples of this transfer of Kim's primitive mental processes to Kipling's narrative form, such as when Kim watches Lurgan Sahib juggle "globules of light," or when he temporarily falls prey to Lurgan's hypnotic manipulation of the broken jar. At these moments, even more radically than with Sherlock Holmes's "magical" investigative activities, the reader is also plunged into "darkness," bereft of the necessary descriptive data to organize Lurgan's activities by logic or natural law. The novel, in other words, partly structures itself according to an epistemology of sympathetic magic, through which the reader's gaze merges with Kim's "mazement." Kipling's ideological priorities demand, however, that such instances of the eclipse of rationality by sentimentality remain relatively scarce. Predictably, as with *The Hound*, *Kim*'s overall form enacts the hierarchical subordination of the latter modality to the former, just as Kim's training demands the subordination of his "negro" to his "white" characteristics.

Given the articulation of these two levels of Kipling's narrative—character and form—through the free indirect discourse centered on Kim, it would be reasonable to expect that the novel's resolution might entail a coalescence of the two beneath the civilizing logic of Kipling's agenda. Such a merger is precisely what seems to occur during the famous passage in which Kim's Anglicization reaches fulfillment:

> "I am Kim. I am Kim. And what is Kim?" His soul repeated it again and again. . . . He did not want to cry . . . but of a sudden easy, stupid tears trickled down his nose and with an almost audible click he felt the wheels of his being lock up anew on the world without. Things that rode meaningless on the eyeball an instant before slid into their proper proportion. Roads were meant to be walked upon, houses to be lived in, cattle to be driven, fields to be tilled, and men and women to be talked to. They were all real and true—solidly planted upon his feet—perfectly comprehensible—clay of his clay, more or less. (331)

No longer is Kim "leagued with the Powers of Darkness"; now, having passed through the crucibles of British education and the "Great Game," he views the world with eyes cleared of the "mist" of magical epistemology. Meaninglessness becomes meaning, and formlessness comes into "proper proportion."

"Solidly planted on his feet" and with his face turned toward a "perfectly comprehensible" world, Kim's very biology melds with British-administered reality as colonially occupied India becomes "clay of his clay." Ignoring the sage lessons of his mentor Teshoo Lama to spurn "Maya," the illusory "wheel" of human desire, Kim's mobile, changeable being, echoing his seizure-like awakening from primitive epistemology under the guidance of Lurgan Sahib, "lock[s] up anew on the world without" in fulfillment of the proclivities of his "white," Saxon component.

This is not to suggest, however, that Kim's other racial element, the "negro" component that enables him to integrate with native India, falls away at novel's end. Kim's exceptional value to the British enterprise in south Asia derives from his ethnological flexibility as an Irish Celt, as a compound of both civilized and primitive characteristics who can serve as a go-between, a mediator and translator coordinating hierarchical relations between British colonizer and Indian colonized. It is Kim's Irishness that makes him, in the words of Zohreh Sullivan, "a type of super colonialist, simultaneously of the people and yet above them" (176). If *Kim* finishes on a "white" note, therefore, this is not to be taken as a racial homogenization of its protagonist. Kipling must find a way to clinch the novel's imperialist ideology and establish once and for all that Kim's loyalties are to the occupying power, but his service to that power must, inferentially, persist in the same liminal racial modality as heretofore. To see Kim as donning a full, homogeneous "sahib" identity at novel's end would thus be to misunderstand this crucial aspect of its design.

Kim's mixture of features is then not to be equated, as many readings of the novel have argued, with that of one of the novel's other liminal characters, the Hindu agent for the Secret Service, Hurree Babu. Kipling openly labels the ill-fitting hodgepodge of Hurree's partially native, partially Anglicized identity an abomination, and does so appropriately, given the anthropological context my reading has adduced, according to his inability to surmount the primitive epistemology of his race. Hurree parodies scientific rationality, proclaiming himself a "good enough Herbert Spencerian" to recognize the fundamentally illusory character of displays like Lurgan's but continuing to believe in magic long after his initiation into the Great Game (272). While fancying himself an amateur researcher for the British Royal Society, Hurree, "with a lively belief in all Powers of Darkness," does not realize that he is himself a specimen of the class of human that is its primary object of study (228). His awkward, "schizophrenic" marriage of primitive and civilized epistemologies makes Hurree the novel's central illustration of "the monstrous hybridism of East and West" (288).[24]

As we have seen, Kim experiences no such schizophrenia. His "hybridism" is set apart by Kipling from that of the Babu as an ideal form of ethnological mixture. The blend of primitive and civilized elements that is monstrous in Hurree is harmonious in Kim. This contrast then produces a final affirmation of Irish hybridity as the preferred modality of British imperialism in India. As the cases of Hurree and the "Hindu boy" demonstrate, there is some *essential* resistance in Indianness to Britain's assimilative mission; by implication, there must also be an obverse resistance in civilized Britishness to full integration with India's native population. In this determinist framework, only Irishness, as a hybrid compound of both sets of evolutionary characteristics, can mediate between these poles and hold together the fabric of the Anglo-Indian enterprise. Irishness is the suture or glue holding together the Empire; without its binding capacity, colonizer and colonized would remain opaque and antagonistic to one another. Likewise, only an Irish character can bind together a narrative devoted to chronicling the differential epistemology of the imperial ethnological interface, because only such a character is flexibly equipped to inhabit or "possess," demon-like, both magical and rational modalities. This racial logic implies that without the translating apparatus that is Irishness, it would be impossible to fashion an aesthetic capable of rendering both sides of this interface. Irishness so conceived provides what Thomas Richards calls a "utopian epistemology," a comprehensive perceptual modality with the potential to depict global difference *in toto*, and Kipling's totalizing purposes thus make Irishness not only a logical, but an inevitable aesthetic choice (44).

"East is east, and west is west, and never the twain shall meet," runs what is perhaps the most famous line of poetry Kipling ever penned. Postcolonial readers of Kim have taken this as an indication of the fundamentally "Manichean" or binary nature of Kipling's imperialism.[25] In the case of Hurree Babu, that ramshackle assembly of "eastern" and "western" elements, this proves emphatically to be the case. As Hurree himself unwittingly affirms with reference to this geographical dichotomy, "you cannot occupy two places in space simultaneously. Thatt [*sic*] is axiomatic" (299). In the case of Kim, however, such Manichean oppositions equally emphatically fail to hold up. Kim's every action and every thought throw into stark relief the major blindspot of Hurree's "axiom" and Kipling's poem: Irishness. Ireland's hybrid features in the late nineteenth and early twentieth centuries meant that the island was neither "east" nor "west," but somewhere in between. Kipling's brilliant solution for negotiating the Manichean divide between the British and their Indian subjects was to conscript a fictional Irishman to the cause. Ultimately then, taking up "the white man's burden," in another of Kipling's infamous phrases, is a geopolitical and aesthetic labor only a "white negro" is capable of performing.[26]

## "SCHEMES OF RECONSTRUCTION AND IMPROVEMENT"

Before extending the foregoing discussion into a consideration of British modernism, we must pause to restore one term in particular to the consideration of imperial-romantic uses of the Irish Celt: that of capital. Implicitly, any analysis of the British Empire in settings such as Ireland and India implicates capitalism as well, as it was economic motives that mainly drove the Empire's expansion and upkeep. Imperialist deployments of Celticism and Irishness thus necessarily buttress fantasies of capital's global spread and consolidation. My reading of *The Hound of the Baskervilles* has directly identified it as such a fantasy through its allegorical vision for the achievement of native Irish "prescription" to the Anglo-Irish economic hierarchy. Beyond such implicit links between these racial configurations and the Empire's capitalist undercarriage, however, both texts I have foregrounded above make explicit, if desultory, reference to the underlying economic stakes of the imperial game. These references complete the location of *The Hound* and *Kim* amid the orbit of concerns preoccupying Arnold's original Celticism.

We have in fact briefly glimpsed the economic underpinnings of the former text via the obituary notice for Sir Charles Baskerville, which lauds this "scion of an old country family" for attempting to "restore the fallen grandeur of his line" through "large . . . schemes of reconstruction and improvement" aimed at both the family estate and the surrounding region. Watson reports on the progress these schemes have made by the time of Sir Charles's death upon his and Sir Henry's arrival at Baskerville Hall: "The lodge was a ruin of black granite and bared ribs of rafters, but facing it was a new building, half constructed, the first fruit of Sir Charles's South African gold" (615). Thus Sir Charles's efforts in Devonshire both bear the appearance of infrastructural development and are funded through his furtive success in South African imperial capitalism. Sir Henry, for his part, vows to take up the slack of Sir Charles's mothballed projects by expelling the gloom that lends the region its Gothic mystery: "I'll have a row of electric lamps up here inside of six months, and you won't know it again, with a thousand candle power Swan and Edison right here in front of the hall door" (616). Sir Charles's benevolent landlordism and his legatee's planned continuation of his policies thus promise to root out domestic crime, colonial insurrection, and primordial nature by bringing the Celtic fringe inside the pale of a fully electrified British modernity. This is the ultimate aim consolidated by Holmes's Anglo-Celtic investigations.

The criteria by which Kim defines India as "real and true" during his final Anglicizing epiphany index these same concerns. Kim's revised vision of India parses the nation according to economic utility. "Roads were meant to be walked upon, houses to be lived in, cattle to be driven, fields to be tilled": India's proper proportions obey the logic of capitalist development. Cattle, the sacred animal of the native Hindu population whose treatment has played such a prominent role in India's turbulent colonial history, will no longer roam free but will be herded toward an instrumental fate.[27] The destiny of Indian fields is "to be tilled," in accordance with one of the founding principles of early modern British capitalism and imperialism, the Lockean doctrine of "improvement," which stipulates that land undeveloped is land forfeited.[28] And the proper "proportion" of Indian social life is middle-class British domesticity—"houses to be lived in." One is reminded of Arnold's description of the Teuton's preeminence in "the field of plain sense, of direct practical utility," where the enterprising, industrious, "steady-going Saxon temperament" produces all the amenities of modern civilization, "doors that open, windows that shut, locks that turn, razors that shave, coats that wear, watches that go, and a thousand more such good things" (*Study* 92–93). Kim, it would seem, becomes something of a Philistine, and his hybrid capabilities, now proportioned, like Holmes's, with the Saxon component predominant, ensure the colonial hegemony of civilized economic norms. Indeed, what is this new, more "steady-going" Kim, reformed from his disorderly, "Oriental" proclivities, if not an exemplar of the Irish Celt's potential to don the Teutonic virtue of "industry" in service to the Empire?

Kim's newfound conviction that "roads were meant to be walked upon" bears special significance in this regard, not merely because of the novel's prior, picaresque rambling across the Indian subcontinent, but because roads were a particularly fraught factor in the British colonization of "primitive" peoples during the late nineteenth and early twentieth centuries. Said's discussion in *Orientalism* of Lord Cromer, Evelyn Baring, who served in the Vice-regal administration in India and subsequently as Consul-General of Egypt, highlights this key cog of the civilizing mission. Said gives a prominent place in his genealogy of the title discourse to an essay of Cromer's published in the *Edinburgh Review* in 1908, which urges, "in dealing with Indians or Egyptians, or Shilluks, or Zulus . . . it is essential that each special issue should be decided mainly with reference to . . . the light of Western knowledge and experience" (qtd. in Said 37). With a pretense of benevolence, Cromer promises that by his administrative methods, "the subject races," "[e]ven the central African savage[,] may eventually learn to chant a hymn in honor of Astrea Redux," but he pivots quickly to his central guarantee: "More than this, commerce will gain" (qtd. in Said 37). Said glosses the rest of Cromer's account scathingly: "Orientals or Arabs are . . . gullible, 'devoid of energy and initiative' . . . given to 'fulsome flattery,' intrigue, cunning . . . Orientals cannot walk on either a road or a pavement (their disordered minds fail to understand . . . that roads and pavements are meant for walking); Orientals are inveterate liars . . . are 'lethargic and suspicious,' and in everything oppose the clarity, directness, and nobility of the Anglo-Saxon race" (38–39). Lord Cromer's racist and capitalist wisdom not only avers the centrality of issues such as "industry" and epistemology foregrounded in this and the previous chapter; it relates these virtues to the specific issue of roads, where, in keeping with their larger illogic and lethargy, "Orientals" cannot avail themselves of the infrastructural advantages of a magnanimous Empire. That Kim's identity "lock[s] up anew on the world without" with reference not simply to the agricultural or domestic components of modernization but also to this particular infrastructural component clinches the economic trajectory of Kipling's vision. Kim's unique compound of traits and affinity both for primitive, "Oriental" India and the civilizing endeavors of the Sahibs subtend this larger fantasy, commissioning both the Irish Celt himself and British imperial-romantic Celticism through him not just for imperial but for capitalist service.

CHAPTER 3

# The Uses of Irishness, II

## *British Modernist Celticism*

In the preceding chapter, we saw how two leading writers of imperial romance utilized hybrid Celtic figures to devise solutions to the problems and anxieties created by colonial difference. In the subsequent, modernist phase of British Celticism, the mediating function of the Celtic hybrid—henceforward, as in *Kim*, the Irish Celt proper—remains, for the most part, a constant. However, for these writers, the hybridity that had been instrumental to the imperialist fantasy of a global British capitalist modernity instead aids in puncturing that fantasy. British modernist Celticism inverts the racial hierarchy of imperial romance, instead imagining the ascendancy of primitivity as a means of recalibrating an overly civilized world. This chapter will trace this shift by recovering the Irish Celt's contributions to the work of two canonical "primitivist" modernists, Joseph Conrad and D.H. Lawrence.[1]

A brief revisitation of the formal features of *Kim* will help limn the reshuffling of racial and political terms that occurs in British modernist Celticism. During the Lurgan Sahib chapter of the novel, as we have seen, Kim is subjected to a bewildering series of perceptual stimuli designed to test his fitness for participation in the Great Game. Initially, Kim's primitive features prevent him from comprehending these stimuli, from Lurgan's necklace of pearls to the phonograph and water jug, but, through his civilized, white resources, he eventually reduces these "magical" items to their objective proportions. What occurs in the interval between the initial stimulus and its ultimate comprehension is a formal device characteristic of modernist narrative: *delayed decoding*. Kipling dabbles in the defamiliarizing gambits of early modernist fiction as a means of representing the succession between primitive, sympathetic perceptions of phenomena and civilized, rational ones. These brief departures from the novel's dominant realist mode gesture toward the inversion of anthropological terms that characterizes British modernist Celticism. Just as Arnold does through his preference for the Apollonian over the Dionysian resources of the "composite English genius," so Kipling implies that a subordination of the Irish Celt's sentimental perceptions to the protocols of "measured" representation goes hand in hand with upholding hegemonic values. For imperial romance, modernist disorientation is, in effect, an evolutionary error to be rectified by the alignment of epistemology, colonial society, and literary form with Saxon norms.

The modernist successors of Kipling and Doyle would choose instead to linger in the interval preceding the rationalization of primitive perceptions. Seizing on the "magical" resources of the Irish Celt as the medium instead for estranging and displacing British norms, in their hands, this figure becomes not the safety valve on the "machinery" of empire and capital, but a "monkey" wrench precipitating their breakdown. In the first text examined here, Conrad's *The Nigger of the "Narcissus,"* this breakdown specifically addresses the complex knot of racial and economic ideologies clustered around the figure of the colonized, black laborer. Conrad's tale of the fin-de-siècle British merchant marine conducts an extraordinary interrogation of the stereotype of black indolence held by white British workers, and it suggests that in situations of increased interracial contact, this racial-economic conception begins to break down. Somewhat unexpectedly, given this white–black emphasis, *The Nigger of the "Narcissus"* arrives at this destabilization of the racial, imperial, and economic infrastructures of the British Empire through the mediating labors of an Irish Celt. In the second text examined here, *The Plumed Serpent*, Lawrence likewise deploys this figure toward a counterhegemonic agenda, a primitivist vision in which Irishness joins in a global, pan-aboriginal revolution against an ascendant, Teutonic capitalist modernity. The innovations Conrad and Lawrence devise cultivate the radical potential latent in Kim's confused perceptions, in the investigative methods of Holmes, and in Arnold's "genius." In so doing, they also presage and, in Lawrence's case, explicitly ally themselves with the contemporary Celticist innovations ongoing in the cultural movement with which the next two chapters of this study will be concerned, the Irish Revival.

## "A SENTIMENTAL LIE": IRISHNESS AND LABOR IN *THE NIGGER OF THE "NARCISSUS"*

The work of Joseph Conrad may seem an unexpected place to come upon the footprints of the Irish Celt. Studies of race in the Conrad oeuvre have focused almost exclusively on the binary, black-white dimensions of the imperial interface and have thus scanted the liminal presence of Irishness. This presence has been outright ignored in the text that represents perhaps Conrad's first major modernist breakthrough, *The Nigger of the "Narcissus."* Though the text's foremost racial concerns are adequately reflected in its inflammatory title, and though they thus conform, on one level, to the white–black emphasis of Conrad studies, the novel's processing of these concerns is pivotally tied to an Irish character. Indeed, the text's radical and disturbing vision of the racial reorganization of the British Empire at the fin de siècle depends upon its equally radical reworking of the imperial-romantic conception of the Irish Celt.[2]

Before introducing Conrad's Celt, the novel's broader white–black racial situation requires comment. *"Narcissus"* presents something of a unique case in the annals of canonical late-nineteenth- and early-twentieth-century British fiction by virtue of its attention to the British mercantile marine. Where much of such fiction featured either domestic plotlines inflected with colonial traces or colonial plotlines driven by imperialist adventure, Conrad's story regards one of the few sites in the network of Empire where colonizing and colonized populations would have been forced into proximity on relatively equal terms. As recent work by historians of ethnic British labor attests, the merchant marine was a highly multicultural workforce in which white, British sailors mingled not only with other Europeans but also with the Empire's "black" populations. Propelled by the needs of British capital, trading companies increasingly employed both native labor in the colonies and immigrant labor at home—that labor being prejudicially perceived as cheaper, more energetic, and more docile than its white counterpart. This gave rise to tensions between Britain's white and black populations, such that white union activity began to focus on the threat of black competition. Historian Diane Frost describes that "The National Sailor's and Fireman's Union" "campaigned vigorously" against "employment of all foreign labor," while "in a petition to the then Prime Minister—Henry Campbell Bannerman—in 1906, British seamen complained of the cheapness of foreign sailors and fireman, who were seemingly doing British sailors out of a job" ("Racism" 26). Such activism helped generate "high levels of unemployment" among immigrant communities, which in turn "led to a Parliamentary Inquiry in 1910—'The Committee on Distressed Colonial and Indian Subjects' . . . [which] highlighted the distress of colonial seamen, and found that approximately three in five of 'distressed' black people were seamen" ("Racism" 26). Conrad's tale of the disturbance produced aboard a British merchant vessel by a black British seaman cannot be understood absent awareness of this racial-economic context.[3]

With this information in hand, we can begin to decipher the response of the white members of the *Narcissus* to their black competitor's arrival. Wait's perceived alienness is immediately thrown into relief when his cry of "Wait," intended to announce his belated arrival at the ship's roll-call, is misread as insubordination, as a command to its indignant captain to delay the embarkation he has just ordered (10). An ambiguity radiates from the very name of the title character, positioning him as an outsider beyond the pale of the ship's normative protocols. The crew's response to Wait once he is visible, encapsulated in the infamous description of his face as the "misshapen," "brutal," "repulsive mask of a nigger's soul," gives this disturbance a specific racial focus (11). When the crew begins to view Wait's inactivity during the first phase of their journey from India to England as an imposture, their prejudice begins to take an even more precise form: the stereotype of the lazy, parasitic black.[4] Where the managers of such companies as owned vessels like the *Narcissus* might have viewed black labor as more productive and cheaper, in keeping with the sort of economic animus reflected in British seamen's 1906 petition to Prime Minister, the white rank and file of the ship unsurprisingly embrace this more self-serving preconception. The entirety of the novel becomes a sort of laboratory experiment probing white–black economic tensions, as the white crew must decide whether to read Wait's increasing debility as either confirming or complicating the stereotype of black indolence.

The interpretive dilemma Wait presents for his white counterparts—truly infirm, or mendacious and lazy—is gradually stoked into a full-blown existential crisis rupturing the crew's racial-economic identity. Initially, the collective embrace of the stereotype of black laziness generates a consensus that he is indeed "shamming." By novel's end, however, following the unassailable fact of his death, a diametrically opposed consensus emerges in which racial antipathies yield to a sympathetic avowal of common humanity. Conrad modulates the crew's initial racism into a revised reading of Wait affirming a super-racial, ontological common denominator, and in doing so leverages the interpretive conundrum he presents to produce a tectonic shift in the essential bedrock of white, British identity. It is this shift that underlies the aesthetic estrangements for which *The Nigger of the "Narcissus"* is famous.

The conundrum in question begins to take center stage in the novel's second chapter. At this point, while they cannot shake the suspicion that Wait's condition is an imposture, the crew find themselves equally unable to disbelieve him. The enigma of Wait dominates their thoughts: "He fascinated us. He would never let doubt die. He overshadowed the ship. Invulnerable in his promise of speedy corruption he trampled our self-respect; he demonstrated to us daily our want of moral courage; he tainted our lives. Had we been a miserable gang of wretched immortals, unhallowed alike by hope and fear, he could not have lorded it over us with a more pitiless assertion of his sublime privilege" (40). Wait's indeterminacy emits an overpowering fascination, a preoccupying "doubt" that "taint[s]" the crew's "self-respect" and sense of "moral courage." If Wait is indeed "shamming," his ruse mocks and exploits the crew's white work ethic. His "promise of speedy corruption," however, makes him "invulnerable," conferring basic human rights before which they feel paralyzed. Serving him in his makeshift infirmary "with rage, and humility, as though [they] had been the base courtiers of a hated prince," they are trapped in a state of "moral" ambivalence, powerless alike to shed or assuage their racist preconceptions (34).

As they are not a "gang of wretched immortals" and are thus thoroughly caught up in emotions of "hope and fear," Wait's condition presents an unbearable reminder of their own mortality. His deterioration throughout the remainder of the voyage affirms this significance, as he gradually sheds his racial associations to embody mortality itself. When the ship nearly capsizes in chapter 3, the crew focalize their racism, their fear of death, and their hope of survival simultaneously in the effort to rescue "Jimmy" from his cabin. The rescue scene manifests their ambivalence and illustrates their transition from a racial to an ontological view:

> though at the time we hated him more than ever . . . we did not want to lose him. We had so far saved him; and it had become a personal matter between us and the sea . . . We could not get rid of the monstrous suspicion that this astounding black man . . . had been malingering heartlessly in the face of our toil, of our scorn, of our patience . . . in the face of death. Our vague and imperfect morality rose with disgust at his unmanly lie . . . we hated him because of the suspicion; we hated him because of the doubt. We could not scorn him safely—neither could we pity him without risk to our dignity . . . The secret and ardent desire of our hearts was the desire to beat him up viciously with our fists about the head; and we handled him as tenderly as though he had been made of glass. (58–59)

The crew "hate" Wait "more than ever" because of the "monstrous suspicion" of his "malingering," of a racially congenital, "unmanly" indolence that would disrespect their "toil," but they resolve to "stick to him" because the ontological risk of death's arrival exceeds the "moral" one of racial subornation. The crew's racial-economic ideology has been thrown into relief by death's proximity and now appears "vague and imperfect." They reside in a liminal psychic state, clinging to their former reading of Wait but coming to adopt an altogether different view of his significance.[5]

Later, when the imminence of his demise becomes unmistakably apparent, Wait's significance becomes entirely tied to his common humanity. The description of this thematic verge, at which the crew finally accepts the illness that Wait himself now denies, is worth quoting at length for its depiction of his influence on the ship's collective psyche:

> Falsehood triumphed. It triumphed through doubt, through stupidity, through pity, through sentimentalism. . . . Jimmy's steadfastness to his untruthful attitude in the face of the inevitable truth had the proportions of a colossal enigma—of a manifestation grand and incomprehensible that at times inspired a wondering awe. . . . The latent egoism of tenderness to suffering appeared in the developing anxiety not to see him die. His obstinate non-recognition of the only certitude whose approach we could watch from day to day was as disquieting as the failure of some law of nature. He was so utterly wrong about himself that one could not but suspect him of having access to some source of supernatural knowledge. He was absurd to the point of inspiration . . . he seemed to shout his denials from beyond the awful border. He was becoming immaterial, like an apparition. . . . He was demoralizing. Through him we were becoming highly humanized, tender, complex, excessively decadent: we understood the subtlety of his fear, sympathized with all his repulsions, shrinkings, evasions, delusions—as though we had been over-civilized and rotten, and without any knowledge of the meaning of life. We had the air of being initiated in some infamous mysteries. (104–5)

A better description of Wait's status as the center of the ship's psychology could scarcely be conceived. His "obstinate non-recognition" of mortal "certitude" he previously broadcast so brazenly is "absurd to the point of inspiration," heartening the crew against death through the psychic mechanism of a "latent egoism." Formerly unsophisticated, they become "humanized," "tender" and, "complex" through sympathetic identification with Wait's plight. This Wait is no longer the racially differentiated subject of the novel's beginning, but embodies a super-racial, ontological meaning.

When Wait does finally die, his departure leaves his shipmates metaphysically adrift. His influence on them has grown so profound as to outlive its source, continuing to exert destabilizing effects on their conception of "the meaning of life." "Jimmy's death, after all, came as a tremendous surprise," the narrator recalls, elaborating, "We did not know how much faith we had put in his delusions . . . his death, like the death of an old belief, shook the foundations of our society. A common bond was gone; the strong, effective and respectable bond of a sentimental lie" (116–17). Wait's death has the status of a religious event, shaking the very "foundations" of the ship's "society" by removing the "common bond" of the "sentimental lie" that he might survive. The crew's view of Wait has shifted so completely that his loss alters their very cosmology, imbuing it with generalized uncertainty: "doubt survived Jimmy" (117).

As one might expect, this newfound white–black intimacy creates profound ripple effects in the economic landscape that was formerly defined by racial difference. These effects are dramatically marked prior to Wait's death in the famous "strike" scene, in which the ship's white seamen agitate in favor of their former competitor. This further turn of the novel's racial-economic screw is instigated by one of its other key characters, the cockney rabble-rouser, "Donkin," who, like Wait, is initially perceived by the rank and file as prone to "unmanly" indolence. Donkin's "ignoble" parasitism, thinly disguised beneath faux-Marxist protestations of his "rights," positions him as an expert arbiter of the initial, racist interpretation of Wait's illness (15). At that stage, Donkin offers the most influential reading of Wait's inactivity: "Donkin grinned venomously . . . told Jimmy that he was a 'black fraud'; hinted to us that we were an imbecile lot, daily taken in by a vulgar nigger" (37). Donkin pours poison into the crew's ears, taunting their "morality" and "self-respect" and herding them toward the stereotypical reading of Wait as a "black fraud."

Later, however, Donkin instead advocates for the revised view of Wait. He "officiates" in a series of quasi-religious observances outside Wait's cabin, which "had, in the night, the brilliance of a silver shrine where a black idol, reclining stiffly under a blanket, blinked its weary eyes and received our homage" (81). His newfound faith inspires him to lead a strike against the ship's captain, Allistoun, who, at the point when Wait, believing himself recovered, asks to return to work, still clings to the initial view of his illness as an imposture and orders him confined to his cabin as punishment. The crew's response to this decree is rendered collectively, with only Donkin's contributions receiving specific attribution: "'D'ye mean to say, sir,' he asked, ominously, 'that a sick chap ain't allowed to get well in this 'ere hooker? . . . Are we bloomin' masheens?,' inquired Donkin . . . 'Soon show 'em we ain't boys'—'the man's a man, if he is black'—'We ain't goin' to work this bloomin' ship shorthanded if Snowball's all right'—'He says he is.'—'Well then, strike, boys strike!'" (91). Donkin's current agitations decry the very same assumptions his former ones avowed, and they define the ensuing strike as a symbolic advocacy for Wait's common humanity. Wait is brought, suddenly, into the economic fold of the *Narcissus*, whose white laborers revolt against its captain for violating his equal rights. "The man's a man, if he is black": this culminating protest completes the dismantling of the "moral" ideology the crew originally espoused, to the point that they are now willing to sacrifice what one historian has called—though in a different national context—"the wages of whiteness."[6]

The crew's renunciation of its white privilege in favor of a larger, multicultural cause enables us to link the novel's racial and economic themes with the otherwise curious tenor of its famous "Preface," where Conrad specifies "solidarity" as the animating ideal of his aesthetic agenda. His desire to speak "to the subtle but invincible conviction of solidarity that knits together the loneliness of innumerable hearts; to that solidarity in dreams, in joy, in sorrow, in aspirations, in illusions, in hope, in fear, which holds men to each other, which binds together all humanity—the dead to the living, and the living to the unborn," may be read in this light as a coded defiance of Victorian racial attitudes ("Preface" 145–46). "Solidarity in mysterious origin, in toil, in joy, in hope, in uncertain fate": such descriptions give a precise name to the crew's ultimate, sympathetic posture, which overrides Wait's racial particularly in recognition of his human universality ("Preface" 147). The word "solidarity," with its connotations of left-leaning political and economic activism, provides an apt suture between the post-racial labor agitations depicted by the novel and the stated aesthetic intentions of Conrad's manifesto. *"Narcissus"* uses the prod of solidarity to unsettle the Victorian anthropological equation of civilized and primitive races with a respective aptitude and inaptitude for capitalist "toil," and it is the erosion of this "moral" code by the "egoistic" embrace of super-racial identity in mortality that drives the novel's famously unsettled form.

This reading, however, tells only half the story. For if the text's aesthetic and ideological implications would seem to push beyond the racist assumptions of Victorian anthropology, the novel nonetheless preserves the husk of the fictional genre most allied with those assumptions, that of imperial romance. *"Narcissus"* proves a striking example of what Michael Valdez Moses, with reference to *Lord Jim*, has described as "Conrad's hybridization of literary form, his extensive use of heterogeneous generic forms within a single narrative" ("Disorientalism" 65–66).[7] Beneath its modernist breakthrough, the infrastructure of imperial romance endures through the novel's treatment of its lone Irish character, nicknamed "Belfast." Paradoxically, the novel only arrives at its revolutionary, post-anthropological rapprochement between whiteness and blackness by deploying a "primitive," anthropological notion of Irishness. Through Belfast, Conrad indicates that it is through the imaginative resources of a Celticist Irishness that Wait's transformative significance can best be deciphered.

Conrad's portrayal of Belfast draws on both the Arnoldian notion of sentimentality and the imperial-romantic deputation of the Irish as mediating colonial agents. It is sentimentality that outfits Belfast with the epistemological capacity to register the deep ontological disturbance produced by Wait's illness and death. Belfast's keen sensitivity and "melancholy" proclivities predispose him to the revised, sympathetic reading of Wait and position him as a sort of mediator between Wait and his white detractors. Thus, just as *Kim* deploys its Irish protagonist as a resource for managing the unruly "black" population of India—as an entity through which the antinomies of civilized and primitive can be hierarchically resolved—so *"Narcissus"* deputizes Belfast to resolve the antagonism between James Wait and the ship's white crew. But where the Irishman's mediations in imperial romance consolidate the genre's hegemonic priorities, Belfast's contribute to their demolition.

Belfast's early responses to Wait in fact hew closely to a specific post-Arnoldian Irish stereotype identified by Curtis in *Apes and Angels*, that of the "melancholeric" Celt. According to Curtis, this figure combined the melancholy of Arnold's "sentimental" Celt with a violent, "choleric" trait perceived by the British as the source of the nationalist agitations of the 1860s, '70s, and '80s discussed earlier in the context of *The Hound of the Baskervilles* (L.P. Curtis, *Apes* 96). As the narrator describes, Belfast's reactions to Wait's illness swing wildly from passionate sympathy to pugnacious resentment—from melancholy to choleric emotional states. As he records, "emotional little Belfast was for ever on the verge of assault or on the verge of tears" (23). At one moment, "illogical little Belfast reproached our nigger with great fury," but soon after, "he looked round at us from Jimmy's bedside, his comical mouth twitching, with tearful eyes" (24). Through his melancholeric proclivities, Belfast becomes a privileged gauge of the ambivalence of the ship's response to Wait, lurching from extreme, sympathetic identification with him to an equally extreme, antipathetic disparagement of him.

In keeping with the stereotypical sentimentality of this "comical," "illogical," "emotional" Irishman, Belfast is described as an early convert to the belief in Wait's ability to elude death, to the quasi-religious faith that is dubbed, significantly "a sentimental lie" in the passage quoted earlier. At the point when the majority of the crew has begun to view Wait sympathetically, the narrator recalls, "It was at this time that Belfast's devotion—and also his pugnacity—secured universal respect. He spent every moment of his spare time in Jimmy's cabin. He tended to him, talked to him. . . . But outside he was irritable, explosive as gunpowder, somber, suspicious, and never more brutal than when most sorrowful. With him it was a tear and a blow: a tear for Jimmy, a blow for any one who did not seem to take a scrupulously orthodox view of Jimmy's case" (86). Not only does Belfast's "view of Jimmy's case" earn "universal respect" for its prescience; this "view" is unmistakably fueled by the traits of the melancholeric Irish Celt, whose emotional vacillations could hardly be more succinctly rendered than with the phrase "a tear and a blow." Whereas his earlier, sentimental posture shifted suddenly from tender sympathy for to combative antipathy toward Wait himself, here, in keeping with the novel's transformation from a racial to an ontological theme, Belfast shifts equally suddenly from sympathy for Wait to antipathy toward those doubting him. Belfast's sentimentality renders his the privileged perspective toward Wait's "sublime" condition. The novel thus positions him as a paradigm for the ultimate perceptual posture of the "Narcissus," and of the novel itself. The narrator's account simply replicates the stages of antipathy, doubt, sympathy, grief, and residual anxiety through which he describes Belfast as passing.

This is to say, in short, that the aesthetic texture of the novel's exploration of black/white economic conflict and reconciliation is encoded as racially Irish. It is thus Irishness, not blackness, that most shapes the novel's aesthetic agenda and that Conrad commissions to accomplish his central artistic purpose: "by the power of the written word . . . to make you see" ("Preface" 147). What innumerable critics, following Ian Watt and Fredric Jameson, have called Conrad's "impressionism" is here revealed as indebted to the Arnoldian definition of Celtic sentimentality.[8] In search of an epistemological apparatus to transmit his "vision" of that solidarity which "binds men to each other and all mankind to the visible world," Conrad settles on the makeup of the Irish Celt as a sort of biological model ("Preface" 147). Conceiving of his project as distinct from that of the "scientist" who, "impressed" by its "aspect," settles on a rational epistemology of "facts" as his medium of engagement with the world, Conrad, likewise impressed, lights on the primitive, "magical" epistemology of the Celt—that which makes him recoil from "the despotism of fact"—as a parallel for his aesthetic purposes ("Preface" 145). Belfast, and with him the novel's narrator, gains "sublime" access to that most primitive fact of the human universe, mortality, via the "sympathetic magic" of Celtic sentimentality. Through them, the reader gains a like access and will have instilled in him/her, subtly but invincibly, the universal "moral" posture of solidarity.[9]

Conrad affirms Belfast's position as the novel's aesthetic center of gravity twice more, first during the scene of Wait's burial at sea, and second during an encounter between the narrator and Belfast after the crew's disembarkation in London. During the former scene, just as Belfast mediates the relationship between the white and black subjects of *"Narcissus"*—as a sort of racial ambassador bringing Wait into the fold of the ship—so he receives the honor of ushering the deceased back out of its ranks. Belfast's special connection with Wait moves him to take the lead in his burial preparations: "it was he, and no other man, who would help . . . prepare what was left of Jimmy for a solemn surrender to the insatiable sea" (97). "Overcome with sorrow, dropping tears" on Wait's shrouded form, Belfast superintends the ritual, inspiring the crew to wonder what makes him "take on so" on Jimmy's behalf (97). These measures complete, Wait is draped in "the folds of the Union Jack," again reflecting his incorporation into the British "society" that formerly excluded him (98). But Wait's white welcome now begins to wear thin. As if purging the ship of Wait's moral "taint," the boatswain "snatche[s] off the Union Jack" and tries to jettison his remains (99). Wait's corpse, however, refuses to move. It is only when Belfast urges his deceased comrade to "be a man" and "go!," "his fingers touch[ing] the head," that "the grey package start[s] reluctantly to whizz off the lifted planks all at once, with the suddenness of a flash of lightning" (99). Reaffirming his status as the racial mediator binding Wait to the crew, only Belfast succeeds in ejecting the "unfair burden," upon which "the crowd stepped forward like one man" to utter "a deep Ah—h—h!" (99).

It would seem, then, given this collective relief, that the racial-economic breakthrough of "solidarity" ultimately fails to stick. This ethos has taken firm root with the "sentimental" Irishman, but its seeds have found less arable ground in the white, British psyche. Belfast's final appearance seems conceived to punctuate precisely this point. This scene, depicting the crew's disembarkation in London, is formally noteworthy through the modulation of the novel's famously protean narrator into a first-person, limited role.[10] Declining to join his shipmates for a farewell drink, the newly-embodied narrator encounters the Irishman:

> I came upon Belfast. He caught my arm with tremendous enthusiasm.—"I couldn't go wi' 'em," he stammered, indicating by a nod our noisy crowd, that drifted slowly along the other sidewalk. "When I think of Jimmy . . . Poor Jim! When I think of him I have no heart for drink. You were his chum, too . . . but I pulled him out . . . didn't I? Short wool he had . . . Yes . . . He wouldn't go . . . He wouldn't go for nobody." He burst into tears. "I never touched him—never—never!" he sobbed. "He went for me like . . . like . . . a lamb." (106)

Belfast's appeal to the narrator as a fellow "chum" of Wait's again implicates the latter, and through him the novel's aesthetic, in the "sentimental" view of its events. Belfast's melancholy attachment leaves him with no heart for celebration, and by implication, the narrator's refusal to accompany the "noisy crowd" also results from the psychic disturbance of Wait's demise. Here, however, he rebuffs Belfast's appeal: "I disengaged myself gently. Belfast's crying fits generally ended in a fight with some one, and I wasn't anxious to stand the brunt of his inconsolable sorrow. Moreover, two bulky policeman stood nearby, looking at us with a disapproving and incorruptible gaze" (106). At the final moment, the novel "disengages" from its earlier, super-racial sympathies, whose remnants are relegated to the "melancholeric" mentality of the Irish Celt. The sudden involvement of the police clinches this turn, as Belfast's excessive "sorrow" draws the ire of the "incorruptible" British law, whose hegemonic gaze, Sherlock Holmes–like, will not countenance the text's earlier investments.

This late twist to the novel's perspective enables us to engage two final, related questions, the first being the relationship of *"Narcissus"* to Conrad's reputed political conservatism, and the second the relationship of the text's Celticist primitivism to the forces of imperial capital. The early phase of the ship's journey indeed seems to bear out the received image of Conrad as endorsing a traditional Englishness, here represented by the white, seafaring work ethic Wait perturbs. During this phase, "Belfast's devotion" to a Wait given to the congenital laziness and devilish mendacity of the Empire's black subjects would position him as, in effect, the dupe of such schemes. Belfast's exceptional attachment to Wait and his facilitation of the crew's subornation would then implicate both the sentimental Celtic trait of unfitness for "industry" and the Irish position as colonial and racial intermediary. His susceptibility to what the narrator calls Wait's "unmanly lie" would, indeed, square perfectly with the Arnoldian classification of the Celt as *feminine*—and thus unsuited to mental and economic self-mastery. In this reading, the interstitial features of the Irish Celt so advantageous for the imperial-romantic fantasy of colonial suppression bear the negative flipside of providing a structural breach in the ship of Empire—an access point through which primitive forces may infiltrate the metropole. The same Anglo-Celtic liminality that ensured the hegemony of British imperial capital for Doyle and Kipling would thus become, rather, a *permeability* that must be foreclosed to shore up that hegemony.[11]

This reading is hard to square, however, with the text's modulation from the certitudes of the Victorian racial-economic code to a post-racial commonality centered on Wait's mortality. This modulation highlights that code's limitations irrevocably, both by tying its racism to the "sublime" threat of death and by insisting on the title character's possession of the humanity it would deny. Following such a transition, white, mercantile, British capital can never recover its self-assurance. And just as it figures as the conduit for racial-economic subversion in the text's initial register, so Celtic Irishness serves as the central conduit for its later post-racial humanism. Its feminine, sentimental, sublime proclivities thus indeed serve to destabilize the Empire's racial-economic infrastructure, but this destabilization bears a truth value that cannot be overridden by the narrator's closing reflections. Conrad himself may have wished otherwise, and he does indeed traffic in the negative associations of Arnoldian and popular Irish stereotypes, but his aesthetic honesty in probing the tensions produced when white–black contact deviates from the anthropological script yields an irreversible glimpse into the leveling, multicultural tendencies of fin-de-siècle British capital. Through the novel's fraught, wondering aesthetic, the Manichean, late Victorian worldview dehisces, leaving in its wake a frighteningly jumbled geopolitical cognitive map. The book's modernism inheres in—indeed consists of—this disorientation. By mediating the relationship of the crew and Wait and limning the mental posture Wait's disturbance of working-class whiteness would inspire, Irish Celtic hybridity and sentimentality provide the inspiration for "solidarity" as a fully counterhegemonic ethos.

## CELTICISM, PAN-ABORIGINALITY, AND TRANSNATIONALISM IN LAWRENCE

The implications of the modernist shift in British Celticism are further illuminated by the case of another of the nation's best-known primitivist writers, D.H. Lawrence. Even more fully than Conrad, Lawrence, chiefly in mid-1920s texts such as *Fantasia of the Unconscious*, *St. Mawr*, and *The Plumed Serpent*, deploys the Celt to overthrow the aesthetic, political, and economic norms of the high imperial moment. Lawrence's Celticism, however, also forms something of an endpoint to British fictional explorations of the Irish Celt's potential by expressing a new perspective not yet glimpsed in either phase of British Celticism: disillusionment. Lawrence's mid-'20s works, in particular *The Plumed Serpent*, represent both an extension of the project of British Celticism and its discontinuation, both an additional instance of the urge toward Celtic otherness and a valediction to that urge's historical viability. Though Lawrence hungers for a primitive otherness accessible via the Celt, he ultimately declares the foreclosure of such access by the globalizing march of capitalist modernity. Pronouncing the Teutonic term of the Anglo-Celtic agon the historical victor, Lawrence brings full circle the British Celticist heritage that began with Matthew Arnold.

As with Conrad's early work, Lawrence's work of the mid-'20s has been treated by critics in a predominantly binary racial mode, as pursuing a prototypical primitivist agenda in which an enervated European whiteness seeks to coopt the vitality of modernity's non-white others.[12] The full complexity of Lawrence's project has not yet been properly appreciated, partly because his numerous Irish characters, being "white" and European, have been read as bearing a strictly "civilized" racial orientation. As we have seen, however, the anthropological discourse on which late-nineteenth- and early-twentieth-century British authors relied defined at least one white group, the Celts, along partly primitive lines. In keeping with this discourse, Lawrence himself did not conceive of the division between civilized modernity and primitive indigeneity in Manichean terms, as is evident in an oft-cited passage from *Fantasia of the Unconscious*:

> The great pagan world which preceded our own . . . had a vast and perhaps perfect science of its own, a science in terms of life . . . this great science . . . once was universal. . . . Asia, Polynesia, America, Atlantis and Europe. . . . In that world men lived and taught and knew, and were in one complete correspondence over all the earth . . . the interchange was complete, and knowledge, science was universal . . . cosmopolitan as it is today. . . . Then came the melting of the glaciers, and the world flood. The refugees from the drowned continents fled . . . some degenerated naturally into cave men . . . some retained their marvelous innate beauty and life-perfection . . . some wandered savage in Africa, and some, like Druids or Etruscans or Chaldeans or Amerindians

> or Chinese, refused to forget, but taught the old wisdom, only in its half-forgotten, symbolic forms. More or less forgotten, as knowledge: remembered as ritual, gesture and myth-story. . . . And so, the intense potency of symbols is part at least memory. . . . And so it is that these myths now begin to hypnotize us again. (13)

Lawrence outlines what we may call a pan-aboriginal theory of human vitality, in which it is not only nonwhite peoples such as "Amerindians" who once possessed an idealized primitive knowledge—a "science in terms of life"—but white groups such as the "Druids." Like the work of the anthropologist on whom he relied most, James Frazer, Lawrence viewed the ancient world as almost undifferentiatedly primitive, and within this schema, both nonwhite and white peoples possessed what he calls "the old vision" (*Fantasia* 15–16). It is the white groups he admits into his aboriginal pantheon, in particular those Celtic groups of which the Druids, masters of "the old wisdom," were the forebears, that thus present the greatest challenge for readers of his mid-'20s texts, as it is these which, though possessed of vestigial primitive characteristics, had been incorporated into the civilized ontology of capitalist modernity by the time of his writing. The "revival" of the ancient "science in terms of life" toward which he looked could thus be expected to be especially preoccupied with the status of this uniquely mixed racial group.

Lawrence's mid-'20s fiction both avers the inclusion of the white Celts in his pan-aboriginal vision and situates them as the historical bellwether for modernity's impending foreclosure of that vision's revivalist potential. Lawrence's Celts play this wishbone-like role across his oeuvre, from *St. Mawr* to "The Princess" and the text that is in many ways the culmination of Lawrence's primitivist aesthetic, *The Plumed Serpent*. Appropriately, given the sociohistorical context established in this and the foregoing chapter, this text, through its protagonist Kate Leslie, situates the Irish as the privileged example of the liminal, hybrid ontology of the modernized aborigine. The novel deploys Kate to probe the viability of a resuscitated primitive vitality in the context of the Mexican Revolution of the 1910s, which Lawrence recasts as an indigenous religious movement devoted to reviving the Aztec God, Quetzalcoatl. Lawrence further affirms his Irish preoccupations by linking this fictional revolution to contemporary Irish events such as the Anglo-Irish War of 1919–22 and the Irish Civil War of 1922–23, in the former of which Kate's husband, James Joachim Leslie, fought and died. Lawrence gestures toward a deep, transnational affinity between Ireland and Mexico even beyond their revolutionary political movements that extends to a shared descent from his pantheon of "primitive" races. In both senses, racial and political, Kate's experience in the country confirms the assessment of the Oxford-educated leader of the revived Mexican religion of Quetzalcoatl, Don Ramón Carrasco, that "Mexico is another Ireland" (69).

*The Plumed Serpent* is filled with descriptions of Kate's essential Irishness. Kate displays an "Irish contempt" for and "Irish malice" toward the populace of Mexico City before her journey to Ramón's country stronghold at Lake Sayula, and Lawrence points to her "Irish mind" to explain her revulsion at cultural practices such as the bullfight (7, 14). At the "Tea-Party in Tlacolula" where she meets Don Ramón, Kate's aloofness is attributed to her being "too Irish, too wise" (37). Soon, however, as she is initiated into the revivalist movement of Ramón and his first lieutenant, Don Cipriano, such superficial attributions give way to a deeper affinity. As she is introduced to the mysteries of Ramón's neo-paganism, Kate's being responds to its irrationality; she reflects, "All a confusion of contradictory gleams of meaning, Quetzalcoatl. But why not? Her Irish spirit was weary to death of definite meanings, of a God of one fixed import" (54). From this point on, Kate's embrace of the movement reflects the answering call of her chthonic, Celtic Irishness to its fully manifest Mexicanness.

Indeed, Kate's portrayal invokes Celticism directly. On the night of her fortieth birthday, she accepts an invitation to a dinner party at Don Ramón's estate with her two American companions, Owen and Villers. Her appearance "in a simple gown with a black velvet top and a loose skirt of delicate brocaded chiffon, of a glimmering green and yellow and black," with an accompanying "long string of jade and crystal," prior to their departure from their Mexico City hotel, explicitly recalls one of British Celticism's foundational figures (56). Lawrence telegraphs the association: "It was a gift she had, of looking like an Ossianic goddess, a certain feminine strength and softness glowing in the very material of her dress" (56). Kate appears an "Ossianic goddess," a female version of the ancient Celtic hero Ossian, the figure at the center of the first wave of British Celticism in the eighteenth century inspired by James McPherson's fabricated epic, *Fingal* (1763). Ossian or Oisín in Celtic mythology was the son of Finn MacCool, the leader of the Fianna or Fenians, an ancient, demi-godly Irish race that defended the island from Norse invaders in the third century CE. The Celticist lineage that began with McPherson and would reach its culmination in Revivalist Ireland in the work of W.B. Yeats and others defined this warrior bard as the quintessential Celtic, and specifically Irish, figure, a mythic personification of the island's primordial essence.[13]

Several other aspects of the above passage help elucidate Kate's place in the novel's design. Most revealing is Lawrence's emphasis on Kate's femininity, the "feminine strength and softness glowing" from her dress and deportment, which ties her to the definition of the Celts as "feminine" in *The Study*—whose own epigraph comes directly from McPherson's sham epic (1). Lawrence further invokes this gendered conception of the Celts at the conclusion of the same chapter, when Kate meets the man who will later become her husband, General Don Cipriano, head of the military arm of Ramón's movement. Cipriano grows infatuated as Kate describes her husband's death in the Anglo-Irish War, and Lawrence implies that his attraction stems from her elemental femininity: "He looked at her soft, wet hands over her face, and at the one big emerald on her finger. . . . The wonder, the mystery, the magic . . . flooded him again. He was in the presence of the goddess, white-handed, mysterious, gleaming with a moon-like power and the intense potency of grief" (67). The feeling of "wonder," "mystery," and "magic" that floods through Cipriano arises from a Celtic source. Kate, in the grip of an intense, *melancholy* attachment to her husband, "gleam[s]" with a "moon-like power" that recalls "the people in the moon," the fairy gods of Celtic mythology in *St. Mawr*, while the "big emerald on her finger" curbs her Celticness in a specifically Irish direction (*St. Mawr* 128). Kate becomes a *genius loci* of the "emerald isle," an essentially feminine, divine descendent of the legendary Fianna.

This Irish essence secures Kate's membership in the divine triumvirate in whom Don Ramón seeks to incarnate his religion of Quetzalcoatl. Though the symbolic meaning of this religion is convoluted, it is clear that Lawrence wished it to embody a union of complementary ontological states. The misogynistic rituals orchestrated by Ramón all entail the ceremonial melding of traditional gender roles through Ramón's native, peasant followers. Above these masses, Lawrence positions Cipriano, Kate, and Ramón in a trinity symbolizing respectively an essential masculinity, an essential femininity, and their dialectical fusion. Cipriano's cosmic, essential maleness—"inert and heavy, unresponsive, limited as a snake or a lizard . . . [but with] a curious power . . . the mystery of the primeval world!"—eventually persuades her to marry him and assume her place in Ramón's pantheon (308). "What a marriage! How terrible! And how complete!" she thinks while "submitting, succumbing" to Cipriano, who radiates the "gift" of "the ancient phallic mystery, the ancient god-devil of the male Pan" (308). Like her husband James Joachim, the Irish nationalist martyr, before her, Kate, succumbing to Cipriano's "dark," phallic maleness, realizes her feminine destiny as one of what the narrator calls "the white, self-sacrificing gods," thus securing the dialectical union of the universe's gender principles and restoring the sundered vitality of Lawrence's pan-aboriginal ontology (386).

Lawrence affirms this symbolism during Kate and Cipriano's subsequent marriage ceremony. Cipriano and Ramón both envision her apotheosis into the goddess Malintzi alongside Cipriano as Huitzilopochtli and Ramón as Quetzalcoatl, the god of the "Morning Star" who represents the *Aufhebung* of Kate's femaleness and Cipriano's maleness. Kate's ascent to the pantheon of Ramón's religion was foreshadowed when she descended the hotel staircase in "glimmering green and yellow and black," a description that symbolically imbricates the green of Ireland with the yellow and black associated with Mexico throughout the novel. Lawrence gradually heightens the verdure of Kate's dress and accessories as the ceremony draws near, outfitting her with a "soft velour hat of jade green," along with her "string of jade and crystal" and emerald ring (319). Cipriano envisions her bedecked in green for their marriage ceremony: "you, too, shall come, in a green dress they shall weave you, with blue flowers at the seam, and on your head the new moon of flowers" (321). As the preparations begin, Kate tries on her Indian-made Celtic wedding gown, tailored according to his specifications, "of green, hand-woven wool . . . showing a bit of white, full underdress, and fastened on the left shoulder . . . strange and primitive, but beautiful" (329). Initiated into the mysteries of Ramón's cosmic vision, and into the mystery of her own chthonic, untapped Celtic divinity, Kate becomes "green-robed Malintzi," "watching the bud of her life united with" Cipriano's "soft, deep Indian heat" on the altar of Quetzalcoatl (383, 392). The "tufts of greenish flowers" and the "dream"-like "perfume" of the "greenish lilac" that adorns her chair clinch the Celtic symbolism of her essentially feminine godhead (392).

Kate and Cipriano's union is freighted with further symbolic associations as well. Both characters represent the incarnation of heavenly bodies in addition to their cosmic gender roles, as Kate's Celtic essence becomes the moon to Cipriano's sun—his elemental, "deep Indian heat." Don Ramón as Quetzalcoatl, the Morning Star, forms the apex of the celestial trinity, the *logos* sublating both. Together, the three gesture toward a modified version of the "old vision" informing *Fantasia of the Unconscious*. The pan-aboriginal vitalism sketched there undergoes a slight retooling, whereby Lawrence assigns gender roles to its constituent races, the Celtic and Indian, now recoded as essentially, cosmically feminine and masculine. This newly gendered vision brings forth the realization of Lawrence's primitivist project, as together Kate, Cipriano, and Ramón form a sort of summit gathering of the world's aboriginal races. Each proves his/her worthiness of inclusion amid the elect whom Ramón dubs "the natural aristocrats of the world," the racial congress that would revive the ancient "science in terms of life":

> Only the Natural Aristocrats can rise above their nation; and even they do not rise beyond their race. Only the Natural Aristocrats of the World can be international, or cosmopolitan, or cosmic. . . . The peoples are [not] capable of it. . . . So if I want Mexicans to learn the name of Quetzalcoatl, it is because I want them to speak with the tongues of their own blood. I wish the Teutonic world would once more think in terms of Thor and Wotan, and the tree Igdrasil. And I wish the Druidic world would see, honestly, that in the mistletoe is their mystery, and that they themselves are the Tuatha de Danaan, alive, but submerged. And a new Hermes should come back to the Mediterranean, and a new Astaroth to Tunis; and Mithras again to Persia, and Brahma unbroken to India; and the oldest of dragons to China . . . then the earth might rejoice, when the First Lords of the West met the First Lords of the South and East, in the Valley of the Soul. (246–47)

Ramón envisions a transnational conclave of "natural aristocrats," plenipotentiaries of the Mexican, Teutonic, Celtic, Mediterranean, Persian, Indian, and Chinese races, whose collective grounding in ancient mythology will found the utopian ontology of the future.

Ethnological Irishness in *The Plumed Serpent* is then merely one primitive agency among a global network of equivalent entities. Though peculiarly feminine, Kate's Celtic Irishness places her on ostensibly equal footing with the masculine, Indian Mexicanness of Cipriano, and their coupling models the kind of trans-aboriginal synergy that Ramón's natural aristocracy would produce. However, the fulfillment forecast by Don Ramón and by *Fantasia* is only temporarily realized. This utopian future is imperiled by the global dominance of a machinelike, artificial modernity that Lawrence ultimately suggests is too firmly entrenched to be counteracted. Lawrence's mid-'20s work persistently highlights humanity's compromised vitality amid the mechanized modalities of the modern. Characters like Clifford Chatterley, maimed and rendered impotent by World War I and confined, cyborg-like, to a motorized wheelchair, or the shell-shocked Native American, Phoenix, from *St. Mawr*, index the monstrous subjection to modernity's imperatives, a set of forces that Lou Witt, the protagonist of the latter work, refers to simply as "the evil" (*St. Mawr* 99). For her, as for Lawrence, the epicenter of this "evil" regime is contemporary England, which is "not real . . . except poisonously" (*Plumed* 154). This assessment echoes the refrain of perhaps the most famous British modernist text, T.S. Eliot's "The Waste Land," where the metropolises of modernity, from London to Jerusalem and Alexandria, are "unreal" as a result of abandoning their cultural and mythological roots. Like Eliot, Lawrence bemoans a world populated by what Kate Leslie calls "mechanical cog-wheel people," lifeless automata held in thrall by capitalist modernity's developmental logic (*Plumed* 101).

Through the fate of its protagonist, *The Plumed Serpent* affirms that despite their inclusion in his primitive pantheon, the Irish Celts, for Lawrence, occupy a signal place in the world's compromised ontology. After seemingly consummating Ramón's religion of Quetzalcoatl through her union with Cipriano, Kate finds herself gradually but irresistibly withdrawing from the neo-aboriginal culture of postcolonial Mexico. After weeks of vacillation, Kate resolves to return home, and in this recoil, the symbolic orientation of her Irishness shifts. Where her participation in Ramón's "science in terms of life" had once affirmed her Celtic primitivity, Kate's detachment from the revived Pan aligns her instead with the makeup of that other Celtic figure, the Irish "white negro." Through her ultimate failure to cultivate her potential, Kate affirms both the irreversibility of modernity's clouding of "the old vision" and the representative status Lawrence accords to the hybridizing effects of Irish sociohistoricity.

Cipriano senses Kate's hesitancy very early, and their subsequent interaction is colored by his concern that her British conditioning will stunt her potential. An early reflection of Kate's presages one of his more pointed interrogations of her earnestness: "Here and here alone, it seemed to her, life burned with a deep new fire. The rest of life seemed wan, bleached, and sterile. The pallid wanness and weariness of her world! . . . surely this was a new kindling of mankind! . . .Yet she preferred to be on the fringe. . . . She could not bear to come into actual contact" (119). When Cipriano later ventriloquizes this description, it becomes clear that she is out of kilter with this "new kindling of mankind." Sensing her distaste for the movement's native, peasant rank and file, Cipriano asks her, "You don't like brown-skinned people?" to which Kate replies, "'I think it is beautiful to look at,' she said. 'But'—with a faint shudder—'I am glad I am white'" (187). This striking admission leads Cipriano to press her further: "You feel there could be no contact?" to which she responds, "Yes! . . . I mean that" (187). As in her reflections above, Kate denies the potential for real "contact" with aboriginal Mexicanness, founding her belief in the notion of a magnetic repulsion between brown and white peoples. Such discussions ultimately convince Cipriano that Kate may be correct in denying the potential for their interracial "contact," but he explains the cause of Kate's distance in very different terms. He accuses her: "You think like a modern woman, because you belong to the Anglo-Saxon or Teutonic world" (204). Kate's insular posture derives not from an inherent antipathy but from an artificiality instilled by her British background and "American education" (204).

Kate's feelings of distance thus emphasize that the barriers to Lawrence's pan-aboriginal vitality have "Anglo-Saxon or Teutonic" origins. Kate is herself one of the "mechanical cog-wheel people" whose artificial, rational ontology she later comes to decry, one of the modernized automata whose geopolitical hegemony "poisons" the world and spreads a fully metaphysical "evil" among its peoples. Lawrence, however, demonstrates the falsehood of her modern sensibilities through her apotheosis as one of the gods of Ramón's movement. Kate's "white," Celtic primitivity becomes the direct route by which she achieves "contact" with "brown-skinned" Mexico. Given that Ramón's "Natural Aristocracy of the World" seems to reserve a place for a Teutonic delegate, Lawrence's racial schema is a bit contradictory on the nature of the "Teutonic" influence Kate has fallen under, but, whether essential or artificial, it is an Anglo-Saxon source from which Kate derives mistaken views of herself and the Mexican other. She is burdened with Teutonic mental habits that breed racial prejudice, and it is these, the Anglo- aspects of her hybrid Irishness, that she must cast off to join Lawrence's natural aristocracy.

Kate's realignment with the "evil" Teutonic world expresses a dire augury regarding the fate of the Irish Celt. Though she cannot deny her primitive responsiveness to Ramón's movement or its larger philosophical validity, her "Teutonic" conditioning proves insuperable:

> Kate was more Irish than anything, and the almost deathly mysticism of the aboriginal Celtic or Iberian people lay at the bottom of her soul. It was a residue of memory. . . . Something older, and more everlastingly potent, than our would-be fair-and-square world. . . . She knew more or less what Ramón was trying to effect: this fusion! . . . It was the leap of the old, antediluvian blood-male in unison with her. And for this . . . her innermost blood had been thudding. . . . Ireland would not and could not forget that other old, dark, sumptuous living. The Tuatha De Danaan might be under the western sea. But they are under the living blood, too. . . . Now they have come forth again, to a new connection. And the scientific, fair-and-square Europe has to mate once more with

> the old giants. . . . But meanwhile, a strange, almost torn nausea would come over Kate. . . . She knew she must go back to Europe, to England and Ireland, very soon. . . . The inner nausea, was becoming too much to bear. (414–19)

Despite the Celtic primitivity that "lives on from the pre-Flood world" "at the bottom of her soul," that is "more everlastingly potent" than the artificial modalities of the modern, and that has begun to reemerge in Revivalist Ireland, Kate cannot yield to her instincts. She is seized with "a strange, almost torn nausea" and a panicked urge to "spare herself" and must return "to Europe, to England and Ireland" to recover equilibrium.

Lawrence's emphasis on Kate's being "more Irish than anything" at the moment in which she abandons her primitivism is of particular significance. The quintessentiality of Kate's Irishness derives not only from the ethnological essence of her "living blood," an inheritance from the mythological Tuatha De Danaan, but also from the very feelings of "nausea" and "torn"ness that lead her to seek refuge in British artificiality. Kate's is not simply an ethnologically Celtic, but a properly historical Irishness. Her vacillations demonstrate the sequential eclipse, first, of the latter by the former, as Kate accesses her primitivity and throws off "Saxon" allegiances, and then of the former by the latter, as she embraces those allegiances once more. Kate's thought process prior to departure illustrates this reversal pointedly: "Christmas was coming! . . . Holly-berries! England! Presents! Food—If she hurried, she could be in England. . . . It felt so safe so familiar, so normal, the thought of Christmas at home, in England. . . . And all the exciting things she could tell. . . . And all the exciting gossip she could hear!" (430). Kate's enthusiasm for the trappings of an English Christmas, the "holly-berries," "presents," "food," and the "exciting gossip" she will share and hear, reflect a thorough enmeshment in Saxon civilizational forms, whose superficiality she thinks of as "safe, "familiar," and "normal." Retreating from the self-awareness she has gained, she no longer resembles the divine version of herself, the "Ossianic goddess" called "Malintzi." Challenged by Ramón's wife, Teresa, on the shallowness of her reasons for leaving, Kate "petulantly" expresses her desire "To get back to simple life. To see the 'buses rolling . . . in Piccadilly, on Christmas Eve, and the wet pavements crowded with people under the brilliant shops!" (430–31). Kate's recrudescence could hardly be more loudly announced than by the urge to join the yuletide pilgrimage of consumers to the display windows of London. In response to Teresa's incredulous reply, "Is that life, to you?," she unflinchingly exclaims, "Yes!" (431).

This conclusion bears out the assessment of one of the most astute critics of Lawrence's primitivism, Michael Bell, that *The Plumed Serpent* is "a peculiarly complex and illuminating failure," while also complicating that assessment (*D.H. Lawrence* 165). If, as Bell describes, the novel falls short of fulfilling the "holistic metaphysic" that was Lawrence's ideal and is unable to achieve what earlier texts such as *The Rainbow* and *Women in Love* achieve, namely "to make that metaphysic the dynamic principle of his narrative language," this reading suggests that, in another sense, its comparatively sterile aesthetic is in fact perfectly suited to its subject matter (166). *The Plumed Serpent* documents the failed transformation of an Irish Celt too entrenched in capitalist modernity to realize the vital potential of her primitive being. Given this insight, which can only be reached through an awareness of the concerns attending Irishness as both an ethnological and a sociohistorical entity, Lawrence's narrative should, perhaps, be seen as aptly rendering the compromised ontology the novel chronicles. If Kate Leslie proves incapable of casting off the "mechanical," Anglo-Saxon habits of her Irishness to inhabit the more fertile ontology dormant in her Celtic makeup, it is only fitting that the novel's aesthetic transmits an equally mechanical and inauthentic experience to its readers.

## MODERNISM AND THE BRITISH CELTICIST HERITAGE

A complete account of British modernist Celticism would extend the foregoing discussion of Conrad and Lawrence into the work of at least two other major figures, T.S. Eliot and Wyndham Lewis. An Irishness complicatedly indebted to Celticism takes center stage in major works by both authors during the 1910s and '20s, from Eliot's "Sweeney poems"—"Sweeney Erect," "Sweeney Among the Nightingales," and "Sweeney Agonistes"—and *The Waste Land* to Lewis's satirical magnum opus, *The Apes of God*. The latter's portrayal of a dim-witted young Irishman named Dan Boleyn as a supposed artistic savant offers an ironic paean to the Celt's inborn aesthetic prowess, while the figure of "apeneck" Sweeney links Eliot's major early work to the broader pop-anthropological view of the Irish as "white chimpanzees" marrying elements of primitivity and civilization.[14] A comprehensive account of Eliot's place in the British Celticist heritage would also range into the excised manuscript materials of *The Waste Land*, in particular the original opening section "He Do the Police in Different Voices," which consists of a ribald chorus of vernacular Irish-American personae. Why does Lewis choose an Irishman as the vehicle for his lampoon of the 1920s London art scene? Why would the original overture for Eliot's vision of an enervated modernity offer a variation on a music hall song with the lyrics, "I'm proud of all the Irish blood that's in me, / There's not a man can say a word agin' me"?[15] Much work remains to be done in linking the major authors and texts of British modernism to the tradition of British Celticism traced here, work that promises to be mutually illuminating of both that tradition and those modernisms.

Such a comprehensive account lies beyond the scope of this study. In the absence of a more capacious survey, we may nonetheless use the examples of Conrad and Lawrence to highlight some of British modernist Celticism's larger implications. It must first be stressed, again, that both writers' representations preserve the basic terms by which Irishness is defined in the imperial romances of Doyle and Kipling, encompassing both Arnold's original, ethnological notion of the Celt as sentimental and the broader, sociohistorical and popular-cultural image of the Irish as metrocolonial hybrids of civilized and primitive traits. Both Conrad's Belfast and Lawrence's Kate Leslie evince a preternaturally sensitive, Celtic epistemology, and both are situated on the boundary between the broader antinomies of race, empire, economics, and aesthetics that define the British geopolitical order at the turn of the twentieth century. We might, in this sense, view them as the less-well-behaved siblings of Arnold's "composite English genius," Doyle's Sherlock Holmes, and Kipling's Kim, sharing the same Anglo-Celtic compound of traits yet cultivating them to destabilize, rather than consolidate, the hegemony of British capitalist modernity. The aesthetic forms to which their narrative points of view give rise are likewise destabilizing of the representational protocols of imperial romance, whose rational interface they supplant with a primitive, "magical" epistemology. In terms of plot content, aesthetic form, and the reader experience these together convey, the Irish Celt of the Victorian period here throws off his chains and helps overthrow that period's governing norms and values.

The figure of the Irish Celt proves central to both authors' modernist innovations, not simply through the cultivation of a primitivity conceived on Victorian anthropological lines, but through the way in which this figure provides a unique means of engaging a number of novel and pressing historical developments that had only begun to emerge at the time of their writing. Both the notion of the Celt as sentimental, as preternaturally sensitive to modernity's ontological encroachments, and the view of the Irish as hybrid intermediaries between the British Empire's colonizing and colonized constituencies, contribute to the radical perspectives Conrad and Lawrence generate toward these nascent historical processes. These perspectives also begin to broach the sorts of material obstacles and entanglements that will preoccupy and bedevil the Celticist project in the chapters to follow, where the urge to cultivate the Celt's anticapitalist and aesthetic potential expands from Britain, across the Irish Sea, into the cultural nationalist movement of fin-de-siècle Ireland itself. Already with Conrad and Lawrence, though their primitivist modernisms rest on the foundation of a Victorian Irish Celt, the political problematics, economic contexts, and aesthetic forms of a more practically engaged Irish Celticism begin to come into view. In the case of Kate Leslie, we witness a transnational, aboriginal political revolution extending from North America to Europe and Asia explicitly pitted against a modernity conceived as Saxon and capitalist. Irish Celtic sentimentality in Lawrence is both a medium for registering the urgency of resisting this newly global, capitalist world order, which threatens to convert peoples of all races from vital indigenes to "mechanical cog-wheel people," and, through Kate's ultimate capitulation to this threat, a medium for registering its insidiousness and dire consequences. As subsequent chapters will show, the use of a Celtic Irishness in both of these ways—to help define the values of an alternative modernity and to gauge the human costs of losing such alternatives—also distinguishes Irish nationalist Celticisms in their quest to forge a distinctive postcolonial and anticapitalist society. Lawrence's explicit invocation of this movement is not coincidental.

The case of Conrad's Belfast presents an equally distinctive historicization of the British Celticist heritage, one that converges with the problematics of the Revival in some ways, but in others engages a distinctly British set of concerns. Conrad's stunningly prescient diagnosis of the impending racial leveling and multiculturality of imperial capital situates the Irish Celt at the heart of the estrangement of these nascent postcolonial processes. Indeed, he becomes once more the privileged gauge or, in the words of this study's introduction, the "detector" of this estrangement. Here, in an especially creative determinist vision, this figure's sentimental epistemology and imperial liminality become a mediating agency normalizing such processes for both the white maritime laborer and the novel's white readership. Celtic Irishness is thus positioned as the hub of the sort of multiracial labor network more characteristic of the later twentieth and early twenty-first centuries both in Euro-America and beyond, and there, his sentimental susceptibilities serve to model the kinds of egalitarian intersubjectivity such networks will increasingly encourage. In a strange and unforeseen twist, the Victorian definition of the Irish Celt thus becomes a medium by which, through the black-white rapprochement Belfast facilitates, a novel, post-anthropological and post-binary racial dispensation begins to emerge. Alongside the pan-aboriginal politics of *The Plumed Serpent*, the radical racial vision of *"Narcissus"* also suggests that in British modernist Celticism, the primitive categorization originally devised to justify the oppression of Irish and "black" subjects of Empire begins to inspire a trans-racial and trans-colonial sensibility.[16]

With regard to the specific Revivalist concerns addressed going forward, it is the disruptions this emergence generates within the capitalist "machinery" of the *Narcissus* that hold the primary interest. The receptivity to super-racial "solidarity" modeled in Belfast's sentimental response to James Wait is profoundly disruptive to this machinery, to the point of precipitating not simply a strike, but, indeed, a *riot* directed at the ship's entire economic hierarchy. If this would seem an idiosyncratic outcome to the modernist cultivation of Irish Celtic traits as defined in British Celticism—one perhaps unlikely to be replicated outside the unique laboratory conditions of Conrad's early work—we must recall that we have already noted the potential for such an outcome in the convergences between Arnold's Celticism and Marx's early theory of Communism. Nor were such affinities a mere figment of the British literary and economic imagination, for, as we shall see in the chapters to follow, they would again emerge in the hands of the Irish nationalist movement, whose efforts to theorize and implement alternatives to British capitalist modernity would light once more upon the notion of a Celtic Communism.

PART II

# Irish Celticism

CHAPTER 4

# "A Nation of Imitators"

## *Anticapitalisms of the Irish Revival, 1885–1910*

> I am going to talk a little philosophy. If I was addressing an English audience I would not venture to even use the word philosophy, for it is only the Celt who cares much for ideas which have no immediate practical bearing. At least Matthew Arnold has said so, and I think he is right, for the flood-gates of materialism are only half-open among us yet here in Ireland; perhaps the new age may close them before the tide is quite upon us. Remembering those but half-open gates, I venture into criticism of the fundamentals of literature, and into the discussion of things which, I am proud to say, have never made two blades of grass grow where one did before, or in any other fashion served the material needs of the race.
>
> —W.B. Yeats, "Nationality and Literature" (1893)

Thus far, this study has traced the legacies of Celticism in just over half a century of British literature and culture. Beginning with the theories of Matthew Arnold and concluding with the primitivism of D.H. Lawrence, it has tried to demonstrate the ways in which Celticism responded to some of the central concerns of capitalist modernity during this seminal period. For the figures in question, Celticism provided an imaginative space for the pursuit of varied, even opposite agendas toward this encroaching regime. Whether recalibrating its rigid ontology, promoting the expansion of its hegemony across the British Empire, chronicling that hegemony's racial and "moral" subversion, or envisioning its total overthrow, each writer has affirmed Celticism's intimacy—both as an ethnological theory and as an aesthetic practice—with British capitalism, and the utility of the former to gauging the nature and consequences of the latter. As we have also seen, British Celticism is intimately bound up with the unique dynamics of Anglo-Irish colonialism. Whether in the Fenian backdrop of Arnold's *Study*, the allegorical Land Wars of Doyle's *Hound*, the Hiberno-Indian espionage of Kipling's *Kim*, the racial-economic mediations of Conrad's Belfast, or the Irish Revival of Lawrence's *Plumed Serpent*, British Celticism remains in close contact with these dynamics, whose hybrid features provide the flexibility to interrogate binary oppositions such as magic/reason, primitive/civilized, and black/white, all of which index a historical trajectory in alignment with capitalist modernization. The mixed, metrocolonial aspects of fin-de-siècle Ireland shape, and indeed make possible, the innovative solutions these authors devise in response to the geopolitical challenges of British modernity.

Ireland's unique colonial makeup becomes even more central to the Celticist genealogy as we move to examine its deployment during the Irish Revival proper. If Ireland's fusion of metropolitan and colonial elements outfits British Celticists with the tools for defusing or aggravating the antinomies of empire, for nationalist writers working to define Irishness during this period, this fusion instead becomes a dilemma and a practical problem. As this chapter will chronicle, one of the primary forms in which Irish cultural nationalists posed this problem followed from the central opposition built into Celticism from its Arnoldian foundation between capital and the aesthetic. When Arnold codified this opposition as the manifestation of an essential racial difference between Teuton and Celt, he initiated a dialectical chain reaction in which both British Celticists and their Irish counterparts became implicated. Against his own hegemonic intentions, Arnold also produced a notion of the Celt as resistant to the modernizing energies of British capital. In the hands of British modernists like Conrad and Lawrence, this resistant potential formed the basis for political ideals, economic visions, and aesthetic forms very much at odds with the discourse's original purposes. It is in this same space that turn-of-the-century Irish Celticism performs its labors.

Chapter 1 of this study located the foundations of Arnold's Celticism in the economic history of mid-nineteenth-century Ireland and argued that the antinomy between the Celtic sentimentality and capitalist industry was based on events like the Great Famine that seemed to British political economists to demonstrate the Celt's economic impotence and, conversely, the essentially Saxon character of capital. As chronicled in chapter 2, the decades following this catastrophic rupture of Ireland's Gaelic civilization witnessed its accelerated incorporation into British structures and mores, such that by the time of the Revival, despite the efforts of organizations such as the Land League and the Fenians to Arnoldian (and Doylean) prescription, the nation's economic lifeworld, in particular the portion known as the Pale, had in many ways become indistinguishable from that of the metropole. Especially in Dublin, the geographical epicenter of the Revival, daily life had melded with that of England so fully as functionally to render the city a node in the domestic British marketplace.[1] The Celticist anticapitalism of the Revival would therefore be directed not simply against the external presence of Empire but also against internal forces generated by decades of assimilative pressure.

This chapter identifies three strains in the Revival's anticapitalist campaign and traces their development during the height of the movement's influence between roughly 1885 and 1920. The first consists of the straightforward identification of British capital as a racially alien force adulterating the nation's Celtic essence. This dual anti-imperial and anticapitalist claim served as one of the Revival's most pervasive ideological elements, and it would transcend the various agendas cohabitating under the tent of Irish cultural nationalism. The second strain entails the splintering of this consensus along the fault line between the movement's two main constituencies: middle-class, Catholic nationalism and the mostly Protestant nationalism of the so-called Literary Revival. These factions, while meeting amicably on the common ground of opposing British capital, diverged over the specific substance of this opposition, with the Catholic faction defining its anticapitalism in *moral* terms and the Literary faction defining its own in terms of *high culture*. This splintering of Revivalist anticapitalism was signally evident in the domain of consumption, where, in opposition to the imported commodities of British popular culture, these groups expressed radically divergent views of Ireland's ethnic identity. Indeed, the commodity critique of the Revival became a privileged staging ground for what can best be characterized as a Gramscian war of position between Catholic and Literary nationalists for the allegiance of the Irish populace.

The third strain of Revivalist anticapitalism is, in many ways, the most remarkable, and it represents a response to many of the tensions and conflicts, both ideological and factional, evident in the first two, and in the history of Celticism since Arnold generally. While the notion of the Irish Celt as resistant to capitalism proved highly galvanizing, and while it stimulated a sophisticated critique of capital's forms, there remained a pivotal question: what form of economic production better suited the Celt? If Arnold and his British successors could embrace the Celt's status as an economic nonentity from the comfort of their armchairs, for Irish thinkers, writers, and activists seeking to forge an independent nation, such an embrace was far more problematic. Thus, as the Revival progressed, there emerged a widespread effort to envision and begin constructing a Celticized Irish economic sphere—a modernizing national economy imbued with characteristics viewed as inherently Celtic. Toward the close of the Revival, the idea of such a sphere would momentarily offer a sophisticated, dialectical alternative to the doomed choice between the economic ineffectuality of Arnold's Celt and the Saxon modernity of the imperial era. It would represent, in short, a sophisticated theory of an Irish alternative modernity, one capable of holding its own in national and international affairs while also spurning the insidious features of a globalizing British capital.

## "SITTING ON THE LAST VERGE": REVIVALIST ANTICAPITALISM

It is a commonplace in Irish Studies to characterize the Revival as opposing British "materialism," or some other term designating the British economic forces encroaching on turn-of-the-century Ireland, and as motivated by the desire to purge the nation of this potent force of Anglicization.[2] Little sustained energy has been devoted, however, to interrogating the intricacies of the movement's anticapitalist discourse. A closer examination reveals that this Revivalist ideological mainstay is highly rich and complex, with the following emerging as recurring themes: the idea that British capital blights the Irish landscape; the complementary idea that it blights the Irish language; the notion that in both land and language resides a Celtic essence that must be preserved; the idea that British capitalism is the product of alien, Saxon proclivities; the idea that the nation's Celtic essence, though unsuited for "industry," bears a corresponding aesthetic potency; and the idea that British capital, despite its pretensions to universality, is merely an overgrown particular obscuring a truly universal, aesthetically charged, primitive ontology of which Celtic Irishness is paradigmatic. Such themes served as common ground among the Revival's diverse constituencies.

We may begin surveying this common ground via the Language Movement, with the words of the co-founder of the Gaelic League, Douglas Hyde.[3] In an 1886 essay titled simply "A Plea for the Irish Language," seven years before the League's founding, Hyde defines what would be its mission—"to arrest the [Irish] language in its downward path"—in anticapitalist and essentialist terms. Anticipating in his audience a "materialistic *cui bono*" in response to his "plea," he declares, "I must . . . confess, that what I advocate brings with it no substantial or material advantages at all. It will make neither money nor help to make money; but I hope that this confession will not put us out of court with an Irish audience, as I know it would an Anglo-Saxon one" (75). The revival of Gaelic is a fundamentally non-profit enterprise, as the "*cui bono*" of capitalism is an alien, Teutonic preoccupation. "Englishmen have very noble and excellent qualities which I should like to see imitated here," Hyde continues, "but . . . I like our own habits and character better, they are more consonant with my nature" (75–76). The Gaelic-speaking Ireland of the future may accommodate some English "qualities," but the country's "character" and "nature" will resist adoption of the Saxon's "material" obsession (76).[4]

Hyde goes on to describe Gaelic as the repository of aestheticized, anti-capitalist qualities that emanate from the Irish landscape. "The language of the Gael is the language best suited to his surroundings," he explains; "it corresponds best to his topography, his nomenclature and his organs of speech, and the use of it guarantees the resemblance of his own weird and beautiful traditions" (77). "Every hill . . . *lios* . . . crag and gnarled tree and lonely valley has its own strange and graceful legend attached to it, the product of the Hibernian Celt in its truest and purest type, not to be improved upon by change" (77–78). Gaelic thus mimes the peculiar features of Irish "topography," both at the level of "nomenclature" and at the more advanced linguistic level of "legend." Hyde goes on to sharpen his depiction of the "change" that threatens these Celtic resources through a portrait of "the east" of Ireland, where, amid the "Pale" of British influence, "the character of the people has deteriorated" and "the halo of romance . . . exquisite and dreamy . . . has been blown away by the brutal blast of the most realistic materialism" (78).

"The Necessity for De-Anglicizing Ireland" couches its advocacy in these same terms. Just before the peroration of this seminal lecture before the National Literary Society in November of 1892, Hyde proposes a thought experiment to convey his admonition against the adulterating influence of British capital. "Let us suppose for a moment," he begins, "that there were to arise a series of Cromwells in England . . . able administrators of the empire, developing to the utmost our national resources . . . making Ireland a land of wealth and factories, whilst they extinguished every thought and every idea that was Irish" (121–22). Hyde presents a frightening, dystopian vision of the total imposition of the "improvement" process, in which, by Cromwellian fiat, the "utmost" development of the nation's "resources" goes hand in hand with the extinction of Irishness. In such an Ireland, its hereditarily Celtic people, now "fat, wealthy and populous," have grown indistinguishable from their occupiers, "the fact that [they] were not of Saxon origin dropped out of sight and memory" (122). Luckily, however, Hyde comforts his listeners, "the difference between the English and the Irish race" determines that while

"Nine Englishmen out of ten would jump to make the exchange . . . nine Irishmen out of ten would indignantly refuse it" (122–23).[5]

Taken together, Hyde's writings of late '80s and early '90s propose an Ireland that is Gaelic speaking, of Celtic "character," laden with aestheticized ecological and ethnological features, and united in opposition to an inherently Saxon capitalist modernity. This economic regime drives the effacement and potential extinction of the three wellsprings of that "character," the land, the corresponding "nature" of its inhabitants, and the language that crystallizes these. The terms of such an analysis are fundamentally Arnoldian: as in the *Study*, Teutonic "industry" "blight[s]" the beauty of this "romantic" milieu, and this economic order must be uprooted to ensure the survival of those "magic" features Arnold called "sentimental." In fact, though Hyde never references Arnold, later in the same lecture he utilizes this very term to describe the source of nationalist resistance, stating, "When the picture of complete Anglicization is drawn for [us] in all its nakedness *Irish sentimentality* becomes suddenly a power and refuses to surrender its birthright" (123, emphasis added). Resistance to the steamrolling of the nation's identity is sentimental, deriving from a "power[ful] attachment" (to recall Dr. Mortimer's phrase in *The Hound of the Baskervilles*) to its environment and traditions. It is because this sentimentality has not been active enough in combating the "fact" of British capital that "one of the quickest, most sensitive, and most artistic races on earth are now only distinguished for their hideousness" (118).

For those familiar with the Revival, it will be obvious that this outline of Hyde's Language program borders on the ideology of the notorious "Celtic Note," the racial ideal advanced mainly by Literary Revivalists like W.B. Yeats. This should not surprise, considering the extent of Hyde's alignment with the Literary Revival (delivering his seminal lecture at one of its most prominent institutional nodes, giving the first performance of his Gaelic-language play *Casadh an tSúgáin* at another, the Irish Literary Theatre, and becoming a vice president of its successor, the National Theatre of Ireland or Abbey Theatre).[6] It is important to recall, however, that Hyde's brand of Revivalism received the endorsement of even the most venomous critic of the "Celtic Note," D.P. Moran. Moran's endorsement derives from a number of convergences between Hyde's program and his own, the most obvious being the emphasis on the preservation of Gaelic as a carrier of essential Irishness (though like Hyde, Moran accepts that as a result of its centuries of Anglicization only a bilingual Ireland is now viable).[7] However, Moran's accord with Hyde can also be explained through a less remarked convergence between them, namely their definition of Irishness as antagonistic to British capitalism.

Moran's view of the relationship between Irishness and economics is more complex than Hyde's, but in the series of essays published in the *New Ireland Review* between 1898 and 1900 with which he launched his "Irish Ireland" program, Moran nonetheless espouses an essentialist anticapitalism. In "The Future of the Irish Nation," he advances the thesis that "economic forces make for the obliteration" of Irish identity itself, and like Hyde, he urges readers to pit "sentimental obstructions" against "economic tendency" in order to "stem the tide and endeavor to fight on for the realization of the dream of Ireland a Nation" (23). Moran's most famous work, "The Battle of Two Civilizations," also foregrounds the ethnological assumptions behind his economic admonitions: "The Irish . . . [are] absolutely different from the English. The genius of each nation [is] distinct. . . . There is something, be it instinct or the living sub-conscious tradition of an almost dead civilization, that says to nearly every Irish heart—'Thou shalt be Irish: thou shalt not be English'" (97). Against the incursions of the English—whom "The Pale and the Gael" describes as "a line of sleek, trimming, bread-and-butter Saxon bourgeois, who would have swallowed the devil any day sooner than lose a customer"—Moran advocates for consolidating Ireland's "absolute difference" (51).

Given his lambasting of the "Celtic Note" as "one of the most glaring frauds the credulous Irish people ever swallowed," it is surprising to see Moran elsewhere invoke Celticist watchwords to buttress his economic nationalism ("The Future" 22). Moran, indeed, often deploys the same Arnoldian terms he elsewhere uses to discredit Literary Revivalist Celticism. "Is the Irish Nation Dying?," for instance, points to qualities of "native charm" and "romance," staples of the dubious Note, as inherent to the Gaelic "personality" (5–7), while "The Future of the Irish Nation" contains the following remarkable passage:

> I suppose the Gael is a sensuous creature, liking music, rhetoric and day-dreams, and hating realities when they wear a dour and threatening look. We are the most fitted people in the world for living in a fool's paradise. . . . In many of its manifestations this characteristic of the Gael is his greatest charm. His optimism and hope spring from it; his good humour flows from it; his happiness and content, amid surroundings that would be intolerable to a more matter-of-fact nature, depend upon it. . . . And as we all are proud of the glamour and lightheartedness . . . we must not grumble too much at the disadvantages which they carry. . . . But when these characteristics . . . threaten our very existence as a nation, it is time to call a halt and examine whither

> we are drifting. . . . Even if the Anglo-Saxon race . . . stopped where it is we could not keep on our present way without disaster . . . we must either stand up to it . . . or else get trodden on and swallowed up. (12)

The Celticist tenor of Moran's advocacy for a native movement that will "stand up" to the "Anglo-Saxon race," stressing the "sensuousness," "day-dreaming," "glamour and light-heartedness" of the Gaelic "disposition," is unmistakable. Though grudgingly, Moran accepts the Arnoldian premise that the Gael revolts against the "despotism of fact," while the Saxon's "more matter-of-fact nature" is better suited to material success.

The case of Moran, then, suggests that it is somehow incumbent even on a brand of nationalism that professes contempt for the "Celt" to characterize Irishness as essentially, "sentimentally" opposed to British capital. This premise becomes even more prominent in the writings of nationalists far better known than either Moran or Hyde for sounding the Celtic Note. The first major figure in this regard is the mystic, poet, and playwright George Russell, also known as AE. In "Nationality and Imperialism," AE leverages Celticist resources to refute the prevalent view (notably espoused by Moran) that Irish prosperity is best secured through continued participation in the Empire.[8] Against this Gladstonian notion, AE warns that the benefits of such participation would be outweighed by its harm to the nation's Celtic features. "What can it profit my race if it gain the empire of the world and yet lose its own soul?" he asks, and proceeds to construct a stark series of oppositions between Ireland's "reservoir of spiritual life," "divine origin," "dreams and longings," and "English materialism," "the deadness, the dullness, the commonplace of English national sentiment" (16–18). AE justifies the rejection of Home Rule by asserting that severing this link will secure the "liberty" needed for "shaping the social order in Ireland to reflect [its] own ideals," among which, just before this passage, he lists "the music of an eternal joy, the sentiment of an inexorable justice, the melting power of beauty in sorrow, [and] the wisdom of age" (16). The Irish qualities that contrast with the commercial "English national sentiment" echo the opposition in Arnold's *Study* between an aestheticized, melancholy Celt and "the gross and creeping Saxon whom he despises" (Arnold, *Study* 88).

A similar typology underpins the essay "Literature and the Irish Language" by the novelist, playwright, and founding member of the Irish Literary Theatre George Moore. First delivered as a lecture before the Theatre's supporters in February of 1900, it advocates for the Gaelic translation of English works, rather than original authorship of plays in Gaelic, which Moore judges too artistically immature. Despite this criticism, he avers that Gaelic houses the essence of the race, and like Hyde and Moran, he distinguishes its merits from Saxon economic utility: "We want our language. . . . Our desire may be foolish, unpractical, unwise, according to the lights of the English race . . . but our desire is our desire, our folly is our own, and if we wish to start ill equipped in the business race of the world . . . shall we be gainsaid like children?" (47). Moore goes on to define the Irish "soul" as the last bastion of an "art world which was in antiquity . . . of which some traces linger," but which "is passing away" before "the commercial platitude which has arisen in England," taking with it all "those who believe [in] dreams, beauty, and divine ecstasy" (50–51). "Sitting on the last verge" of this ancient regime, the Irish can see the British Empire "extending over the whole world," a "universal suburb, in which a lean man with glasses on his nose and a black bag in his hand is always running after his bus" (50–51).

With Moore, we thus encounter the final Revivalist theme described at the outset of this section: the assertion that it is not capitalist modernity but a premodern primitivity that is the natural modality of all human societies. In this theme, we see an attempt to reposition Irish "sentimentality" not as a deviation from the human norm, but *as* that norm. Revivalist Celticism hereby sanctions its anticapitalist efforts by drawing on the historical framework developed by anthropologists like E.B. Tylor, Andrew Lang, and James Frazer—the same framework cultivated by British modernists like Lawrence—which defined the "magical" practices explored in chapters 2 and 3 as universal at an early stage of human history. But where this framework assigned an ascending scale of value to the supersession of "magical" ways by "religious" and, later, "rational" ones, the Revival, in a Nietzschean "transvaluation of values," defines Ireland's "primitive" traditions as the source of its civilizational greatness.[9]

This historical narrative of the eclipse of a magical, universal primitivity by a rationalizing capitalist modernity also appears in AE's *Co-Operation and Nationality*, which constructs an elaborate portrait of "the wild child humanity" being "caught and put in harness" during a "modern race for wealth" spearheaded by English "business methods," as well as in the text which, perhaps more than any other, exemplifies the Revival's debts to a specifically Arnoldian Celticism, Yeats's "The Celtic Element in Literature" (AE, *Co-Operation* 16). This 1897 essay begins by proposing to distinguish the Celt's characteristics from those described by Arnold. Once the moment arrives to make explicit the qualities Yeats views as distinctively Celtic, however, he affirms the very same traits that define Arnold's Celt, from "worship" of the "beauty" and "abundance of nature" to "unearthly ecstasy" and "imaginative passion" (Yeats, "Celtic" 175, 178). Indeed, he accepts what is perhaps the key term of Arnoldian "sentimentality": "natural magic." Yeats, like Moore, merely transvalues this term into a universal, stating of Arnold, "I do not think he understood our 'natural magic' is but the ancient religion of the world" (176).

Yeats's reliance on Arnoldian ethnological premises despite his occasional protestation to the contrary of course extends to the notion of a primitive Irishness opposed to English capital. The epigraph of this chapter, taken from the essay "Nationality and Literature," delivered as a lecture to the National Literary Society on May 19, 1893, unequivocally avows this dichotomy and credits Arnold directly ("Matthew Arnold has said so, and I think he is right") with the argument that "it is only the Celt who cares much for ideas which have no immediate practical bearing" (268). These premises continue to undergird Yeats's commentaries on more specific, topical matters throughout the Revival. The *Samhain* writings of the early 1900s, in which Yeats reflects on the early gains made by the Irish Literary and National Theatres, deploys them to distinguish the Theatre movement from its competitor, the commercial theater of England. The 1901 *Samhain* proposes to combat Irish demand for the latter through the formation of a "joint stock company" to produce Irish plays and foreign "masterpieces," both of which would help rejuvenate "the national character, which is so essentially different from the English . . . [that it] is at present like one of those miserable thorn-bushes by the sea that are all twisted to one side by some prevailing wind" (76). The 1904 *Samhain*, similarly, stresses the need to put the "modern theatre," which the English "wind," carrying with it "the vulgarity of commercial syndicates, of all that commercial finish and pseudo-art she has done so much to cherish," has blighted, back in touch with "the living impulse of life" ("Dramatic" 129). Yeats's ecological metaphors convey the dual imperative to cast off the artificial influences of British theatrical capital and infuse the Irish theater with an essential, ethnological primitivity.

Yeats elsewhere invokes other key themes of Revivalist anticapitalism by defining the language and the landscape as repositories of an indigenous, Irish primitivity in need of both conservation and cultivation. In the *Memoirs* that formed the first draft of his *Autobiographies*, he reflects on the aesthetic inspiration he derived from staying with Hyde at Frenchpark in County Roscommon in April of 1895:

> On a visit to Dr Hyde I had seen the Castle Rock, as it was called, in Lough Key. There is a small island entirely covered by what was still

> a habitable and empty castle. . . . All around were wooded and hilly shores, a place of great beauty. I believed the castle could be hired for little money, and had long been dreaming of making it an Irish Eleusis or Samothrace. An obsession more constant than anything but my love itself was the need of mystical rites—a ritual system of evocation and meditation—to reunite the perception of the spirit, of the divine, with natural beauty. . . . Commerce and manufacture had made the world ugly; the death of pagan nature-worship had robbed visible beauty of its inviolable sanctity. . . . I meant to initiate young men and women in this worship. (123–24)

Castle Rock inspires a utopian vision of the reestablishment of a "pagan nature-worship" whose "mystical rites" will "reunite the perception of the spirit, of the divine, with natural beauty" and uproot the forces of "commerce and manufacture" that have "made the world ugly." The "ritual system" of Yeats's art will battle British capital for possession of the Irish landscape, and on the outcome of this battle hinges the ontological fate of its inhabitants.

Yeats also took pains to link his anticapitalist "system" with the extant "primitive" practices of the Irish people themselves in such works as *Fairy and Folk Tales of the Irish Peasantry* (1888), *Irish Fairy Tales* (1892) and *The Celtic Twilight* (1893). As in "The Celtic Element in Literature," however, the Celtic qualities portrayed in these texts are mostly cordoned off from the capitalist forces whose advance motivates their recovery.[10] In the Revivalist text that is most famous for chronicling Ireland's extant, Gaelic civilization, however, the dissonance between Celt and capital plays a far more visible role. The 1907 publication of J.M. Synge's *The Aran Islands* represents the fullest realization of the Revivalist trend of identifying the nation's essence with this far western locale. Reading Synge's account of his travels there between 1898 and 1901, however, one is struck not only by the urge to affirm this identification, but also by the short-circuiting of this effort by the encroaching forces of capitalist modernity.[11]

Among the many pre-modern attributes Synge identifies on Aran, from the lack of female "conventionality" to hatred of English Law, the lack of a distinction between the natural and supernatural, and the lack of modern temporality, those related to economic production are perhaps most telling. He describes common, homemade Aran objects such as "curaghs and spinning-wheels . . . tiny wooden barrels . . . homemade cradles, churns, and baskets" as "full of individuality" and as affirming the "natural link between the people and the world that is about them" (13–14). His depictions of labor practices such as cottage "thatching" are similarly idealized in contrast to the capitalist alternatives poised to eclipse them:

> Like all work that is done in common on the island, the thatching is regarded as a sort of festival. From the moment a roof is taken in hand there is a whirl of laughter and talk . . . and, as the man whose house is being covered is a host instead of an employer, he lays himself out to please the men who work with him. . . . It is likely that much of the intelligence and charm of these people is due to the absence of any division of labour, and to the correspondingly wide development of each individual. . . . Each man can speak two languages. He is a skilled fisherman, and can manage a curagh with extraordinary nerve and dexterity. He can farm simply, burn kelp, cut out pampooties, mend nets, build and thatch a house, and make a cradle or a coffin. His work changes with the seasons . . . keep[ing] him free from the dullness that comes to people who have always the same occupation. The danger of life on the sea gives him the alertness of a primitive hunter, and the long nights he spends fishing . . . bring him some of the emotions that are thought peculiar to men who have lived with the arts. (83–84)

The "division of labor" that has reified human endeavors and the ontological "dullness" it instills provide the backdrop against which this "wide development of each individual" becomes both legible and beautiful. Labor in the islands, free from the repressive-productive dynamic of industrial capitalism, is "a sort of festival," rife with "laughter" and "charm," and in the more perilous activity of fishing is generative of sublime "emotions that are thought peculiar to men who have lived with the arts."

Synge, however, maintains his readers' awareness of capital's proximity to this last bastion of Gaelic civilization.[12] He does so not simply by invoking it as a frame of reference, but also by closing each part of the book with an ominous reminder of its westward creep. At the close of Part I, for example, "com[ing] out of an hotel full of tourists and commercial travelers" in Galway City, which, for all its "wild human interest . . . seems a tawdry medley of all that is crudest in modern life," Synge gazes back at Aran across "Galway Bay" and experiences an "indescribably acute" "yearning" for its idyllic world (56). The contrast between indigenous ideality and capitalist modernity, however, is not strictly an island-mainland distinction; it has infiltrated the islands themselves, as illustrated near the end of Part II, when Synge contrasts the islands of Inishmore and Inishmaan. "Looking out" from the former toward the latter, Synge finds it "hard to believe that those hovels . . . are filled with people whose lives have the strange quality that is found in the oldest poetry and legend," while the "increased prosperity" that has taken hold in Inishmore has brought "the anxiety of men who are eager for gain" (69). Capital has so extinguished the "charm" they once "share[d] with the birds and the flowers" that even their "eyes and expressions are different," giving off a dulled, "indefinable modern quality" (69). A well-known passage from the first of Synge's Aran notebooks forecasts the engulfment of even the Inishmaan Gael by such dehumanization: "The thought that this island will gradually yield to the ruthlessness of 'progress' is as the certainty that decaying age is moving always nearer the cheeks it is your exstacy to kiss. How much of Ireland was formerly like this and how much of Ireland is today Anglicized and civilized and brutalized?" (qtd. in Robinson, xliii).

Synge's depiction of an essential Irishness threatened by British capitalist modernity, though complicated by realistic elements that trouble the halcyon tenor of the Celtic Note, replicates each of the central themes that define the Revival's cultural nationalist agenda. The Irishness of the islanders is anchored in both the Gaelic language and the geography of Aran, and as a result of this "natural link" their lives evoke comparisons to the aestheticized, universally primitive lifeworld of "the oldest poetry and legend." Synge's figuration of this extant civilization draws deeply from the wellspring of Revivalist Celticism, and in this frame the encroachment of British capital on native Irish "charm" becomes both legible and execrable. Synge's researches reinforce and advance both the specific bullet points and general anticapitalist agenda of Irish cultural nationalism, providing them with empirical corroboration and amplifying their dire urgency.

## "OUTWARD AND INNER THINGS": THE REVIVAL'S COMMODITY CRITIQUE

By the time of *The Aran Islands*' publication in 1907, however, the anticapitalist consensus of the Revival had already begun to fracture along the fault line between its Catholic and Literary constituencies. We may pursue this schism through an examination of the Revival's critique of the Irish consumption of the commodities of British popular culture. As we shall see, while both Catholic and Literary nationalists opposed such consumption as productive of Anglicization, their articulation of this opposition reflected radically divergent visions for Ireland's post-British future. The commodity critique of the

Revival reveals a full-blown Gramscian war of position between these factions for the "spontaneous consent" of the Irish populace, a hegemonic struggle that in turn enables us to identify the discourse of Revivalist anticapitalism as one of the primary vehicles through which the tensions that would define revolutionary and postcolonial Irish society began to entrench themselves.[13]

It is crucial to note that the hegemonic struggle between Catholic and Literary advocates of decolonization takes place within a political domain already proscribed by perhaps the most potent ideological force in Irish life at the turn of the century, the Catholic Church itself. The profound influence of Church doctrine on mainstream Irish life has in fact been implicit throughout the preceding section of this chapter through the near-total absence of the word "capitalism" from Revivalist agitations against its influence. There is a tacit yet clear and consensus avoidance of the nominal denunciation of capital throughout the texts surveyed above that can only derive from the tactical calculation to avoid identification with socialism/communism, which the contemporary Church famously defined as anathema. As chronicled by historian Emmet Larkin in "Socialism and Catholicism in Ireland," particularly during the later Revival period of 1909–14, nationalists like James Connolly and James Larkin who avowed socialist allegiances openly "drew sustained fire from the clergy and hierarchy of the Church of Ireland," who viewed the movement as incompatible with Catholic values (67). Prominent Irish clergy such as Father Kate, Father John Gwynn, and Cardinal Logue built on the opposition to socialism initiated by Pope Leo XIII in the seminal "Rerum Novarum" on the "Rights and Duties of Capital and Labor" in 1891 and thus solidified the Irish Catholic antagonism to the alternative economic models of the political left. In this atmosphere, practical efforts to de-capitalize Ireland would need to skirt the association with socialism/communism to appease to the entrenched hegemony of the Church. It is for this reason that anticapitalist advocates like Hyde, AE, Moore, Yeats, and Synge specify only "materialism," "commerce," "improvement," "wealth," or "industry" as the bêtes noires of the nationalist agenda. Such terms serve as a metonymic code for the capitalist system Irish nationalism was interdicted from naming by the anticommunism of the Church hierarchy. As we shall see by tracking the course of Revivalist nationalism's commodity critique, this prior delimitation of the ideological field in fact foreshadows—indeed partly predetermines—the ultimate victory of the Catholic faction over its Literary competitor in their hegemonic struggle.

I have already alluded to the fundamental difference separating the commodity critique of Catholic nationalism from that of the Literary Revival, namely that the former defines its opposition to the British popular-cultural products that had become ubiquitous in Ireland by the late nineteenth century in *moral* terms, while the latter couches its objections in the terminology of *high culture*. This conflict of "Irish Ireland versus Anglo-Irish Ireland," in F.S.L. Lyons's phrase, turns on divergent conceptions of Irish human nature.[14] Specifically, Catholic nationalism, premised on both church doctrine and the mores of the peasant social institution of "familism," promulgates a repressive ideology that defines the consumption of British popular culture as a kind of dissoluteness or moral incontinence, while Literary nationalism, premised instead on humanist principles, promulgates an expansive, vitalist ideology that defines such consumption as producing ontological desiccation or impoverishment. "Irish Ireland" sees the consumption of British commodities as spurring a *centrifugal* dissolution of the national being, while "Anglo-Irish Ireland" sees it as spurring a *centripetal* contraction thereof.

We begin with the former faction, and with a historical disagreement that has emerged in recent years over the origins of the ideology of fin-de-siècle Catholic nationalism. One prominent narrative in Irish Studies interprets the moral tenor of the movement as arising from an attempt to project a purified national image to the metropole, one which, by conforming to the mores of Victorian respectability, would help secure British sanction for Irish independence.[15] The flaw in this picture lies in part in its attribution of Catholic nationalism's *modus operandi* to an imitation of imperial norms rather than to norms immanent to Irish Catholic culture itself. As we shall later see, this view in fact replicates the analysis of one of the Catholic nationalism's most venomous critics, W.B. Yeats, who refused to identify in its ideological makeup any indigenous Irish dimension. But while some aspects of Catholic nationalism were certainly directed toward the Victorian gaze, a more persuasive account is offered by studies such as *Writing Ireland*, by David Cairns and Shaun Richards, that view the movement as organically linked to traditional peasant institutions such as "familism" and the Catholic Church itself. Because the majority of the nationalist constituency in urban centers like Dublin had only recently emigrated from the countryside (often as a result of the Famine), Catholic culture in these locales still adhered to the codes instilled by these institutions. The moral emphasis of Catholic nationalism, in particular its obsession with *sexual* morality, must be read in this native frame as well as in the imperial one emphasized in recent studies.[16]

This preoccupation with sexual morality came to the fore in such watershed historical events as the Kitty O'Shea controversy (the adulterous affair that spelled the political demise of Charles Stewart Parnell) and the so-called

"Mahaffy/Atkinson Affair" (which pitted Trinity College dons John Pentland Mahaffy and Robert Atkinson with the Irish Catholic Primate and Cardinal Michael Logue against defenders of Gaelic such as Hyde over the question of the language's reputed "indecency" and "immorality"), and in the later controversies surrounding Yeats's *The Countess Cathleen* and Synge's *The Shadow of the Glen* and *The Playboy of the Western World*.[17] Nowhere, however, is Catholic nationalism's emphasis on sexual morals more marked than in its critique of the commodities of British popular culture. Examples of this particular anti-imperial tack date from the very beginning of the Revival period. In an 1884 letter to the founder of the Gaelic Athletic Association, Michael Cusack, later published in *The Nation*, Archbishop Croke, an outspoken supporter of both the GAA and the Land League, provides one of the earliest examples of the moral critique of British products, warning that England's "accents, her vicious literature, her music, her dances, and her manifold mannerisms . . . [are] not racy of the soil, but rather alien . . . as are for the most part, the men and women who first imported and still continue to patronize them" (qtd. in Lloyd, "Counterparts" 139). Croke's definition of British literature as "vicious" tars this litany of commodities with the brush of sexual immorality and implies that their consumption by Irish "men and women" who have "imported" or "patronize[d] them" constitutes a licentiousness tantamount to a national betrayal. Sexual vice is English, but this racially "alien" force can be communicated to Irish bodies via such products. From his prominent, nationalist perch, Croke promulgates a conception of Irishness defined by sexual continence and opposed to a salacious British commodity culture. Through such clerical interventions, as well as through the preconditioned receptivity of Ireland's Catholic middle classes, a sexualized anticapitalist discourse idealizing the interlocking values of "purity, piety and simplicity," in the well-known phrase of Sir Charles Gavin Duffy, made its bid for hegemony within Irish cultural nationalism (12).[18]

Many of the figures introduced in the previous section also invoke this discourse while elaborating their opposition to British commodities, none more so than D.P. Moran. We have already begun to highlight the relationship between Moran's Catholicism and his anticapitalism through his castigation of the "Saxon bourgeois" who would "swallow the devil" rather than "lose a customer." This economic Catholicism extends from his opposition to British capitalism as a whole to criticism of the very same commodities pinpointed by Archbishop Croke, in particular that which, in the "Statement of Principles" that opens the first number of *The Leader*, he calls "British gutter literature" (116). Such a description, by equating such literature with filth, reflects the reliance of Moran's critique on the same sexual morality that Croke deploys, where the Irish consumption of British commodities spreads a "vicious," tainting influence throughout the nation. A more extended description of the salacious, Anglicizing effect of consuming the "gutter literature" of England occurs in "The Battle of Two Civilizations," where Moran bids to expose the "fraud" of "Anglo-Irish literature" by linking its emergence to "the great rise of cheap periodicals . . . in England": "it soon became evident that Ireland was largely feeding upon a questionable type of British reading matter. And the commandment—'Thou shalt be Irish'—was all the while troubling Irish hearts" (102). If there be any doubt as to the moral inflection on the word "questionable," it is dispelled by the religious terms that furnish its context, where not only are British periodicals a metaphysical "evil," but to consume them is to violate a national "commandment" to "be Irish." Such consumption is sinful, and in "troubling Irish hearts," inspires an unmistakably Catholic guilt.

Moran's praise for the Gaelic League is replete with similar descriptions of British commodities, whose immoral tide he views the League as devoted to stemming. In "The Gaelic Revival," he calls the League's effort to resuscitate the language as "an opportunity of vast moment, a good deed shining in a naughty world," and defines the "genius" of the League as "another name for the moral essence of the Irish nation" (75, 86). Moran then constructs a portrait of the Irish populace as fallen from grace through the consumption of British products:

> The Gaelic League has . . . a motley gathering to work upon. Observe it in the music halls . . . yelling at low jokes and indecent songs; watch it coming from a patriotic meeting roaring 'The Boys of Wexford' . . . see it in petticoats in its thousands filing into the circulating libraries and . . . penny novelette shops for reams of twaddle about Guy and Belinda; listen to it in the literary clubs discussing . . . the ideas of English literary men, and never . . . becoming conscious that God gave it . . . a head which He intended it to use in some original and independent manner. . . . How can any one conclude that it can ever be licked into Irish shape? It is . . . a blessed dispensation that faith can move mountains. (80)

The "motley gathering" that for Moran stands synecdochically for the nation shows a perfunctory patriotism by "roaring" the 1798 ballad "The Boys of Wexford," but this behavior is juxtaposed with their indulgence in the "low jokes and indecent songs" of the London "music halls." The same tendency is evident in the "thousands" of "petticoats" flocking to the "circulating libraries" and "penny novelette shops" to read "twaddle about Guy and Belinda," a description that intensifies the immoral associations of such commodities by invoking the staple Catholic nationalist ideal of the chaste female. As in the previous indictment of "cheap periodicals," the consumption of such "gutter" literature and of British popular music violates God's plan for an "independent" Ireland. Only a redoubled "faith" in his "blessed dispensation" holds out hope that it this "motley" populace "can be licked into Irish shape."

Moran had legitimate warrant for nominating the League as the standard bearer of Catholic morality. The League attracted significant allies in clerics like Father O'Growney and Father O'Hickey, and as F.S.L. Lyons records in *Culture and Anarchy in Ireland*, its co-founder, Eóin MacNeill, "was in no doubt that the true religion and the native language were deeply interfused," so much so that he declared, "When we learn to speak Irish, we soon find that it is what we may call essential Irish to acknowledge God, His presence, and His help, even in our most trivial conversation'" (80). For MacNeill, Gaelic and Catholicism were coextensive, "essential Irish" characteristics. Lyons also quotes the League's other co-founder, Douglas Hyde, as calling "the Irish Gael" "pious by nature" (80). In Hyde, however, Moran's claim of League sanction for his Catholic nationalist program encounters an obstacle. For though Hyde's work is in many ways responsible for the critique of British commodities as a source of national adulteration, Hyde's objection to these commodities is based not on religious premises, but on the Arnoldian premises of Literary Revivalist Celticism, which align much more closely with secular, humanist principles than Catholic ones.

Though Hyde does occasionally invoke Catholic ideals such as "piety" in his definitions of essential Irishness, the terminological bent of his criticism of British commodities tends in this contrary direction. It is here that the first piece of Revivalist prose cited by this study, from "The Necessity for De-Anglicizing Ireland," assumes its full significance. This essay is filled with denunciations of British commodities, including many of the same ones singled out by Croke and Moran—in particular music-hall songs and sensational literature. Hyde laments that "English music-hall ballads" have eclipsed the "old airs" of "travelling fiddlers and pipers," and hopes that "the revival of Irish music may go hand in hand with the revival of Irish ideas and Celtic modes of thought" (155–56). The subsequent passage cited in this book's introduction elaborates on this case to propound a more general opposition between Irishness and an array of "English" influences encompassing printed matter such as "penny dreadfuls, shilling shockers, and the garbage of vulgar

English weeklies like *Bow Bells* and *The Police Intelligence*," and other English "fads" in "music, games, fashions, and ideas" (159). Hyde's classification of such fare as "garbage" comes close to striking the moral key of Croke and Moran, where such "cheap" publications hold a symbolic place in the "gutter" of national life. As also quoted above, however, Hyde's definition of the original Ireland such influences threaten to engulf is "Celtic to the core," home to "one of the most original, artistic, literary, and charming peoples of Europe" (159–61).

Hyde's deployment of the watchwords of Arnoldian sentimentality at such moments is unmistakable. In this regard, it is not the word "garbage" that signals the fundamental basis of the essay's conception of British commodities, but the word "vulgar." Though this adjective could no doubt be assimilated to the sexualized moral discourse of Catholic nationalism, Hyde applies the term in a manner that figures it not as eroding sexual continence, but artistic sensibility. Where a Catholic nationalism such as Croke's identifies in the consumption of such commodities a licentious loosening of sexual mores—a simultaneous dissolution of "purity" and "piety"—Hyde perceives the desiccation of a naturally fecund and creative Irish being. If for Catholic nationalism British commodities impel the national being in a centrifugal, expansive direction, for the Literary Revival, they impel it in a centripetal, contractive one.

This emphasis on the artistic exfoliation of "Celtic modes of thought" aligns the commodity critique of the Literary Revival with the heritage of European humanism, which, from its Greco-Roman inception, promoted the creative cultivation of human species potential. For the Literary Revival to define British commodities as producing an impoverishment of Irish ontology further allies the movement with the specifically economic humanism of Karl Marx addressed in chapter 1. Marx's "anthropological" critique of the "estrangement" of capitalist labor converges unmistakably with the Celticist definition of Irishness underlying such passages as Hyde's above. Like Marx, who conceives of the species as bearing a utopian "sensuous potentiality," and building upon the work of Matthew Arnold and its critique of British "wealth," the Literary Revival conceives of "Irish human nature" as bearing a creative potential whose cultivation should be the independent nation's founding principle. Resting on this humanist foundation, Literary Celticism aestheticizes Irishness as the site of an ontological plenitude that capital threatens with extinction.

This critique underpins the Literary Revival's identification of British commodities as "vulgar." The deployment of this term signals the movement's corresponding investment in the ideology of high culture as a bulwark against the onslaught of capitalist reification. In keeping with this study's opening commentary on Celticist "alternative modernities," Literary Revivalist nationalism figures the domain of the aesthetic as both a model for and a stimulus to the ideal development of human societies—as, in other words, the privileged vehicle of the Arnoldian "study of perfection."[19] This dimension of the Revival will come more directly to the fore in chapter 5, which will probe the literary modernism devised by its aesthetic practitioners to navigate the challenges of anticapitalist decolonization. At this point, however, the commodity critique of the Literary Revival that so crucially underpins Irish modernism requires both further substantiation on its own terms and further elaboration vis-à-vis that of its Catholic nationalist competitor. Both purposes can be served by examining the especially caustic criticism directed by Literary Revivalists against two primary social nodes of the Irish consumption of British commodities: the rural Irish town and the Dublin theater.

In *Co-Operation and Nationality*, AE outlines the "new social order" the creation of which he views as the purpose of Sir Horace Plunkett's Irish Agricultural Organization Society. The specific components of the "rural civilization" promoted by the IAOS will be addressed in this chapter's final section. More pertinent to the Literary Revival's commodity critique are AE's descriptions of the existing rural characteristics he hopes to see the organization supplant. In the midst of a harangue on the "little country towns" of central and western Ireland, "social parasites" that "produce nothing" but subsist on resources imported from other Irish locales and from Britain, AE highlights their consumption of British literary "garbage" as paradigmatic:

> Here and there you will find a yellow assortment of ancient penny novelettes or song-books in a window . . . or a row of sensational tales in gaudy colours. . . . Better the ignorance of great literature—which left the Gaelic poets centuries ago to their own resources, their own traditions and folk tales, out of which came songs as natural and sweet as the songs of the birds—than these dust heaps of cheap prints, without high purpose, and glimmering all over with the phosphorescence of mental decay. . . . Towns ought to be conductors, catching the lightnings of the human mind and distributing them all around their area. The Irish country towns only develop mental bogs about them. (43)

The inventory of the country bookstore, a shabby "assortment" of "penny novelettes" and "sensational tales," sits at the lowest depths of the "mental bog" the "rural civilization" of the future must drain. The high-cultural key of AE's objection to these "cheap prints," lacking "high purpose" and "glimmering . . . with the phosphorescence of mental decay," echoes his assessment of ten years earlier in "Nationality and Imperialism," where "Police gazettes," "penny novels," and "hideous comic journals" spread an Anglicizing "vulgarity of mind" among Irish consumers ("Nationality" 19). In place of the "lightnings of the human mind" that coursed through Gaelic Ireland, these commodities stimulate vulgarity and "mental decay."

AE's inclusion of "song-books" among the rural Irish town's vulgar fare, and his juxtaposition of their commercialized airs to the "sweet" and "natural" songs of "the Gaelic poets," similarly recalls the earlier text's lament that where "the music of fairy" once "enchanted the elder generations," only "the songs of the London music halls" can now be heard ("Nationality" 19–20). Again, literature and music are singled out as powerful engines of the conversion of Irish beauty to British vulgarity. These same commodities preoccupy an even more vehement passage on "mental decay" in rural towns by Yeats in the *Samhain* of 1906, subtitled "Literature and the Living Voice," which recounts his recent pilgrimage to the grave of the Gaelic poet Anthony Raftery, Killaneen in County Galway. Yeats contrasts the experience of a commemorative ceremony put on by the "townspeople" there with the milieu of Galway City, through which he passed en route back to Dublin:

> A few days after, I was in the town of Galway, and saw there, as I had often seen in other country towns, some young men marching down the middle of a street singing an already outworn London music-hall song . . . with a rhythm as pronounced and as impersonal as the noise of a machine. In the shop-windows there were . . . the signs of a life very unlike that I had seen at Killaneen: halfpenny comic papers and story papers, sixpenny reprints of popular novels, and, with the exception of a dusty Dumas or Scott strayed thither, one knew not how, and one or two little books of Irish ballads, nothing that one calls literature, nothing that would interest a few thousands who alone out of many millions have what we call culture. A few miles had divided the sixteenth century, with its equality of culture, of good taste, from the twentieth. (204)

The journey from Killaneen to Galway City takes Yeats through a time warp, an impossibly rapid shift from the Gaelic Ireland of Raftery to the Anglicized Ireland of the twentieth. The "equality of culture" and "good taste" of the Killaneen villagers have been driven out by "halfpenny comic papers," "sixpenny reprints of popular novels," and "outworn London music hall song[s]," which, like poetry from an Orwellian "versificator," fill Yeats's mind "with a rhythm as pronounced and as impersonal as the noise of a machine." The contrast between the organic high culture of the "village" and the mechanical vulgarity of the "town" is further marked in terms of "fashion": the former locale is distinguished by indigenous "bawneens . . . clothes that had been adapted to their calling by centuries of continual slight changes," while in the latter, "nobody was well dressed; for in modern life, only a few people . . . set the fashions . . . and as for the rest, they must go shabby" (204).

"Literature and the Living Voice" derives an anthropological principle from Yeats's amateur fieldwork that makes explicit the central premise of the Literary Revival's commodity critique: "outward and inner things answer to one another" (204). This principle also informs the movement's critique of another central site of Irish access to British popular culture, the Dublin theater. We have already encountered the primary bête noire of the Revival's dramatic propaganda through Hyde's, AE's, and Yeats's condemnation of "the music hall": the genre of British "musical comedy." This genre had come to dominate both British and Irish popular taste by the time of the Revival's first stirrings. As the Irish Literary and National Theatres began to take shape as competitor organizations around 1900, musical comedy became one of the main targets of the Literary Revival's high-cultural agitations.

The February 1900 issue of *Beltaine*, "The Organ of the Irish Literary Theatre" edited by Yeats, provides a pristine specimen of the Theatre Movement's critique. The number consists of contributions by George Moore, Edward Martyn, Alice Milligan, and Lady Gregory, as well as three by Yeats himself, all of which celebrate the Movement's early success in reviving the Irish faculty of aesthetic appreciation. Moore's essay "Is the Theatre a Place of Amusement?" is particularly revealing. Its title, he explains, arose from the fact that while a recent London production of Ibsen's *Hedda Gabler* "did not pay its expenses," "a play called *The Dancing Girl*, which interested no one, drew large audiences" and "made money" (7). Moore draws from this perplexing mismatch between artistic quality and commercial success the following lesson: "People seek amusement, not pleasure, in a theatre. To obtain pleasure in a theatre, a man must rouse himself out of the lethargy of real life; his intelligence must awake, and the power to rouse oneself from the lethargy of real life is becoming rarer in the playgoer and more distasteful to him" (7–8). Artistic and commercial value are oil and water in the British theatrical market: "only with musical comedy," though "there is probably nothing in life so low as a musical comedy . . . can 1500 people avid for amusement be amused nightly" (9–10).

Martyn's contribution, titled simply "A Comparison between Irish and English Theatrical Audiences," goes so far as to pronounce the Literary Theatre already victorious in its bid for the allegiance of the Irish public. He paints the Theatre as offering an indigenous version of the universal aesthetic value Moore locates in Ibsen, exulting that in place of the "parade of wealth and commerce . . . vast cosmopolitanism and vulgarity . . . shoddy literature and drama" through which "certain persons and institutions" have sought to "create in Ireland a sort of shabby England," Ireland is instead busy cultivating "an idealism founded upon the ancient ideals of the land . . . a great intellectual awakening . . . and . . . a curiosity and appreciation for the best" (11–12). As evidence for this assessment, Martyn points to the "Dublin audiences," who, he declares, "have awakened to the insipidity of the modern English theatre," such that "when the big successes are brought over, the audience comes away wondering how the Londoners could have made it such a success" (12–13).

For the cultural nationalism of the Literary Revival, then, both sites, the rural town and the Dublin theater, are prime targets by virtue of their immersion in the "vulgar" commodity culture of the metropole. British literary, theatrical, sartorial, and other commodities threaten the resurrection of those "ancient ideals" that will form the indigenous basis for the nation's Celticist humanism, and their eradication is indispensable to this "high purpose." The fundamental divergence between this outlook and the moral outlook of Catholic nationalism determined that the alliance of the two factions against British capital and its popular-cultural products was highly unstable. Each faction of the Revival thus became forced to fight its anticapitalist battle on two fronts, on one of which loomed the imperial enemy, and on the other its domestic competitor for the consent of the Irish people.

The hegemonic struggle would even extend to the leveling of charges by both factions that their opponents were agents of British economic forces. The spat that emerged in the wake of Yeats's *The Countess Cathleen* between Yeats and the prominent Catholic nationalist F. Hugh O'Donnell provides a fascinating example. O'Donnell, in two publications, the broadside pamphlet "Souls for Gold: A Pseudo Celtic Drama in Dublin" and the longer work *The Stage Irishmen of the Pseudo-Celtic Drama*, famously indicted Yeats for his play's depiction of "the baseness which is utterly alien to all our national traditions, the barter of Faith for Gold" ("Souls" 260). O'Donnell's dually Catholic and anticapitalist attack won the immediate approval of Cardinal Logue, who, without having read the play, remarked in the *Daily Nation* in May of 1899 that "an Irish Catholic audience which could patiently sit out such a play must have sadly degenerated, both in religion and patriotism" (qtd. in Cairns and Richards 72). O'Donnell's language in the latter, 1904 text is even more aggressive, declaring that "The rapt gaze and ethereal contemplations of the Mystic Minor Poet are quite compatible with sound commercial principles," and classing him dually as a "Professor of Extreme Nationalism and Dramatic Entertainer to Dublin Castle" (8–9). In O'Donnell's hands, Yeats's brand of Celticism becomes just that, a commercial *brand* bearing the stamp of an immoral British capitalism.

In the essays following the *Countess* controversy, Yeats rationalized the play's failure by reciprocating O'Donnell's tactics and casting Catholic nationalism as itself a "Castle" commodity, one allied to the Anglicizing influence of two symbolic figures identified in the 1902 essay "Edmund Spenser" as "the Puritan and the Merchant" (364). These figures emblematize an array of repressive religious and economic traits, "the timidity and reserve of the counting house," by which Yeats, particularly in the *Samhain* writings, tried to leverage the Celticist, anticapitalist consensus against his Catholic opponents ("Edmund" 365). Texts such as "Moral and Immoral Plays" (1903) and "First Principles" (1908) identify Catholic Ireland's preference for moral over artistic achievement as a thinly veiled incarnation of British capitalist vulgarity. In the former, Yeats, describing a "Connacht Bishop" who "told his people . . . that they 'should never read stories about the degrading passion of love,'" argues that the priest's "puritanism is but an English cuckoo" (113). In the latter, addressing not just *Countess* but the more recent controversies generated by Synge's *The Shadow of the Glen* and *The Playboy of the Western World*, he asserts, "the attacks which have followed us from the beginning . . . have arisen out of conceptions of life which . . . are essentially English. . . . These patriots, with an heretical preference for faith over works . . . continually attack in the interest of . . . some reflection from English novelists" (232–33).

Like O'Donnell, then, Yeats leverages the tools available to him within the hegemonic discourse of Revivalist anticapitalism to define his nationalist opponents as being in traitorous alignment with British economic forces. Because both factions of the Revival are committed to a position of general opposition to British capitalism, they naturally couch their objections to each other in the terms of this established discourse. Refracted through the bifocal lens of the Revival, nationalist anticapitalism vis-à-vis the imported commodities of British popular culture would become the medium for articulating the competing factional ideals of the movement's Catholic and Literary constituencies. Thus, for O'Donnell, "the Yeatsite drama" is a "Castle" commodity furthering the nation's dispossession by a British capitalist system figured as licentious, immoral, and ontologically expansive, while for Yeats it is views such as O'Donnell's that bespeak Ireland's commodification and dispossession by a British capitalism instead figured as repressive, vulgar, and ontologically contractive.

The commodity critique of the Irish Revival can thus be seen as a signal conduit for both the general nationalist antagonism to British capital and the factional infighting that would precipitate the foundational ideals of the postcolonial state. That this nationalist war of position would issue in the establishment of some form of Catholic nationalism as hegemonic was more or less preordained by the organic linkage between this faction's ideals and those of Ireland's middle-class, Catholic population. The Literary Revival's attempts to secure this population's spontaneous consent for its high-cultural vision were confronted with the impossible task of fundamentally reshaping its deeply ingrained beliefs, and thus, in spite of its more liberal agenda, it failed. However, even as the Literary Revival's efforts in the domain of consumption began to founder, another attempt to extricate Irish culture from capital had already begun to emerge in the domain of production, where a number of important movements sought to reshape the nation's economy in accord with Celticist ideals.

## TRANSVALUING THE *DAMNOSA HEREDITAS*: CELTICIZING THE IRISH ECONOMY

The passage from Yeats's "Nationality and Literature" that opens this chapter foregrounds one of the central challenges of the nationalist embrace of the Arnoldian Celt. Founding Irish independence not just on antipathy to the "flood-gates" of British capital, but on the premise of a racially congenital impracticality, might succeed in galvanizing decolonization, but wholesale disregard for "the material needs of the race" would surely imperil the nation's viability. This study's account of Celticist anticapitalism here returns to the problematic addressed by numerous exponents of postcolonial theory and remarked on in this study's introduction, namely the "double bind" of colonial binary oppositions—the definitional dilemma whose horns puncture any effort toward a Nietschean "transvaluation" of their negative terms. Not only in terms of legitimizing the colonized's claim to independence, but also in terms of the subsequent, practical creation of a flourishing postcolonial society, the embrace of stereotypes of drunknenness (as opposed to sobriety), irrationality (as opposed to rationality), and ungovernability (as opposed to civility) would appear inherently disabling.[20]

The Irish nationalist embrace of the "primitive," Celtic alternatives to British capitalist modernity provides an especially significant illustration of this problematic. In a world dominated by capital, a complete rejection of capitalist imperatives—of the need to make "two blades of grass grow where one did before"—could only disable the effort to begin developing a viable, independent Irish society. Recognizing this turn of the colonial screw, a number of leading Revivalists thus undertook efforts to spur economic development. Remarkably, however, even in the domain of practical economics, the Celticist ideals that so powerfully facilitated Revivalist nationalism's alternative cultural vision would play a major role. By attempting to Celticize the Irish economy, Revivalists attempted simultaneously to preserve the "primitive" forms on which this alternative vision depended and to satisfy the "civilized" economic dictates of modernity.

Such efforts began to emerge through the "Irish manufactures" or "native manufactures" campaign spearheaded by Moran's *Leader* and *The United Irishman* of Arthur Griffith around the turn of the century. Moran's statement of purpose in the first number of the former publication—already quoted above vis-à-vis Revivalist opposition to British "gutter literature"—exemplifies this advocacy. Complaining that Ireland has become "a dumping-ground for English and Scotch commercial enterprise," Moran promises to devote *The Leader*'s space to promoting this particularization of the (to his mind) capitalist universal: "We will never cease driving home the necessity for economic development if this country is to be regenerated, and we will support every effort no matter from what quarter it comes that helps on the material prosperity of Ireland without militating against her distinct nationality" (117). Read alongside his lament in "The Battle of Two Civilizations" that "Ireland, because she has lost her heart, imports today what on sound economic principles she could produce herself," one receives the impression that "Irish manufactures" will spur the nation's economy not only in the direction of simple independence from British capital but along a "distinct," Irish trajectory consonant with Moran's signature combination of Catholic and Arnoldian Celticisms.

The "Hungarian Example" on which Griffith modeled Sinn Fein proposed a similar program. The 1904 pamphlet *The Resurrection of Hungary* locates its economic component within the British anthropological framework that defines capital as inherently Saxon. In his fight against the Teutonic Austrian Empire, the Hungarian Magyar confronted many of the same economic stereotypes as the Irish Celt now confronts. "Forty years ago," Griffith explains, "the Austrian Press and . . . statesmen assured the world, as the English . . . assure it now about Ireland—that the people of Hungary were fickle, inconstant, lacking in application—in a word, devoid of the great Teutonic virtues of sobriety, patience and industry" (78). In contrast, however, to Hungary, who have "shown the world how Austria lied . . . Irishmen have been found to believe the libel . . . that . . . we lack the staying power of the Saxon," with the result that "of the two nations both seemingly helpless . . . in 1849—the one that believed in itself has since become a great nation . . . [while] the one that sought succour from its masters is, perhaps, to-day the most miserable and most forgotten in Europe" (78). Ireland must follow Hungary and repudiate the Teuton's economic slander through its own, native "sobriety, patience and industry." This will only be possible, Griffith argues, by withdrawing Irish MPs from Westminster and assembling a "Council of Three Hundred" Irish representatives in Dublin to superintend "a system for the Protection of Irish manufactures" from British competition (94). If this would seem to propose the adoption of "Teutonic virtues," his "Sinn Fein Policy" would insist elsewhere on Ireland being "a distinct nation," a statement which, given the ethnological premises of the above passage, could only be interpreted as recommending a Celticization of these normative qualities.[21]

Other prominent venues like *The Shan Van Vocht* of Alice Milligan, *An Claidheamh Soluis*, the organ of the Gaelic League, and *The Irish Homestead*, the publication of the IAOS, also used the "Manufactures" campaign to promote economic Celticization.[22] Milligan, in an editorial titled "Industrial Ireland" in the 7 November 1898 *Shan Van Vocht*, insists on her Irish readers "preferring Irish manufactures to all others" and warns English "visitors" to Ireland that "they are coming to a country very different from that of the Sassenach, and that it is in studying these differences, not denouncing them, the benefit of travelling there lies" (206–207). Such print exhortations help contextualize a number of striking economic developments, among them one chronicled by Hugh Oram's history of Irish advertising, *The Advertising Book*. In 1905, Oram records, after "the Dundalk family firm of Carroll's bought its first cigarette making machine," it proceeded to brand its first two lines "'Anti-Combine,' a reference to the monopoly held in the Irish market . . . by the big English companies such as Players and Wills," and "'Emerald Gem'" (29). Such campaigns clearly constitute attempts to capitalize not just on the anti-English posture of the manufactures movement, but on Celticist themes. Though such ploys are perhaps exploitative and tokenistic, even the possibility for such opportunism reflects the extent to which the Celticization of the economy had influenced public sensibilities.

If the promotional efforts of the "Irish manufactures" campaign display an obvious, and perhaps necessary, vagueness about their plan to Celticize such "Teutonic" characteristics as "industry," other Revivalist efforts would yield a more precise formula for a distinctively Celtic economy. Sir Horace Plunkett's Irish Agricultural Organization Society represents one such effort. Founded in 1894 as a species of "Constructive Unionism"—to borrow F.S.L. Lyon's label for those Unionists who in spite of their politics worked to foster Irish economic development—by autumn of 1903, according to Plunkett's *Ireland in the New Century*, "considerably over eight hundred societies had been established," of which "360 were dairy, and 140 agricultural societies, nearly 200 agricultural banks, 50 home industries societies, 40 poultry societies . . . [and] 40 others with miscellaneous subjects" (192).[23] While reading this text, which summarizes both the Society's efforts during its first decade and its underlying motives, the Unionist and Anglicizing intent underlying such advances becomes clear. Plunkett addresses a mainly British readership and promises that the book will help rectify the root problem of colonial Ireland's lack of prosperity, "the failure of the English to see into the Irish mind" (13). Once that problem has been addressed, he declares, a "strengthening of the Irish character" will ensue that will enable the nation to "contribute a factor of vital importance to the life of the British Empire" (70, 59). When Plunkett defines the vehicle for this change as "the development of a commercial morality, without which there can be no commercial success," he appears to advocate for Irish assimilation to British norms, and it would thus seem that his Society's aims leave little room for national distinctiveness (18–19).

But Plunkett elsewhere warns that the Irish economy of the future "will have to accord with national sentiment and be distinctively Irish" (41). It is in fleshing out this "national sentiment" and the particularizing force it must exert on British "commercial morality" that *Ireland in the New Century* indicates the IAOS's contribution to Irish economic Celticization:

> The problem of mind and character with which we had to deal in Ireland presented this central . . . discouraging fact. In practical life the Irish had failed where the English had succeeded, and this was attributed to the lack of certain English qualities . . . undoubtedly essential to success in commerce and industry. . . . It was the individualism of the English economic system . . . which made these qualities indispensable. The lack of these qualities in Irishmen to-day may be admitted. . . . But those who regard the Irish situation as industrially hopeless . . . ignore the fact that there are other qualities . . . which can be developed by Irishmen and

> may form the basis of an industrial system . . . qualities which come into play rather in association than in the individual, and to which the term "associative" is applied. So that although much disparaging criticism of the Irish character is based upon the survival in the Celt of the tribal instincts, it is gratifying to show that . . . our preference for thinking and working in groups may not be altogether a *damnosa hereditas*. If, owing to our deficiency . . . we cannot at this stage hope to produce . . . the 'economic man' of the economists, we think we see our way to provide, as a substitute, the economic association. (166–67)

Plunkett's efforts to instill those "English qualities" that have produced "success in commerce and industry" have encountered an obstacle, one that suggests the Irish will never transform into the *homo economicus* of Adam Smith. "The survival in the Celt of the tribal instincts," which "come into play rather in association than in the individual," recommends that a "substitute" be devised for the maxims of political economy. Adapting the IAOS's economic program to the Celtic raw materials of the Irish population, Plunkett submits that a compromise system, "the economic association," provides the only viable route for accomplishing its goals.

If Plunkett is too conservative to call such an association by its proper name, his partner in "co-operation," AE, displays no such compunction. Where Plunkett speaks merely of "developing the industrial qualities of the Celt on associative lines" (170–71), AE's *The National Being* refers to the IAOS as "the pivot round which Ireland has begun to swing back to its traditional and natural communism" (20). For AE, it is full-blown *communism* that best describes the economic system implicit in the traits of the Irish Celt. The entry of this term into the discussion of Revivalist economics brings immediately to mind the figure most responsible for the notion of a "Celtic communism," the founder of the Irish Socialist Republican Party, James Connolly. Two texts of Connolly's in particular, the pamphlet *Erin's Hope: The End and the Means*, and the *Shan Van Vocht* essay "Socialism and Nationalism," both published in 1897, propound an economic system in tune with both Celticist and modernizing ideals. A passage from the former text explaining the origins of the "Irish question" begins to outline this system by locating "its real origin and inner meaning in the circumstances that the two nations held fundamentally different ideas upon the vital question of property in land" (6). Invoking "recent scientific research" in such British anthropological texts as Lewis Morgan's *Ancient Society*—as well as on such seminal Young Ireland precursors as Thomas Davis's "Udalism and Feudalism"—Connolly explains

Anglo-Irish conflict as stemming from a clash between the English preference for a "feudal" system founded on private property and an Irish preference for the kinds of "common ownership" that "formed the basis of primitive society" (6). Against the anthropological characterization of such "primitive Communism" as unevolved, Connolly defines the communism of the Irish Celt as civilized to a high, utopian degree—as "part of the well defined social organizations of a nation of scholars and students, recognized by Chief and Tanist, Brehon and Bard, as the inspiring principle of their collective life" (6).

This Celticist economic theory informs the more famous argument in "Socialism and Nationalism" that mere political separation from England will not generate true independence. Rather, Connolly warns, "the whole brutally materialistic system of civilization" that is British capitalist modernity, consisting of "those insidious but disastrous forms of economic subjection—landlord tyranny, capitalist fraud, and unclean usury," constitutes the essence of Ireland's colonial subjection (25). The formula for complete decolonization thus resides not in "hoist[ing] a green flag over Dublin Castle," but in "a reorganization of society on the basis of a broader and more developed form of that common property which underlay the social structure of ancient Erin" (25). Making Ireland a "Socialist Republic" through the cultivation and "development" of the nation's inborn, Celtic economic qualities, is the linchpin of true nationalism, and Connolly's efforts both in the ISRP and, later, the Irish Transport and General Workers Union and Irish Labour Party all spring from this central motivation.[24]

In *Irish Times*, David Lloyd offers a compelling rereading of Connolly's "Celtic Communism" within the frame of Dipesh Chakrabarty's theory of the two histories of capital, which views the colonial expansion of European capital as precipitating a schism between the pre-capitalist social practices adaptable to its imperatives and those which required elimination for capital's global ascendancy. Modifying Marx's *Theories of Surplus Value*, Chakrabarty designates the first set of practices "History 1" and the second "History 2," according to their respective ability and inability to "contribute to the self-reproduction of capital" (63–64). Lloyd's reading of Connolly's Celticist economics identifies in them an attempt to radicalize the recalcitrant, capital-resistant elements of an indigenous, Irish "History 2," whereby the vestigial elements of "ancient Erin," through their unassimilability to the "iron logic" of capitalist modernity, provide the basis for the nation's "alternative future" (126). Connolly's innovations are thus recuperable for the postcolonial theoretical project of "mapping the interface between colonial modernity and the counter-modern formations that emerge in relation to it" (126).

The concept of a "relational" rejection of capitalist modernity enables us to interpret Connolly's "Celtic communism" as refusing the choice between the disabling terms of the dual imperial binaries of primitive/civilized and sentimentality/industry. More than a simple "transvaluation" of economic primitivity, the notion of a Celtic alternative modernity existing differentially alongside that of Britain envisions a middle way between the Scylla and Charybdis of either adopting capitalist norms wholesale or embracing the doomed historical choice of rejecting modernization outright. Connolly's Celticized Irish economy thus represents a visionary formula for breaking out of this particularly snarled facet of the dialectic of Celt and capital. By embracing and radicalizing the implications of Revivalist Celticism, Connolly's communism moves beyond the limitations of either the "Irish manufactures" movement, which is often unable to commit to substantive modifications of the industrial capitalist model of England beyond a few tokenist adjustments, or the "cooperative movement" of Sir Horace Plunkett's IAOS, which, in spite of the correspondences between its "economic associations" and Connolly's program, figures such associations as simply a reluctant compromise between an unremitting British ideal and the putative backwardness of the Irish populace.

It is important to note, however, that Connolly's communism is but the most radical, practical incarnation of the widespread Revivalist effort to define a Celtic Irishness against a Teutonic British capitalism. The work of such other figures as Hyde, Moran, Yeats, AE, and Synge provides the context necessary to trace the cultural filiations of Connolly's "national Marxism," and if their ideas for disentangling Ireland from colonialism and capital are less sophisticated than his (with the possible exception of AE), his theories could scarcely have emerged outside of the intellectual atmosphere they helped produce. Indeed, it would not be overly hyperbolic to identify in the less self-consciously economic endeavors of the Gaelic League or the Theatre Movement a similar attempt to reactivate the indigenous Irish elements of "History 2" and to leverage such characteristics toward the production of an alternative modernity. Especially through such efforts as these, in fact, efforts founded on the ontologically liberatory, humanist Celticism of its Literary participants, the anticapitalist decolonization movement that was the Revival suggests just such a reading.

CHAPTER 5

# "In Front of the Cracked Looking-Glass"

## *Revivalist Modernism, the Irish Female Consumer, and the Colonial Spectacle*

As the previous chapter has begun to show, the Irish Revival was both an intellectually sophisticated and a practically minded effort to use the resources of Celticism to supplant the capitalist norms attending Ireland's colonial subjection. The dual Arnoldian stereotype of the Celt's unsuitability to "industry" and proclivity for aesthetic sensitivity provided the basis for a broad anticapitalist consensus among Irish nationalists, all of whom could agree, despite differences as to motive, method, and extent, that the Ireland of the future should jettison the economic modes of the imperial era. As I have also argued, Celticism proved an especially dynamic resource in the hands of one nationalist faction in particular, that of the Literary Revival, whose anticapitalist agenda bespoke a more liberal vision than that of its Catholic counterpart. This chapter builds upon these claims by reading a selection of Literary-Revivalist works as modernist attempts to decolonize and Celticize the Irish marketplace.

I will begin addressing these efforts via a reading of Yeats's *The Land of Heart's Desire* and a related consideration of the popular success achieved by Yeats's and Lady Gregory's *Cathleen ni Houlihan*. *The Land*, I will argue, stages a confrontation between the vulgar consumer tastes bred by British popular culture and the "Titanic," sublime resources of Celtic sentimentality. This confrontation situates the play at the beginning of a highly innovative Revivalist modernism whose aesthetic strategies of de-Anglicization constitute a significant contribution to the broader nationalist vision of a Celticist alternative modernity. As the ensuing discussion of *Cathleen* will show, however, as a result of the friction between his generic preference for the high-cultural aesthetics of tragedy and the play's achievement of popular success via the "low" devices of melodrama, Yeats would soon abandon his early Celticist tactics and retreat into the elitist posture that would define his middle and late career.

The chapter will then show how two subsequent texts, Synge's *The Playboy of the Western World* and James Stephens's *The Charwoman's Daughter*, likewise adopt modernist strategies of de-Anglicization but go further than Yeats to achieve an immanent critique of the forms of British popular culture. Where the elitist Yeats scorned the "vulgar" genres to which Irish taste had grown attuned, Synge and Stephens both draw on such genres in order to reshape the mental habits of the Irish consumer. In so doing, both *Playboy* and *Charwoman's Daughter* achieve a radical insight into the nature of the capitalist culture industry, one that anticipates later twentieth-century theories of postmodernism: that the consumption of pop-cultural media reifies human perceptions and values, and that in a colonial context, such consumption threatens to contribute to reproducing the thralldom of the colonized to metropolitan and capitalist norms. Drawing specifically on the theories of the French Marxist Guy Debord, I call this phenomenon "the colonial spectacle." Synge's and Stephens's efforts to defuse this phenomenon represent some of the most innovative aesthetic extensions of the Revival's Celticist anticapitalism, and they represent the fulfillment of the Celt's potential as an instrument of capitalist critique.

As the readings below will gradually underscore, the Literary Revival's modernist innovations were frequently aimed at one Irish demographic in particular: that of the young, female consumer. Concern over the exposure of this specific group to the influence of the metropolitan culture industry in many ways represents a further, movement-wide theme in addition to the three adumbrated in the preceding chapter's anatomy of Revivalist anticapitalism. More specifically, the Revival's commodity critique would highlight the reification of the Irish female's Celtic sensibilities by such Anglicizing products as tabloid reporting, Romance fiction, and sartorial fashion. This chapter will show that many of Literary modernisms' most dynamic formal innovations would constitute sophisticated extensions of these concerns. It will then conclude by taking stock of the implications of such modernist reform efforts in relation to the work of the Revival's own, feminist participants, and within the history of Celticism more broadly.

## *THE LAND OF HEART'S DESIRE* AND THE REBIRTH OF CELTIC TRAGEDY

W.B. Yeats's 1894 play *The Land of Heart's Desire* is, in many ways, a prototypical Literary-Revivalist work, and it shares with other major, early productions carried out under the movement's aegis such as Edward Martyn's *The Heather Field* (1899) and *Maeve* (1900), George Moore's *The Bending of the Bough* (1900), and even a text such as George Bernard Shaw's *John Bull's Other Island* (1904), a leveraging of Celticist ideals against an Irishness overrun by British capital. Additionally, in keeping with the hegemonic bid of Literary-Revivalist Celticism, *The Land* also targets the influence of Irish Catholicism, which it depicts, along with capitalism, as stunting an inborn, expansive Irish ontology. The play thus offers a signal instance of Yeats's lifelong crusade against "The Puritan and the Merchant," and it is against these interlocking agencies of Anglicization that its Celticism is trained.

The play's primary symbols, the cross and the heart, focalize its critique. Yeats's stage directions place "a crucifix on the wall" of the Bruin household, and the play's dialogue soon alerts the audience to this prop's thematic relevance. In response to his mother Bridget's complaint that his wife, Mary, "because I bid her clean the pots," "took that old book down out of the thatch" of the Bruin cottage and "has been doubled over it ever since," thus shirking her feminine duties, Shawn Bruin remarks, "Mother, you are too cross" (34). When Bridget further explains, "She would not mind the kettle, mild the cow, or even lay the knives and spread the cloth," it becomes clear that her "cross" disposition results from being beset by domestic chores (35). The religious impulse behind such economic duties as Mary avoids appears through the counsel of the Bruins' "old priest," Father Hart. Hart assures Bridget that Mary's waywardness will dissipate as she matures: "I have seen some other girls / Restless and ill at ease, but years went by, / And they grew like their neighbors and were glad / In minding children, working at the churn, / And gossiping of weddings and of wakes" (36). Mary, then, seems fated to grow as "cross" as Bridget under the allied pressures of domestic economy and clerical surveillance.

The symbol of the heart surfaces through the activity that distracts Mary from her chores. Maurteen Bruin recounts the history of an "old book" his daughter-in-law reads, establishing it as the catalyst of her "heart's desire" to escape the play's normative regime. "My father told me my grandfather wrote it," he explains, and proceeds to denigrate its contents for having "filled his house with rambling fiddlers, and rambling ballad-makers and the like," which frivolous activities, were he to indulge them, would prevent him from bequeathing his son and daughter-in-law a "stocking stuffed with yellow guineas / . . . when I am dead" (35). He accordingly warns Mary, "You should not be filling your head with foolish dreams" (35). Mary's subsequent description of the book's contents signals its Celticist filiations. "A daughter of a King of Ireland," she summarizes, "heard a voice singing on a May eve like this," which she "followed, half awake and half asleep / Until she came to the Land of Faery, Where nobody gets old and godly and grave / . . . crafty and wise / . . . and bitter of tongue" (36). In keeping with Celticism's staple oppositions, the "cross" influences of "grave" religion and "crafty" economy are barred from this realm, whose inhabitants are instead "busied with the dance," enjoying a carefree vitality (36).

Mary's attraction to this "dream" overpowers Father Hart's warning that "it was some wrecked angel . . . / Who flattered [the princess's] heart with merry words," as well as Maurteen's enticements to be a "good girl" through reminders of the "hundred acres of good land" the family possesses, the "golden guineas" the land has brought, and the "content and wisdom" such possessions bring to the "heart" (38–39). She then calls to the "Good People" of the "Faery":

> Come, faeries, take me out of this dull house!
> Let me have all the freedom I have lost;
> Work when I will and idle when I will!
> Faeries, come take me out of this dull world,
> For I would ride with you upon the wind,
> And dance upon the mountains like a flame. (39)

The cruciform pressures of economy and religion are then the source Mary's "heart's desire," a dream of escape to a Celtic paradise where "freedom" and revelry displace "dull" duty.

Before Mary's entreaty is answered, the play suggests that there is in fact already potential for realizing such freedom in the material world. Hearing Mary's lament for their "dull" life, Shawn defends himself against the charge of complicity with his parents and Father Hart. "Do not blame me," he soothes, "Sit down beside me here—these are too old, / And have forgotten they were ever young" (40). According to Yeats's stage directions, at this moment, Mary "would put her arms around him, but looks shyly at the priest and lets her arms fall" (40). Noting her reticence, Father Hart encourages the couple's affectionate display but does so in terms that reassert his oppressiveness: "My daughter, take his hand—by love alone / God binds us to Himself and to the hearth / That shuts us from the waste beyond His peace, / From maddening freedom and bewildering light" (40). Shawn affirms his desire to gratify Mary's greater urges, assuring her, "Would that the world were mine to give it you, / And not its quiet hearths alone, but even / All that bewilderment of light and freedom, / If you would have it" (40). Mary appears satisfied by Shawn's attentions, telling him, "Your looks are all the candles that I need" (40). It would therefore seem that in the absence of the domestic-economic and religious nagging of the elder Bruins and Father Hart, Mary and Shawn, through their youthful vitality and passion, might achieve an earthly freedom sufficient to render her utopian dreaming superfluous.

Mary's fate, however, has already been sealed through her appeal to the Celtic "faeries," whose power is augmented by the play's setting on Beltaine, the "May eve" during which the "wrecked angels" of the Irish wood have increased sway over human affairs. A "child of the gentle people" soon arrives to convey Mary to the Land of Fairy and succeeds in "coaxing" the cottage's inhabitants to surrender to her designs. Maurteen, noting the change in Bridget upon her arrival, tells her, "mother was quite cross before you came," while Father Hart, in spite of his earlier assurance that the crucifix on the wall "will keep all evil from the house," accedes to the child's request to remove "that ugly thing on the black cross" (43). A heated struggle for Mary's soul then ensues between Shawn, Father Hart, and the child in which Hart, sans crucifix, is rendered powerless. Shawn fares better in his efforts to "bind" Mary to the world, despite the child's reminder that by remaining, Mary will "grow like the rest; / Bear children, cook, and bend above the churn, / And wrangle over butter, fowl, and eggs, / Until at last, grown old and bitter of tongue, / You're crouching there and shivering at the grave" (45). His appeals seem to turn the tide when Mary states, "I think that I would stay—and yet—and yet—," but, finally, "Mary Bruin dies" and is transubstantiated to the realm of "faery" as a "white bird" (46). The play's conclusion bears out the prophetic song chanted by the child, as, beneath the "cross" pressures of domestic economy and religion, "the lonely of heart is withered away" (47).

*The Land of Heart's Desire* thus uses Celticism to throw the oppressive conditions of Irish society into relief. Mary's Celticist dream is both negatively spurred by the "cross" demands of capitalism and Catholicism and positively geared toward defining an ideal society to replace this religious-economic regime, a world of "light," dancing, love-making, and "freedom" from its repressive-productive dynamics. This critique, however, only begins to identify the play's contribution to the Revival's anticapitalist campaign. We may begin to further define that contribution by spotlighting an additional textual detail, one that links the play directly to the Irish marketplace. Though Yeats's stage directions indicate that it is set in "a remote time," and though it might thus seem equally remote from Revivalist concerns over commodity consumption, the play subtly invokes this anachronistic context by depicting Mary Bruin as a consumer of *fashion*. As Bridget complains to Maurteen before

Mary's entreaty to the fairies, "I must spare and pinch that my son's wife / May have all kinds of ribbons for her head" (38). Lest there be any doubt about the importance of this detail, it reappears twice: first, when Bridget chastises Mary, "Before you were married you were idle and fine / And went about with ribbons on your head; / And now . . . / [You are] not a fitting wife for any man" (39); and, second, when Maurteen attempts to bribe the fairy child "Not to talk wickedly of holy things" with a gift: "Here are some ribbons I bought in the town / For my son's wife—but she will let me give them / To tie up that wild hair the winds have tumbled" (43). The cumulative effect of these references is to place the play's "remote" setting inside the pale of contemporary Irish commodity culture and to suggest that Mary is a faithful devotee of sartorial fashion.

Registering the economic concerns indexed in Mary's "ribbons" gives sharper definition to the play's design. *The Land* depicts not merely a macro-cultural conflict between the agencies of "the Puritan and the Merchant" and the Celtic values of the title "land," but also a micro-economic conflict between the consumption of "vulgar" popular-cultural commodities and the consumption of high culture. Mary's reading of the Celticist legends authored by Maurteen's grandfather, which once drew to the cottage a retinue of "rambling fiddlers" and "rambling ballad-makers," represents the conversion of an Irish "West Briton" to nationalist values. Underscoring this vein of significance complicates the play's engagement with the agon of Celt and capital and suggests that it is not merely in its plot dynamics that the reader should seek its contribution to the Revivalist cause, but in their *aesthetic tenor.* Regardless of its characters' fate, the play contributes to decolonization through its embodiment of the high-cultural aesthetic values it depicts Mary as preferring over her formerly frivolous consumer tastes.

This aspect of *The Land* exemplifies an extremely common theme among the Revival's dramatic works: the identification of the young, native, female Irish consumer as an especially vital target of de-Anglicization. This theme arises in Martyn's *Maeve*, for example, through the heroine's conversion from the Anglicizing influences of Burren, County Clare, by a Celticist text, "The Influence of Greek Art on Celtic Ornament." In *John Bull's Other Island*, similarly, before her initial encounter with the British capitalist Tom Broadbent, his Irish love interest, Nora, "hums a song—not an Irish melody, but a hackneyed English drawing room ballad of the season before last" (150). Like Mary Bruin, Shaw's Nora has become Anglicized through the consumption of British popular culture. A comment of Shaw's from his "Preface for Politicians" affirms *John Bull*'s intention to criticize such consumption: "When I say

I am an Irishman, I mean that I was born in Ireland, and that my language is the English of Swift, and not the unspeakable jargon of the mid-XIX century London newspapers" (473). Like those of Yeats and Martyn, then, what Shaw calls his "patriotic contribution to the repertory of the Irish Literary Theatre" consists not simply of an attempt to envision a postcolonial, anticapitalist Irish identity, but an attempt to combat British capitalist influence *directly* by deterring the Irish female consumption of British literary "garbage" (473).

How, then, did Literary-Revivalist texts attempt to reshape Irish consumers, and female ones in particular, through an exposure to high-cultural ideals, and in what way were such ideals coded as the vehicle of a de-Anglicizing Celticization of Irish culture? In many ways, answering this question proves a matter of *genre*. As I have shown, Literary Revivalists like Yeats, Martyn, and Moore positioned formulaic British genres such as melodrama and musical comedy as prime targets of their high-cultural agitations in publications like *Beltaine* and *Samhain*. Having now touched upon the content of a number of the Theatre Movement's productions, we are ready to identify their Celticism as motivated by a generic choice geared toward awakening the Irish populace from the "vulgar" slumbers such genres bred. Plays like *The Land of Heart's Desire*, then, illustrate the Revivalist conception of *tragedy* as the genre best suited to breaking the hold of British entertainments on the Irish consumer. In the words of Moore's essay "Is the Theatre a Place of Amusement?," "To obtain pleasure in a theatre, a man must rouse himself out of the lethargy of real life; his intelligence must awake, and the power to rouse oneself out of the lethargy of real life is becoming rarer in the playgoer and more distasteful to him" (7–8). Perhaps a tragic elevation of the Irish theatrical landscape could "rouse" the nation's "intelligence" from its pop-cultural "lethargy." Much of the attraction in Celticism for Literary Revivalists like Moore inheres in its inbuilt utility to such elevation. As Yeats puts the matter in the 1904 *Samhain* essay "The Dramatic Movement," in tragedy, "everything has been changed all of a sudden; we are caught up into another code, we are in the presence of a higher court" (154). Literary Revivalists sought to impanel this "higher court" by exfoliating the tragic undertones of Arnold's "melancholy," "sentimental," "titanic" Celt.

Pursuing Revivalist Celticism's contribution to decolonization further thus necessitates more precise attention to its aesthetic practices. This shift toward a more formal analysis naturally dovetails with the question of whether the Revival was, in fact, a *modernist* movement. If the Revival's aim was to supplant the formal simplicity and vulgar tendencies of musical comedy and melodrama with a more challenging and "titanic" art, this aim would seem to demand some degree of formal innovation. To what extent did the Revival's "titanic," tragic ideals issue in a properly modernist—and therefore, within the context of Irish nationalism's commodity critique, a properly de-Anglicizing—literary practice?[1] Here we must return to the distinction advanced in chapter 1 between a romantic and a modernist primitivism. As argued there, Arnold's *Study* shares with Nietzsche's *The Birth of Tragedy* a desire to restore the "titanic," "Dionysian" power of primitive aesthetics to a Europe enthralled by the "Apollonian" "machinery" of capitalist modernity. Arnold, however, as a result of his imperialist commitments, reins in the radical impulse toward a renewed efflorescence of the Celt's "natural magic," while Nietzsche embraces this potential through the primordial "ecstasy" of the Attic Tragic chorus. The Literary Revival's tragic aesthetics must be read in this Nietzschean, primitivist vein.

What the tragic conclusions of texts like *The Land of Heart's Desire* produce is a properly Dionysian aesthetic effect, an explosion of reason and representational clarity through an irruption of primordial "ecstasy." The profound strangeness and opacity of the representation of Yeats's "fairy child" to both the play's other characters and its audience must be duly emphasized here. Though her descriptions of her "land" provide some definite indicators of an ontological state defined against the repressions of Catholicism and capital, there is a point in her "dreamy and strange talk" beyond which interpretation cannot pass (41). The play's aesthetic at such moments—as in the child's account of the "woods and waters and pale lights," the descriptions of the "small[ness]" of her eating, drinking, and dancing, and her "shriek" in response to the "tortured thing" on the crucifix—itself gives over to "unmeasured prattle" like the child's own and becomes "a place apart" from civilized norms (41–45). Indeed, there is a dimension of *horror* to the play's conclusion and its choric refrain, "the lonely of heart is withered away," that makes it impossible to read Mary's transfiguration as straightforwardly positive or to read the "land" to which she travels as a fully utopian alternative to the Barony of Kilmacowen. Rather, it seems clear that Yeats's central aim in this play set on the pagan occasion of Beltaine is to evoke, in Nietzsche's terms, "the terrible *awe* which seizes upon man, when he is suddenly unable to account for the cognitive forms of a phenomenon, when the principle of reason . . . seems to admit of an exception" (*The Birth*, 3).

Yeats succeeds in producing a fully sublime aesthetic through the play's tragic conclusion, one whose effect is the same as that which Nietzsche locates at the root of his proposed "Rebirth of German myth": "dissonance" (*The Birth*, 91). This term links Yeats's and the Literary Revival's tragic innovations not only with the aesthetic theories of Nietzsche, but also with the arguments of Theodor Adorno discussed in this book's introduction—as well as the sublime subversions of Conrad's "sentimental" narrative in *The Nigger of the "Narcissus."* The dissonance by which Yeats transports his audience "into another code" activates the radical, "titanic" potential of Arnold's Celt to offer what Adorno calls "a counter-image of mere existence," an "image of a space liberated from fetters and strictures." Through the potent estrangement of its tragic Celticism, the play "rouses" its viewers from Moore's "lethargy of real life," liberating their perceptions from the fetters and strictures of Catholicism, domestic economy's repressive-productive dynamic, the colonial influence these (for Yeats) index, the Irish female's frivolous consumerism, and the broader national public's "vulgar" literary taste.

Marjorie Howes's discussion of Yeats's ritualistic stage management during the 1890s and early 1900s is also pertinent on the question of the Revival's modernism, as, of course, is the radical primitivism of other tragedies such as Synge's *Riders to the Sea*, which, in its authentic incorporation of the native "caoine," represents perhaps the most radical illustration of a sublime rebirth of Celtic tragedy. Such tragic effects as Yeats and Synge achieved at the fin de siècle surely meet even the strictest criteria of experimental aesthetics, and the innovative primitivism they index suggests in turn that the full measure of the Revival's modernism can only be taken by attending to its performance history.[2] Unfortunately for the Theatre Movement, however, these same sublime, high-cultural effects seem to have led to its eventual marginalization in the ranks of popular Irish nationalism. The fate of the Literary Revival's modernist campaign to de-Anglicize the taste of the Irish consumer is, indeed, a thoroughly ironic one, in that the very "vulgar" preferences that were the target of that campaign may have prevented its "success."

Such preferences are evident in the reviews of the initial performance of *Riders*. As quoted in Robert Hogan and James Kilroy's history of the Theatre Movement, *Laying the Foundations*, D.P. Moran's *Leader* found the production "the most ghastly . . . ever seen on stage," while Arthur Griffith's *United Irishman*, though admitting that its "tragic beauty powerfully affected the audience," protested, "our stage has not been remarkable for diffusing sunshine around, and we need sunshine badly" (*Laying* 117). But it is the *Independent*'s review that best conveys the popular nationalist press's distaste for the sublime power of Synge's tragedy. "There is nothing," it complains, "of the glorified melodrama which helps to make the popular success of other productions carried out under the auspices of the Irish National Theatre Society" (116–17). Regrettably, "Its appeal is to a cultivated taste . . . more than to a dramatic instinct; its studies in melancholy have hardly the poignancy of other popular works . . . the theme is too dreadfully doleful to please the popular taste" (116–17). Synge's tragedy is both too "dreadfully doleful" and too "cultivated" to appeal to a "popular taste" habituated to the devices of "glorified melodrama." Such sentiments imply what *The Leader* states openly in its review of Yeats's *The Shadowy Waters* earlier the same year: "experiments in Drama, that have only a literary and not a dramatic justification, will in the long run only result in boring and repelling the ordinary man" (*Laying* 114).

The tremendous success of the play to which *The Independent* surely alludes, Yeats and Lady Gregory's *Cathleen ni Houlihan*, can be explained in part by its less "cultivated" textures and greater degree of thematic "sunshine." Roy Foster has speculated that while Gregory seems to have authored the majority of the text, Yeats's contributions to its "glorified melodrama" may have been spurred by *United Irishman* critic Frank Fay's complaint that his prior plays "do not inspire . . . do not send men away filled with the desire for deeds," but abet the national tendency to "shun reality" rather than "face it" (249).[3] What Foster describes as *Cathleen*'s "straightforward, rather heavy-handed," "predictable," and "mechanical" arrangement, may then have derived from an effort to depart from tragedy's "doleful" effects (249). In the context of subsequent developments like the negative reception of Synge's *In the Shadow of the Glen*, Yeats in fact seems to have grown increasingly perturbed by *Cathleen*'s popular acclaim, in tacit avowal of its "vulgar" affiliations. During the patent inquiry for the Abbey in 1904, he protested against the notion that the play pandered to "low" aesthetic taste: "It may be said it is a political play of a propagandist kind. This I deny. . . . I have never written a play to advocate for any kind of opinion and I think that such a play would be necessarily bad art. . . . At the same time I have no right to exclude . . . any of the passionate material of drama" (Foster 249). Yeats vehemently protests the idea that the play courted popular nationalist "opinion," which would reduce it to "a very humble kind of art" lacking in artistic "sincer[ity]" (249). He persists, despite the play's "glorified melodrama," in identifying its success as stemming from the very same "passionate" qualities cited as anathema in reviews of the Theatre Movement's tragedies.

The popular demise of the Literary Revival's combination of Celticism, anticapitalism, and modernism seems, indeed, to have accelerated upon Yeats's digging in the heels of artistic integrity after the dissatisfactions of *Cathleen*. One can only speculate on the degree to which Yeats himself was responsible for stoking what Hogan and Kilroy describe as a "growing tension" within Irish nationalism from 1903 onward "between two views of what the theatre should be": "On the one hand, Yeats, Synge and the Fays . . . thought that the theatre's chief criterion should be artistic excellence. On the other hand, Maud Gonne, Maire T. Quinn, Dudley Digges and others thought that [it] should be primarily a place of patriotic propaganda" (*Laying* 48–49).[4] It seems likely, however, that Yeats was the guiding influence in bringing such tensions to a head during incidents like the Irish National Theatre Society's 1903 rejection of Padraic Colum's play *The Saxon Shillin* based on its "artistic defects," which precipitated Gonne and Griffith's withdrawal from the Society and their immediate founding of a competitor organization, the Cumann na nGaedheal Theater Company, on more "patriotic" lines (Hogan, *Laying* 49).

It is clear, in any event, that through its adherence to modernist aesthetic principles as the preferred route to de-Anglicizing the Irish literary marketplace, the Theatre Movement sowed the seeds of its marginalization. A side comment from the *Freeman's Journal* review of Padraic Colum's play *The Land* on 9 June, 1905, serves as a fitting epitaph for the movement's efforts: "Mr. Yeats has proved a little too abstruse, and Mr. Synge a little too bizarre to get fully down into the hearts of the people" (31). It is worth asking, then, whether Yeats might not have been better served to respond to his fleeting popular success in the opposite fashion. If "comedy" and "melodrama" had such a hold on Irish "hearts," the Literary Revival would, perhaps, have been better advised to utilize these "low" genres as tools capable of aiding its high-cultural mission, rather than dismissing their utility out of hand. The next section of this chapter will suggest that, if Yeats could not see his way clear to embrace popular adaptation, his "bizarre" compatriot would soon make a stunningly innovative attempt at doing just that.

## TABLOID JOURNALISM AND IRISH NATIONALISM IN *THE PLAYBOY OF THE WESTERN WORLD*

Near the beginning of act 2 of Synge's *The Playboy of the Western World*, Pegeen Mike returns to her father's shebeen to discover her newfound beau, Christy Mahon, basking in the attentions of a throng of her female neighbors. Casting out her competitors for his affections in a fit of jealous rage, she purges her irritation by hinting that word of his parricide has reached the authorities. She tells him, "I was down this morning looking on the papers the post-boy does have in his bag. . . . For there is great news this day, Christopher Mahon" (39). Following Christy's panicked response, "Is it news of my murder?" Pegeen continues to needle him: "Murder, indeed. . . . There was not, but a story filled half a page with the hanging of a man. Ah, that should be a fearful end, young fellow, and it worst of all for a man who destroyed his da, for the like of him would get small mercies" (39). She prolongs Christy's punishment until, as he moves to flee, she admits her charade: "I'm after going down and reading the fearful crimes of Ireland for two weeks or three, and there wasn't a word of your murder. They've likely not found the body. You're safe so with ourselves" (42).

To date, critical accounts of *Playboy* have said little regarding what, aside from its entanglement with Anglo-Irish colonial law, appears the most salient sociological aspect of Pegeen's report, namely its engagement with the print culture of contemporary Ireland through the medium of "the papers."[5] This dearth of attention is especially striking given that, as demonstrated in the last chapter, Irish nationalism—routinely adduced as the most significant context for interpreting the play—identified newspapers as a major source of Irish Anglicization. Any reading that takes seriously the relevance of cultural nationalism to *Playboy*'s concerns must take this immersion into account. As we shall see, Synge's richest play advances a very specific response to the nation's enmeshment in the consumer economy of the British metropole. *Playboy* signals that its account of a would-be parricide's rise to and fall from social eminence is deeply engaged with contemporary concerns over the Irish consumption of British print culture, specifically the "vulgar" fare of metropolitan tabloid journalism. This reading suggests not only that Synge shared his contemporaries' belief that Irish minds had become colonized by the pop-cultural forms of British capitalism, but that *Playboy* may be read as an attempt to purge those minds of such colonization. The play does not merely invoke "the papers" as an inert feature of its socio-historical backdrop but rather foregrounds them as a central component in the reproduction of the Anglo-Irish colonial order and its underlying capitalist imperatives. In this light, *Playboy* appears as both a chronicle of the challenges to colonial self-determination posed by capital's expansion and a remarkably innovative attempt to surmount those challenges.

The stories Pegeen describes are specimens of one of the prime targets of Revivalist nationalism's commodity critique, the genre of "The Police Intelligence." This genre achieved popularity in England during the mid-1800s through such publications as the *Illustrated Police News*, *Lloyd's Weekly Newspaper*, and *Reynold's Newspaper*, and would spread to Ireland both through their circulation and through the emergence of homegrown organs like the *Belfast News-Letter* and the Dublin-based *Freeman's Journal*. Through its obsession with legal transgression and other deviations from Victorian respectability, The Police Intelligence was, in effect, a type of sensational literature—printed matter that attracted readers through shock value, gossip mongering, and a fascination with public and domestic violence. An early form of tabloid reporting, it served—along with other subspecies of the "scandalous genre" of "sensation" like the "shilling shocker" and the "penny dreadful"—to index the depravity of British culture in such seminal nationalist texts as Hyde's "The Necessity for De-Anglicizing Ireland" and Moran's "The Battle of Two Civilizations." Nationalist thinkers across factional lines perceived The Police Intelligence as a contaminating form of literary "garbage" threatening to erode Ireland's native characteristics.[6]

Despite the seeming premodernity of *Playboy*'s Mayo setting, such tabloid publications were in fact ready to hand for the region's contemporary inhabitants.[7] As we have seen, Revivalists like Yeats, AE, Martyn, Moore, Hyde, Moran, and Synge himself came to identify as perhaps the primary locus of Anglicization not the urban capital of Dublin, but the rural Irish town. In the words of AE's *Co-Operation and Nationality* quoted in the previous chapter, the bookstores of such locales housed an abundance of "sensational tales in gaudy colors . . . cheap prints, without high purpose . . . glimmering all over with the phosphorescence of mental decay" (43). Pegeen's description of "a story filled half a page with the hanging of a man" and of having perused "the fearful crimes of Ireland for two weeks or three" resonate with this prominent area of nationalist agitprop and suggest that the play's setting resides "within the Pale" of British popular culture.

Pegeen's allusion to The Police Intelligence is but one of a host of related references *Playboy* makes to the genre. Synge signals their thematic centrality almost immediately after Christy's arrival. Having deduced from his inquiries about the police that Christy is on the lam, the pub's denizens try to suss out the specifics of his crime. Philly Cullen speculates, "Maybe the land was grabbed from him, and he did what any decent man would do" (16). Detecting the scent of nationalist land agitation, others inquire whether his crime was directed against "bailiffs," "agents" or "landlords" (16). Christy's response provides the first invocation of The Police Intelligence: "Ah, not at all, I'm saying. You'd see the like of them stories on any little paper of a Munster town. But I'm not calling to mind any person, gentle, simple, judge or jury, did the like of me" (16). Christy's citation of the stories of legal transgression contained in the newspapers of the Munster town affirms his own familiarity with the genre, but it is through his listeners' reaction that Synge begins to highlight its larger significance to the play's development. Upon Christy's implication that his crime is more serious than those typically described in Irish newspapers, the stage directions state that his auditors "all draw near with delighted curiosity" (16). Christy titillates his audience by placing his crime in the framework of this sensational genre. Stimulated by his unwitting self-advertisement, his listeners' speculations escalate quickly in imaginative fervor and transgressive severity. They guess that he mugged a British soldier, married three wives, or "went fighting for the Boers" against the British in South Africa (17). When Christy finally admits to killing his father, the Mayoites respond with "great respect" for the even greater "daring" his act bespeaks. The duration of the play merely exfoliates the social tensions reflected in this initial idolization.

Synge thus grounds the Mayo community's fetishism of parricide in their engagement with the literary "garbage" of the rural Irish town. By associating his crime with The Police Intelligence, Christy transforms himself into something of a tabloid celebrity. If this term seems anachronistic, later developments make clear that, as Paige Reynolds has also argued, celebrity is indeed the appropriate word to apply to his newfound eminence.[8] By the beginning of act 2, Christy's initial response of "surprise and triumph" to the admiration his "murder" has produced has inflated into full-blown egomania (17). He wonders "Didn't I know I was handsome" before the mirror in the shebeen's main room and declares, "I'll be growing fine from this day" (30). The interruption of his self-admiration by "stranger girls" from the surrounding country then initiates a fascinating scene in which Christy's celebrity status is on full display. It becomes evident that the girls have heard tell of Christy's exploit and have traveled there in order to catch a glimpse of him. Upon spying their impending arrival, Christy retreats into an "inner room," leaving them to slake their curiosity by examining his personal effects. "Look at that," observes Honor Blake, "He's been sleeping there in the night . . . it'll be a hard case if he's gone off now, the way we'll never set our eyes on a man killed his father, and we after rising early and destroying ourselves running fast on the hill" (32). Sara Tansey's contribution to the investigation again affirms that the Mayo villagers' fetishism derives from its sensational reading. In response to "Nelly," who asks "Are you thinking them's his boots?," Sara replies, "If they are, there should be his father's track on them. Did you never read in the papers the way murdered men do bleed and drip?" (32). The details of Sara's description clearly allude to the shock-trolling conventions of The Police Intelligence, in which murder and violence come to life through melodramatic narrative and graphic descriptions of physical injury. Combined with Honor's description of their "rising early" and "destroying

[them]selves running" to see Christy, the gifts the girls have brought—eggs, cake, butter, and a "little laying pullet"—become legible as the offerings of a frenzied fan base eager for the favor of their pop-cultural idol (33–34).

The idolization in which the "stranger girls" and Pegeen collectively engage thus also locates *Playboy* in relation to specific Revivalist concerns over the Irish female consumer. To a far greater extent than its men, the play depicts young Irish women as caught—like Mary Bruin before them—within the "Pale" of popular-cultural Anglicization, whose print-cultural agencies deeply inflect their reception of tales of criminality. The direness of Synge's portrait of these dynamics is difficult to overstate. The play's female Mayoites, indeed, provide an illustration of the emergent phenomenon that William Roughead, an early-twentieth-century Scottish pioneer theorist of "true crime," called "the enjoyment of murder." The "taste for blood" that Roughead identified in the popularity of violent crime-related literary fare surfaces unmistakably here and suggests that Christy's elevation derives from his ability to satisfy this novel consumer demand (10).

To grasp the specific brand of celebrity such demand inspired, it is helpful to examine some actual Police Intelligence texts that circulated in fin-de-siècle Mayo. Although "the enjoyment of murder" was surely more pervasive in Ireland's urban centers, its rural inhabitants had plentiful access to the genre through the infrastructural agency from which Pegeen acquires her morning fare: the post office.[9] *The Freeman's Journal*, for example, though published in Dublin, was available in Mayo and contained accounts such as the following, from the 1899 report "The Attempted Murder of a Sweetheart in Cork":

> A young man named Patrick Barry pleaded guilty of having on the night of the 16th of February last attempted to murder his sweetheart, Kate Scully. . . . This occurrence created a great sensation in Cork in February last. Barry and Scully had been courting for some years . . . but [she] refused his offer of marriage. Barry seemed to have felt this keenly. He made an appointment with the girl to meet her . . . she again refused to marry him, and said 'Pat, I must go home.' He . . . pressed her to stay, and putting his arms around her neck feigned an embrace—and drew a razor heavily across her throat. A desperate struggle then ensued. She fought . . . and during her endeavors to free herself he gashed her right and left with the razor. Although she became very weakened through loss of blood she managed to creep to her own door. . . . Barry then fell on her and both had a desperate struggle against the door for possession of the razor. The girl, however, retained possession until the door was

opened, when she fell into the hallway exhausted from loss of blood. ("The Attempted Murder")

The "great sensation" the story describes as arising in the wake of Barry's assault was surely the product of such graphic and melodramatic accounts as this passage instantiates. The continual amplification and reprinting of such "dreadful" details undoubtedly helped whet the "taste for blood" in the Mayo consumer.

Local papers such as *The Connaught Telegraph* also reveal an intense interest in sensational legal fare. The 19 March, 1904, report "The Glosheens Tragedy," for example, describing the "cold-blooded and deliberate murder" of Edward Hopkins by his father, James, bears all the generic marks of The Police Intelligence. The report borrows heavily from the opening statement of the Solicitor General, whose ready-made sensationalism saves the paper much literary labor. The statement adopts the perspective of the primary witness, Edward Hopkins's wife, through which readers learn how she "heard the discharge of the gun and on looking out . . . saw the prostrate form of her husband lying a few yards from the door," then "rushed from the house and lifted him from the ground" ("The Glosheens"). Following threats from "the prisoner, with the gun in his hand," that "if she did not go away he would shoot her dead," Mrs. Hopkins "appealed to him to spare her for the sake of her little baby, and ran away," after which, from "the window of the house, she again saw the prisoner fire the second barrel of the gun into the prostrate body of his son" ("The Glosheens"). To the Solicitor's account the paper adds that of "Acting Sergeant Finn, R.I.C.," who "deposed that on the date of the murder he went to the scene of the outrage, and saw deceased in a pool of blood on the ground, and then went into the prisoner's house and saw Hopkins, senior, taking a cup of tea" ("The Glosheens"). The staple devices of "The Police Intelligence"— privileging of female terror, emphasis on the murderer's cold-bloodedness, and graphic descriptions of bodily injury—are again prominent. Such journalism, from a leading turn-of-the-century Mayo paper, helps contextualize Sara Tansey's panting search for Christy's blood-drenched boots, as well as the Mayoites' general eagerness to speculate about his crime. The circumstances of "The Glosheens Tragedy"—a filial dispute over property distribution following Edward Hopkins's marriage—prove particularly illuminating in that one speculation, voiced by The Widow Quin, proposes a similar scenario: "And you went asking money of him, or making talk of getting a wife would drive him from the farm?" (35).[10]

The criminal case often cited by critics as a source for the play, that of the attempted murderer James Lynchehaun, also received much local coverage, for instance in the *Telegraph* story of 13 September titled "Lynchehaun at Large Again," which describes his "escape from Maryboro Prison" and references the "tremendous sensation" "excited" by the convict's "remarkable career" ("Lynchehaun"). The details of Lynchehaun's original crime on Achill Island in Mayo in 1894, consisting of a vicious assault on his English landlady, Agnes McDonnell, and the subsequent arson of her home, played perfectly into the tropes of tabloid sensationalism. As Susan Cannon Harris describes in *Gender and Modern Irish Drama*, "he attacked a woman that he was reported to be sexually obsessed with, biting and maiming her" (120–21). The *Telegraph* reports that through these initial acts and his subsequent outfoxing of legal authorities Lynchehaun has become "perhaps the most famous convict in Ireland" ("Lynchehaun"). Remarkably, Canon Harris also notes with reference to the play's negative press coverage and the famous "riots" that ensued upon its first performance in Dublin on 26 January, 1907, that "Synge's protestors identified . . . Lynchehaun as the source for Christy," further bespeaking the "fame" generated not just in Connaught but throughout the nation by Lynchehaun's exploits, as well as affirming the savvy of Synge's choice to draw on this particular case through its themes of land agitation, sexuality, murder, and fugitivism (120).[11]

Synge signals an especially significant convergence between the play and The Police Intelligence through Pegeen's classification of Christy's tale as a "gallous story." The etymological root of "gallous" in the noun *gallows* links the play's many references to hanging with the genre's law-mongering conventions, which often involved descriptions, even illustrations, of capital punishment technologies and their application to British and Irish bodies.[12] The case of "The Cavan Parricide," the subject of numerous articles in the *Freeman* and other publications throughout 1898–99, foregrounds this especially ghoulish aspect of the genre. Preceding coverage described a visit paid by "his Eminence Cardinal Logue . . . Primate of All Ireland," to one Thomas Kelly ("The Cavan Murders"), sentenced to death for shooting his father, and the "Arrival of the Executioner" at Armagh Prison ("The Cavan Parricide: Arrival"). Finally, on 11 January, 1899, the *Journal* published "The Execution of Thomas Kelly":

> Whilst standing on the scaffold Kelly turned to the prison chaplain and begged that . . . he might be allowed to live a few minutes longer for . . . completing his prayers. This was granted. At eight o'clock [the executioner] . . . drew the bolt, and Kelly disappeared. . . . A large crowd assembled to witness the hoisting of the black flag, and the people

> did not disperse until it was taken down. . . . Kelly was twenty-seven years of age . . . a man of no fixed occupation . . . [and] spent a great deal of his time in playing cards and shooting through the country. He was particularly expert with the gun, and acquired the notoriety of being one of the finest marksmen in County Cavan. It is a remarkable fact that on the day he shot his father he was actually shooting bottles in his own yard. ("The Cavan Parricide: The Execution")

We have already witnessed Pegeen's fascination with capital punishment through her reference to a "story filled half a page with the hanging of a man." This passage displays just such a story, and it presents an illustration of the very crime of which Christy claims to be guilty, one that corresponds to his account in several key respects: both young men, Kelly and Christy, are idlers dependent on their fathers, and both rise up and murder them in the immediate vicinity of their homes using implements ready to hand, a gun in the former case and a "loy" in the latter. Given her exposure to such fare, it is unsurprising that Pegeen's imagination would run toward the same grim conclusion as The Police Intelligence so readily furnishes.

The "great respect" Christy acquires in turn-of-the-century Mayo thus exemplifies a very specific brand of tabloid celebrity. The community's feverish attendance of Christy manifests the same impulse evident in the crowds that figure so prominently in "The Execution of Thomas Kelly" and innumerable other, contemporary accounts of capital punishment—crowds whose presence can only be explained through consumption of Police Intelligence accounts.[13] This impulse, which I have described as a tabloid-stoked "taste for blood," expresses a popular cathexis of illegality that, however early its historical vintage, can be identified as part of a larger phenomenon of modernity—that of the celebrity criminal. The crowds gathered to consume the thrilling conclusions of "The Cavan Parracide" and "The Glosheens Tragedy" connect not only with Victorian-era examples of celebrity criminality like Jack the Ripper; they also prefigure contemporary crowds assembled near courthouses and in "media villages" to hear the verdicts of the recent murder trials of O.J. Simpson, Casey Anthony, and Amanda Knox.[14] Despite the vestigial premodernity of *Playboy*'s setting, when Sara Tansey dons Christy Mahon's boots and strolls excitedly around the Flaherty shebeen, the play directly anticipates later practices such as the collection of memorabilia associated with killers and accused killers like Simpson, Charles Manson, and Jeffrey Dahmer (33).[15]

Through their treatment of Christy's parricide as Police Intelligence fare, Synge suggests that the Mayoites' moral compass has been led astray through the consumption of tabloid news coverage. The "great respect" with which the Flaherty patriarch greets Christy's "hanging crime" signals this collective derangement by reflecting an outlook attuned more to a desire for sensational entertainment than to the ethical valuation of human acts (18). This derangement is similarly reflected in Pegeen's disdain for The Widow Quin's "murder" of her husband. As she tries to prevent Christy from becoming romantically interested in the Widow, Pegeen tells him, "contemptuously," "She hit himself with a worn pick, and the rusted poison did corrode his blood. . . . That was a sneaky kind of murder did win small praise with the boys itself" (28). The dismissal of the Widow's manslaughter as only deserving of "small praise" reflects the extent to which the Mayoites' engagement with The Police Intelligence—and especially that of Mayo's young women—has generated a "taste for blood" entirely severed from ethical considerations.

The derangement of values brought upon Mayo through exposure to British tabloids expresses a bleak prognosis regarding Irish independence. Following his sudden elevation, Christy manifests an array of characteristics seemingly aligned with Synge's own Celticism-affiliated ideals as expressed by *The Aran Islands*—central among them physical vitality, romantic assertiveness, and an organic aestheticism. His transformation may thus appear an archetypal postcolonial liberation story, serving as the vehicle for the expression of desires repressed in the community through its subjection to the British Empire and Catholic Church. Given, however, that Christy's ascent results also from the convergence of his narrative with the conventions of The Police Intelligence, his feats of athletic, romantic, and poetic prowess incarnate not so much an ideal, self-determined Irishness as a commodity-mediated illusion thereof.[16]

*Playboy* seems to offer ample evidence that Christy's rise is genuinely liberatory. After Pegeen equates the "great rage" of Christy's murder with the "fine fiery" ways of "the poets," his speech escalates in complexity and ornateness until he indeed seems to embody the instinctual artistry Synge identified on Aran (23). Pegeen's comment that "a fine lad" like Christy "should have [his] good share of the earth" then seems to freight his metamorphosis with decolonizing implications (26). The Widow Quin's warning that "there's great temptation in a many did slay his da" further positions Christy's heroism as defying Catholic moral prohibitions (34). Christy's triumph in the local Gaelic sporting contests of "racing, leaping, pitching, and the Lord knows what" then seems to figure his physical prowess as a subversive, Celtic wildness (26–27). "Astride the moon" after his victories, Christy unnerves the local prelate, who, having received the papal "dispensation" to marry Pegeen and

Shawn Keogh, tells Michael, "It's come in the nick of time . . . I'll wed them in a hurry, dreading the young gaffer who'd capsize the stars" (68). This diagnosis of Christy's subversive influence receives decisive corroboration through Michael's decision to void Pegeen's betrothal to the "puny weed" Shawn and give his blessing for her marriage to Christy: "A daring fellow is the jewel of the world," he beams, "and a man did split his father's middle with a single clout should have the bravery of ten, so may God and Mary and St. Patrick bless you, and increase you from this mortal day" (71). Christy's triumph over the repressive regimes of British colonial law and Catholic morality appears complete.

The reified nature of Christy's newfound characteristics, however, soon shows through. From the conclusion of first act, where he exclaims, "I'm thinking this night wasn't I foolish not to kill my father in the years gone by," the play figures his rise as driven by extrinsic incentives of celebrity rather than intrinsic resistance to political and religious oppression (30). Christy becomes increasingly invested in his Police Intelligence–based idolization, to the point that his foremost desire is to maintain the celebrity status he has so felicitously acquired. He even begins to *perform* celebrity criminality around the time the neighbor girls make their pilgrimage. During the subsequent retelling of his murder to The Widow Quin, he begins "shy but flattered" by her interest but soon expresses "growing satisfaction" in reprising his "gallous" feat through the relish with which he devours the "little laying pullet" furnished by Nelly (35–36). He acts out, playing both parts, his argument with his father over his arranged marriage to "The Widow Casey," "brandishing his mug" and "waving" a chicken "bone" for swaggering effect: "He gave a drive with the scythe, and I gave a lep to the east. Then I turned around with my back to the north, and I hit a blow on the ridge of his skull, laid him stretched out, and he split to the knob of his gullet" (37). He then "raises the chicken bone to his Adam's apple" as a culminating flourish (37). If not for its Hiberno-English idiom, Christy's sensational narrative would fit seamlessly among the contents of a typical installment of The Police Intelligence.

Pegeen's complaint that Christy has "told that story six times since the dawn of day" reflects the extent to which, if he hopes to maintain his celebrity, his performance must escalate ever further in sensational intensity to meet consumer demand (39). But the full extent of his reification becomes apparent only when his undead father, "Old Mahon," arrives and threatens to dismantle his status. During the climactic scene in which Christy re-attempts to murder him and is captured, tortured, and nearly executed by the Mayoites who formerly idolized him, Synge indicates how fully his ascendancy derives from his role as a fetishized commodity. As Christy and Old Mahon square off, the "crowd" that attends Christy after his success in "the games below" transfers its spectatorship to the new "sport" their fight provides. They prod, "Keep it up, the two of you," and take sides in supporting the participants: "I'll back the old one. Now the playboy" (75). As Christy lights upon a means of clinching his celebrity and seizes the nearby "loy," the crowd is described as "half frightened, half amused" by his actions, again reflecting their treatment of the struggle as sensational entertainment (74).

After Christy "runs at old Mahon" and "chases him out" of the shebeen, however, the stage directions indicate that the crowd receives more than it bargained for, as "there is great noise outside, then a yell, and dead silence for a moment" (75). Christy "comes in, half dazed" by his own violence, and responds to The Widow Quin's warning that he'll now be "hanged, indeed" in a manner that reflects the extent to which his "daring" stems from celebrity considerations (75). He tells her, "I'm thinking, from this out, Pegeen'll be giving me praises the same as in the hours gone by" (75). When she reiterates the threat of the "gallows tree" and tries to abet his escape by thrusting him—with the steadfast assistance of his number one fan, Sara Tansey—through the back door, he protests, "Leave me go, will you? . . . for she will wed me surely, and I a proven hero in the end of all" (75–76). To Christy, as a result of his education in the commodity-mediated desires of the Mayo villagers, *mere* murder—as distinguished from the genuine act of resistance to oppression embodied in his initial "clout"—provides a certain route to the rewards of heroism.

One of the defining characteristics of tabloid news coverage is that while it invites a vicarious transgression of social and legal norms, it simultaneously reinforces those norms by interpellating the reader as morally superior to the transgressor.[17] It is thus fitting that, following his second attempt on Old Mahon's life, Christy is subjected to a backlash to match his former elevation. Upon their startled recognition of the "great gap between" the "gallous story" of Christy's murder and the "dirty deed" of its duplicated reality, the Mayoites seek to evade legal liability by giving Christy's tale a conventional ending. Taking their cue from The Police Intelligence, Michael Flaherty and the men of the crowd appear "with a rope" and, with Pegeen's assistance, "they drop the double hitch over his head" (76). "Come on to the peelers, till they stretch you now," Michael coaxes, explaining, "If we took pity on you, the Lord God would, maybe, bring us ruin from the law to-day, so you'd best come easy, for hanging is an easy and a speedy end" (77). Horrified by Pegeen's participation in his lynching, Christy exclaims, "And it's your self will send me off, to have a horny-fingered hangman hitching his bloody slip-knots at the butt of my ear" (77). Pegeen responds by "scorch[ing]" his leg with a piece of turf, finally alerting Christy to the gravity of the Mayoites' intentions (77–78). He fights to free himself until Old Mahon's reentry renders the struggle moot, at which point Michael again voices the motivation behind their attempted execution: "It is the will of God that all should guard their little cabins from the treachery of law" (79).

Christy, however, has absorbed the lesson Synge would have the audience learn from this "gallous story" and quickly turns the tables on his assailants. Disdaining the Mayoites as "fools of the earth" for disavowing their complicity in his actions, he not only redirects his violence against them—causing Shawn Keogh in particular to cower before his "holy terror"—but narrates an alternative ending to the play. Fittingly, Christy's conclusion draws openly on the sensational resources of The Police Intelligence. He paints a scene in which the Mayoites regret their betrayal and consecrate him a Celtic folk hero once more: "If I can wring a neck among you, I'll have a royal judgment looking on the trembling jury in the courts of law. And won't there be crying out in Mayo, the day I'm stretched upon the rope with ladies in their silks and satins sniveling in their lacy kerchiefs, and they rhyming songs and ballads on the terror of my fate?" (78). The elaborate aesthetic texture of Christy's portrayal confirms its underlying thesis: that the Mayoites' idolization, though confused and reified, has "turned [him] a likely gaffer in the end of it all" (80). He chastises his auditors for lacking the courage to embrace the hero their desires have unwittingly spawned, and he taunts them with the very generic conventions that stoked those desires. Synge signals his endorsement of Christy's narrative by ending the play with a fulfillment of its imaginary scenario. Just as, on the "day" when Christy is "stretched," the women of Mayo "snivel . . . in their lacy kerchiefs" and compose "songs and ballads on the terror of [his] fate," so Pegeen Mike, "putting her shawl over her head and breaking out into wild lamentations," responds to his departure by "sniveling," "Oh my grief, I've lost him surely. I've lost the only Playboy of the Western World" (80). What began as a play about the radical impact of a "gallous story" on a rural Irish community primed to receive it through consumption of The Police Intelligence thus concludes by subordinating both that community and that genre to the aesthetic authority of the Syngean Celtic hero.

Postcolonial readings of *Playboy*, which often emphasize its critique of the rural impact of British rule and the repressive mores of Irish Catholicism, are immediately complicated by the recovery of this context. In recent years, the fetishism of parricide that Christy inspires has been taken to reflect "the return of the repressed" of both social systems, imperial and Catholic. In Christy, this reading argues, the Mayo villagers identify an outlet for their repressed desires, but then finally reject their former vessel and reinstall the very hegemonic regime whose tyranny motivated the process to begin with. Christy's reciprocation of their rejection, his contemptuous classification of the Mayoites as "fools of the earth," his declaration that they have made him "a likely gaffer," and Pegeen's closing lament have been read by critics like Declan Kiberd as indexing a proto-Fanonian diagnosis of the "the pitfalls of national consciousness." Christy's initial performance of a fetishized criminality is thus viewed as embodying the second, reactive stage of colonial history, wherein the colonized inverts the norms of the colonizer in a simplistic attempt at ideological purgation, and his final rejection of both those norms and their inverse is thus taken to represent a model of postcolonial self-determination.[18]

The play's identification of the Irish incarnation of this archetypal story as mediated by mental habits instilled by British tabloid journalism enriches this reading significantly. *Playboy* suggests that because Irish men and women participate in the same consumer practices as the inhabitants of the metropole, they are more complexly impacted by British colonialism than their counterparts in Africa, South Asia, and the Caribbean, where such practices have yet to be disseminated. In the Irish context, Christy's celebrity suggests, the route to liberation is hindered by an advanced form of capitalist reification. Synge's readers of The Police Intelligence have been transformed into *consumers of their own oppression, and also of their resistance to that oppression*. Their nationalist impulses are refracted through the lens of British tabloid journalism, and are thus doubly hemmed in not simply by repressive colonial norms that set the terms by which resistance must proceed, but also by a reifying epistemology that reduces both oppression and resistance to entertainment. In such a society, the "great gap between a gallous story and a dirty deed," between transgression and its representation, becomes narrow indeed given the entanglement of "real" actions with generic convention. In the case of The Police Intelligence, this entanglement determines that the Irish subject's visions of liberation will remain grounded within a legal and social frame that promotes the reinforcement rather than the overthrow of prevailing norms. Synge suggests, finally, that a postcolonial Ireland purged only of the institutional domination of the Catholic Church or the British Empire and not also of the reifying pop-cultural forms of modern capitalism will never achieve self-determination.

We may now return to the question with which we began the analysis of *Playboy*, namely whether an Irish modernist drama more responsive than the tragic elitism of Yeats to the "vulgar" pop-cultural terrain of the Irish marketplace could better succeed in retraining Irish consumers in the appreciation for high-cultural ideals. As we have seen, Synge's play undertakes a remarkably deft immanent critique of one of the most popular of British pop-cultural genres. By figuring the emergence of national liberation as necessarily accompanied by a casting off of the mental habits of Irish Anglicization, and by structuring his play in a manner geared not only toward transferring awareness of this necessity to his audience but also toward *stimulating* such a casting off *directly*, Synge's dramaturgy unquestionably fulfills the criteria of such responsiveness. If Yeats's drama maintains a "high modernist" disdain for popular culture and is thereby prevented from "getting fully down into the hearts of the people," the modernism of *Playboy* would be better described as *avant-garde* by virtue of its engagement with popular culture, and it would thus seem to bear a far greater potential for reforming the "heart" of the Irish consumer.[19] Indeed, it would not be inappropriate to identify in Synge's manipulation of the epistemological habits accompanying The Police Intelligence a full-blown Brechtian "alienation effect," whereby the theatrical consumer is "roused" from his/her "vulgar" bourgeois slumbers by witnessing an estranging dramatization of that very vulgarity.[20] As is well known, however, for all its alienating aesthetic ingenuity, Synge's masterpiece instead became, through the popular nationalist denunciation of the play and the riots its performance generated, the foremost historical illustration of the obduracy of prevailing Irish taste. It would thus seem that seem that Yeats's disillusionment with the Revival's decades-long effort to reshape the Irish consumer was not entirely misplaced.

## *THE CHARWOMAN'S DAUGHTER* AND THE "CRACKED LOOKING-GLASS" OF IRISH ART

Synge was not the only Revivalist to devise a strategy for combating British popular culture within its own generic domains. James Stephens's *The Charwoman's Daughter*, published in 1912, presented its readers with an equally deft critique of the "vulgar" literature of the metropole. Though it might be called a "late Revivalist" text, appearing on the precipice of the decolonizing events of the 1910s and early '20s, the novel offers a pristine example of the movement's Celticist anticapitalism through its interrogation of the uber-popular genre of Romance fiction, which, much like The Police Intelligence, was identified by Revivalist ideologues as one of the driving forces of Irish

West Britonism. As witnessed in the previous chapter via examples like D.P. Moran's denunciation of the "petticoats in [the] thousands filing into the circulating libraries and the penny novelette shops for reams of twaddle about Guy and Belinda" ("Gaelic" 80), Romance fiction also played an especially prominent role in nationalist discussions of the Irish female consumer. Like Synge does in his portrait of legal tabloid consumption, Stephens's portrait of Romance makes a rich contribution to this gendered commodity critique.

Though ostensibly a "fairy tale," *The Charwoman's Daughter* is in fact a form of "respectable fiction" in disguise, in Nancy Armstrong's seminal definition of the genre as "that which represent[s] political conflict in terms of sexual differences" and which resolves such conflict through "a peculiarly middle-class notion of love" (41). Stephens signals quite early that his fantastical narrative is merely an exaggerated variation on this genre. Just as respectable fiction and the low-brow Romance fiction that was its heir defined the female protagonist's adolescence as leading ineluctably to marriage and domestic economy, so the imaginative horizons of the protagonist, Mary Makebelieve, are confined by this gendered script:

> Her mother spoke sometimes of matrimony as a thing remote but very certain . . . she knew that a girl had to get married, that a strange, beautiful man would come from somewhere looking for a wife, and would retire again with his bride to that Somewhere which is the country of Romance. . . . When the subject of matrimony was under discussion her mother planned minutely the person of the groom, his vast accomplishments, and yet vaster wealth. . . . All these wonders could only concentrate in the person of a lord. Mary['s] questions . . . were searching and minute; her mother's rejoinders were equally elaborate and particular. . . . Mary . . . would have loved to wed a lord. (9)

Mary's self-conception is thus routed through the trappings of Romance from the novel's opening, as its "fairy tale" proceeds in tandem with the marriage plot. Though Mrs. Makebelieve's "elaborate and particular" narratives define the matrimonial ideal as one only a "lord" can fulfill, the novel more properly centers on the "middle-class notion of love" that is the keystone of Victorian respectability.

Mrs. Makebelieve's outlook on her and her daughter's world asserts the novel's initial concern with this British gender code in no uncertain terms. Through Stephens's deft free indirect style, the reader learns, "For her a woman's business was life . . . God did not need any assistance, but man did, bitterly he wanted it, and the giving of such assistance was the proper business of a woman" (78). "Most of the trouble of life," she "divine[s]," is the result of "men and women not doing their duty. . . . A partner, a home and children—through the loyal cooperation of these she saw happiness and, dimly, a design of so vast an architecture as scarcely to be discussed" (78). Mrs. Makebelieve is so ensnared by respectability that she conceives of its contingent dictates as constituting "life" itself. Stephens secures the connection between the respectable mold of Mrs. Makebelieve's philosophy and the novel's Romance narrative by defining the duty of a woman to adhere to this patriarchal template as her "quest" in life. Such descriptions unmistakably suggest that the novel's "fairy tale" structure is—at its outset—merely an embellished version of respectable fiction.

The majority of the novel's female characters have, however, a very conflicted relationship to this middle-class norm because of their working-class status. The code in which they are so heavily invested in fact exacerbates the miseries of their poverty by holding them to an impossible standard. The Makebelieves' neighbor in their Dublin tenement, Mrs. Cafferty, intuits through this mismatch of norms and resources that "something was wrong somewhere, but whether the blame was to be allocated to the weather, the employer, the Government, or the Deity, she did not know" (83). Nor, likewise, "did Mrs. Makebelieve know; but they were agreed there was an error somewhere, a lack of adjustment with which they had nothing to do, but the effects whereof were grievously visible in their privations" (83). Within such a desperate, working-class situation as the Makebelieves and Caffertys inhabit, the enjoinder to middle-class norms heaps misery upon misery. The hardships generated by the "lack of adjustment" in the British capitalist system are compounded by their lacking the means to fulfill the middle-class ideology by which they have been so successfully interpellated.

For Stephens, as for theorists such as Armstrong and Michel Foucault, respectability constitutes nothing short of a *biopolitical technology* ensuring, through its subjects' behavioral self-policing, the reproduction of the linked gender and class ideologies of the Victorian period.[21] *The Charwoman's Daughter*, however, is also keenly attuned to the ways in which this regime is refracted by Anglo-Irish colonialism. Another reflection of Mrs. Cafferty's on respectability's gendered division of labor begins to gesture toward this attunement: "men made the laws and women administered them—a wise allocation of prerogatives, for she conceived that the executive female function was every whit as important as the creative faculty which brought these laws into being" (87). As numerous Irish Studies critics have shown, the British pervasively defined the Anglo-Irish Union as a heterosexual marriage, with the Irish cast in the role of wife. Mrs. Cafferty's endorsement of the arrangement by which "men made the laws and women administered them" as a "wise allocation of prerogatives" resonates with this gendered colonial ideology and suggests that for the Irish, adherence to the biopolitics of "respectability" abets the reproduction of colonial subordination.[22]

It is precisely the function of Mary Makebelieve's courtship with the unnamed "policeman" who pursues her throughout Dublin to secure this insight regarding the dense entanglements of Romance, respectability, and colonial dependency. After the narrative has established Mary's Romantic self-conception, it proceeds to lay the groundwork for this figure's entry with a disturbing passage describing her attraction to male violence. Mary "fancied she would not mind being hit by a man . . . watching the terrible vigor of their movements, she thought they could hit very hard, but still there was a terrible attraction about the idea of being hit by a man" (10). The distance between fiction and reality is again punctuated when Mary "asked her mother . . . had a man ever struck her?," in response to which Mrs. Makebelieve "was silent for a few moments and then burst into so violent a passion of weeping that Mary Makebelieve was frightened" (10). Mary, however, remains oblivious to this response's import, and she soon encounters in the policeman—described as a "monument of solidity and law" (11)—a figure capable of satisfying her desire:

> The massive policeman fascinated her. Surely everything desirable in manhood was concentrated in his tremendous body. What an immense, shattering blow that mighty fist could give! She could imagine it swinging vast as the buffet of an hero, high-thrown and then down irresistibly—a crashing, monumental hand. She delighted in his great, solid head as it swung slowly from side to side, and his calm, proud eye—a governing, compelling, and determined eye. . . . One day her shy, creeping glance was caught by his; it held her mesmerized for a few seconds; it looked down into her—for a moment the whole world seemed to have become one immense eye—she could scarcely get away from it. (12)

The "immense, shattering blow" the policeman's "crashing, monumental" hand seems capable of giving captivates Mary, and although the policeman is not a colonial official but merely an Irish "shoneen" or Anglicized Irish subject, his status as a "governing, compelling" representative of colonial law enforcement clinches the symbolic complicity of her Romantic ideals with

Anglo-Irish colonial rule.[23] The Irish female as embodied in Mary is trained by Romance to desire the violent imperial domination of Irish subjects.

In keeping with this critique, the novel does not merely partake self-reflexively of the generic trappings of Romance; it describes the female inhabitants of Dublin, Mary Makebelieve chief among them, as ubiquitously consuming the genre. Early in the novel, the reader is told of the activities with which Mary occupies herself while her mother chars the city's middle- and upper-class homes. While much of her time is spent wandering its streets and browsing its shops, "Sometimes she did not go out at all. She stayed in the top back room sewing or knitting, mending holes in the sheets or the blankets, or reading books from the Free Library in Capel Street" (17). Should there be any doubt as to the generic gravitation of her reading, it is dispelled by a subsequent description of one of Mary's strolls in search of her newfound beau, which takes her into "wider fields" where "great numbers of children" are "accompanied by one and sometimes two older people, girls or women who lay stretched out on the warm grass or leaned against the tree-trunks reading novelettes" (26). This passage returns us to Moran's "petticoats in [the] thousands filing into the circulating libraries and the penny novelette shops" and suggests that Mary's Romantic proclivities derive from participation in an Irish-female-adolescence-wide consumption of British literary "garbage."[24] The novel reaffirms the normativity of this practice during another walk in which the policeman accompanies Mary to Phoenix Park: "The children ceased from their play to gaze round-eyed at the little girl and the big man; their attendants looked and giggled and envied. Under these eyes Mary Makebelieve's walk became afflicted with a sideward bias which jolted against her companion. She was furious with herself and ashamed" (31). The irresistible "sideward bias" with which Mary's gait is "afflicted" is produced by the giggling, envious attention her accompaniment by such a "manly" figure has drawn from the female "attendants" of the children populating the Park, those who, in the earlier description, read novelettes beneath its trees. Mary's self-conception is thus doubly filtered both through her own engagement with Romance and through her intuitive awareness of the similar engagement of Dublin's other female adolescents.

The novel also links the policeman's shoneen identity to the consumption of British literary "garbage." In keeping with the Revivalist castigation of such "vulgar" fare, he cites "reputable English journals, such as *Answers* and *Tit-Bits* and *Pearson's Weekly*" in support of his assertion that Phoenix Park is "the third largest in the world, but the most beautiful," rather than "the local newspapers, whose opinion," he warns, "might be biased by patriotism" (29).

He even regales Mary with stories that employ the sensational tropes of The Police Intelligence:

> He told her stories also, wonderful tales of great fights and cunning tricks, of men and women whose whole lives were tricks, of people who did not know how to live except by theft and violence. . . . He told her the story of . . . of the Sailor who had been Robbed . . . and of the Old Women who Steal Fish at Night-time, and the story of The Man he Let Off, and . . . a terrible story of how he fought five men in a little room, and showed her a great livid scar . . . and the marks in his neck where he had been stabbed with a jagged bottle, and his wrist watch which an Italian madman had thrust through and through with a dagger. (41–42)

The capitalization of these crime-related tales identifies The Police Intelligence as the source of the policeman's repertoire and suggests that Mary's enthrallment by this "governing, compelling" figure is doubly inspired by British popular culture. Not only her Romance consumption, but also his Christy Mahon–like self-fashioning as a protagonist of this genre prime her to view this colonialist shoneen as an ideal suitor. Like Pegeen Mike, Mary's reading has trained her to see her nation's imperial domination as a source of entertainment.

The remarkable extent to which Mary's self-conception is refracted through empire-abetting genres informs what is perhaps the novel's central symbol, the Makebelieves' "cracked looking-glass." Antedating by five years or so Joyce's cultivation of this image from Wilde's "The Decay of Lying" as a figure for the aesthetic challenges of colonial subalternity, Stephens deploys it to suggest that Mary's "life" imitates the low-brow "art" of Romance and The Police Intelligence and is thus reduced to a distorted, servile imitation of British culture.[25] This symbol first appears during the opening exposition of the Makebelieves' lives, wherein mother and daughter "often stood together before the little glass that had a crack running drunkenly from the right-hand top corner down to the left-hand bottom corner, and two small arm crosses, one a little above the other, in the center" (14). The effects of this item on their impoverished toilette are striking: "When one's face looked into this glass it often appeared as four faces with horrible aberrations; an ear might be curving around a lip, or an eye leering strangely in the middle of a chin" (14). The significance of the visual fragmentation in this passage only becomes clear, however, when the mirror emerges as integral to the sartorial preparations involved in Mary's courtship with the Policeman. After this "monument of solidity" begins to pursue her, Mary's respectable obsession with her appearance intensifies. She tries to achieve an equal, feminine "solidity" to entice his further attentions: "She polished her shoes, put on the white dress, and then did up her hair in front of the cracked looking-glass" (23). Mary arranges herself to conform to her Anglicized conception of Romance, and through this conformity the "cracked looking-glass" takes on associations of pop-cultural West Britonism.

This association is confirmed at the conclusion of her first stroll with the Policeman when Mary, though thrilled by his gentlemanly farewell, is also mortified by a flaw in her dress. At this charged moment, "the first time a man had ever uncovered before her," she becomes hyper self-conscious of her appearance, "wish[ing] frantically that her dress was longer than it was—that false hem! . . . she feared he was looking critically at her short skirt and immodest ankles" (31). That she imagines him "looking critically" at this unrespectable display reflects her mental colonization by the normative, Romantic gaze of this shoneen. Another description just prior to the above explicitly ties these implications to the "cracked looking-glass": "She wished to go away to her own little room where she could look at herself and ask her questions. She wanted to visualize herself sitting under a tree beside a man. She knew that she could reconstruct him to the smallest detail, but feared that she might not be able to reconstruct herself" (31). The Romantic reification of Mary's desires is so complete that she wants to depart from the very scene of their fulfillment to "visualize herself" with the "man" in the privacy of her room. Mary, in effect, fantasizes about composing her own Romantic narrative of the encounter. In that it will entail not simply reimagining her time with the Policeman but a direct visual self-inventory, this process of composition will necessarily hinge upon the disclosures of the Makebelieve family mirror. In keeping with the symbolism of the cracked looking-glass, however, while she is certain of her ability to "reconstruct him to the smallest detail," Mary is not nearly so confident in her ability "to reconstruct herself." A Mary so refracted by the conventions of British Romance can only appear as "horribly" distorted as the female subjects of such canonical Cubist paintings as Pablo Picasso's *Les Demoiselles d'Avignon*.

The duration of the novel is accordingly devoted to "reconstructing" Mary's fractured Irish identity. With the policeman's discovery of Mary's working-class standing, her consequent downgrading from potential wife to intended sexual conquest, and the entry of the "young lodger" into the Cafferty tenement, the narrative affiliations of this "fairy tale" shift subtly from alignment with British Romance to alignment with two different genres of decolonizing, nationalist orientation. As Joseph Valente's reading of the novel points out, the lodger's prototypical nationalist sentiments—his "fervor of passion" for Ireland, his conception of the nation "as a woman, queenly and distressed and very proud," and his "yearn[ing] to do deeds of valor, violent grandiose feats which would redound to her credit"—align him with the male protagonist of the most prevalent of Revivalist genres, the Shan Van Vocht (*The Myth* 90–100). Mary's rejection of the policeman's sexual overtures, her recovery from the disappointment of their courtship through her interactions with the lodger, the Makebelieves' closing of ranks against the policeman during his overbearing marriage proposal, and the lodger's fistfight with him after his departure all realign this "fairy tale" with the "chivalric," "sovereignty"-generating formula of this genre and contribute to the "reconstruction" both of Mary and the nation of which she becomes a Cathleen ni Houlihan–like embodiment.

Although, as Valente argues, the gender politics undergirding this "chivalric" genre "could not but cooperate in the very [shoneenism] it officially reprehends, helping to enthrall its audience in a set of 'non-Irish' values," values which, I have attempted to demonstrate, are those of British respectability, and although, given the novel's deep sensitivity to the retrograde and Anglicizing influence of this norm, Stephens signals his awareness of this nationalist genre's complicity with colonial patriarchy, *The Charwoman's Daughter* ultimately overrides such considerations in favor of a "fairy tale" wish-fulfillment fantasy of achieved decolonization (Valente, *The Myth* 130). By overlaying both narratives, that of Romance and that of its nationalist counterpart, with that of the Celticist "fairy dream," Stephens implies that, at least in its "magic" domain, the Makebelieves can escape the contradictions of the text's real-political resolution. The novel deploys Celticism, in other words, to combat the gender, class, and colonial obstacles confronting Irish nationalism with willful disregard for their material force.

Within this altered frame, the very elements that produced the Makebelieves' hardships become their means for transcending them. Their class privation evaporates when Mrs. Makebelieve's dream of inheriting a fortune from her American émigré brother, Patrick, miraculously comes true, thus overriding the debilitating assumptions of the Celtic trait of "mistaking dreams for reality." During the climactic scene of the Policeman's proposal, Mrs. Makebelieve leverages the similarly disadvantageous tenets of respectability to resist his shoneen overtures, forcing him to admit his failure to do "the right thing" by courting Mary without her knowledge (107–108). The Makebelieves' investment in fashion, formerly integral to the symbol of the cracked looking-glass, likewise becomes a medium of Irish self-assertion through a heightened emphasis on Mrs. Makebelieve's gifts as a seamstress, which take on, through the "freedom and bravery" and "terrifying originality" of her "divinely inspired needle," anticapitalist associations of aestheticized, utopian labor. Through such transvaluative, Celticist gestures, *The Charwoman's Daughter* "give[s] birth to a Dancing Star," achieving a symbolic Irish sovereignty (118–19).

Like Synge, then, Stephens envisions decolonization as proceeding not merely through political or military resistance, but through the extrication of Irish subjects from the popular-cultural forms of British capital. Only after the influence of British literary "garbage" on Mary's self-conception has been combated through immanent, generic critique does the replacement of "West British" cultural ways with Celtic ones become possible. By subtly modulating the reader's experience from immersion in British Romance conventions to immersion in a utopian, Celticist fairy dream, the novel's reader-response transaction ensures that its consumers, especially those female consumers who are most susceptible to the gendered variety of shoneenism bred by the former genre, undergo this epistemological shift directly. If, as its Wilde allusion implies that it hopes, life indeed imitates art, then *The Charwoman's Daughter* offers a potent contribution to the de-Anglicizing and Celticizing of the Irish female consumer and, through her, to the repair of the cracked looking-glass of Irish culture.

## THE IRISH FEMALE CONSUMER AND THE COLONIAL SPECTACLE

In a 1912 issue of *The Irish Citizen*, the publication of The Irish Women's Franchise League, the suffragist Mary Hayden outlined a program for ameliorating the political deficiencies of the "average Irish girl" (343). Titled "Women Citizens—Their Duties and Training," the article argues that because the "boarding schools" at which most girls receive their education fail to attune their pupils to matters of civic import, the Irish female enters adulthood "ludicrously . . . ignorant of public affairs and wholly indifferent to them" (343). Exacerbating this lack of preparation is the fact that after graduation, the young Irish woman is assailed by the blandishments of a frivolous print culture, such that "when she grows up and returns home, she generally contents herself with skimming over the notices of social functions and reading the lists of births, deaths, and marriages; unless indeed, as too often happens, she turns her attention to those more sensational items on account of which she was debarred from newspaper reading during her school days" (343–44). In Irish women citizens' susceptibility to such trivial fare, Hayden discerns dire ramifications for larger, nationalist priorities such as that of "the Irish industrial movement," of which, "up to the present, the majority of women have been very lukewarm supporters" (345). Lamenting that it was not "explained to them in their school-days why they should patronize native goods," Hayden concludes with a striking sketch of a typical "young girl" shopping: "'What do I care where the stuff was made, so that it is pretty?'" (345).

Hayden's brief piece extends the array of concerns outlined in the preceding chapter in a specifically feminist direction, and in so doing helps crystallize the portrait of early Irish modernisms constructed in the present one. Though she does not deploy its specific keywords in advocating for increased print- and popular-cultural discrimination on the part of the "average Irish girl," her invocation of such staple nationalist positions, alongside others like the promotion of "native manufactures," inevitably draws upon the imprimatur of Revivalist Celticism. This connection would be made explicit by other feminist organizations such as Maud Gonne's Inghinidhe na hÉireann, or "Daughters of Ireland," whose mission statement of 1900 lists among its chief "objects" "complete independence"; "the study of Gaelic, of Irish Literature, History, Music, and Art, especially amongst the young"; "to support and popularize Irish manufacture"; and an imperative to "discourage the reading and circulation of low English literature, the singing of English songs, the attending of vulgar English entertainments at the theaters and music halls . . . which is doing so much injury to the artistic taste and refinement of the Irish people" ("Objects of Inghinidhe na hÉireann" 92). Through such efforts, Revivalist Celticism fixed its attention on the adolescent Irish female, whose vulnerability to "low," metropolitan cultural products it identified as a beachhead of Anglicization.

Beyond their preoccupation with the general reification of Irish, Celtic sensibilities by the British culture industry, the Revivalist modernisms surveyed in this chapter find more specific common cause with this feminist agenda. Yeats's portrayal of the adulteration of Mary Bruin's "heart's desire" by a taste for "ribbons" mirrors Hayden's "young girl," who cares not for her fashion's national origins "so that it is pretty," while the Police Intelligence–driven moral derangement of Synge's young, female Mayoites and the Romance-spurred shoneenism of Stephens's Mary Makebelieve mirror both Hayden's readers of "sensational," society column– and divorce report–style tabloid gossip and Gonne's "vulgar" consumers of the literature, theater, and music of England. While it may then be tempting to view such male writers' emphasis on the vulnerability and safeguarding of the young, female consumer as patronizing—as implying that this demographic is especially susceptible to colonial seduction and in need of proportional, male intellectual guidance—it is also important to locate such efforts amid this broader agenda. In this vein, the gender politics of the Celticist, "feminized male" modernist as addressed in this study's introduction forms part of a larger, cross-gendered nationalist campaign to leverage the "feminine" virtues of "artistic taste," "refinement" of sensibility, and "sentimentality" against the "vulgar," desiccating, and reifying tendencies of British capitalism. Though limited by the gender assumptions of its time, the campaign against the Irish female's engulfment by such tendencies figures as a major wellspring of the Revival's Celticist alternative modernity.

What the specifically modernist iteration of this gender politics contributes is a heightened attunement to the imbrication of British colonialism with the perceptual forms of the metropolitan culture industry. More so than the often-formulaic, "propagandistic" works against which Yeats railed, and more even than Yeats's own "sublime" repudiation of the pop-cultural ornamentation of Mary Bruin's flounces, the signal works of Synge and Stephens achieve a potent resistance to such forms through their immanent critiques of British-disseminated literary genres. These critiques may, in fact, be read as identifying the historical emergence of a novel aesthetic phenomenon, one that we might call *the colonial spectacle*. As coined by Guy Debord's seminal postmodernist work, *The Society of the Spectacle*, the relevance of this seemingly anachronistic concept to these texts is evident through the criminal celebrity of Christy Mahon, as well as through Mary Makebelieve's idolization of colonial patriarchy. Both phenomena embody Debord's description of spectacle as a process by which, "where the real world changes into simple images, the simple images become real beings and effective motivations of hypnotic behavior" (18). Synge portrays the Irish as hypnotized into imperial and capitalist obedience through the consumption of the images of crime contained in The Police Intelligence, which train them to fetishize legal deviance for sensational titillation instead of ethical or political empowerment, as well as to desire the ultimate narrative closure of the repressive state apparatus of Empire. Similarly, Stephens portrays Mary Makebelieve as hypnotized through consumption of Romance into desiring male domination and violence and investing in the reproduction of Union through their legal corollary. Both Synge's tabloid-addicted and Stephens's Romance-addicted Irish consumers embody the "spectacular" effect Debord calls "the alienation of the spectator to the profit of the contemplated object": "the more he contemplates the less he lives, the more he accepts recognizing himself in the dominant images of need, the less he understands his own existence and his own desires" (30). Such modernisms highlight that the perceptions of the Irish consumer of imperial media, and those of the young, female consumer in particular, are reified by the contemplation of the generic objects of metropolitan capital, whose "dominant images of need" obscure the distinct existence and needs of the colonized.[26]

The collective Irish subjection to the reifying effects of British popular culture presents a pristine illustration of Debord's observation that "the society which carries the spectacle does not dominate the underdeveloped regions by its economic hegemony alone. It dominates them *as the society of the spectacle*" (57). Synge's Mayoites and Stephens's Dubliners exemplify the manner in which turn-of the-century Ireland's metrocolonial membership in Britain's budding "society of the spectacle" compounds its colonial subordination through the effects of capitalist reification. Their alienation as spectators of the colonizer's "images of need" reifies their identities in accord not only with capital's pop-cultural imperatives but with the metropolitan norms that structure them. Their behaviors in this sense anticipate, and even instantiate, Jean Baudrillard's notion of "simulacra" by demonstrating the "precession" of human action and understanding by media-generated signification.[27] Perceiving in the colonial spectacle an incipiently postmodern cultural process threatening to stall decolonization by reproducing imperial and capitalist perceptions, both authors devised experimental aesthetic strategies for alerting the Irish consumer to these effects and pointing the way beyond them. In so doing, they achieved an ingenious contribution to the Revival's anticapitalist decolonization campaign and also placed that campaign at the beginning of a larger, global story of the spread of capitalist pop culture and its complication of the legacies of Empire.

CHAPTER 6

# The Bathetic Muse

## *Irish Late Modernism*

The contours of the literary-historical movement with which this study's final chapter is concerned are neatly forecast by a text written well in advance of the moment to which it constitutes a response: James Joyce's "Araby." Though composed at the Revival's height, Joyce's tale nonetheless presages the critical interrogation and ironic deflation of Revivalist ideals that would become the calling card of modernist Irish writers in post-independence Ireland, central among them the commitment to cultivating Celticist alternatives to capitalist modernity. "Araby" invokes the Celticist anticapitalism of the Revival as an unconscious touchstone for its protagonist's journey to the title bazaar, an errand motivated by simple adolescent infatuation which he comes to conceive as a sort of Shan van Vocht–cum–grail quest beset by an urban and markedly commercial "throng of foes." The boy's self-casting as the hero of this popular, nationalist genre sustains him in Dublin locales "most hostile to romance," "through the flaring streets, jostled by drunken men and bargaining women, amid the curses of the laborers, [and] the shrill litanies of shop-boys who stood on guard by the barrels of pigs' cheeks," but his fantasy runs aground upon his arrival at "Araby" and the realization that his own objective of retrieving a trinket for his crush bears an identical consumer signature (22–23). Educated through the failed playing-out of his anticapitalist, nationalist ideals, the boy's famous epiphany centers on the "vanity" of his prior self-conception, which fundamentally misgauged the possibilities for transcending the base materialism of the Dublin marketplace (27).

"Araby" mimes the literary-historical process this chapter will chronicle. The image of the boy turning away from his nationalist anticapitalism in embittered recognition of its foolish "vanity" might, indeed, be offered as a symbolic tableau for the entirety of Irish Late Modernism, a literary movement in which the anticapitalist, Celticist goals of the Irish Revival are tried and found wanting on several counts, some ideological and some real-historical. The Catholic definition of "vanity" (of which Joyce was surely aware) as "the idle effort to obtain recognition or respect for what a person does not have a rightful claim to" could appropriately adorn the gravestone which would be placed over the Revival's vision during the several decades following the Anglo-Irish Treaty of 1921.[1] What "Araby" shows, above all else, is the extent to which that vision was predicated upon an immersion in capitalism so thorough as to render any nationalist fantasy tainted by its forms down to its very roots. The boy's distaste for the base money-grubbing of Dublin is the direct impetus for his anticapitalist quest, and that quest is therefore not only indebted to capital at a genetic level, but delusional insofar as it defines Irishness as separate from it. Joyce scathes Revivalist nationalism for failing to forge its ideals from the real constituent elements of turn-of-the-century Ireland, among which capital can only be admitted as central. During the post-independence moment at which the experiment of the Irish nation could be said to have had ample opportunity to take its course, a number of Irish writers—some old-guard nationalists, some part of a new generation—would arrive at the same epiphany as Joyce's protagonist: that the dream of an anticapitalist, Celticist nationality had failed and that Irishness remained inextricably bound up with the forms of capital.

The attempt to define such an aesthetic that resonates most with this chapter's account is that of Tyrus Miller's *Late Modernism: Politics, Fiction, and the Arts between the World Wars*. For Miller, the term designates a set of aesthetic practices prevalent during the interwar years that are distinct from both modernism and postmodernism and represent something of a transitional phase mediating between the "high" formal strategies of the former and the "low," pop-oriented strategies of the latter. As Miller describes, in the effort to highlight the failures of high modernism to contain the pressures attending the rise of "technological culture, mass politics, and shock experience" in early-twentieth-century Europe and America, "late modernist writing . . . reopens the modernist enclosure of form onto the work's social and political environs, facilitating a more direct, polemical engagement with topical and popular discourses. . . . [It] also registers the ways in which intense social, political, and economic pressures of the period increasingly threatened the efficacy of high modernist form" (20). Presaging the later developments of postmodernism, late modernism evinces "a painstaking pursuit of literary 'failure'" in which modernism's strategies of aesthetic mastery begin to dehisce (62).[2]

Miller's schema of Euro-American literary history in the mid-twentieth century might easily be adapted to schematize the tectonic shift that occurs in Irish aesthetics between the Revival and World War II, one that results in large part from the establishment of an independent Irish state and the concomitant opportunity to put Celticist ideals into practice. As a result of a number of factors attending post-independence Irish history, Irish writers came to conclude that the Celticist anticapitalism of the Revival had foundered, and, as a means of registering that failure, they engaged in a "painstaking pursuit" of demonstrating the "failure" of both Revivalist ideals and of the modernist strategies that had been their chief vehicle. In the world of Irish Late Modernism, the Revival's ideals have been all but extinguished by the onrush of an ever-accelerating capitalist world-system. The task of Irish Late Modernism in the texts surveyed here, from Joyce's *Ulysses* to the late poetry and drama of Yeats, Flann O'Brien's *At Swim-Two-Birds*, and Samuel Beckett's *Murphy*, is to register the failure of Revivalist nationalism to achieve its aims. As we shall see, capital forms, perhaps, the central pressure transforming pre-independence conceptions of Irishness. The texts of Irish Late Modernism index the increasingly globalized trajectory of Irish society and its submission to the same capitalist system once defined by Revivalists as utterly alien to the nation's Celtic essence.

## "IN CAPITAL SPIRITS": COUNTER-REVIVALISM IN *ULYSSES*

If "Araby" presages the sensibility of Irish Late Modernism, it is only with the appearance of the opening chapters of *Ulysses* in *The Little Review* in 1917 that its signature aesthetic begins to take shape. As we have seen, the younger Joyce of *Dubliners* shows not only a keen awareness of the imaginative hegemony of the agon of Celt and capital in Revival-era Ireland, but critical insight into the falsehood of that agon's binary premise. Its epiphany's seeming transcendence of the false opposition of nationalist anticapitalism makes all the more curious, then, the fact that the later text that Joyce envisioned as his national epic begins by invoking the racial theories of Matthew Arnold. That Joyce found this necessary suggests that *Ulysses* is preoccupied by some the same concerns as the earlier story, and that it may be useful to consider the protagonist of its opening chapters, Stephen Dedalus, as to some extent shaped by the same ideological pressures as its anonymous narrator.

The opening chapters in which Stephen stars, the "Telemachiad," repeatedly invoke the same Arnoldian oppositions that have preoccupied this study. Stephen, we shall see, inhabits the same fin-de-siècle, colonial intellectual milieu it has been the aim of the foregoing chapters to reconstruct. His ambition, announced at the conclusion of *A Portrait of the Artist as a Young Man*, to "fly by those nets" "flung" at "the soul of man . . . born in this country," figures these specifically Arnoldian "nets" as among the aspiring Irish artist's most formidable obstacles. At the same time as the Joyce avatar of 1904 is bedeviled by the Celticist legacy, however, the novel itself proceeds to perform the later Joyce's fulfillment of this "flying by" through its own aesthetic form. That form, in particular in those chapters starring not Stephen but Leopold Bloom, thus emerges through an implicit repudiation of the Arnoldian assumptions of the Irish fin de siècle. It is no coincidence that the novel's central protagonist—as both a capitalist ad-man and a member of the ethnic group most identified with capital's imperatives, the Jews—embodies the negative terms of the Arnoldian binaries that so influenced Revivalist nationalism. The hero of Joyce's Irish epic takes shape in direct opposition to the Revival's Celticist anticapitalism, and he serves to deflate not only its claims regarding the national essence, but those corresponding aesthetic projects that sought to foment the nation's disentanglement from capital. The novel's counter-Revivalism extends not only to a "realist" admission of the nation's domination by capitalist modernity, but to an embrace of those popular-cultural forms that earlier modernists such as Yeats, Synge, and Stephens viewed as its most insidious feature.

Reconstructing this arc begins with a closer look at the novel's references to Matthew Arnold, all of which arise in relation to Stephen. The eponymous opening chapter of the "Telemachiad" foregrounds the binaries of Hebrew/Hellene and Celt/Saxon almost immediately. The former is explicitly invoked in Stephen's opening exchange with Buck Mulligan, whose mania for "the Greeks" leads him to propose a mock-campaign to "Hellenize" Ireland, while the latter is implicitly cited by the Englishman Haines, the Saxon ethnologist who seeks to convert the Irish phenomena he encounters, among them Stephen's intellect, to specimens of Celtic folklore. As noted in early postcolonial readings by Gregory Castle and Vincent Cheng, Haines's Celticism is subjected to contextual deflation and mockery soon after its introduction through the entry of the "poor old woman" who delivers milk to Stephen and Mulligan's Martello Tower residence. Haines's expectations regarding this ethnographic specimen prove comically out of step with her reality, in particular through her failure to understand his Gaelic, while Stephen's own internal commentary and subsequent interactions with Haines highlight his ironic distance from the Celticist lens through which he and she are viewed.

*Ulysses* thus opens by invoking Celticism, but it links the discourse to the primitivist mindset of the English. Stephen's response to Haines's proposal for "a collection of your sayings" entails a complicated reading of this mindset (1.480). His blunt inquiry, "Would I make any money by it?," in addition to violating English politesse, bucks the specific Celticist expectation of disregard for the world of "fact," leading Haines to beat a hasty, awkward retreat (1.490). Stephen's monetary preoccupation, however, also reflects his all-too-real proximity to the stereotype of Irish economic incapacity. As he tells Mulligan, whose own hope of using Haines for financial gain Stephen has imperiled, "The problem is to get money. From whom? From the milkwoman or from him. . . . I see little hope . . . from her or from him" (1.495–501). His assessment highlights the alternatives available to the aspiring Catholic literary artist at the turn of the century: cater to British ethnographic desire, or serve the prevailing ideal of Irishness propounded by Revivalist Celticism's "poor old woman," the central figure of nationalist genres such as the Shan Van Vocht and texts such as Gregory and Yeats's *Cathleen ni Houlihan*.[3]

While Stephen seemingly dispatches the former option, the latter, as well as the more general set of Irish literary and nationalist ideals circa 1904 of which it is a part, receives a much more extensive treatment throughout the novel. It is here that Mulligan's proposal to "Hellenize" the "island" enters in, along with the text's first explicit Arnold reference. This reference cannot be deciphered alone, however, as Mulligan's notion of the Hellenic also reflects the "series of modulations" that, as Don Gifford describes in his invaluable *Ulysses Annotated*, "Arnold's essentially intellectual distinction underwent" during the late nineteenth century, whereby the binary came to stand for a more general "opposition between the sensual-aesthetic freedom of the Greeks and the repressiveness of late-Victorian Hebraism" (*Annotated* 16). Mulligan's own literary idol is Oscar Wilde, whose aesthetic theories in such texts as "The Decay of Lying" and the "Preface" to *The Picture of Dorian Gray* he invokes while forcing Stephen, the "dreadful bard," to take stock of his disheveled appearance in the mirror he uses for his morning shave (35). Mulligan's quip, "The rage of Caliban at not seeing his face in a mirror. . . . If Wilde were only alive to see you!," and Stephen's retort regarding the broken mirror, "It is a symbol of Irish art. The cracked lookingglass of a servant," enact an extremely intricate pantomime of ethnic and aesthetic identifications (1.143–46). The Anglo-Irish Mulligan's depiction of Stephen as a "Caliban" indeed seems to slight his native status, as many commentators have suggested. Mulligan's subsequent references to Stephen having "more spirit than any of them" and having to "beg from these swine" seem to allude to the predominantly Anglo-Irish Dublin literati amid which later chapters will depict him as marginal (1.150–60). But the specificity of the reference in question adds another layer to its significance. Namely, in Wilde's "Preface," the "rage of Caliban at not seeing his face in the glass" is equated with a specific aesthetic viewpoint:

"the nineteenth-century dislike of Romanticism" (Wilde, "Preface"). The larger suggestion, then, is that Stephen does not like what he sees because of a disproportion between his ideals or aspirations and the "Romantic" image the "glass" contains.

Stephen's famous response regarding the "cracked lookingglass" then points to a potential basis for this mismatch: the Irish artist, positioned as colonial "servant," finds the very medium of artistic creation riven by power dynamics. Mulligan pokes fun at Stephen's aspirations for being both overblown and unfulfilled, but Stephen's response suggests that the native Irish writer confronts an especially complex challenge of literary mimesis of which Mulligan is only dimly aware. It is in this vein that Stephen's first, stream-of-consciousness reference to Matthew Arnold arises. Upon Mulligan's offer to "rag" Haines for his disruptive night terrors just as he and his Oxford peers once did "Clive Kempthorpe," Stephen has a vision:

> Young shouts of moneyed voices in Clive Kempthorpe's rooms. Palefaces. . . . A scared calf's face gilded with marmalade. I don't want to be debagged. . . . Shouts from the open window startling evening in the quadrangle. A deaf gardener, aproned, masked with Matthew Arnold's face, pushes his mower on the somber lawn, watching narrowly the dancing motes of grasshalms. . . . To ourselves . . . new paganism . . . omphalos. (1.166–75)

Stephen thus associates both Haines and Mulligan, as "Oxy chaps," with Matthew Arnold. While Stephen's companions are products of the educational environment tended emblematically by Arnold, Arnold himself is "deaf" to the violence and squabbles therein and is instead—as a symbolic "gardener"—preoccupied with myopic considerations of "culture." Both ideas may then apply to Stephen's immediate circumstances, in which two devotees of Arnoldian cultural ideals—Celtic and Hellenic—seek to incorporate him into their respective schemes, while oblivious to the socioeconomic violence to which they subject him.

Cheng reads the passage's final bits as Stephen "combating Mulligan's hailing of Stephen as fellow Hellenist . . . with a 'new paganism' and . . . an echo of the Irish nationalist slogan Sinn Féin ('We ourselves'), celebrating his . . . otherness like a quietly defiant Caliban" (154). This assessment, however, misses the passage's second, crucial allusion to Oscar Wilde, whom Joyce, in the 1909 essay "Oscar Wilde, Poet of 'Salome,'" describes as having "deceived himself by thinking that he was the harbinger of the good news of neo-paganism to the suffering people" (*Occasional* 150–51). Joyce elaborates, "Wilde, far from being a monster of perversion that inexplicably arose in the midst of the modern civilization of England, is the logical and inevitable product of the Anglo-Saxon college and university system, a system of seclusion and secrecy" (150–51). Stephen's "combating" of Mulligan's Hellenism, then, does not in fact entail an embrace of primitive, "neo-pagan" otherness, but instead identifies that Hellenism with such primitivism. The location of his vision amid the "Anglo-Saxon university system" neatly ties together all of the above references to suggest that Arnoldian Hellenism and Wildean decadence, along with Haines's Celticism, are equivalent, "Romantic" responses to an Anglocentric, "late-Victorian repressiveness."

Stephen implicitly recognizes and rejects these models as "cracked," non-self-identical bases of self-fashioning and artistic inspiration, yet he himself—like the similarly Wilde-affiliated protagonist of *The Charwoman's Daughter*—embodies a number of allied, derivative ideals. As Jennifer Wicke notes in *Advertising Fictions*, although the novel as a whole is thoroughly bound up with the language and phenomenology of advertising, "Stephen unnaturally escapes advertisement altogether" (159). Stephen assiduously cultivates the anti- or non-capitalist posture of the bohemian, decadent aesthete, which gestures implicate him in both Mulligan's Wildean counterculture and the "reaction" against capital's "despotism" that Haines seeks in his Celtic specimens. It may be, then, that part of Haines's surprise at Stephen's request for monetary compensation derives not from simple ethnological prejudice, but from Stephen's own deliberate cultivation of an anti- or non-capitalist persona. The convergence between Stephen as aesthete and the image of the Arnoldian Celt may in turn signal something of a wry joke on Joyce's part regarding his ur-self: simply by espousing the countercultural impulses of the decadent, an Irish Catholic such as Stephen moves into unwitting alignment with prevailing stereotypes. Such an implication would entail both a structural diagnosis of Irish Celticism as simply a local incarnation of broader, European aesthetic and economic currents, and a mechanism by which Stephen's youthful artistic aspirations ironically draw him back into the "pale" of the national influences he would "fly by."

It is thus fitting that in "Proteus," when the reader finally encounters one of Stephen's literary compositions, it proves deeply indebted to preceding literary models, the Celticist among them. Indeed, his initial mental draft of the poem that will later be quoted in full in "Aeolus" offers a pronounced illustration of Wilde's dictum in "The Decay of Lying" that "the more imitative an art is the less it represents to us the spirit of its age" (321): "Omnis caro ad te veniet. He comes, pale vampire, through storm his eyes, his bat sails bloodying the sea, mouth to her mouth's kiss" (3.395). As many critics have noted, Stephen borrows heavily from at least two major textual precedents, Douglas Hyde's *Love Songs of Connaught* and Bram Stoker's *Dracula*. Through its reference to the former, he and his work become further realigned with the Celticism of Haines, who is later depicted as acquiring a copy of Hyde's Revivalist opus in "Scylla and Charybdis." Through the latter, Joyce establishes a series of complex "vampire" thematic resonances that may likewise highlight Stephen's literary and personal parasitism. Critics have found the vampire image a particularly dense and ambiguous one, and have read it as a figure for several different characters, from Stephen himself, to his mother, to Buck Mulligan. The notion of Stephen as vampire would comport well with the contents of the Hyde poem he mentally quotes, "My Grief on the Sea," which depicts a native Irishwoman's "keen" at the loss of her lover through emigration to America.[4] Just as the poem's speaker laments her lover's departure, so Stephen may figure as a "vampire" émigré returning to Ireland at his dying mother's plaintive call. The sense in which his returning "mouth" "kisses," and is thus symbiotic with hers, may derive not only from familial interdependency, but from his recitation of the song "Who Goes with Fergus?" from Yeats's *The Countess Cathleen* at her request. Given that the Joyce of 1901, in the essay "The Day of the Rabblement," would make the "vulgar," "popular" reception of this INTS play a leading illustration of the nation's status as "the most belated race in Europe," Stephen's sense of himself as a "vampire" may reflect his sense that his catering to his mother's demands perpetuates his relationship with prevailing Irish taste (*Occasional* 50). Whether Stephen's Hyde-based composition merely indexes, or sardonically reflects upon, such parasitism, the avowal of ongoing entanglement is the same.

The poem's vampire reference may also be read as alluding back to the novel's opening scene, where Stephen and Mulligan's banter over the "cracked lookingglass" parallels the famous shaving scene at the beginning of Stoker's novel. The parallels are suggestive: just as Jonathan Harker shaves before a mirror in which the Count's image fails to appear, so Mulligan shaves before a mirror in which Stephen, "Caliban"-like, fails to see himself. Stephen, in his role as "kinch," the knife blade, may then symbolically serve as an accessory in the wealthier Mulligan's toilette, but he may also, Dracula-like, hunger after the blood of the latter, which implication would comport with his financial indebtedness to his roommate, as well as the intellectual companionship that Stephen will later seek to discontinue. Reversing the image, Mulligan becomes invisible as Stephen ponders his own face, in which case the former becomes the vampire-like parasite, perhaps in reflection of his

Haines-like dependency on Stephen's intellectual stimulation, as well as on the shorter-term financial boom created by Stephen's teaching wages. The notion that the two companions' relationship is mutually vampiric would find further support in that both—Stephen through refusing to pray for her, and Mulligan through his disrespectful remarks regarding her "beastly" death—prey, ghoul-like, on the dying May Dedalus.[5] In this vein of association, the "cracked lookingglass" symbol, more than suggesting that Stephen's self-image is refracted through a servant-like dependency on Arnoldian ethnic and aesthetic ideals, may reflect a deeper investment—familial, financial, and intellectual—on surrounding Irish circumstances. The migratory colonial dynamics numerous recent critics have read into the figure of Dracula—who before emigrating to England steeps himself in the study and emulation of English ways—may provide another parallel to Stephen's present situation, in which he has been forced to immerse himself further in the Anglicizing Irish influences he would otherwise spurn. A close reading of his poem according to the Wildean representational principle established above, then, not only reveals its "vampiric," dependent relationship with prevailing, Irish intellectual currents at the level of subject matter; in its very form, his composition proves riven by the "crack" of colonial reification.[6]

One other "vampire" resonance is worth exploring briefly, one that extends the ruminations of "Proteus" forward into the later chapter containing the novel's last explicit depiction of Matthew Arnold: "Circe." As noted by David Earle, the novel's vampire theme intersects with another major symbol: that of absinthe. Earle reads absinthe as symbolic of the culture of fin-de-siècle decadence embodied in Stephen, whose center of gravity was the Symbolist France to which he has recently made a pilgrimage. When, in "Proteus," just prior to his mental draft of the vampire poem, Stephen recalls his absinthe-drinking interaction in Paris with the Fenian "wild goose," Kevin Egan, his language may link vampirism with Irish nationalism. As Earle describes, "The poem's vampire imagery seems to emerge from Stephen's reminiscence of Egan: 'the green fairy's fang thrusting between his lips' and 'Green eyes, I see you. Fang, I feel.' . . . To a certain extent, Stephen's poem is indeed inspired by the green muse, albeit via Egan" (695). In this sense, Stephen—here figured as the vampiric victim—is bitten by a very specific "fang" in addition to that of French decadence: that of nationalist Irishness, for which, indeed, the "green fairy" would be an apt, Celticist emblem.

Later, in "Circe," when Stephen descends, through an over-indulgence in absinthe, into a mental phantasmagoria in which are legible all the sources of conflict he confronts throughout the day, the idea that his overall psychology is infected with the vampiric pull of contemporary Irishness becomes more compelling. Such a link would confirm the earlier implication that through his countercultural aestheticism, Stephen unwittingly falls in line with Celticist stereotypes, and it is no coincidence that the novel's opening references to Matthew Arnold resurface here in specific relation to his financial profligacy. Deep in the clutches of the "Green Fairy," Stephen is visited by "The Siamese twins, Phillip Drunk and Phillip Sober, two Oxford dons with lawnmowers," both of whom "are masked with Matthew Arnold's face" (15.2512–14). The two figures, representative of proverbially foolhardy and wise states of decision-making, respectively, engage in an argument over Stephen's squandering of his wages that alludes not only to the earlier Arnold image but to other, preceding scenes such as Stephen's interview with his Anglophilic, capitalist boss, Garrett Deasy. Significantly, upon Phillip Drunk's ironic invocation of the Deasy-an, "Saxon" economic principle "I paid my way" to justify Stephen's drunkenness—the thorough current violation of which Phillip Sober punctuates by computing the tab of his bender—the chapter's mock stage directions suggest that the former's Arnoldian "lawnmower begins to purr" (15.2525). Stephen, in short, bitten by the "Green Fairy" of Irishness, now embodies a well-nigh comic, stage-Celticism whose stereotypicality is again measured against the standard of Arnoldian "Culture."

It is at this crisis point that the chapter's other Arnold allusion, raised during Stephen's music-theoretical dispute with the "cap" worn by his companion, Lynch, enters in and sets the stage for the larger, dialectical union of ethnic principles embodied in the father-son relationship of the novel's dual protagonists: "Jewgreek is greekjew" (15.2098). To comprehend this turn, however, further explication of the novel's representation of the Revival is needed, because only through that representation does the text's larger relationship with prevailing racial thought grow clear. As it happens, the chapter in which the Revival takes center stage, "Scylla and Charybdis," entails a whole series of further, though less explicit, engagements with Arnold. The chapter in fact subtly extends the novel's Celticist joke regarding Stephen upon the reentry of Mulligan, who tracks him down at the National Library of Ireland, where he has stopped in search of a publishing venue for Deasy's letter on hoof and mouth disease. Stephen's resentment of Mulligan and Haines has led him to stand the two up at the drinking appointment agreed upon in "Telemachus," and he has sent in his stead a telegram which reads: "The sentimentalist is he who would enjoy without incurring the immense debtorship for a thing done" (9.550–52). As Mark Osteen shows in *The Economy of Ulysses*, Stephen's missive entails a complex, and contradictory, quotation of the novel

*The Ordeal of Richard Feverel*, by George Meredith: on the one hand, "the wire accuses Mulligan of failing to pay his debts" to Stephen, while on the other, "ironically . . . Stephen might be accused of sentimentalism," since "he owes more than twenty-five pounds to various people," including nine pounds to Mulligan himself, "and shows little likelihood of repaying any of it" (Osteen 217). Given the context in which preceding chapters place Stephen, it would be difficult to miss not just the hypocritical irony of his accusation, but the larger coincidence of his financial haplessness with the Arnoldian definition of the Irish Celt as "sentimental." Stephen's indictment of Mulligan for the same failing of which he is himself guilty—and his seeming ignorance of the contradiction—thus constitutes a quintessentially Celtic "reaction" against "the despotism of fact." Such a contextually pointed invocation of the word "sentimental" might, indeed, help explain Joyce's selection of the seemingly ill-fitting, idiosyncratic Meredith quotation as a vehicle for Stephen's spleen.[7]

Beyond further highlighting Stephen's structural alignment with Celticist stereotypes, the chapter's meditation on his relationship to Arnoldian ideas also proceeds through the intellectual currents against which Stephen struggles to articulate his theory of Shakespeare. "Scylla" consists of a dialogue between Stephen and four interlocutors: Thomas Lyster, director of the National Library; Richard Best, the assistant director; the assistant librarian William McGee, also known as John Eglinton; and a figure we have encountered extensively in preceding chapters, George Russell (AE). It is in this epicenter of Literary Revivalism that the novel's "Hamlet chapter" proceeds. Appropriately, Lyster broaches the discussion with a complex, dual allusion to Arnold, conveyed through a paraphrase of Goethe's description of Hamlet in *Wilhelm Meister's Apprenticeship*: "The beautiful ineffectual dreamer who comes to grief against hard facts" (9.9–10). As Gifford notes, the idea of Hamlet as "beautiful" and "ineffectual" is cribbed from Arnold's essay on Percy Shelley in his *Essays in Criticism: Second Series* (1888) (Gifford 193). Lyster's phrasing also converges unmistakably with *The Celtic Element in Literature*, where the opposition of ineffectual, aesthetic "dreaming" to "facts" is the defining characteristic of the Irish Celt. The tone of the chapter's dispute over Hamlet is then set, and it is against a distinctly Arnoldian and Celticist reading of Shakespeare that Stephen's performance plays out.[8]

It is not Lyster's ideas, however, that take center stage in the ensuing dispute, but those of Eglinton and AE. Eglinton, who in the words of Richard Ellman wrote "essays in a graceful style modeled on Matthew Arnold" (118), affirms his Arnoldophilia by borrowing one of his contributions from an Arnold sonnet on Shakespeare: "of all great men he is the most enigmatic. We know nothing but that he lived and suffered. . . . Others abide our question. A shadow hangs over all the rest" (9.360).[9] Stephen seems to show awareness of the Arnoldian basis of Eglinton's position through an oblique, mental recollection of the novel's opening scene. Upon Eglinton's warning, "if you want to shake my belief that Shakespeare is Hamlet you have a stern task before you," Stephen presses his more intricate biographical reading through a characteristically Wildean analogy: "As we, or mother Dana, weave and unweave our bodies . . . from day to day, their molecules shuttled to and fro, so does the artist weave and unweave his image. And as the mole on my right breast is where it was when I was born, though all my body has been woven of new stuff . . . so through the ghost of the unquiet father the image of the unloving son looks forth" (9.370–81). When Stephen then politely grants Best's suggestion that Hamlet's "passages with Ophelia" more so reflect the pubescent interests of a "son" than Shakespeare's roles as father and husband, stating wryly, "that mole is the last to go," Eglinton is described as responding with a "nothing pleasing mow" (9.392). As well as being Elizabethan English for "a mocking expression," the word "mow" may recall the opening chapter's depiction of the "deaf gardener" with "Matthew Arnold's face" who "pushes his mower" on the lawns of Oxford (Gifford 218). Such a connection would suggest that Eglinton's resistance to Stephen's theory is founded on the very same imperially affiliated Arnoldianism—Hellenic and Celtic—established earlier with Mulligan and Haines.[10]

Eglinton later solidifies this theme when he wonders aloud, "Has no one made him out to be an Irishman?" (9.519–20). The mention of "Dana," however, extends such implications to the domain of Revivalist literary production. Stephen grows painfully conscious of his literary and financial marginality in this world when Lyster mentions an impending "literary surprise" of a "sheaf of our younger poets' verses" to which Stephen has not been invited to contribute, and he forces himself to "listen" to the enumeration of its details (9.290–300). Lyster's description alludes to an actual work, *New Songs: A Lyric Selection*, published by AE (to whom, the episode indicates, Stephen is also a pound in debt) in 1904 (Gifford 212). Stephen's second-class status is punctuated not only by his exclusion from the volume, but by the insider status of his nemesis, Mulligan, who unlike Stephen has been invited to attend a gathering of the involved literati that evening. Mulligan's real-life counterpart, Oliver St. John Gogarty, would in fact publish a "literary notice" in praise of the "sheaf" in a periodical launched by Eglinton earlier in 1904: *Dana: An Irish Magazine of Independent Thought*, so named after the mother goddess of those Celtic idols, the Tuatha de Danaan. Stephen's "weaving" together of his Hamlet theory of the aesthetic "image" with this reference should then be read not as appeasing his Celticist auditors, but as an attempt to outflank them through a defiant assertion of aesthetic autonomy.

AE's appearance in the chapter, though briefer, is just as crucial as Eglinton's to its portrayal of Stephen's, and the novel's, relationship to Revivalist Celticism. Though Stephen identifies the two figures as kindred "seekers on the great quest" to the land of "Tir na n-og," the episode distinguishes between Eglinton's Arnoldianism and AE's Theosophy-based literary nationalism. The latter is reflected in Russell's remark, "All these questions are purely academic . . . whether Hamlet is Shakespeare or James I or Essex. . . . Art has to reveal to us ideas, formal spiritual essences . . . Plato's world of ideas" (9.45–50). Stephen's inner monologue then incorporates a direct Hamlet reference, the full, original text of which indexes the pressure Stephen feels before AE's idealist Celticism: "Fie, upon't! Foh! About, my brain!" (qtd. in Gifford 198). Indeed, the description that appears the strongest candidate for a direct invocation of the chapter title suggests that AE constitutes the "Charybdis" of Stephen's mindset, with the Oxford-affiliated Arnoldianism of Eglinton, Mulligan, and Haines serving as his "Scylla": "Between the Saxon smile and the Yankee yawp. The devil and the deep blue sea" (9.139–40). The "Saxon smile" refers once more to Haines, whose pleasant exterior conceals an implacable, predatory intent equated with "the horns of a bull" and the "heels of a horse" (1.732). On one side, Stephen confronts such "hard" obstacles, which resemble the "rock" on which the monster, Scylla, resides in *The Odyssey*, while on the other, he confronts the "deep blue sea" in the form of a "Yankee yawp," which phrase entails a complicated reference to AE.

In "Aeolus," at an earlier stop on his publishing errand, Stephen learns that he has recently been a subject of discussion between Eglinton ("Professor Magennis") and J.J. O'Molloy. O'Molloy inquires what Stephen "think[s] really of that hermetic crowd . . . A. E. the mastermystic," and informs him that AE "has been telling some Yankee interviewer that you came to him in the small hours of the morning to ask him about planes of consciousness" (7.781–89). This incident, based on a real interaction between AE and Joyce chronicled in the American writer Cornelius Weygandt's book *Irish Plays and Playwrights* (1913), suggests that Stephen's rousing of his "brain" against AE bespeaks a very recent dependency, as does his inner response to O'Molloy's report: "Speaking about me? What did he say? What did he say? What did he say about me? Don't ask" (7.789–90). If, then, Arnoldian Revivalism is Stephen's intellectual Scylla, these references position AE's Theosophical Revivalism as his Charybdis. Stephen skirts the former peril by reading Shakespeare through a Wildean autonomy, while his attempts to bypass the latter can be comprehended via the mirror symbolism of "Telemachus." Just as Stephen "rages" at "not seeing his face" in the Romantic "glass," so he expresses an aestheticist "rage" at the image of Irishness propounded by AE, which he equates with the primitivist "yawp" of the American Romantic, Walt Whitman. Weygandt's account of the young Joyce—"an exquisite who thought the literary movement was being vulgarized," and who rejected AE's "Absolute" in favor of "Pater's relative"—corresponds perfectly to Stephen's efforts to escape the gravitational pull of AE's Revivalist "Charybdis" throughout the episode (Weygandt 121).

AE's Theosophy also provides two further dialectical contributions to the ur-Joyce's development, both of which help clarify the novel's relationship to the Revivalist influences the chapter documents. The first is highlighted by another link between "Scylla" and Stephen's conversations with Dublin pressmen in "Aeolus," one that centers on Irish perceptions of ancient Egypt. Theosophy such as AE espouses is tied in Stephen's mind to Madame Helena Blavatsky's founding "textbook" for the movement, *Isis Unveiled* (1876), which derived a comparative, spiritualist philosophy from Indian, Jewish, and Egyptian doctrines, among others. In "Aeolus," however, Egypt takes on rather different associations than those of quasi-Celtic mysticism, in particular through its Biblical role as an imperial oppressor of the Jews. The *Evening Telegraph*'s employees, including O'Molloy, Myles Crawford, and "professor MacHugh," engage in an "impromptu" discussion of a 1901 dispute between the Conservative Lord Justice Gerald Fitzgibbon and the nationalist journalist John F. Taylor regarding the Gaelic Revival, in which the latter, according to MacHugh, compared Fitzgibbon's censure of the movement to that of an "Egyptian highpriest" scolding a "youthful Moses": "Why will you jews not accept our culture, our religion, and our language? You are a tribe of nomad herdsmen: we are a mighty people. You have not cities nor wealth . . . You have but emerged from primitive conditions: we have a literature, a priesthood, an agelong history and polity" (7.844–50). MacHugh's evocation of the Babylonian captivity as an analog for the imperial captivity of the Irish remains on Stephen's mind in "Scylla," where it tellingly resurfaces upon AE's departure. In the "rest" that follows his exit, Stephen "ponders things that were not . . . what might have been: possibilities of the possible as possible: things not known," among which ousted futures he seems to include his potential Theosophical apprenticeship to AE: "Coffined thoughts around me, in mummycases. . . . Thoth, god of libraries, a birdgod, moonycrowned. And I heard the voice of an Eyptian highpriest. . . . They are still. Once quick in the brains of men. Still: but an itch of death is in them, to tell me in my ear a maudlin tale, urge me to wreak their will" (9.349–58). Stephen's thoughts offer a complex network of suggestions regarding his relationship to AE's brand of Revivalism. In keeping with the Joycean biographical incident described by Weygandt, he views AE's Egyptological mysticism as imperiling his aestheticist independence. At the same time, he seems to identify himself with the Jew in MacHugh's parable: just as the Jews are urged to accept Egyptian culture, so Stephen feels the urge to embrace the Egypt-affiliated ideology of this prominent Revivalist.

Stephen thus adapts the "Aeolus" opposition between colonizing Egypt and colonized Jew from an analog for Irish imperial subjection to one highlighting his own marginality among the predominantly Anglo-Irish Revival. Through these Egyptological ruminations, the novel's investment in the figure of the Jew begins to grow clearer. As the manuscript materials for *Ulysses* document, Joyce was deeply committed to the notion of a kinship between the Irish and the Jews. "Aeolus" and "Scylla" together establish one basis for this identification in the parallel, Jewish and Irish occupation of a colonially oppressed position. Part, then, of the novel's answer to the anxieties Stephen feels between the "Scylla and Charybdis" of Revival-era Irish thought is to privilege not Egyptian or imperial models, but those Jewish models with which Irish subalternity, in particular Catholic Irish subalternity, had more in common. The emergent centrality of Leopold Bloom, then, to the novel's portrait of Irishness extends Stephen's thoughts about the imperialist affiliations of AE's Theosophy and suggests that Joyce adopted Jewishness as more appropriate to his colonial chronicle. Bloom's increasing prominence as the novel progressed away from its initial designs as a sort of *Portrait* sequel likewise reflects Joyce's response to the episode's "Scylla": where Stephen is hemmed in on all sides by the racial thought of Matthew Arnold, which privileged Hellene and Celt as idealized alternatives to Hebraic/capitalist values, Joyce opts to privilege the latter, reviled terms of these oppositions.[11]

Indeed, Stephen's Shakespeare theory soon undergoes an improvisatory modulation that may be read as a defiance of his auditors' racial investments. This modulation follows the appearance of Bloom, whom Mulligan receives with venomous, caricature anti-Semitism ("The sheeny! . . . Ikey Moses"), after having just encountered him in the National Museum of Ireland (9.605–607). After Eglinton prompts him to resume his explanation, Stephen invokes a number of biographical and textual details that identify Shakespeare as, in effect, a Saxon capitalist: "Twenty years he lived in London and, during part of that time, he drew a salary equal to the lord chancellor of Ireland. His life was rich. His art . . . is the art of surfeit. . . . The gombeenwoman Eliza Tudor had underlinen enough to vie with her of Sheba. . . . He was a rich country gentleman . . . a capitalist shareholder, a bill promoter, a tithefarmer" (9.624–31, 710–12). Flouting his auditors' urge to view him as "an Irishman," Stephen insists upon Shakespeare's wealth, and that wealth's relationship with signifiers of Irish colonial oppression. The characterization of Queen Elizabeth I, the inaugurator of the plantation system of Irish subjugation, as a "gombeenwoman" initiates an even more specific series of references that characterize the Bard as not just a Saxon capitalist, but a Jewish userer: "He drew Shylock out of his own long pocket. . . . The son of a maltjobber and moneylender he was himself a cornjobber and moneylender, with ten tods of corn hoarded in the famine riots" (9.741–45). Having sussed out his Revivalist auditors' Arnoldian reading of Shakespeare, and keenly aware of both Mulligan's anti-Semitism and his view of him as a hapless Celt, Stephen modulates his Wildean, aestheticist reading of Shakespeare to foreground a Saxon and "Hebraic" materialism.

Joyce's choice of the Jewish Bloom as his protagonist is thus overdetermined by a number of defiant urges toward prevailing aesthetic and nationalist ideologies.[12] But it is not merely in abstract, schematic terms that the chapter's "Scylla and Charybdis" stimulate the ur-Joyce's budding self-conception. The latter symbol, as embodied in AE, provides a second, pivotal clarification of the novel's agenda. Early in the chapter, Best describes having inspired Haines to purchase a copy of *Love Songs of Connaught* from "Gill's." AE seizes the opportunity to give vent to his distinctive version of the Celticist, anti-capitalist hobby-horse:

> People do not know how dangerous lovesongs can be. . . . The movements which work revolutions in the world are born out of the dreams and visions in a peasant's heart on the hillside. For them the earth is not an exploitable ground but the living mother. The rarefied air of the academy and the arena produce the sixshilling novel, the musichall song. France produces the finest flower of corruption in Mallarme but the desirable life is revealed only to the poor of heart, the life of Homer's Phaeacians. (9.153)

The "peasant" idealism of AE's Revivalist Celticism motivates a spurning of popular genres and media so extreme as to extend even to Hyde's canonical text, which is classed as "dangerous" by virtue of its nominal convergence, as a collection of "lovesongs," with the Anglicizing fare of such venues as the "musichall." Joyce directly invokes the rhetoric of Revivalist screeds by AE such as "Nationality and Imperialism" as a feature of his aesthetic "Charybdis," and in doing so suggests that *Ulysses* will spurn not only Celticism's primitivist "yawp," but the commodity critique that was its ubiquitous, hegemonic counterpart.

The novel itself immediately makes good on this implied promise through the thorough immersion of its next chapter, "Wandering Rocks," in the "vulgar," urban, popular-cultural space of the Dublin streets, where its emergent, "Hebraic" protagonist, in search of a gift for his wife, purchases not a mere "sixshilling novel" such as AE reviles, but a work of pornography titled *Sweets of Sin*. The very title of the episode, which refers to an alternative seagoing route past Scylla and Charybdis that Odysseus, in fact, never traveled, highlights the book's intention to skirt those Revivalist alternatives by embracing the demotic realities of 1904 Ireland. Stephen's vow to "fly by those nets" comes to fruition through his author's proffer of Bloom—not merely a Jewish ad-man but an avid consumer of a host of genres defined as nationalist anathema—as his epic hero. Bloom's *flâneurie* across Dublin and the thoroughly pop-culturally oriented texture of the book's later chapters serve to demonstrate Joyce's view of the wrongheadedness of the Literary Revivalist ideologies chronicled in chapter 4 of this study, which seek to define Irishness in idealist, Arnoldian abstraction from its genuine, everyday, capitalist realities.

Not only those chapters controlled by Bloom's stream of consciousness such as "Sirens" and "Cyclops," but those centered on the consciousness of Irish women such as "Penelope" and "Nausicaa," stage with their every phrase the errancy of the Revivalist modernisms contemporary with the novel's plot. The former episode's portrait of Molly Bloom plunges the reader into a stream-of-consciousness monologue that imbricates personal recollections with references to soft-core pornography, music hall productions, newspaper accounts of divorce proceedings, and "Police Intelligence" reports. The latter episode, "Nausicaa," provides a corresponding portrait of young, Irish femininity in Gerty McDowell, whose mental landscape is replete with similar materials derived from Romance "novelettes," patent medicine advertisements, and beauty magazine advice columns. Joyce, indeed, uses "Nausicaa" to deliver a stinging joke at AE's expense, as it is in the corresponding episode of *The Odyssey* that "the life of Homer's Phaeacians"—whose Irish equivalent he would find anything but "desirable"—is depicted.[13]

*Ulysses*, then, uses Bloom to transcend the opposition between nationalist ideology and everyday, capitalist reality so memorably captured in the jejune fantasies of "Araby," and invoked through the novel's portrait of the Literary Revival. This transcendence yields a fresh aesthetic dynamic that repudiates the modernist strategies documented in the foregoing chapter, all of which sought to consolidate this opposition by demonstrating the injurious effects of popular, Anglicizing aesthetic genres. This pivotal, post-nationalist shift, which I have labeled Irish late modernism, requires some direct explication beyond the preparatory, theoretical work embodied in Stephen Dedalus. One might almost select illustrative passages at random from the later chapters of *Ulysses*, as these consist almost entirely of formal imitations—parodies, pastiches—of the pop-cultural genres modernists such as Yeats, Synge, and Stephens sought to purge from the national consciousness. For readers seeking to extend the previous chapters' narrative of Irish femininity as imperiled by such influences, "Nausicaa" and "Penelope" serve as rich veins of reference highlighting Joyce's specific rejection of this protective discourse, and his determination to chronicle Irishness in all of its "vicious" sexuality (to recall the foremost, Catholic watchword) and "vulgar" pulpiness (to recall its Literary counterpart). Idealized notions of the Irish female propounded by nationalist ideologues are ruthlessly, relentlessly deflated, until the subsumption and bathetic undermining of such notions becomes one of the novel's foremost aesthetic principles.

But perhaps the novel's best illustration not simply of the manner in which *Ulysses* shows up prevailing, nationalist ideals, but of its parallel agenda of taunting Joyce's anticapitalist, modernist precursors, occurs in its most nationalist chapter: "Cyclops." It is no coincidence that "Cyclops" is also the book's most vehemently anti-Semitic episode. It is here that the novel's portrait of Irish nationalism manifests the more tendentious and insidious potential of its Arnoldian ethnological underpinnings, the "Hebraic" term of which is not made explicit in "Telemachus" or "Scylla" aside from the brief invocations of Buck Mulligan. The figure of the Jew proves pivotally significant for the "physical force" Irish nationalism this later chapter so memorably chronicles. As Amy Feinstein has argued, the racist venom spewed by both its title character—famously a rendering of a figure mentioned briefly in chapter 4, Michael Cusack of the Gaelic Athletic Association—and by its narrator, the "Nameless One," demonstrate the tendency of Irish nationalists to deflect taboo, British political associations they fear apply to themselves onto the Jewish other.[14] Similar purgatory gestures are visible earlier in the book's other prominent anti-Semites such as Garrett Deasy, who complains that "England is in the hands of the Jews. In all the highest places: her finances, her press" (2.346–48), but whose own, Shakespearean ethos is "Put but money in thy purse" (2.239). In contrast to the Anglophilic and capitalist Deasy, the Citizen's racist treatment of Bloom in Barney Kiernan's pub displays all the hallmarks of nationalist anticapitalism. "Those are nice things . . . coming over here to Ireland filling the country with bugs" (12.1141–42), he comments in Bloom's direction after O'Molloy has reported the outcome of the "Canada swindle case," in which "one of the bottlenosed fraternity" defrauded a number of Irish men and women after promising passage to Canada for "twenty bob" (12.1086–93). The Citizen's equation of "Saxon" and "Hebraic" capitalism grows yet more pronounced as he describes the Jews as "Swindling the peasants . . . and the poor of Ireland," and quotes *Cathleen ni Houlihan* as a warrant for their deportation: "We want no more strangers in our house" (12.1150–51). Upon Bloom's exit from Kiernan's, the Citizen further tightens the equivalence between Bloom as Jew and the Saxon "invader," declaring, "Beggar my neighbor is his motto" (12.1491). The episode is careful, however, to suggest that the Citizen himself might be vulnerable to the same indictment in that he is afraid to "go down and address his talk to the assembled multitude in Shanagolden where he daren't show his nose with the Molly Maguires looking for him to let daylight through him for grabbing the holding of an evicted tenant" (1311–16). That the Citizen is reputed to have committed a scab-like exploitation of the Irish peasant clinches Joyce's suggestion that nationalist ideology is driven to a disingenuous disavowal of its participation in the capitalist practices of the "Sassenach." The Nameless One's own contradictions—working as a "collector of bad and doubtful debts" for Moses Herzog, a Jewish merchant, but spewing anti-Semitic venom throughout his narrative—serve as but one more example of such hypocrisy (12.24–25).

But it is not simply through the theory-praxis contradictions of the Citizen or the Nameless One that "Cyclops" demonstrates the "vanity" (to recall the keyword of "Araby") of Irish nationalism vis-à-vis capital. Indeed, the episode's mock-epic style lampoons both the contemporary, Celticist fantasies of Irish nationalism and the prevailing, "shoneen" popular-cultural discourses of which Irish daily realities contrarily consist. One such discourse is uniquely positioned both to deflate those fantasies and to signpost the chapter's larger departure from the protocols of the Revival's Celticist modernisms: that of The Police Intelligence. The milieu of Barney Kiernan's, located in Dublin's legal district and bedecked in memorabilia of trials, executions, and legal events of national-historical significance, is of a piece with that of the Mayo shebeen so powerfully captured in Synge's *Playboy.* Joseph Valente's reading of the Kiernan's patrons' engagement with the contents of the American-based *National Police Gazette* also helps decode their engagement with the broader, Police Intelligence–filtered legal world the chapter documents. Just as, in Valente's reading, these patrons are both repulsed and titillated by the "transgressive pleasures" the *Gazette* vicariously provides, so Joyce parodies the legal tabloid discourse of such publications to suggest that they are dually offended by the Irish subjection to British law and "turned on" by that subjection ("The Novel" 17). The chapter's suffusion with such discourse goes beyond merely suggesting that because Irish subjects partake in the consumption of British literary "garbage," the high-cultural pieties of the Celticist nationalisms invoked in "Scylla" misrepresent real, everyday Irishness, to suggest further that the burgeoning popularity of tabloid journalism helps to petrify the nationalist mind in a state of pleasurable dependence upon the prevailing imperial order.

Joyce's treatment of *Police Gazette* thus repeats the insight of Synge's *Playboy* by suggesting that Dubliners' entanglement with the budding culture industry of the metropole undermines their would-be nationalism, positioning them as consumers of both their oppression and their resistance to it. But where Synge sets Christy Mahon apart through his extrication from the effects of the colonial spectacle, in *Ulysses*, no such extrication seems possible. Instead, what the reader experiences is an incessant re-subsumption of nationalist discourse in general, and of its Celticist variety in particular, by the newly dominant, already transatlantic, and incipiently global forces of capital. One parody in particular affirms this claim, namely that which ensues upon Alf Bergan's unveiling of "hangman's letters" authored by H. Rumbold, a British executioner offering his services to the High Sheriff of Dublin. The (lengthy) parody's subject is the execution of the United Irishman, Robert Emmet:

> The deafening claps of thunder and the dazzling flashes of lighting which lit up the ghastly scene testified that the artillery of heaven had lent its supernatural pomp to the already gruesome spectacle. . . . Considerable amusement was caused by the favourite Dublin streetsingers L-n-h-n and M-ll-g-n who sang *The Night Before Larry Was Stretched*. . . . Our two inimitable drolls did a roaring trade with their broadsheets among lovers of the comedy element and nobody who has a corner in his heart for real Irish fun without vulgarity will grudge them their hardearned pennies. The children of the Male and Female Foundling Hospital who thronged the windows overlooking the scene were delighted with this unexpected addition to the day's entertainment. . . . The viceregal houseparty which included many wellknown ladies was chaperoned by Their Excellencies to the most favourable positions on the grandstand while the picturesque foreign delegation known as the Friends of the Emerald Isle was accommodated on a tribune directly opposite. . . .

> The arrival of the worldrenowned headsman was greeted by a roar of acclamation. . . .The learned prelate who administered the last comforts of holy religion to the hero martyr when about to pay the death penalty . . . offered up to the throne of grace fervent prayers of supplication. Hand by the block stood the grim figure of the executioner . . . as he awaited the fatal signal . . . of his fell but necessary office. . . . On a handsome mahogany table near him were neatly arranged the quartering knife, the various finely tempered disemboweling appliances (specially supplied by the worldfamous firm of cutlers, Messrs John Round and Sons, Sheffield). . . . Quite an excellent repast consisting of rashers and eggs, fried steak and onions, done to a nicety, delicious hot breakfast rolls and invigorating tea had been considerately provided by the authorities for the consumption of the central figure of the tragedy who was in capital spirits when prepared for death. . . . The *nec* and *non plus ultra* of emotion were reached when the blushing bride elect burst her way through the serried ranks of the bystanders and flung herself upon the muscular bosom of him who was about to be launched into eternity for her sake. . . . She swore to him as they mingled the salt streams of their tears that she would ever cherish his memory, that she would never forget her hero boy . . . and, oblivious of the dreadful present, they both laughed heartily, all the spectators, including the venerable pastor, joining in the general merriment. That monster audience simply rocked with delight. (12.525–668)

This fascinating passage stages the subsumption of the nationalist significance of the "hero martyr," Emmet, by the sensational devices of tabloid journalism. A "ghastly," "gruesome spectacle" of the very same kind that fascinates the Mayo villagers in *Playboy*, Emmet's execution becomes an "entertainment," before which Viceregal and nationalist-affiliated delegations alike emit a "roar of acclamation." Political antagonisms dissolve beneath an array of literary techniques derived not only from Police Intelligence–style reportage but from other genres such as Romance fiction, catalog advertisement, and society column gossip-mongering. The combined "monster audience"—itself an allusion to the midcentury mass meetings organized by the Young Ireland "Liberator" Daniel O'Connell—"simply rock[s] with delight," bursting the bounds of national and factional allegiance. Joyce's use of the phrase "in capital spirits" in his depiction of the commodifying discourses that dissolve the pathetic force of tragedy and render this canonical event fodder for comedy could hardly be more apt.

This parody ties the mature aesthetic of *Ulysses* to the many threads adduced thus far, all of which serve to mark the distance of Joyce's agenda from the anticapitalist Celticism of the Revival. The novel's reconstruction of Stephen Dedalus's struggles to break free of the Arnoldian assumptions of the 1904 Irish literary world point the way toward such passages, wherein the false fantasies of contemporary nationalism take their rightful place amid the broader, metrocolonial array of cultural-industrial discourses they would repudiate. If the arrival of Leopold Bloom in Stephen Dedalus's life provides for the practical rescue of the latter's Celticism-inflected, impoverished aestheticism—according to the twin principles of "jewgreek meets greekjew" and of a "Hebraic" corrective to "sentimentality"—so it likewise provides for the reunion of that aestheticism with the entity of which it claimed to be the representative: Irishness itself. The novel's early chapters mark the young Joyce's dissatisfaction both with prevailing, Revivalist philosophies, and with his own, high-cultural conception of Irish art, while its later ones release such tensions through a ludic and bathetic embrace of all those values—"Saxon," "Hebraic," capitalist—those notions conceived as anathema. *Ulysses* thus becomes the signal post-Revivalist text, conducting an autopsy on both the theoretical and practical failures of the Celticist anticapitalism of Irish nationalism and Revivalist modernism. Its ebullient embrace of the aesthetics of the colonial spectacle provides a preview of the broader fate not just of Irish modernity, which would soon abandon the alternative ideals of the Revival, but of those later Irish modernisms that bore witness to that abandonment, all of which would replicate some version of the novel's all-encompassing, value-dissolving aesthetic flux.[15]

## OFFICIAL IDEOLOGIES AND CULTURAL REALITIES IN IRELAND AFTER 1922

In the wake of the Irish Civil War, the newly established Free State government ushered in an official milieu in keeping with the tenets of the Catholic faction of Revivalist nationalism, thereby attempting to foment from the top down the regenerated, post-British civilization that had long been that nationalism's dream. The vast body of historical research chronicling this early independent period emphasizes such repressive measures as the Censorship of Films Act (1923), the 1925 Dáil Éirann bill to outlaw divorce, and the Censorship of Publications Act (1929), as some of the most significant steps taken by W.T. Cosgrave's Cumann na nGaedheal government toward such fomentation. These measures reflect the thorough continuity between prominent turn-of-the-century nationalists such as D.P. Moran and the ideology of the figures superintending the Free State in its opening decade, and have led to an impression that Irish life at this time deviated wholesale from both the shoneen mores of the colonial period and the aesthetically minded, cosmopolitan resistance to such mores by the Literary faction of the Revival. A "joint pastoral" issued by the Irish Catholic hierarchy—the agency that was to have perhaps the greatest influence in crafting both official state policy and, particularly through its control of the nation's educational system, everyday life during this period—in 1927 reflects the extent to which such longstanding popular notions informed these measures, declaring, "the evil one is ever setting his snares for unwary feet. At the moment, his traps for the innocent are chiefly the dance hall, the bad book, the indecent paper, the motion picture, the immodest fashion in female dress—all of which tend to destroy the characteristics of our race" (qtd. in Brown, *Ireland* 33). Aside from the addition of "the motion picture," these sentiments evince total continuity with the Catholic contingent of Revivalist nationalism, which, as we saw in chapter 4, sought to define Ireland's immersion in British capital as a dangerously ontologically expansive state of affairs. Presented for the first time with a practical opportunity for choosing between a repressive or expansive set of ideals, the Free State government affirmed an unequivocal commitment to the former, to the detriment of those cosmopolitan values so passionately promoted by the Revival's Literary participants.

Following the global economic crisis of the late 1920s, an event whose nightmarish fallout seemed to recommend a further severance of Irish ties with capital, the Irish public opted to install the Fianna Fáil party of Éamon de Valera, a veteran nationalist who participated in the Easter Rising, in power in 1932, in part to effectuate such severance. De Valera's loyalty to the economic doctrines of Griffith's Sinn Féin, central among them "self-sufficiency," "exploitation of native resources," and the pursuit of "industrial development behind protective tariffs," affirmed the State's endorsement of longstanding anti-British economic thinking as a response to contemporary exigency (Daly, *Industrial* 38). De Valera's broadcast on the state-sponsored station, Radio Éireann, on 6 February, 1933, in which he called on Ireland to help "save Western civilization from the scourge of materialism," further reflects the endurance of Revivalist anticapitalism under Fianna Fáil's rule from 1932 to 1948 (Brown, *Ireland* 31), as would, even more emphatically, his oft-cited broadcast on St. Patrick's Day, March 17, 1943, six years after a new Constitution had given birth to the first fully independent Irish state, Éire, and in the midst of the "Emergency" measures taken by the new government in response to the continental rage of World War II:

> The Ireland we have dreamed of would be the home of a people who valued material wealth only as a basis of right living, of a people who were satisfied with frugal comfort and devoted their leisure to the things of the spirit; a land whose countryside would be bright with cosy homesteads, whose villages would be joyous with the romping of sturdy children, the contests of athletic youths, the laughter of comely maidens; whose fireside would be the forums of the wisdom of old age. It would, in a word, be the home of a people living the life that God desires that men should live. (qtd. in Garvin, 35)

De Valera's vision of an Ireland whose citizens "valued material wealth only as a basis of right living," who would be "satisfied with frugal comfort" and whose "leisure" activities would bespeak a commitment to "the things of the spirit," as a sort of mission statement of the newly founded state, incarnates the Revivalist dream of establishing an Irish economic sphere whose links with global capitalism would be as slender and few as possible, and whose practices would accord with perceived "native" values. Irish macroeconomic policy during the 1930s and '40s thus extended the motivation underlying the microeconomic legislation of the Free State in the '20s by aligning Irish society yet more closely Catholic Revivalism's vision of the Irish nation as "the home of a people living the life that God desires that men should live."[16]

Yet, in recent years, a modified account of Irish reality in the decades following independence has emerged that suggests that the nation's severance of ties with an increasingly global capitalist modernity was far from complete. As Brian Fallon's *An Age of Innocence: Irish Culture 1930–1960* argues, though official state and Church proclamations and policies during this period projected an image of Ireland that accorded with Revivalist ideals, the nation's popular-cultural reality in fact closely resembled its shoneen predecessor. As Fallon describes, circa 1930, "English importations flooded the market, censors or no censors," feeding an ongoing, ever-increasing popular taste for "thrillers, Westerns, popular love stories . . . and their like"—literary and cinematic—and a general "Anglo-American domination" of Irish culture (11). In Fallon's estimation, "when all this is taken into account, the accepted picture of a culturally chauvinistic statelet shutting its doors on international currents turns out, in several respects, to be almost the reverse of the truth"; "instead, Ireland, badly in need of developing a national culture of her own, was hopelessly outgunned by external forces—mainly commercial—over which her leaders had little control, and few institutions or public bodies knew how to combat these forces effectively" (11). The alternative modernity toward which Revivalist nationalism labored seems, given this more comprehensive, bottom-up picture of the newly independent nation, never to have arisen, in spite of the best efforts of de Valera and his administrative and clerical compatriots. In its place, there instead emerged an Ireland still immured in the pop-cultural forms identified during the Revival as the foremost threat to autonomy from the civilization of the "Saxon robber."

The composite portrait constructed here, of an independent Ireland attempting to realize the nation's longstanding ideal of extrication from capitalist modernity through censorship and tariffs but unable to combat an ever-mounting tide of popular culture emanating from that modernity, provides the background against which Irish Late Modernism after Joyce emerges as a coherent movement. Each of the late-modernist practitioners this chapter will move on to survey—the late Yeats, Flann O'Brien, and Samuel Beckett—was inspired by this complex array of contradictory social conditions, and, most importantly, by the marked deviation of such conditions from the ideals of the Revival, especially the Celticist ideals of its Literary faction. Aligning themselves with the "cosmopolitan" tenor of this faction, but perceiving, like Joyce, an actually existing Irishness instead both ontologically repressive and culturally "vulgar," these writers cultivate an "aesthetics of failure" (in Miller's phrase) whose primary target is the Celticist modernism of the Literary Revival. Irish Late Modernism after Joyce, training its gaze on the results of almost four decades of Revivalist nationalism, chronicles the manner in which those results incarnate a set of values and cultural practices entirely at odds with that nationalism's anticapitalist, Celticist ideals. Whether emphasizing the repressive Catholicism of Irish life under the Free State and Éire or the ongoing Irish immersion in popular-cultural habits of consumption associated by the Revival with an Anglicizing capitalism, the aesthetic aim of Irish Late Modernism is a constant: to demonstrate the collapse of the Revival's Celticist ideals by staging both their reification and the bathetic deflation of the modernist aesthetic practices that were their most potent vehicle. In short, Irish Late Modernism narrates the destruction and collapse of the alternative modernity envisioned by Revivalist nationalism amid an Ireland increasingly suffused by the globalizing forces of capital.

## "IF FOLLY LINK WITH ELEGANCE": CAPITALISM AND TRAGICOMEDY IN LATE YEATS

In the previous chapter, we saw how both the Revivalist nationalism and the modernism of W.B. Yeats were pivotally bound up with considerations of genre. Yeats's early Celticism hinges on the amenability of the Arnoldian Celt to the aesthetic and ontological elevation he associated with tragedy, and which he opposed to the vulgarity of empire and capital. Such works as *The Land of Heart's Desire* thus position the Celt's primordial "ecstacy" as an Adornoan and Nietszchean alternative to the homogeneous, empty time of British capitalist modernity. Not merely through the Celt's critical, contrastive potential, but through cultivation of the high-cultural key of his "titanic" features, Yeats hoped to usher an Anglicized Irish populace into a new state of "tragic" transcendence. His later retreat into an elitist spurning of the nationalist movement was, in turn, inspired by encounters with the "vulgar" taste of the Irish populace and the popular forces he viewed as retrenching British sensibilities. Such retrenchment centrally transpired through the consumption of degraded genres such as melodrama—whose associations with *Cathleen ni Houlihan* he anxiously denied—and that longstanding Revivalist foil, (musical) comedy. The latter, indeed, served as the antagonist of a generic master narrative through which Yeats envisioned Ireland's decolonization and extrication from capital. As he put the matter in a *Land*-era essay on the poetry of Sir Samuel Ferguson, "This faithfulness to things tragic and bitter, to thoughts that wear one's life out and scatter one's joy, the Celt has above all others. Those who have it, alone are worthy of great causes. Those who have it not, have in them some vein of hopeless levity, the harlequins of the earth" (53).

Yeats maintained this narrative, by which Irish independence would embody a tragic departure from the "harlequin" comedy of colonial capitalism, throughout his life; only his perception of Ireland's position along its continuum would change. This claim is borne out by the poem that in many ways marks the beginning of Yeats's aesthetic response to the Ireland of the postcolonial era, "Easter, 1916." The poem's account of the significance of the Easter Rising and the martyrdom of its participants openly affirms their tragic transcendence: in place of a colonial Ireland "where motley [was] worn," a world of "casual comedy," the martyrs' "sacrifice" performatively establishes a new national era of sublime, "terrible beauty" (lines 14–40). This "transformation" is not merely a nascent, postcolonial one, but encompasses the jettisoning of the capitalist modalities with which British rule was coextensive.

The poem opens by recalling routine encounters "at close of day"—a phrase that smacks of familiar economic terminology such as "close of business" and "end of day"—amid the same office- and shop-based settings, "counter" and "desk," which earlier, anti-popular Yeats poems such as "September, 1913" had so scathingly castigated (1–3). This "polite, meaningless" workaday world, however, once the inspiration for "mocking tale[s]" and "gibe[s]," has been "transformed utterly," such that the very temporality of its comedic routines must be rethought (10). Yeats's speaker, in search of a metaphor for the martyrdom's finality, lights first upon the image of "nightfall" that earlier marked the "close of day," but such conventional signifiers of duration no longer serve: "No, no, not night but death" (66). The future Ireland whose arrival the occasion may mark will escape the homogeneous, empty time of capital, just as its citizens in "time to be" will exchange the "harlequin" garb of the British culture industry for a Celtic "green" (78–79).[17]

"Easter" may also signal the fulfillment of the "tragic," anticapitalist potential of Yeats's Celt through its emphasis on the faculty for which that figure had been noted from his pre-Arnoldian inception in the work of Ernest Renan: dreaming. As described by Yeats himself in "The Celtic Element in Literature," Renan's "Celtic race . . . 'has worn itself out in mistaking dreams for realities" (173). It is these "thoughts," perhaps, that lead the Celt of Yeats's Ferguson to "wear [his] life out and scatter [his] joy," just as they feed forward, in his reading, to inspire the cardinal feature of the Celt of Matthew Arnold: "a passionate, turbulent, indomitable reaction against the despotism of fact" (173). While averring the Celtic tendency to react against the specific "despotisms" of empire and capital, however, Yeats's revolutionaries achieve something remarkable: "their dream," an "excess of love" likened to a "stone / To trouble the living stream," transfigures the domain of "fact" itself, displacing its comedic status quo through the Celt's tragic "turn" (43–44, 70, 38). Not simply defying the stereotype of Celtic impracticality, but defying it through the pragmatic fulfillment of those very same, aestheticized, "dreaming" tendencies long thought to underlie his "wearing out," the poem may be read to augur nothing less than the achievement of an alternative, Celticist modernity.

This fulfillment, however, is only provisional. In addition to the poem's many markers of ambivalence toward the Rising—among them the question of whether Home Rule might have been achieved without it—its anxieties also stem from uncertainty regarding the Irish future that will follow the tragic break.[18] As Elizabeth Butler Cullingford has recently put the matter, "the tragic mode does not on the face of it offer much practical assistance to a colonized people hoping to throw off the imperial yoke" (45). Though this observation more regards the practical, political contradictions of what the previous chapter of this study labeled the "rebirth of Celtic tragedy," and though, as we have seen, this rebirth was often, for Yeats, more an aesthetic than a practical matter, its insight regarding the challenge of converting Celticist ideals into an embodied, independent Irishness is a crucial one. Would the Ireland whose arrival the Rising set in motion, and whose formation followed the 1919–21 War of Independence and the Irish Civil War of 1922–23, bear out the projections of "Easter" by jettisoning not just Empire, but the capitalist norms that bedecked the nation in "motley"? As suggested in the foregoing overview of Irish political and cultural trends of the '20s and '30s, there would be ample basis for a mindset such as Yeats's to answer in the negative. Indeed, while there is evidence that Yeats reserved judgment regarding the nation's direction in the immediate wake of independence, he would ultimately conclude that Ireland under the Free State and Éire regimes recrudesced into many of the same "comedic" tendencies that defined the colonial era.

While it would thus maintain his lifelong opposition between British, capitalist comedy and an Irish tragic mode linked inextricably to his early Celticism, as his work progressed in response to the events of the '20s and '30s, it underwent an unprecedented shift. In contrast to the received narrative of Yeats's career—according to which, following his early Celticism, he would embrace the minority ideals of the Anglo-Irish "Big House" in his middle period and the racist and authoritarian doctrines of eugenics and Fascism in his final years—his 1930s work reveals a further phase which, in many ways, repudiates the putative, hermetically sealed elitism of the previous two. This work reveals a "late" turn that has only recently begun to be appreciated by scholars, with the recent edited collection *Yeats and Afterwords* (Howes and Valente) being perhaps the leading example.[19] With regard to this study's narrative of Yeats's Celticist anticapitalism, his late drama and poetry reveal a surprising twist whereby he no longer simply depicted the nation as yet-ensnared by shoneen, capitalist mores, while he himself stood apart in fulfillment of the Celt's alternative, high-cultural potential. Rather, a careful reading of his late work reveals that the very opposition between comedic and tragic values begins to break down. More than simply asserting that the late Yeats admitted his own marginality and "defeat" at the hands of a still-capitalist, majority Catholic Ireland, this reading suggests that Yeats would allow those forces to inflect and shape his work as never before. By attending to his late work's handling of the comedic/tragic opposition in which he continued to encode the binary of Celt and capital, the reader can witness the remarkable development by which his late work stages not simply the collapse of his nationalist project, but its absorption by the very "vulgar," comedic values he opposed throughout his life.

As late as 1932—for instance, in the essay "Ireland, 1921–1931," published in *The Spectator* on June 2—Yeats can be found uttering positive sentiments about the fledgling Free State government, in spite of several earlier confrontations, primary among them the 1925 Senate debate over outlawing divorce, in which his and its stated values came into direct conflict.[20] For the duration of his life, however, one witnesses a mounting displeasure with the nation's official and cultural tendencies that, beginning with *Parnell's Funeral* in 1935, seems precipitated especially by the policies of de Valera's Fianna Fáil. The title poem presents a scene in which a gathering of Irish citizens before Parnell's tomb bespeaks the ignominious role of popular opinion in destroying the nationalist leader's career, reputation, and life. Yeats writes, with a bitterness reinvigorated by current events, that "all that was said in Ireland is a lie / Bred out of the contagion of the throng," thus calling into question whether even the halcyon nationalism of the fin-de-siècle period can any longer pretend to freedom from the "low" influence of the "crowd" (lines 26–27). He speculates that recent Irish history might have run along a different course "had de Valera eaten Parnell's heart" and thereby infused his government with the "bitter wisdom" that "enriched" the latter's "blood" (II, 2, 12). Instead, however, Ireland is at the mercy of a "loose-lipped demagogue" whose "school" was that very popular "contagion" (II, 3). The poem's final stanza measures the distance between Yeats's former ideals, both Revivalist and "Big House," and the current Irish status quo, as its speaker, catching himself in the act of composing a list of national figures that resembles the heroic roll of honor in "Easter, 1916," suppresses his bardic impulses to declare, "I name no more" (9). In the Free State of the 1930s, the high offices of bardic commemoration are vacant, the ideals that were their raison d'être being brought low by the forces of popular nationalism.

The later poem "Church and State" makes clear that the Catholic values that so deeply inform such nationalism are at the root of Yeats's disapproval. "What if the Church and the State / Are the mob that howls at the door! / Wind shall run thick to the end / Bread taste sour," its speaker bemoans, suggesting that an alliance of the Catholic and Free State/Éire hierarchies has spurred Ireland's descent into "mob" (lines 9–12). As several of the poems from the penultimate volume Yeats would release before his death, *New Poems* (1938), make clear, however, Yeats's definition of "mob" hinges to just as great an extent on capitalism. In "The Curse of Cromwell," the speaker complains that "Nothing but Cromwell's house and Cromwell's murderous crew" rules the land, driving out the "lovers," "dancers," "tall men," and "horsemen" who have indexed national ontological plenitude throughout Yeats's career (2–4). The poem's second stanza specifies capital as perhaps this decline's central catalyst, whereby "All neighborly content and easy talk are gone / . . . for money's rant is on" (9–10). In such a dystopia, "He that's mounting up must on his neighbor mount / And we and all the Muses are things of no account" (9–12). Yeats continues to identify in contemporary Ireland the capitalist characteristics he has always defined as British, and the nation's ongoing enthrallment by "money's rant" defines its popular mores as yet shaped by colonial norms. In such an Anglicized, capitalist Ireland, both "neighborly" intercourse and the values of the "Muses" are "things of no account."

Even more direct indictments of contemporary Ireland's failure to throw off its capitalist chains arrive in "The Great Day" and "Parnell." The former undercuts its opening patriotism, "Hurrah for revolution and more cannon shot," by defining both the period before revolution, in which "a beggar on horseback lashes a beggar on foot," and the period after, in which "the beggars have changed places but the lash goes on," as controlled by what I (following Moishe Postone) have called *social domination*—a capitalist system in which all participants regardless of class position experience an ontological siphoning of their vital energies (1–4). The Ireland before revolution, where the Anglo-Irish "beggar on horseback" was preeminent, is identical to that which has succeeded, where the subaltern, Catholic class, the "beggar on foot," has gained the upper hand, by virtue of the utter lack of departure from the systemic "beggaring" of the human subject under capital. The two-line poem "Parnell," portraying a brusque encounter between the leader and a "cheering man" to whom he prophesies, "Ireland shall get her freedom and you still break stone," puts the same argument yet more succinctly (1–2). To the mid-to-late-'30s Yeats, Ireland bears all the marks of continued immersion in the British colonial order, as its subjects continue to "break stone" under capitalist domination.

But it is not only in those poems whose primary subject is capital that Yeats defines Ireland as yet subject to its "low" dictates. Even in those texts whose predominant focus is eugenic, Yeats gestures toward capital as a powerful catalyst of national "degeneration."[21] His most eugenic play, *Purgatory*, advances this implication through the downfall of the ancestral, "Big House" genetic line of the "Old Man." The play's argument, in which the "Old Man," finding his son unreceptive to warnings about the cause of their house's demise, murders him in an attempt to "finish . . . all that consequence" attending his mother's errant choice of a groom as a sexual and marital partner, is Yeats's most fully realized embodiment of the eugenic prescriptions of the contemporaneous prose tract *On the Boiler.*[22] The Old Man links the lowly occupation to which he has been reduced, that of a "peddler on the roads" (433), with his mother's degenerate desire by defining it as "no good trade, but good enough / Because I am my father's son, / Because of what I did or may do" (433). Finding his lessons regarding the proper, class-bound outlet for noble female desire unheeded by his son—who, in response to his assertion that when his mother's "mother never spoke to her again, / . . . she did right," displays his own degeneracy by asking, "What's right and wrong? / My grand-dad got the girl and the money," and by then attempting to "to slip away" with the "bag of money" accumulated through the Old Man's labors (434)—the latter determines to halt his line's downward genetic spiral with a "jack knife," just as he murdered his mother's lover sixteen years earlier (431). The Old Man hopes this act will right the family legacy and free his mother's trapped soul according to the Catholic principle that transgressions "upon others" may be atoned for by others, while those begotten "upon [oneself]" must be absolved by God (431), but, upon reaching out to retrieve the money, he again hears the "hoof-beats" that announce his father's drunken arrival and a further reenactment of his mother's sexual crime (436). Irish degeneration proceeds in tandem with capital's ascension, and the debased Irish populace embodied in the Boy's money-grubbing proclivities will bear in its awry genetic code a marked capitalist trait.

The Old Man's eugenic murder represents an attempt to eradicate degenerate, capitalist values by redemptive force. Inspired, however, by the muse of Irish late modernism, this attempt fails, and the alternative values professed by the Old Man collapse back into the low sexual and economic domain that inspired them. In the world of Yeats's late dramaturgy, a degenerate, sexually indiscriminate, capitalistic Irish status quo smothers any attempt to revive the high aims of Revivalist nationalism. Nowhere is this warning borne out more than in those late works that engage with questions of genre, all of which stumble in the effort to recapture and revive the "tragic" ideals of Yeats's Celticist nationalism. Yeats's late aesthetic goes beyond a mere return to pre-independence practices of comedic recrimination to suggest that in contemporary Ireland, not only is a tragic elevation of the nation no longer viable; the very distinction between tragedy and comedy no longer makes sense. This Ireland is, to Yeats's eyes, so suffused with "low" values as to render any "high" alternative inconceivable. In this regard, perhaps the most fitting epigraph for his late turn is offered by the *New Poems* work "The Old Stone Cross," whose speaker declares,

Because this age and the next age
Engender in the ditch,
No man can know a happy man
From any passing wretch
If Folly link with Elegance
No man knows which is which. (lines 9–14)

This stanza combines Yeats's newfound, eugenic mode of valuation with his longstanding, generic one to argue that in the benighted Ireland of the present "age," which "engender[s]" in the symbolic "ditch," the "folly" of comedy and the "elegance" of tragedy are indistinguishable. The Ireland of Yeats's early "dreams" has been subsumed by the homogeneous, empty time of capitalist modernity so completely that even his own art capitulates to its bathetic trajectory.

To corroborate this late complication in Yeats's generic mythopoesis, we need look no further than *The Death of Cuchulain* (1939). The play's jarring opening speech, delivered, according to stage directions, by an unmistakable Yeats avatar, "A very old man looking like something out of mythology," partakes of the traditional Yeatsian indictment against popular Irishness, but goes further to suggest that the crucial value distinction on which that indictment hinges can no longer be confidently drawn (438). The "Old Man" informs his audience, "I have been asked to produce a play called *The Death of Cuchulain* . . . I have been selected because I am out of fashion and out of date like the antiquated romantic stuff the thing is made of," thus distancing his high, mythological values from the current "fashion" he assumes they collectively obey (438). That this late play requires an overtly antagonistic frame itself bespeaks the extent to which the "elegance" of the "antiquated" ideals of Yeats's nationalism has been eclipsed by the "folly" of contemporary Irish reality, but it is the interlinkage and mutual indistinction of these opposed sets of values that is most noteworthy. The Old Man's description that "When they told me that I could have my own way, I wrote certain guiding principles on a bit of newspaper," is a fitting encapsulation of such "linkage" (438). Though the arrangement of this "guiding" charter is not specified, the "principles" in question must either be consigned to the margins left untouched by the journalism of the "throng"—in which case their relationship to such discourses is self-evident—or superimposed *over* it—in which case those discourses' infection of the play is even more "contagious" (438).

Yeats's ability to "have his own way" is not, in the latter scenario, simply circumscribed by the current status quo; it is thoroughly infused with it and can only take the form of a palimpsest on its more "fashionable" content. But it is the Old Man's complaint that he is unable to "find a good dancer" to perform the role of Emer, who later dances about the severed head of Cuchulain "in adoration or triumph" (445), that offers the most glaring evidence for the parallel indistinction of aesthetic and national-historic genres:

> I was at my wit's end to find a good dancer; I could have got such a dancer once, but she has gone; the tragi-comedian dancer, the tragic dancer, upon the same neck love and loathing, life and death, I spit three times. . . . I spit upon the Dancers painted by Degas. I spit upon their short bodices, their stiff stays, their toes whereon they spin like peg-tops, above all upon that chambermaid face. They might have looked timeless . . . but not the chambermaid, the old maid history. I spit, I spit, I spit. (439)

The old man's definition of the prevailing aesthetic norm among dancers as a "tragi-comedian" one that fails to distinguish between properly distinct emotions and states such as "love and loathing, life and death," affirms the unbreakable "link" between Yeats's late aesthetic and the debased materials of Irish modernity. Yeats must now utilize low generic means in pursuit of high-cultural ends. The "chambermaid face" of such dancers indexes their degeneracy, but no matter how vehemently he spits on them or the downward-spiraling history they incarnate, the Old Man has no alternative but to *employ* them.

The extent to which capitalism informs the Old Man's vision of historical degeneration is indicated by Yeats's choice to delegate the decapitation of his preeminent Celtic hero to "the Blind Man of 'On Baile's Strand,'" who, driven by the promise "that if I brought Cuchulain's head in a bag / I would be given twelve pennies," reduces this tragic symbol to the comedic plane of exchange value (444). It would seem, however, that the play's concluding verses, uttered by the "Street Singer" who, in its opening speech, the Old Man vowed to "teach . . . the music of the beggarman, Homer's music" (438–39), protectively enclose a kernel of high aesthetic and cultural value through their evocation of the statue of Cuchulain installed in the Dublin General Post Office. Unlike in the late poem "The Statues," however, in which this momument symbolizes the "proper dark" of a "plummet-measured" Irishness set apart from the "formless, spawning fury" of the "modern tide" in which actually existing Irishness is engulfed (28–32), the import of this closing song, recited in tandem with "the music of some Irish fair of our day," is far from stable (445). First, the "Street-Singer" places the "elegant" music of Homer in the mouth of a "harlot," who "sings to the beggar man" about Celtic heroes, "Conall, Cuchulain, Usna's boys, / All that most ancient race," but whose degenerate sexuality calls into question her fitness to deliver such encomia (445). Second, as the song proceeds, it becomes clear that as a result of Ireland's continued immersion in the "tide" against which the play's title character once warred in "tragic ecstasy," the values such an act would instantiate are now only imperfectly comprehensible. "I adore those clever eyes, / Those muscular bodies, but can get / No grip upon their thighs," the "harlot" complains, and continues by describing that instead of such heroic meat, "the flesh my flesh has gripped / I both adore and loathe" (445). The compound of adoration and loathing to which contemporary "flesh" gives rise in the "harlot" serves as an affective corollary to the tragicomedy described at the play's outset, rendering physiologically the generic indistinction the Old Man bemoans in the prevailing dancing "fashion."

If it would seem that the song's final two stanzas enshrine a high, nationally resonant set of values through their "Statues"-esque litany of ruminations on "what" it was that "stood in the Post Office / With Pearse and Connolly" on Easter 1916, this impression is undercut by the lines, "No body like his body / Has modern woman borne, / But an old man looking on life / Imagines it in scorn" (446). As David Lloyd has memorably shown, Yeats's mature poetics adopts a syntactic indeterminacy in protest of the rigid, monological values emanating from the Free State government.[23] In the preceding lines, such an indeterminacy obtains with regard to the antecedent of the final pronoun, "it." Does the "it" "imagine[d] . . . in scorn" by the "old man" refer to "life," or to the very "body" of Cuchulain whose "lineaments" would seem to incarnate Yeats's nationalism? If the former, a high, tragic, "proper" set of ideals might indeed be set apart from the play's "tide" of tragi-comic leveling, but if the latter, then those very high ideals might be the object of "scorn" rather than the "life" that is busy dismantling them. This last possibility, considering the Old Man's bitter self-description as an "antiquated" piece of "mythology," cannot readily be dismissed, and the play's closing verses might therefore be read not as "dancing" before Cuchulain's statue, Emer-like "in adoration or triumph," but instead as a renunciation of the figure who, throughout Yeats's career, has perhaps most embodied his ideals. Having already referred to the "popular" audience for whom he expects the play to be performed, one made up of "people who are educating themselves out of the Book Societies and the like," as "pickpockets" in the play's opening monologue, this reading strongly points to the idea that Yeats viewed contemporary Ireland and its adulterated,

State-sponsored nationalism as having stolen his foremost icon, repurposed it for comedic purposes, and thereby converted it to an object of "scorn" in the eyes of his creator. Removed from his aesthetic control and subjected to popular iconography, Cuchulain has been degradingly converted to a kind of currency, in perfect correspondence to the fate of his severed head, exchanged by the Blind Man for a handful of coins. That the interpretive choice between this, negative reading of the closing lines and the alternative, positive one is syntactically undecidable only further reinforces the play's endorsement of the generic-historical assessment of "The Old Stone Cross."[24]

A further, yet more powerful endorsement of that assessment is offered by the poem which, more than any other, incarnates the defeatism and fatigue of Yeats's late aesthetic, "The Circus Animals' Desertion." "Being but a broken man" at this final moment of his life and career (line 3), Yeats reviews the menagerie of figures accumulated during more than half a century of devotion to the nationalist cause—"that sea-rider Oisin," The Countess Cathleen, Cuchulain—and finds them all equally compromised by their lowly origins in the "vain" "dreams" of his "embittered heart" (11–13). Unable to imagine an alternative "theme" to transcend the predicament by which each ideal is stained by the low-cultural materials that inspired it, Yeats, in keeping with the bathetic linkage adumbrated by his other late plays and poems, instead undertakes an even more merciless demolition of his former work:

> Those masterful images because complete
> Grew in pure mind but out of what began?
> A mound of refuse or the sweepings of a street,
> Old kettles, old bottles, and a broken can,
> Old iron, old bones, old rags, that raving slut
> Who keeps the till. Now that my ladder's gone
> I must lie down where all ladders start
> In the foul rag and bone shop of the heart. (33–40)

Yeats methodically dismantles the "masterful images" that "grew" to "completeness" and ideal perfection in his "pure mind" by tracing their origins in the detritus of a decidedly urban and capitalist modernity, the world of "refuse," street "sweepings," scrap "iron," abandoned, "broken" utensils, moldering clothes, and "raving," slatternly cashiers that gave rise to the "ladder" of his entire literary, political, and personal life.

The aesthetic hallmark of Irish late modernism, the deflation of the Revival's Celticist ideals by the same capitalist forces that inspired them, could hardly be more fittingly rendered than in the poem's closing couplet, in which Yeats's "heart's desire" collapses in a heap in the same symbolic locale he viewed as the epitome of anathema, the "shop." No aspect of Yeats's nationalism, from his early Celticism to his "Big House" and eugenic phases, was as vehement or steadfast as his assault on the Irish "shopkeeping" mores he identified as emanating from the shoneen hegemony of "the Puritan and the Merchant." Yeats's earliest writings had sought to rezone these Irish values as unnatural imports of a vulgar, British capitalism, while in later moments of heightened national significance like the "Playboy Riots" and the Easter Rising, he would try the nation and find it worthy or wanting based on its seeming adherence to or departure from them.[25] The latter event, in particular, as we have seen, appeared to him to signify the potential broaching of an alternative, postcolonial and post-capitalist Irish modernity, one whose "tragic," Celticist textures would be set in relief against the "grey," comic routines of "counter and desk." It is, thus, difficult to conceive of a more fitting gesture by which to declare the bankruptcy of the nationalist "dream" than for Yeats to define his career-long contribution to it as itself but one more instance of the "shopkeeping," retail practice of buying and selling.

## "THE HIGHEST AND THE LOWEST IN THE SAME STORY": *AT SWIM-TWO-BIRDS*

Flann O'Brien's *At Swim-Two-Birds* has been nominated for membership in a large array of aesthetic categories over the past several decades, from "postmodernism" to "absurdism" and the "carnivalesque" tradition of Mennipean satire.[26] While the novel's formal plasticity certainly renders it amenable to such labels, amid its shifting sea of signifiers, several buoys of meaning emerge that perhaps align it best with Irish late modernism. What distinguishes this movement from such protean designations is not so much its historical sensibility—Irish late modernism, as with late modernism as a general phenomenon, partakes of an incipient phase of a now-global regime of capitalist reification, and is thus homologous in many of its formal tendencies to postmodernism—but that it aims this sensibility at a set of values that are inextricably tied to the modernist moment. In the case of *At Swim*, the novel's primary concern is to demonstrate the extent to which the distinctions that drove both the nationalism and the Celticist modernisms of the Revival—between high and popular culture; Catholic morality and modern depravity; literary creation and capitalist production—have become untenable as a result of '30s Ireland's suffusion by the relentlessly destabilizing forces of capital. In this regard, the novel's primary model is *Ulysses*, a text in which the constituent elements of Irishness are incessantly melded together in the teeming cauldron of reification. Where the novel differs from its predecessor is in its later historical vantage, being written after roughly a decade and a half of independence, and in a Literary Revival-esque depiction of the nation's continued, "low" proclivities as aesthetically anathema. Despite these Literary allegiances, however, O'Brien's aesthetic corroborates the prognostications of Joyce, as, in the novel's madcap world, the reification of Irishness becomes its defining characteristic.

The novel's narrator raises the topic of modernism repeatedly both in his expositions and in conversation with his college classmate and confidante, Brinsley. He stocks his bedroom with books "recognized as indispensable to all who aspire to an appreciation of contemporary literature" (3), among them works by Huxley and Joyce, and his oft-quoted explanation of the "daemon" of his own work-in-progress further declares his modernist allegiances:

> The novel, in the hands of an unscrupulous writer, could be despotic. . . . A satisfactory novel should be a self-evident sham to which the reader could regulate at will the degree of his credulity. It was undemocratic to compel characters to be uniformly good or bad or poor or rich. Each should be allowed a private life, self-determination and a decent standard of living. This would make for self-respect, contentment and better service. . . . Characters should be interchangeable as between one book and another. The entire corpus of existing literature should be regarded as a limbo from which discerning authors could draw their characters as required, creating only when they failed to find a suitable existing puppet. The modern novel should be largely a work of reference. . . . A wealth of references to existing works would acquaint the reader instantaneously with the nature of each character, would obviate tiresome explanations and would effectively preclude mountebanks, upstarts, thimbleriggers and persons of inferior education from an understanding of contemporary literature. (19–20)

At different points, the passage advocates for both a high-modernist elitism—according to which the "modern novel" should, à la *The Waste Land*, incorporate a "wealth of references" to "preclude . . . persons of inferior education from an understanding of contemporary literature"—and a similarly Eliotic conception of modern authorship as the addition of individual talent to an existing tradition. Along with such elitist erudition, the utopian freedom promised the characters populating such a novel may be taken as further invoking the larger modernist goal of compensating for material dissatisfactions with aesthetic autonomy.

Such hallmark modernist aims, however, immediately dehisce into the mutually negating poles of Irish late modernism. Are the novel's readers subject to the writer's mastery, or may they disregard it? Is the purpose of the "wealth of references" to "preclude" reader access, or to sate authorial laziness? Does the novel enshrine high culture, an "appreciation of contemporary literature," or is any attempt at such enshrinement a "self-evident sham"? The narrator poses, yet provides only the most contradictory answers to, these perennial questions. And while it may seem that such instabilities flow mainly from O'Brien's irrepressible comic muse, what one discovers throughout the novel is not, in fact, a mere ludic or satiric irreverence, but a flux of meaning driven by capitalist reification. Brinsley's discovery that "there are two ways to make big money . . . to write a book or to make a book," a principle that asserts the identical functionality of authorship and bookmaking, or gambling, as routes to a financial windfall, immediately destabilizes the "great divide" between the author's high-modernist ethos and the low-cultural materials associated with "persons of inferior education" (19). When the novel itself begins to deploy the strategy of "reference" portended by the narrator's manifesto, it becomes clear that such a technique inevitably contaminates modern fiction through the encroachment of such materials. So it is that, finding a portion of his manuscript wanting in "high-class" characteristics such as "structural cohesion and . . . literary style," the narrator chooses to "present in its place a brief resume (or summary) of the events which it contained, a device frequently employed by newspapers to avoid the trouble and expense of reprinting vast portions of their serial story" (59). The ensuing "synopsis, being a summary of what has gone before, for the benefit of new readers," repudiates the narrator's "preclusive" philosophy and demonstrates that the aesthetic of "reference" will serve to collapse the distinction between the literary high and low (59). This particular reference, an "Aeolus"-like incorporation of the practices of the modern newspaper, delivers the novel's agenda into the hands of the ill-informed, convenience-minded consumer.

As distinct from high-modernist allusiveness, O'Brien's strategy of "reference" issues in a formal technique of cut-and-paste that portends the acceleration of Ireland's merger with capitalist modernity and its reciprocal deviation from the program of Revivalist nationalism. The referential aesthetic of *At Swim* reveals that it is the very same genres of pop-cultural fare against which the Revival railed that provide the average Irish man or woman of the 1930s with his or her daily sustenance. The novel repeatedly incorporates "relevant excerpt[s] from the press" in comic exposition of its plot developments, excerpts which consist of Police Intelligence–style narration—as when Paul Shanahan regales the recently created villain, Furriskey, with an account of the pilfering of "negro maids" from the cattle ranch of his former "employer," the pulp novelist William Tracy—as well as inflecting the subplot of the moralist writer Dermot Trellis with elements of both Romance fiction and its cruder cousin, pornography. Additionally, in keeping with what F.S.L. Lyons, discussing the 1929 Censorship Act's targeting of the increasingly popular cinematic fare of Hollywood, calls the "Californication" of Irish culture during the first decades of independence, the novel also "refers" ubiquitously to film genres like the Western, thus further infusing its aesthetic with lowbrow materials the Revival viewed as anathema to the national cause (*Ireland Since the Famine* 677). This conglomeration of literary and cinematic genres constitutes the primary pole toward which the novel's high ideals persistently gravitate, rendering the text a rich index of the accession of mainstream Irish culture to an already transatlantic and buddingly global popular culture.

Beyond the general level at which these materials puncture the Revivalist fantasy of an anti- or post-capitalist Irishness, the novel presents a number of specific Revivalist institutions as driven to extinction by the low aesthetic predilections such consumption has engendered. These institutions fall into two categories, each defined by the values of one of the two main factions of the nationalist movement, the Literary and the Catholic. With the first, the primary target for bathetic deflation is the "mythological" figure of Finn MacCool. Most of the novel's parodies of the Celticist values enshrined in this figure take their lead from the mock-epic style of the "Cyclops" chapter of *Ulysses*. The early statement that "three fifties of fosterlings could engage with handball against the wideness of his backside," and later passages in which Finn himself "relates" tales from ancient Celtic legends, all mimic this Joycean vein (2). These passages specifically mock the Arnoldian Literary wont to assign aesthetic value to the Celt, such as when Finn adumbrates to his fellow Celtic heroes "the attributes that are to Finn's people" (10). He describes that "till a man has accomplished twelve books of poetry, the same is not taken for want of poetry but is forced away," and explains that if a man be unable to "sit on the brow of a cold hill with twelve-pointed stag-antlers hidden in his seat" without "cry[ing] out," "eat[ing] grass stalks," or "desist[ing] from the constant recital of sweet poetry and melodious Irish," that man "is not taken but is wounded" (10). Such descriptions signal unmistakably that it is the Celticist ideal of an inherently artistic Irishness that O'Brien targets for ironic demolition.

O'Brien also scathes Literary Celticism by depicting Finn's comically inflated narrative style as received with disdain and incomprehension by a group of characters representative of average, working-class Irishness. Just after the "birth" of John Furriskey, the character who will go on to serve, in the hands of Dermot Trellis, as a model of sexual depravity and rapine, he arrives at the room in the "Red Swan Premises" where his lower-class retainers, Shanahan and Lamont, have gathered in anticipation of his arrival. Both men have been regaled in the meantime and have grown increasingly annoyed by Finn's tall tales. Referring to him derisively as "Mr. Storybook," and as a "terrible man for talk" whose yarns one must receive with a "grain of salo," the two men brace Furriskey for his further "relations" (62). At the prompting of his legendary compatriot, Conan, Finn narrates "the account of the madness of King Sweeny . . . on a madman's flight through the length of Erin" (63). His tale, full of "staves" of "sweet poetry" recited by the mad king while perched in the trees of Ireland, is interrupted by Shanahan, who shuns such legendary fare and proffers in its place the doggerel verse of his own favorite poet, Jem Casey, the "poet of the people" (74). Paying lip service to the inestimable value Finn's "stuff," the "real old stuff of the native land," has contributed to the nation, Shanahan complains that "it's not every man could see it," and therefore proposes the Casey ballad "Workman's Friend" as a more demotic alternative (76). The poem's subject, a "drink of porter," which elixir it figures as a panacea for human ills from starvation to debt and sickness, exemplifies the low literary species that it was the Literary Revival's chief aim to purge from the national marketplace. Upon completing his recital, Shanahan highlights the scene's destabilization of high/low distinctions by asking "Mr. Storybook" for his impression of Casey's work, asking, "Tell us, my Old Timer . . . What do you think of it? Give the company the benefit of your scholarly pertinacious fastidious opinion" (80). Finn has fallen asleep in the interval, but rouses and resumes his narration, which Lamont dismisses as "more of your fancy kiss-my-hand" (80).

This crucial scene should be taken to model the entirety of the novel's assessment of the high-cultural ambitions of Literary Revivalists such as Yeats and Synge. The absurdity of attempting to make such working-class, pop-culturally primed figures as Shanahan, Lamont, and Furriskey receptive to the Celticist aestheticism of Finn's legends and Sweeny's "melodious Irish" poetry emphasizes the Revival's disregard for the actually existing Irishness of the early twentieth century. The normative Irishness of the 1930s such "vulgar" characters represent could hardly be less amenable to such Revivalist productions or the "fancy" values they promoted. Declan Kiberd argues that "the versions of the Sweeny poetry" that populate Finn's narrative are not subject to a similar destabilization, and asserts that these "staves" "remain exempt from O'Brien's corrosive parody" and "provide . . . a point of rest, a still center" amid the novel's all-encompassing, ironic "daemon" (*Irish Classics* 506, 509). However, during the later scene in which, led by the novel's other key mythological figures, the Pooka and the Good Fairy, Sweeny—along with Jem Casey and two other working-class Irishmen whose names, features, and dialogue clearly allude to Western literary and cinematic fare, "Shorty" Andrews and "Slug" Willard—makes a pilgrimage to attend the birth of Orlick, the bastard son of Dermot Trellis, his poetry is subjected to the very same deflation as Finn's folktales. As this motley crew await Orlick's arrival, they engage in an activity whose low associations we have already encountered: gambling. After the Pooka, the Good Fairy, Slug, Shorty, and Jem have all anted, Sweeny, prompted by Slug's inquiry whether he has "any money," "address[es] himself to the utterance of this stave": "They have passed below me in their course, the stags across Ben Boirche, their antlers tear the sky, I will take a hand" (150). That this particular "stave" is delivered in prose punctuates the message communicated by its jarringly discrepant contents—wherein lines that seem in keeping with high aesthetic standards are succeeded by a final line declaring Sweeny's readiness to gamble—namely that all Revival-derived or -inspired attempts to erect an idealized aesthetic domain founder amid an Irishness dominated by "vulgar" cultural proclivities. The comic conclusion of Sweeny's quatrain not only bespeaks the reification of Celticist values by capital but also a parallel, formal process wherein high, Revivalist ideals are contaminated by the low influences they would purge. Sweeny's poetry thus transmogrifies into a doggerel reminiscent of Jem Casey's "Workman's Friend."

O'Brien's bathetic modus operandi targets not only the Literary Revival, however, but also the Catholic values of that faction's competitor for political hegemony. These values are given a compound meaning in that they relate not only to turn-of-the-century nationalist ideology but also to its descendant, the official nationalism predominant after 1922. The pop-cultural and lower-class reference modality serves as one route by which Catholic mores are punctured. The Pooka and Good Fairy, for example, set aside their common investment in "respect" and "propriety" and their revulsion at the predilection for "vulgarity and smut" shown by many of their fellow characters to participate enthusiastically, along with Sweeny, in the ribald poker game that transpires during Orlick's birth (127). Popular culture is not the only means by which O'Brien lampoons Catholic nationalism's pretense to an Irishness purged of capitalist modernity's taint, however. O'Brien also suggests that Catholic nationalism itself is but capital by another name. Through the author-narrator's uncle, "holder of [a] Guinness clerkship the third class" who harps repeatedly on the "sin of sloth" (2) and the need to maintain "a good record, a clean sheet" (23), Catholic moral dictums begin closely to resemble the capitalism-attuned Protestant work ethic bemoaned by both Matthew Arnold and Max Weber in this study's opening chapter. The uncle's preparations for a gathering of the local branch of the Gaelic League—his refusal to allow an "old time waltz" to be danced, as the "clergy" are "opposed" to it (143); his insistence on a token inclusion of "a few words in Irish" (145); and his demand that the organizers employ "three clean respectable women to cut the bread" for the "strict" prelate who will be in attendance (147–48)—bespeak his representative status relative to the repressive, provincial philosophy of de Valera's Fianna Fáil. If such priorities seem to confirm the antimodernity of contemporary Irish culture, however, the uncle's hegemonic mix of respectable mores and "native" pieties nonetheless directly abets the capitalist forces that it would repudiate. His advice to the layabout Brinsley that "To the flesh we say: thus far and no farther" gestures toward the deep alignment of contemporary Catholic values and the repressive-productive dynamic of capitalist labor (177). The very figure who may seem to represent Ireland's departure from capitalist modernity thus emerges as a prime representative of its ongoing subjection to the alliance of "the Puritan and the Merchant."

Dermot Trellis, another character who like the uncle represents the supposedly antimodern values of the Irish status quo, ultimately serves to reveal the identity of those values with capital in an even more central register: that of literary production. Devising his own characters through "aestho-autogomy," a mode of authorial immaculate conception whose rationale—in addition to the goals of obviating "uncalled for fecundity" (37) and eliminating "the mortifying strategems collectively known as birth control" (38)—is to provide reproductive "issue . . . born already matured, teethed, reared, educated and ready to essay those competitive plums which make the Civil Service and the Banks so attractive to the younger bread-winners of to-day," thus transforming procreation "from the sordid struggle it often is to an adventurous business enterprise of limitless possibilities"—Trellis both seconds the uncle's fusion of repressive Catholic morality and capitalist productivity and adapts this religious-economic regime into an aesthetic principle (37–38). Through this literary adaptation of the stifling norms of the 1930s, Trellis illustrates the narrator's warning that "the novel, in the hands of an unscrupulous writer, could be despotic": "He is compelling his characters to live with him in the Red Swan Hotel so that he can keep an eye on them and see that there is no boozing" (30). Trellis's demand that his current work, a "book on sin and the wages attaching thereto" (30), be bound in green further aligns his repressive authorship with the official culture of de Valera and the tokenist nationalism that is its popular counterpart. "All colors except green he regarded as symbols of evil and he confined his reading to books attired in green," a monomania that "for many years" prevented him from "obtaining a sufficiency of books to occupy his . . . inquiring mind" (104–105). Upon the emergence, however, of "publishers of Dublin" who "deemed the colour a fitting one," he not only benefited from a boom in "green" texts "on the subject of Irish history and antiquities"; by virtue of his strict preference, "Trellis came to be regarded as an authority thereon and was frequently consulted by persons engaged in research, including members of the religious orders" (104–105). Trellis's empty observance of "purity" and "piety" through the avoidance of non-green books satirizes the conglomerated national, religious, and economic ideals of such regimes as the Censorship Act of 1929, as this essentially Irish color exclusively bears associations of "good" and only Dublin publishers, not their "evil" London counterparts, acknowledge this principle. At every level, Trellis embodies the "despotic" '30s regime of Catholicism-cum-capitalism, and at each such level, his tokenist practice bespeaks the betrayal and destruction of the expansive ideals of Literary Revivalist modernism.

Indeed, Trellis's repressive aesthetic provides perhaps the primary target for the novel's own "cosmopolitan" agenda. In keeping with the text's incipiently postmodern historicity and destabilizing, referential aesthetic, this monological philosophy proves self-contradictory and auto-deconstructive, as its logocentric emphasis on sexual purity collapses bathetically into its opposite through its necessary engagement with the popular marketplace. The narrator explains to Brinsley that because "Trellis wants his salutary book to be read by all" and "realizes that purely a moralizing tract would not reach the public . . . he is putting plenty of smut into his book" (30–31). Trellis's pornographic seasoning of his moralistic fiction bespeaks both the contemporary dominance of vulgar, entertainment-based fare and the more general historical collapse of formerly stable value distinctions. His violation of his own beliefs renders these destabilizing tendencies with even greater comedy, as, having already directed his story's villain, Furriskey, to assault a "domestic servant" named Peggy, Trellis, "in order to show how an evil man can debase the highest and the lowest in the same story," he "creates a very beautiful and refined girl called Sheila Lamont" whose beauty is so "blind[ing]" "that he so far forgets himself as to assault her himself" (60–61). Trellis's lapse bespeaks the indistinction to which oppositions of good and evil, or of sexual purity and depravity, have been reduced by the thorough reification of both the conditions of literary production and the conditions of subjectivity in general in an incipiently postmodern and globalized Ireland.

But the primary vehicle by which the novel satirizes the morally repressive and aesthetically debasing agencies routed through Trellis's authorship is the literary rebellion of his aestho-autogamously bred son, Orlick. In Orlick, O'Brien in effect resurrects the defunct institution of Literary Revivalist modernism as a high-cultural bulwark against these assembled forces. Following six months of tutelage under the Pooka, who "sow[s] in his heart throughout that time the seeds of evil, revolt, and non-serviam" (163), it becomes evident upon his fellow characters' discovery of "a manuscript of a high-class story" that "Orlick has inherited his father's gift for literary composition" (178). Importuned by Furriskey, Shanahan, and Lamont to join them in resisting Trellis's tyranny, and "smouldering with resentment at the stigma of his own bastardy . . . and incited by the subversive teachings of the Pooka, he agrees" to author a counter-text in which Trellis will be subjected to similarly "despotic" control, thereby freeing his characters for "self-determination" (178). Orlick's initial, "high-class" plot, however, fails to satisfy his co-conspirators, who complain that it does not gratify their desire for revenge quickly enough: "This is a bit too high up for us. This delay, I mean to say. The fancy stuff, couldn't you leave it out or make it short, sir?" (181). Orlick protests, "You overlook my artistry" (181), but, after Shanahan insists that the story be recalibrated to the cruder attention span and taste of "the man in the street," he agrees to accelerate its pace by enlisting the magical services of the Pooka, who arranges a full-blown "stasis of the natural order" wherein Trellis is subjected to a degree of torture and torment otherwise unbearable by the human body, to the sadistic delight of Furriskey et al. (191). Not only, then, is Orlick's "high-class story" aligned with the ideology of Literary Revivalists like Yeats, Synge, and Stephens, who likewise sought to eradicate Ireland's dependence on the "vulgar" fare of Anglo-American popular culture; upon its subjection of its fictional world to the physical law-violating magical powers of the mythological Pooka, that story also becomes aligned with the primitivist, Celticist aesthetics of Literary Revivalist modernism. Orlick's counter-text is thus nothing short of a late specimen of Literary Celticism, whose hallmark practices it resuscitates to criticize the impoverished ontology of 1930s Ireland.

Orlick's revised tale, however, continues to dissatisfy his audience, whose demands for brevity and "simplicity" impinge on its "high-class" fabric. Indeed, after Orlick excuses himself from this increasingly antagonistic exchange to recover his composure, his advisors commandeer his story and subject it, through the authorial stylings of Shanahan, to their low aesthetic preferences. Orlick then returns, armed with a renewed strategy for purging his work of "vulgar" incursions and informs them, "I have devised a plot that will lift our tale to the highest plane of great literature" (200). His strategy—to insert a brief passage flattering each of his critics—bespeaks the extent to which any high-cultural work is doomed to bowdlerization by the low consumer demand of the Irish marketplace. However, just as his Revivalist predecessors, Synge and Stephens, devised an ingenious, hybrid aesthetic in which, Trojan horse–like, a "high" aesthetic agenda is concealed behind a popular generic façade, so Orlick conceives a culminating "torment" for Trellis that promises to "lift" his "tale" in the manner described.

What then ensues is a remarkable scene in which Trellis is put on trial for violating the rights of his characters, who serve as judges, witnesses, and jury while the Pooka secures his submission to the ribald proceedings. As characters such as "Slug" Willard and Shanahan take the stand, the scene's larger design becomes clear. "Slug," referring to Trellis as his "employer," proceeds to lodge various complaints against him, such as that he failed to honor "a claim which [he] advanced of compensation for impaired health" (215). When Shanahan follows with a similar testimony, describing how "he presented a petition to the accused praying relief from certain disabilities and seeking improved pay and conditions of service" (221), it becomes evident that Trellis's characters have *unionized* and that their rebellion will now take an overtly *Communist* or, recalling the term used by the Good Fairy during an earlier Jeremiad on the state of the nation, "Bolshevist" form (128). O'Brien thus reunites the Revivalist Celticism of Orlick's "high-class story" with its one-time ally against capital's "despotism," the Irish Socialist tradition whose zenith was the Celtic Communism of James Connolly. Orlick resurrects these ontologically expansive, Celticist forces to combat the contractive, tokenistically Celtic, literarily degrading, present Irish regime, in effect attempting to reverse three decades of Irish history and return to the moment of Revival, at which, allied against empire and capital, Irish cultural politics seemed poised to generate a truly alternative modernity. Warning his assistants of "importance of the step that is about to be taken," Orlick raises his pen to deal the death blow to the errant national order that has eclipsed that moment's radical, utopian vision (227).

The novel's tripartite conclusion, however, quickly quarantines this vision and restores the hegemonic mores of 1930s Irishness. The bathetic humor with which the mock-trial is freighted portends this outcome by undermining the novel's revitalized Celticism, but even that portion of aesthetic freedom that endures in its "referential" modality is dissipated by the ensuing destruction of Orlick's manuscript and the narrator's parallel submission to his uncle's "respectable" dictates. Having "passed [his] final examination" with a "creditable margin of honor" and earned the right to enter the ranks of workaday Irishness (228), the narrator receives what seems poised to become another lecture from his uncle on his leading character flaw: "Lord save us . . . there is no cross in the world as heavy as the cross of sloth . . . idleness leaves you a very good mark for the sinful schemes of the gentleman below" (233). On the contrary, however, to his "great surprise," the narrator instead receives the hearty congratulations of his uncle and his friend, Mr. Corcoran, for having "done the trick" of securing his credential (234). The reader braces for a further repudiation of Catholicism and capital by the narrator's sardonic wit, but the latter suddenly reverses course and expresses only "thanks, utilizing formal perfunctory expressions" previously anathema to him (234). His transformation is completed when he receives, again "without verbal dexterity or coolness," a gift of the object perhaps most emblematic of respectability, a watch (234–35).[27] Deviating from his previous "descriptions" of his uncle throughout the novel as a "rat-brained," "cunning," "concerned-that-he-should-be-well-thought-of" "holder of Guinness clerkship the third class," the narrator views him anew, seeing instead a "simple, well-intentioned . . . responsible member of a large commercial concern" (236). Struck by "an emotion of surprise and contrition extremely difficult of literary rendition or description," his aesthetic powers are crippled by acculturation to the impoverished ontology of mainstream Irishness (236).

Clinching the late-modernist significance of the narrator's capitulation, the novel's "penultimate" conclusion rescues Dermot Trellis from Orlick's Celtic-Communist counter-tale by allowing "Teresa, a servant employed at the Red Swan Hotel," to cast it into the fire in Trellis's bedroom (236). Returning to the hotel after his release from the Pooka's torments, Trellis, ascending to his quarters and staring at the posterior (or "arse") of his "slavey," "mutter[s]," "doubtful as to whether he had made a pun," "ars est celane artem" ("it is true art to conceal art"), thus signaling to the reader that his vulgar sensibilities will be reinstalled as the normative aesthetic (237). The consolidated Irish world that wins out in the novel's battle of high and low, conservative and progressive, ontologically contractive and expansive values, is thus perhaps best emblematized by the narrator's realization, upon hearing the "peal" of the "Angelus far away," that his new watch is six minutes slow (236). Ireland's false alternative modernity, existing only slightly out of kilter with the rapidly globalizing new world order of capital, is aptly rendered by such an image, as is the more general sensibility of Irish late modernism, for which the window of potential for any real alternative has all but closed.

## "UBI NIHIL VALES, IBI NIHIL VELIS": *MURPHY*

The recent trend in Beckett criticism toward increased emphasis on Ireland and Irishness has initiated something of a historicist shift away from the philosophical issues long thought to control the oeuvre's meaning. Yet the former considerations are, in fact, far from incompatible with the latter in that the diverse, transnational endeavor to envision an Irishness that would supplement or even supplant capitalist modernity, an endeavor I have called Celticism, necessarily traffics in the same philosophical concerns perennially applied to Beckett's work, foremost among them the Cartesian binary of mind and body.[28] The Celticist diagnosis of modernity as subjecting humanity to ontological repression and as in need of an "imaginative," expansive recalibration, and the constitution of the figure of the Celt as a wellspring of such energies, may indeed be viewed as a content-thick iteration of this formal philosophical divide. Given the emergence of mind/body dualism as perhaps the central problem of philosophy at the early modern moment of Descartes, a moment in which capital began to commandeer human history and rearrange it according to the imperative for ever-more-productive uses of the body, it is not surprising that Celticism's ontological problematic vis-à-vis capitalist "industry" bears the marks of this same dualism. Indeed, Beckett's most openly Irish novel, *Murphy*, overlays its interrogation of the dualism of modernity with a direct invocation of the Celticist heritage. Through this palimpsestal alignment of philosophical, economic, ethnological, and aesthetic concerns, *Murphy* crystallizes the ontological dynamic that informs Celticism from its Arnoldian inception. By anatomizing the failure to resolve or transcend the mind/body antinomy in a modernity controlled by the repressive-productive logic of capital, the novel also crystallizes the particular inflection given this dynamic by Irish late modernism.

*Murphy*'s exploration of this antinomy pervades the novel and is imbricated with the forces of capital from the start. The opening scene in which Murphy "sat naked in his rocking-chair of undressed teak, guaranteed not to crack, warp, shrink or corrode, or creak at night," as, outside his condemned London "mew," "a cuckoo-clock . . . became the echo of a street-cry, which now entering . . . gave *Quid pro quo! Quid pro quo!* directly," immediately establishes the economic impetus for Murphy's quest to become "free in his mind" (2). Murphy's efforts to "quiet" his body as a prerequisite to the attainment of mental freedom are more than incidentally related to the exchange value–suffused modern world his body inhabits: "He worked up the chair to its maximum rock, then relaxed. Slowly the world died down, the big world where *Quid pro quo* was cried as wares and the light never waned the same way twice" (6–7). The physical world Murphy seeks to exit is defined by capital, and even his most successful efforts to escape it depend upon some level of submission to its imperatives. His rocking chair, as the first quotation above makes clear, is tied to these through the language of advertisement, and, as described to Murphy's former mentor Neary by his new pupil, Wylie, later in the novel, another, even more extreme strategy of Murphy's for chastening his body requires some startup capital: "The last time I saw him . . . he was saving up for a Drinker artificial respiration machine to get into when he was fed up breathing" (49).

If, as assessed by Neary at the outset of its plot, Murphy's "conarium," the mechanism by which, in Cartesian philosophy, the body is linked to the spirit, "has shrunk to nothing"—thus indicating that his attempts to sever the dual components of his being have made some headway—the duration of the novel consists mostly of a Romance fiction–type love story through which Murphy is re-bound to the physical through his attraction to the Irish-born London prostitute, Celia (6). Celia's alignment with the forces that impinge on Murphy's mental freedom is evident in the narrator's free indirect description that, within his composite being, "the part he hated craved for Celia, [while] the part that he loved shriveled up at the thought of her" (8). Through the biopolitical tenets of bourgeois romance, Murphy's mind is re-moored to a capitalist foundation. Like her predecessor Miss Counihan, at whose behest Murphy migrated to London from Ireland, Celia views love through the bifocal lens of domestic economy and respectability, whose materialist imperatives render it a kind of "commerce" (6). Spurred on by her uncle, Willoughby Kelly, who is aghast at her report that Murphy "belonged to no profession or trade," "came from Dublin," "did nothing that she could discern," and lives on "small charitable sums" acquired from an eccentric uncle (18), Celia, holding her sexual services hostage, forces Murphy to "enter the jaws of a job" (38) to provide for their "domestic establishment" (19). Murphy's protestations that "he could not earn," "that he was a chronic emeritus," and that his reluctance to work is "not altogether a question of economy" but is based on "metaphysical considerations" (21), are silenced by Celia's command, "You can get up out of that bed, make yourself decent and walk the streets for work" (38). Murphy submits, but not before uttering a warning that foreshadows much of the novel's subsequent plot: "What have I now? . . . I distinguish. You, my body and my mind. . . . In the mercantile gehenna . . . to which your words invite me, one of these will go, or two, or all. If you, then you only; if my body, then you also; if my mind, then all" (39–40). Celia proves impervious to Murphy's preview of the consequences employment will bear for the metaphysical and physical aspects of his being, and their negotiations conclude with Murphy's cowed query, "Look is there a clean shirt" (41).[29]

Given the novel's, and Beckett's own, disdain for the life and literature of the contemporary "Saorstat," we might hesitate to read Murphy's transition from economic cipher to productive laborer as bearing a specifically Irish significance.[30] In view of its satirical representative of contemporary Irish literature, "Austin Ticklepenny," the "pot poet for the County of Dublin" whose doggerel verse, a "Gaelic pseudoturfy" composed as a "duty to Erin" (89), bears out the castigations of the essay "Recent Irish Poetry" (1934)—where Beckett savages poets who employ Celticist "themes" (among them the model for Ticklepenny, Austin Clarke) as "antiquarians" neglecting the pressing concerns of modern life—the novel seems to rule out any potential convergence between its own aesthetic practice and Celticism's aesthetic heritage (70). Its similar impatience with the prudery of life under the Free State—evident in Wylie's praise for Miss Counihan as "the only nubile amateur . . . in Twenty-six Counties who does not confuse her self with her body," as "one of the few bodies, in the same bog, equal to the distinction" (216–17), and in the narrator's description of her as "exceptionally anthropoid" for an Irishwoman by virtue of her rejection of the mind-body conflation protested in "Censorship in the Saorstat" (1935)—seems to sever its ties to matters Irish in no uncertain terms (118). Reading these essays, however, one discovers that Beckett's central complaint against both the life and literature of the Free State concerns their "flight from self-awareness," in the words of the former essay, and their concomitant abandonment of aesthetic experimentation (71). As we have seen, the literary heritage of Celticism has been concerned first and foremost with these very priorities—the path toward more expansive self-cultivation and more radical aesthetic forms. Beckett's professed admiration for Synge and these texts' numerous respectful references to Yeats suggest that there were certain exceptions to his contempt for Irish writers deploying Celticist "themes" and that his contempt concerned not the innovative, imaginative visions of the Literary Revival but the degraded, reified, popular version of such themes propagated by the newly founded state. *Murphy*'s central tableau of an Irishman's imaginative "freedom" hemmed in by forces of capital—amid whose rationality he constitutes an unassimilable "surd"—is thus more than satirically related to the literary and cultural heritage whose underlying binary code is the agon of Celt and Capital (77).

The taxonomy of mental "forms" adumbrated in "section six" of the novel provides a further basis for linking Murphy's journey with this code, as its distilled account of the mind-body antinomy feeds directly into considerations of aesthetic imagination. The narrator describes that "Murphy's mind pictured itself as a large hollow sphere, hermetically closed to the world without," and proceeds to identify this division as the basis for generating a mental realm capable of redressing the degradations of the physical: "The mental experience was cut off from the physical experience, its criteria were not those of physical experience, the agreement of part of its content with physical fact did not confer worth on that part. It did not function and could not be disposed according to a principle of worth" (108). "Self-sufficient and impermeable to the vicissitudes of the body" and its principle of "worth," "Murphy's mind" consists of three distinct zones: a first, consisting of "forms with parallel" in the physical world, where he indulges in "the pleasure [of] reprisal, the pleasure of reversing the physical experience"; a second, consisting of "forms without parallel" in outer experience and defined by "contemplation"; and a third, consisting of a chaotic, primal "flux of forms," a "matrix of surds" where he becomes "a mote in the darkness of absolute freedom" (111–12). Murphy's quest to become "free in his mind" centers on the first and second of these "zones," because in them he is "sovereign" and subject to "no rival initiative" and may therefore conceive a virtual reality purged of modernity's imperatives (112). His potent faculty for inventive redress of the "Quid pro quo!"-governed external world converts its "fiasco" to "a howling success" (111).

Prior to "Celia's triumph over Murphy," he had spent increasing amounts of time in the third zone, the "absolute freedom" of "non-Newtonian" chaos, in hopes of ascending ever farther from the domain of "worth" (113–14). Hailed irresistibly by that domain through her enjoinder to gainful employment, Murphy requests that she couch her demand in the language of a system that, like his own mental one, will confer on ignoble wage labor a higher significance. He requests therefore that "she kindly procure a corpus of incentives based on the only system outside his own in which he felt the least confidence, that of the heavenly bodies," informing her of "a swami who cast excellent nativities for sixpence" in nearby Berwick Street (23). When she returns with this new "life-warrant," Murphy surprises her by declaring that its contents will form the basis for a further avoidance, rather than an embrace of work (31). Compelled by her threat to deprive him of sex, however, Murphy submits to its specifications. The "Thema Coeli" devised by "Ramaswami Krishnaswami Narayanaswami Suk" identifies a dazzling series of heaven-ordained characteristics in Murphy, a number of which bear striking similarity to those by which Celticism defines Irishness. "His highest attributes being Soul, Emotion, Clairaudience and Silence," "Few minds are better concocted than this Native's" (32). Possessed of a "great Magical Ability of the Eye," bearing "a great desire to engage in some pursuit, yet not," given to "Success terminating in the height of Glory" that will nonetheless "injure the Native's prospects," Murphy, "with regards to a Career . . . should inspire and lead, as go between, promoter, detective, pioneer, or, if possible, explorer, his motto in business being large profits and a quick turnover" (32–33). Thus armed with a satisfactory pretext to "enter the jaws of a job," Murphy sets out in obedience to Celia's extortionate demands.

There is undoubtedly an element of Revivalist parody to Murphy's "Thema Coeli." Culled from an Indian immigrant "swami," this "life-warrant" alludes to the Theosophist bent of leading Revivalists like Yeats and AE, who viewed the "sentimental" characteristics of the Celt as giving rise—*Kim*-like—to a cosmic insight closely resembling that of Indian mysticism.[31] Murphy is described as possessing such characteristics, as his leading attributes of "Soul, Emotion, Clairaudience and Silence" combine with a "great Magical Ability of the Eye" to produce a constellation of traits redolent of the "natural magic" of Arnoldian sentimentality. The contradictory description in which "Success" will result in "injur[y]" to the "Native's prospects" is particularly difficult to read apart from the Celt's economic haplessness, the unsuitability for "high success in the world of fact" that formed the point of origin for Celticism's resistance to capital. In typical late-modernist fashion, however, this roll-call of Celticist attributes is already subordinated to those very imperatives, as the "thema" outfits Murphy with a "sixpence worth of sky" in delusory support of his vulgar, materialist agenda. That such "magical," "Native" characteristics should become the basis for "profits and a quick turnover" punctuates Beckett's bathetic inflection of Murphy's quest.

However, a residue of genuine ideological convergence between Beckett and the Literary Revival persists whereby the Celticist spin to Murphy's pursuit of mental "freedom" and "sovereignty" accentuates that pursuit's aim of escaping reification. Celticism thus provides a semi-genuine touchstone for the motive energy behind Murphy's quest. The outcome of that quest—now imperiled by Celia's domestic-economic demands—may thus be read as bearing on the historical fate of Celticism's alternative project. The comic mismatch between Murphy's investment in such metaphysical values and the physical demands of his economic activity already foreshadows the novel's eventual dehiscence of this unstable compound of elements. Temporarily, however, from the point at which he pours his life into the mold of "Suk's heaven," *Murphy*'s narrative inhabits an aesthetic mode inflected by Celticism's aim of recalibrating modernity's ontological impoverishment. Thus, following his acceptance of a position as a custodian in the Magdalen Mental Mercyseat asylum, "this sixpence worth of sky, from the ludicrous broadsheet that Murphy called his life-warrant, his bull of incommunication and corpus of deterrents, changed into the poem that he alone of the living could write" (93). Murphy's chosen occupation seems uniquely well-suited to unite his desire for mental freedom and imaginative "sovereignty" with his need to secure Celia's love via capital's "quid pro quo," and thus seems to present an opportunity to aestheticize modernity and render it more commodious to metaphysical values.

Indeed, the metaphysical-physical combination achieved by Murphy's "mad" labor is so commodious that of the three agencies distinguished earlier—his mind, his body, and Celia—it is the third of these that "goes." Murphy abandons Celia in favor of the company of the Mercyseat inmates, who not only "cause Murphy no horror" in stark contrast to their effect on his fellow custodians, but inspire in him "feelings" of "respect and unworthiness" (168). His "impression" of these deranged subjects upon their first encounter is "that of self-immersed indifference to the contingencies of the contingent world"—the very state of mental freedom "he had chosen for himself as the only felicity"—and of having finally discovered the "race of people he had so long despaired of finding" (168–69). Perceiving "the patients not as banished from a system of benefits but as escaped from a colossal fiasco," Murphy reflects: "If his mind had been on the correct cash-register lines, an indefatigable apparatus for doing sums with the petty case of current facts, then no doubt the suppression of these would have seemed a deprivation. But since it was not, since what he called his mind functioned not as an instrument but as a place, from whose unique delights precisely those current facts withheld him, was it not most natural that he should welcome their suppression, as of gyves?" (177–78). Utterly severed from the world of "facts" arranged "on correct cash-register lines," Murphy identifies in them "what he would be" if he were to press his quest "freedom" to its conclusion: "It meant that nothing less than a slap-up psychosis could consummate his *life's strike*" (184, emphasis added).

Murphy later arrives at this consummation by imitating the near-catatonic state of his favorite patient and mentor in madness, Mr. Endon. Following an utterly nonsensical chess match between the two, Murphy kneels before him, "[takes] Mr. Endon's head with his hands and [brings] his eyes to bear on his," and, "seeing himself stigmatized in those eyes that did not see him," he temporarily achieves the state he sees as a "strike" against modernity's "quid pro quo" (249). "Murphy began to see nothing, that colourlessness which is such a rare postnatal treat, being the absence . . . not of percipere but of percipi," and is finally at "peace," a "mote" in the "absolute freedom" of "nothing" (246).

Though this state of separation from the imperatives of the "body" and the capitalist system that binds it fulfills Murphy's most fervent desire, however, "it was his experience that this should be stopped" (252). He thus decides to forego the absolute freedom of psychosis and resume the compromised agency of life with Celia. But his fate has been sealed as a result of his obsessive flight from physical involvement, and, returning to his "garret" in the Mercyseat dormitory, Murphy perishes in the "superfine chaos" of the flammable "gas" emitted by his makeshift radiator (252–53). Murphy's final hour thus oscillates between the physical and metaphysical extremes with which we have grown so familiar throughout this study. In his delirious, psychotic state of achieved mental freedom, we can discern the features of the sublime, primordial ecstasy that I have associated with the modernist embrace of the Celt, just as, in the ultimate self-destruction of that freedom and consequent reintegration with the gross, determinist domain of the body, we can discern the ontological features of the total reification of the modern subject. Given the text's Celticist inflection of Murphy's quest, it is no great leap to identify in Murphy's achieved ecstasy a late iteration of the Celt's proclivity for spurning the world of "fact" for the aesthetically attuned realm of the imagination. Likewise, we can identify in Murphy's final recoil from this posture a further instance of the compromise between aesthetic and economic values that has defined so many visions of a Celticist alternative modernity.

But rather than affirming the viability of such a compromise, the consequence of Murphy's temporary commitment to a primitive ecstasy loosely yet recognizably linked with the features of the Irish Celt bears out the historical diagnosis of Irish late modernism. His quest for freedom thus runs aground, repossessed by the capitalist system whose despotism first inspired it, when his corpse is incinerated, at the instructions of a motley crew of friends and lovers, in "a small close furnace of the reverberatory type, in which the toughest body, mind and soul could be relied on to revert, in under an hour, for the negligible sum of thirty shillings, to ash of an eminently portable quantity" (272). Fittingly, given Celticism's long identification of that system as "Saxon" in origin and "vulgar" in destination, Murphy's cremains are finally scattered on the premises of a London pub, "freely distributed" among its filthy detritus, "the sand, the beer, the butts, the glass, the matches, the spits, the vomit" (272–74).

# Conclusion

## *Post-Celticism*

Is Murphy, then, along with the other protagonists manqué of Beckett's fiction—Watt, Molloy, Malone, the Unnamable—a Celt? The parallels between his and their characteristics and those of this study's central figure—a penchant for magical thinking, an aversion to the repressive-productive ethic of capital, a proclivity to cultivate the former at the expense of the latter, and a proclivity for that cultivation to issue in failure—are suggestive. At least one recent critic has read these characteristics as a commentary on the values of the movement I have in effect defined as Celticism's heyday, the Irish Revival.[1] Murphy's oft-cited, unfulfilled wish for his cremains, "body, mind and soul," to be "placed in a brown paper bag and brought to the Abbey Theatre" and flushed, "if possible during the performance of a piece," down the toilet of the "necessary house" located "on the right as one goes down to the pit," would seem, perhaps, to call such affiliations into question, although one eminent commentator has read this satirical swipe instead as a Revivalist tribute (*Murphy* 269).[2] It may, ultimately, be impossible to respond to this question with a confident "yes," despite this and the novel's other invocations of Celticist and Revivalist precedent, because of the aesthetic quality of Beckett's work that Duncan McColl Chesney has recently described as "a minimalist reduction of recognizable elements (settings, objects, characteristics), which opens his works onto a greater domain of pertinence to ours, while rendering interpretation always *impertinent* because it always fills in the gaps with unwarranted external material from *our* worlds, expressing *our* concerns" (644).

The fact that Beckett's oeuvre is amenable to a Celticist reading may, then, merely reaffirm its protean ability to mirror a seemingly infinite range of reader preoccupations. We have seen enough, however, of *Murphy*'s array of "recognizable elements" to be sure that capitalist modernity forms one of its central "domains of pertinence," and to register the text's implication that even its more metaphysical "domains" are now routed through its "quid pro quo." Perhaps, then, the very indefiniteness of the novel's Celticism forms its most fitting illustration of Irish Late Modernism, in which the constituent elements of the Celticist project are either swallowed up by capital or retrofitted in accordance with its reifying logics. The same indistinction we have tracked through Joyce's info-tainment parodies, Yeats's generic motleys, and O'Brien's merger of high and low thus comes to implicate not simply literary content and form, but our own literary-critical practice, which, with Beckett, is forced to mimic modernity's identity- and value-confusing trajectories. It is something of a grim salute to Irish Late Modernism's prescience that such a practice also limns Ireland's own twentieth-century fate, which, already with the Anglo-American, pop culture–dominated era of "de Valera's Ireland," but all the more so following Taoiseach Sean Lemass's "Programmes for Economic Expansion" in the late 1950s and early '60s and the finance- and technology-based Ireland of the 1990s "Celtic Tiger," has ceded any alternative space to capital's global despotism.[3]

Murphy's "life's strike," then, whether viewed as a simple revolt against capital or a specifically Celticist one, takes its place alongside the many modes and figures of resistance to capitalist modernity this study has chronicled, from the "composite English genius" of Matthew Arnold, to Conrad's Belfast, Lawrence's Kate Leslie, Yeats's Mary Bruin, Synge's Christy Mahon, Stephens's Mary Makebelieve, Joyce's Stephen Dedalus, the late Yeats's innumerable, angry old men, and O'Brien's Orlick Trellis. Like both his British and his Literary modernist forebears, the Celt of Irish Late Modernism shows a marked affinity for resisting—through critique, through strikes, through riots, through revolutions—capital's hegemony. It is fascinating to note in this regard that, even at this final moment in Celticism's transnational history, the terminology of what O'Brien's Good Fairy calls "Bolshevism" continues to arise. Though here given a comic inflection—through Murphy's one-man revolt and Orlick's magical literary unionizing—Celticism's vision of an alternative modernity continues to converge with Communism, the twentieth-century's most radical, practical incarnation of such an alternative.

Though this study lacks the scope to take stock of the latter movement, Irish Late Modernism's diagnosis of the culture industry, the signifying apparatus of late capital, as perhaps the central underlying cause of the collapse of the Irish alternative surely has a more general applicability, in addition to bearing out Revivalist nationalism's dire prognostications. This diagnosis is evident particularly in Joyce and O'Brien, but also in the late Yeats, who, in poems such as "The Circus Animals' Desertion" and plays like *The Death of Cuchulain*, increasingly foregrounds the economic materiality of his work, figuring himself as an employer and purveyor of debased theatrical productions and a shop-owning retailer of "deserted" literary values. It is easy to imagine what Yeats's reaction might have been when in 1966, on the fiftieth anniversary of the 1916 Rising and amid Lemass's expansionist "fever," the Central Bank of Ireland, in near-perfect fulfillment of the rueful conclusion of his final play, issued a ten-shilling commemorative coin featuring an image of Oliver Sheppard's *The Dying Cuchulain*.[4]

For a further and final illustration of Irish Late Modernism's bathetic muse, of Ireland's impending economic future, and of Celticism's own historical fate, we may return to *At Swim-Two-Birds*. As we have seen, O'Brien expresses a "late" allegiance to the Literary Revival's Celticist modernism through the authorship of Orlick Trellis, which draws on that modernism's high-cultural, primitivist, and anticapitalist strategies to subject Dermot Trellis to a magical, "Bolshevist" trial for "low" aesthetic crimes. Even before its incineration by Dermot's "slavey," however, the perishability of this Celticist fantasy is already foreshadowed by Paul Shanahan, who interrupts Orlick's composition to describe the venue in which the trial is poised to occur, "a large hall not unlike the Antient Concert Rooms in Brunswick Street (now Pearse Street)": "That place is a picture-house now, of course, said Shanahan's voice as it cut through the pattern of the story, plenty of the cowboy stuff there. The Palace Cinema, Pearse Street" (213). That Orlick's Celticist resistance proceeds in this specific space bespeaks its prior suffusion by the forces of the culture industry, which by the 1930s had, indeed, converted this site of national and high-cultural significance—in which Revivalist works by the Irish Literary Theatre were once performed, and in which a young tenor named James Joyce once competed in a *feis ceoil*—to a "picture-house," a cinema, featuring the very "vulgar" aesthetic fare the Revival agitated against.

The subsequent history of this landmark is equally instructive: it would continue to serve as a hybrid theater, music hall, and cinema until 1956, when it was renamed "The Academy Cinema" and dedicated strictly to films; it was damaged by fire in 1975, and would sit abandoned for over three subsequent decades; buoyed by the boom of the Celtic Tiger, whose Dublin hub, "Silicon Docks," sits nearby, it was then restored to serve as office space in the early 2000s, after which it would house, among other entities, the EMEA (European, Middle Eastern, and African) headquarters of an American company devoted to the commodification of information and value in its purest form: Twitter.[5] It would be difficult to conceive of a space in which the archeological record of Ireland's efforts to resist incorporation into capitalist modernity, those efforts' subsequent collapse into parody, and their final defeat and foreclosure—literal and figurative—would be as concentratedly visible. It is, conversely, breathtakingly easy to conceive of a rewritten version of this scene in which it is not the cinematic stylings of the Western, but the rapid-fire, spectacle-driven, selective-amnesiac mediations of the Twitterverse that "cut through the pattern" of Orlick's "high-class story."

# NOTES

## INTRODUCTION

1. For discussions of the Celt in Irish Studies, see Deane, *Celtic Revivals* 17–27; Lloyd, *Nationalism and Minor Literature* 6–13; Cairns and Richards, *Writing Ireland* 42–49; Corbett, *Allegories of Union* 149–64; Gibbons, *Transformations in Irish Culture* 149–64; Johnston, "Cross-Currencies in the Culture Market"; Kiberd, *Inventing Ireland* 29–32; O'Connor, *Haunted English* 25–32; and McCormack, *Ascendancy and Tradition in Anglo-Irish Literary History* 221–28. As will become clear above, the Celt of this study is specifically that of Arnold and those British and Irish figures who build on his conception; the Celt of linguistic, anthropological, or archeological studies falls outside my concerns. For a more general history of Celticism, see Cairns and Richards, ch. 2–3, and Brown, *Celticism*.
2. Recent comparative treatments of British and Irish literatures include Begam and Valdez Moses, *Modernism and Colonialism*; Daly, *Modernism, Romance, and the Fin-de-Siècle*; and Esty, *Unseasonable Youth*.
3. For their views of Arnold's Celt vis-*à*-vis the Revival, see Castle 46–52 and Garrigan Mattar 21–27. Castle's distancing of the Revival Arnold occurs mainly through his reading of W.B. Yeats, who, in his account, "seemed instinctively to understand that his own ideas about the Irish primitive had to be defined more or less overtly against" Arnold's (46). Garrigan Mattar's account situates Arnold amid an "'old school' of primitivist popular Celticism" that "had to be put in its place if 'Celtology' was to succeed" (27). I do not contest either Castle's or Garrigan Mattar's readings for the duration of this study with a few occasional exceptions, nor do I dispute the claim that the particular representations of the Revival sometimes complicated Arnold's characterizations. I simply claim that such complications should not obscure the fundamental, overarching convergence of Revivalist nationalism's racial definitions with Arnold's notion of the Celt as essentially antithetical to an inherently Saxon capitalism.
4. The development of this "postcolonial conventional wisdom" is too complex to trace here, but Fanon's *The Wretched of the Earth* and *Black Skin, White Masks*,

themselves built upon the teachings of Aimé Césaire as represented in such texts as *Discourse on Colonialism*, may be taken as a point of origin. Chatterjee's work has been influential in bolstering Fanon's notion of decolonizing nationalisms as "derivative" of imperial models in both *Nationalist Thought* and *The Nation and Its Fragments*. Much work in postcolonial studies has proceeded from the premise that the adoption of metropolitan conceptual categories is inherently disabling and has thus been geared toward redefining colonial nationalisms apart from such categories. Homi Bhabha's work in *The Location of Culture* is representative.

5. Spivak explains the concept of "ab-use" in relation to Schiller in *An Aesthetic Education in the Era of Globalization*. She proposes a repurposing of Schiller's notion of aesthetics as providing women, in the absence of the rational capacity for access to abstract truth, a "sensible," "figural" surrogate for such access, whereby what is for Schiller a female disadvantage becomes, through a critical ab-use, instead a valuable alternative modality to the overly rational, Enlightenment-based contemporary world order. See pages 30–34 for this discussion.
6. See the chapter "On National Culture" in *The Wretched of the Earth* for Fanon's analysis of the three stages of the dialectic of decolonization. For commentaries on Fanon's foundational tripartite theory, see Bhabha, *The Location of Culture*, ch. 2; Said, *Culture and Imperialism* 267–78; Kiberd, *The Irish Writer*, ch. 8–10. Kiberd places Fanon's theory specifically in contact with Irish nationalism.
7. See Chrisman, "Nationalism and Postcolonial Studies," for her account of the empirical shortcomings of poststructural theories of postcolonial nationalism. The work of Lazarus, Timothy Brennan, and Benita Parry has also advanced the materialist critique of postcolonial theory as insufficiently attuned to the historical realities and political imperatives of colonies, former colonies, and the "imperial" nature of contemporary global power more generally. See Lazarus, "The Fetish of 'the West'" and *The Postcolonial Unconscious*; Brennan, "From Development to Globalization" and "Postcolonial Studies between the European Wars"; and Parry, "Liberation Theory" and *Postcolonial Studies*.
8. It is difficult to acquire information regarding the spread of the "late" facets of modern capitalism—those attending consumption and the "culture industry"—to such sites in the former British Empire and beyond. The contributions to the edited volume *Alternative Modernities* (Gaonkar) tend to place the spread of such phenomena closer to mid-century (the '30s, '40s, and '50s), while Ireland had been caught up in them since the turn of the century. Arjun Appadurai's work in such texts as *Modernity at Large*, *The Future as Cultural Fact*, and the edited volume *Globalization* is helpful in conceptualizing the implications of this spread, but it tends to limit its gaze to more recent, contemporary decades. Michael North criticizes the recency bias, as it were, of Appadurai's work in the introduction to *Reading 1922*, which dates the emergence of media phenomena usually identified with postmodernism as far back as the 1860s (18–19). The recent edited volume *Global Culture Industry* (Scott and Curry) also displays such a bias.

9. For histories of Irish economic modernization, see Lee, *The Modernization of Irish Society*, and Cormac O'Grada, *Ireland*, ch. 9–14. I prefer Joseph Valente's term "metrocolonial"—as propounded in texts such as *The Myth of Manliness in Irish National Culture*—to designate fin-de-siècle Ireland's unique mixture of colonial and metropolitan characteristics, rather than other terms designating the same characteristic such as "metropolitan colony," in Kiberd's *Inventing Ireland*; "semicolonial," in the edited volume *Semicolonial Joyce* (Attridge and Howes); and "internal colonialism," in Michael Hechter's *Internal Colonialism*.
10. On the Marxist concept of "uneven development" or "combined and uneven development," see Lenin, *Imperialism*; Trotsky, *The History of the Russian Revolution*; and Smith, *Uneven Development*. On the implications of the theory for postcolonialism, see San Juan, "Postcolonialism and the Problematic of Uneven Development," and Deckard and Lawrence, *Combined and Uneven Development*.
11. The notion of a "Neo-Marxist" theoretical shift depends primarily on the departure from the notion of the "superstructure" of human culture being precipitated by the "base" of economic production to a conception of the former as self-transforming and in many ways primary in the constitution of human social organization. The notion of postmodern reification that I trace here from Adorno and Horkheimer to Debord and Baudrillard may be summed up as arguing that human identity in the postmodern period is determined directly by the nature of commodification, advertising, and media imagery. Any number of quotations from these texts could be taken as representative, and I will revisit these works subsequently in those chapters where Celticism plays a diagnostic role in identifying the reifying tendencies of British commodities in Ireland. For now, a brief description from Adorno and Horkheimer will serve: "The most intimate reactions of human beings have been so thoroughly reified that the idea of anything specific to themselves now persists only as an utterly abstract notion: personality scarcely signifies anything more than shining white teeth and freedom from body odor or emotions" (167). Fredric Jameson's essay *Postmodernism, or, The Cultural Logic of Late Capitalism* remains perhaps the best synthesis of the theoretical advances made by such Neo-Marxist theorizations of postmodern identity and aesthetics. The original Marxist concept of reification is of course that of György Lukács in *History and Class Consciousness*, where he elaborates the theory that the human organism is "qualitatively" alienated in its relationships to itself, to other human beings, and to the products of its labor, by unfolding the implications of Marxism's theory of commodity fetishism. See 83–92 for this theory, and see Marx, *Capital*, vol. 1, 163–77, for the original passage on which Lukács relies.
12. For Kant's sublime, see the *Critique of the Power of Judgment*, vol. 1, sec. 23–30.
13. Moishe Postone offers a compelling analysis of "social domination" as the foundational insight of Marx's mature work that is germane to the consideration of the term's deployment in Adorno and in "Western Marxism" more generally. See

his *Time, Labor, and Social Domination*. Adorno's own definition of "domination," however, often tends to evince what is for Postone the problematic attribution in "traditional Marxism" of dominatory effects to the ownership of the means of production and class antagonism, rather than to the underlying, abstractive dynamics of the capitalist production of value.

14. My emphasis on the reformative and critical nature of the Adornoan sublime bears affinities with Luke Gibbons's discussion of the utility of the Burkean sublime to colonial resistance and cross-colonial solidarity in *The Colonial Sublime*. As Gibbons describes with reference to Irish colonial history circa 1800, "the tradition of the oppressed is charged with the disruptive force of the sublime, deriving its energies from the fact that the originary violence of conquest has never been put to rest. . . . This is the prospect raised by the colonial sublime . . . that the transformative power of terror would pass from master to slave, in keeping with the logic of the sublime whereby the endangered subject appropriated to itself part of the force which threatened to overwhelm it" (*Edmund Burke and Ireland* 233).
15. On Adornoan negative dialectics, see Buck-Morss, *The Origin of Negative Dialectics*; Martin Jay, *The Dialectical Imagination*; and Jameson, *Late Marxism*.
16. On Nietzsche's significance for modernist aesthetics, see Bell, *Literature, Modernism and Myth* 22–37.
17. In addition to Bell, Seshagiri, and Platt, see Torgovnick, *Gone Primitive*; North, *The Dialect of Modernism*; Barkan and Bush, *Prehistories of the Future*; and Winkiel, *Modernism, Race, and Manifestos* for general discussions of modernist "primitivism." For a specific discussion of Irish primitivism, see Culleton and McGarrity, *Irish Modernism and the Global Primitive*. Prior to the recent repudiation of the primitivist model's conceptions of race, we might also cite the moment of "modernist anthropology," in which readings of modernist writers drew parallels not to the binary racialisms of Victorian anthropology but rather to the more ambivalent, self-troubling anthropology of such figures as Franz Boas and Bronisław Malinowski, whose method of "participant observation" involved a more direct engagement with Europe's others. The work of Marc Manganero is of particular note. See his *Modernist Anthropology* and *Culture, 1922* for considerations of modernism's post-Victorian anthropological models. Castle's *Modernism and the Celtic Revival* also exemplifies this approach.
18. Adorno's concept of the sublime is itself closely attuned to a notion of the primitive. He affirms this linkage in relation to what he calls "the dialectic of the elemental and the spirit" in art: "Art is spiritualized not by the ideas it affirms but through the elemental—the intentionless—that is able to receive the spirit in itself; the dialectic of the elemental and the spirit is the truth content. Aesthetic spirituality has always been more compatible with the *fauve*, the savage, than with what has already been appropriated by culture. Spiritualized, the artwork becomes in itself what was previously attributed to it as its cathartic effect on another spirit: the sublimation of nature" (196).

19. Of interest on the negative political implications of modernist uses of the primitive are Edward Said's summary of modernism in *Culture and Imperialism* as "in one sense reproduc[ing] the aggressive contours of the high imperialist undertaking" (188–89); Howard Booth and Nigel Rigby's "Introduction" to *Modernism and Empire*, which takes issue with Bell's account of the primitive in particular by arguing that "there are many authors and texts from the modern movement that are extreme and violent in their attitudes to race and empire, rather than respectful and hybrid—and whether any author found a place wholly outside the dominant discourses of race and empire can be questioned" (5); and Andrzej Gasiorek's assessment of D.H. Lawrence's primitivism, "War, 'Primitivism,' and the Future of the West." Winkiel, for her part, though she pursues postcolonial and "alternative" racial modalities by tracking the global spread of the manifesto form in locales such as the Caribbean and Africa, still views modernists as relying on a straightforwardly primitivist view of the racial other as a "foil."
20. I address the question of whether the Revival produced a modernism in more detail in chapter 5, but I am alluding specifically to Dobbins, who argues, in *Lazy Idle Schemers*, "In the Irish case, the more experimental formal qualities of modernist writing . . . signal an important break from the stylistic patterns of the Revival" (16).
21. Along with North, Nicholas Daly's *Modernism, Romance and the Fin de Siècle* and David Chinitz's *T.S. Eliot and the Cultural Divide* represent early attempts to reread modernism for its pop-cultural affiliations and repudiate the image of the movement as divorced from and antagonistic to such forces. The studies that have followed in the wake of these early efforts are too numerous to recount here, but for an overview and some exemplary recent readings in addition to those mentioned above, see the "Introduction" and constituent essays of the recent *Cambridge Companion to Modernist Culture* (ed. Celia Marshik).
22. Though I do not extend this argument above, the concept of the unique materiality of Anglo-Irish colonialism providing for an "archipelagic" sensibility among both British and Irish Celticists contributes to the ongoing effort in transnational modernist studies to devise alternative geographical categories to the dominant, traditional paradigm of the nation state. Exemplary texts in this project of "critical geography" include Hegglund, *World Views*; Walkowitz, *Cosmopolitan Style*; Berman, *Modernist Commitments*; and Doyle and Winkiel, *Geomodernisms*. Sanjay Krishnan's discussion of the problematic aspects of the concept of the "global" in *Reading the Global* and Appadurai's discussion of "moving geographies" in *The Future as Cultural Fact* are also pertinent.
23. Felski's study is among several feminist works to challenge the notion of a predominantly male modernity, alongside others such as Nancy Armstrong's seminal *Desire and Domestic Fiction*. Regarding the Victorian doctrine of the "separate spheres" to which such works offered a response, see such classic works as Sandra Gilbert and Susan Gubar's *The Madwoman in the Attic* and Mary Poovey's *Uneven*

*Developments*. My choice to use male pronouns as the default reference for the Irish Celt is simply the product of Arnold's own, original gendering of the Celt as male, if a "feminized" one. As later examples of female Irish Celtic characters throughout this study will show, Celtic capacities were by no means conceived as limited to male subjects.

24. A number of arguments have been advanced in recent years for redefining modernism as extending to more subtle formal modulations, including those undertaken within the very mode against which modernism was for so long defined, namely realism. The edited volume *A History of Irish Modernism* (Castle and Bixby) endorses such a redefinition, in particular through its introduction and its sixteenth chapter, devoted to the novelist Kate O'Brien. Many such efforts have taken inspiration from Paul Saint-Amour's influential advocacy for a "weak" reconceptualization of modernism in a 2018 issue of *Modernism/Modernity*. For my purposes, however, it is worth preserving the distinction between realist and modernist formal experimentations in contexts such as those this study explores because of the greater alignment of the former with the prevailing, popular norms of the marketplace, and thus with those aesthetic media Celticist modernisms advocated explicitly against. The work of Elizabeth Bowen must be mentioned here as well. Bowen's modulations of traditional forms in texts such as *The Last September* undoubtedly qualify as modernist, but her emphasis on Anglo-Irish, "Big House" culture leads her work away from engagements with Celticism.

25. Spivak's account in *An Aesthetic Education* of "the double bind" as a methodological snare by which increased attention to the global sacrifices local nuance and vice versa is pertinent here. See the "Introduction."

26. In addition to Hart, Walkowitz, Berman, Kalliney, Esty, Friedman, and Krishnan, noteworthy recent attempts to nuance modernist studies in relation to both the global and the postcolonial can be found in Ramazani, *A Transnational Poetics*; Jay, *Global Matters*; Quigley, *Empire's Wake*; Keane, *Ireland and the Problem of Information*; and Pearson, *Irish Cosmopolitanism*. In the words of Jay, "If globalization offers a critical framework that moves the disciplines of literary and cultural studies toward a new transnational coherence, it will only do so if its relationship to postcolonial studies can be thought through in a responsible way" (4).

27. The volume for which Gaonkar's essay serves as the introduction, *Alternative Modernities*, in many ways codified this theoretical paradigm upon its publication in 2001. Among its contributions, Charles Taylor's "Two Theories of Modernity" also offers a noteworthy elaboration of a "cultural" theory of modernity opposed to what he calls the "acultural" understanding of modernity as unified or unifying (convergent, or "societal," in Gaonkar's terms). Much of the impetus behind this paradigm comes from preceding work in Subaltern Studies by Ranajit Guha, Dipesh Chakrabarty, and Spivak. Guha's *Elementary Aspects of Peasant Insurgency in Colonial India* and *Dominance without Hegemony*, Spivak's "Can the Subaltern Speak?" and *A Critique of Postcolonial Reason*, and Chakrabarty's

*Provincializing Europe* are representative examples of the group's methods, as is the volume *Selected Subaltern Studies* edited by Guha and Spivak. The work of David Lloyd in texts like *Irish Times* has also been at the forefront of the effort to conceptualize and recover "alternative modernities." For a useful discussion of the stakes and major features of alternative modernities theory, see Esty, *Unseasonable Youth* 195–204. The recent edited volume *Comparison* (Felski and Friedman) may also be read in the context of the "divergent" claims advanced by alternative modernities through its concerted interrogation of the limits of comparison as a theoretical and literary-critical practice. Friedman's essay "Why Not Compare?," Stam and Shohat's "Transnationalizing Comparison," and Loomba's "Race and the Possibilities of Comparative Critique" bear on this question most directly, with the last explicitly posing its discussion in relation to alternative modernities.

28. On the concept of a "minor transnationalism" attuned not to top-down, majority-minority theoretical comparisons but to linkages between subaltern/minority groups, see the introduction to the volume of the same name edited by Shu-mei Shih and Françoise Lionnet. In the context of British and Anglophone literary studies, the work of Elleke Boehmer, in texts such as *Empire, the National, and the Postcolonial*, is of particular note in shifting focus from diffusionist, metropole-colony models of influence to connections and collaborations between colonized writers.
29. For accounts of the heated responses to Chibber's polemic, see Subir Sinha and Rashmi Varma, "Marxism and Postcolonial Theory: What's Left of the Debate," and Alf Gunvald Nilsen, "Passages from Marxism to Postcolonialism," both in *Critical Sociology*. Spivak herself promptly published a reciprocally acerbic review of the book in the *Cambridge Review of International Affairs*.
30. Michael Rubenstein's study of infrastructure in postcolonial Ireland in *Public Works* offers an exemplary theorization of the potential consonance between development theory and the "alternative" of divergence and incommensurability. Comparing James Joyce's *Ulysses* and the novel *Texaco* by the Martiniquais writer Patrick Chamoiseau, Rubenstein argues that "for the underdeveloped identity, and for the postcolonial writer, the teleological arc of personal development culminates in taking on . . . the role of the development. . . . Joyce and Chamoiseau conjure the public utility, in its idealized distance from capital and the state, as a fetishistic reminder of the post-colonial writer-developer's commitment . . . to the development of the common good" (13). Spivak, whom Rubenstein cites on this point, provides another example of this *rapprochement* when she argues in *An Aesthetic Education*, "We want the public sphere gains and private sphere constraints of the Enlightenment; yet we must also find something relating to 'our own history' to counteract the fact that the Enlightenment came, to colonizer and colonized alike, though colonialism, to support a destructive 'free trade,' and that top-down policy breaches of Enlightenment principles are more rule than exception" (4).
31. Esty's discussion of the "difference versus development" debate undergirding the alternative modernities paradigm is extremely perceptive in identifying the nature

of its theoretical impasse. Juxtaposing the "alternative" view of Chakrabarty with the Marxist one of Jameson's *A Singular Modernity*, he wonders, "What methods might allow us to navigate between Chakrabarty's claim that a singular modernity imposes a false, unilinear narrative of transition and Jameson's claim that alternative modernity makes it impossible to describe transition at all?" (200–201).

32. Though Ireland's capitulation to and accelerated integration into the capitalist world-system from the mid-twentieth century onward are beyond the scope of this study, accounts are available in the introduction to Cleary, *Outrageous Fortune*; Brown, *Ireland*, ch. 8; Garvin, *Preventing the Future*; Kirby, Gibbons, and Cronin, *Reinventing Ireland*; and Daly, *Sixties Ireland*.

## CHAPTER I

1. In addition to Young, *Colonial Desire* 55–89, the following offer ethnological readings of Arnold: Anderson, *The Powers of Distance* 91–118; Appiah, "Against Races," in Appiah and Gutman, *Color Conscious* 30–73; Pecora, "Arnoldian Ethnology"; Ragussis, *Figures of Conversion* 211–33; and Daniel Williams, *Ethnicity and Cultural Authority* 33–71. Also of note is Faverty, *Matthew Arnold the Ethnologist*.
2. For an instance of the tendency to identify the racial filiations of Englishness in *Culture and Anarchy* with the "Indo-European humour" epitomized by the Hellene, see Pecora 362. For the instabilities of Arnold's racial thought, and the instabilities in mid-century race theory more generally, see Appiah 47 and Young 86.
3. See Collini, *Arnold* 76–77, for this composition history.
4. In addition to Mandler, see Stocking, *Victorian Anthropology* 62–69, and Curtis, *Anglo-Saxons and Celts* 66–74, for discussions of Teutonic discourse. See also Curtis's *Apes and Angels*.
5. See Wood, *Empire of Capital* 73–88.
6. See Postone's *Time, Labor and Social Domination*. Terry Eagleton offers an interestingly similar anatomization of the ontology of modernity in his chapter on Marx, "The Marxist Sublime," in *The Ideology of the Aesthetic* 196–233.
7. The major Irish Studies readings of Arnold are Deane, *Celtic Revivals* 17–27; Lloyd, *Nationalism and Minor Literature* 6–13; Cairns and Richards, *Writing Ireland* 42–49; Corbett, *Allegories of Union* 148–84; Gibbons, *Transformations* 149–63; Johnston, "Cross-Currencies in the Culture Market"; Kiberd, *Inventing Ireland* 29–32; and McCormack, *Ascendancy and Tradition* 221–28.
8. In this vein, my reading aligns with the sorts of progressive political views offered by ethnological critics such as Young, Anderson, and Ragussis. In their readings, Arnold appears as a sort of postcolonial theorist *avant la lettre* who, by promoting the fusion of putatively divergent racial identities, presaged recent critical efforts toward conceptualizing the sort of liberatory intersubjective modalities designated by terms like *hybridity*, *multiculturalism*, and *cosmopolitanism*. In such readings,

in spite of its manifest imperialist intentions, Arnold's ethnological thought bespeaks a latent urge toward an alternative, non-Manichean identity formation.

9. See Eagleton, *Heathcliff and the Great Hunger* 11–26, for his reading of the Famine. For another study of the racialization of British economic discourse at mid-century vis-à-vis the Irish, see Peart and Levy, "Not an Average Human Being."
10. See Renan, *The Poetry of the Celtic Races*, for his reading of the title group as "essentially feminine."
11. Critical accounts of Arnold's racial ideals have persistently conflated these two figures. Daniel Williams, for example, refers to "the Hellenistic appreciation for nature found among the Celtic peoples," in effect erasing any distinction between the two figures (41). Similarly, Johnston, couching his description of Arnold's utopian vision for England's future in the terms of "The Function of Criticism," defines this regenerated era as "a more expansive Celtic/Hellenic epoch," thus, again, rendering Celt and Hellene as identical (50). Pecora, though for the most part more sensitive to the ethnological nuances of Arnold's thought, at times also slips into equating the two, as when he asserts that the "Celtic aptitude for sentiment and beauty" imbues the Saxon with Hellenic attributes (374).
12. See Stocking 219–28 for these distinctions. The division of human epistemological evolution into magical, religious, and scientific stages arises most famously in James Frazer's compendium of Stocking's title discipline, *The Golden Bough*. See Frazer 15–44 for Frazer's descriptions of primitive or "homeopathic" epistemology.
13. For the origins of aesthetic discourse as a reintegrative social medium, see Guillory, *Cultural Capital*, ch. 5, and Eagleton, *The Ideology of the Aesthetic*. See also Cascardi, *The Subject of Modernity*, and Habermas's oft-cited essay "Modernity: An Incomplete Project."

## CHAPTER 2

1. The term "anomalous" is intended to allude to one of the central texts of Irish Studies, David Lloyd's *Anomalous States*. Lloyd's use of the term, however, refers mainly to "anomalous" cases of Irish artists and thinkers resisting the politics of the Irish Free State, founded in 1923 in the wake of the Anglo-Irish War and Irish Civil War.
2. See Cleary, "Misplaced Ideas," and the introduction to David Lloyd's *Ireland After History* for refutations of the "revisionist" tendency to discount the colonial aspects of Irish history.
3. For further examples of research on British racial views of the Irish, see L.P. Curtis, *Anglo-Saxons and Celts*; Liz Curtis, *Nothing but the Same Old Story*; Lebow, *White Britain and Black Ireland*; Nelson, *Irish Nationalists and the Making of the Irish Race*; and Pittock, *Celtic Identity and the British Image*.
4. Nelson arrives at similar conclusions regarding Beddoe. See *Irish Nationalists*, 39–40.
5 See Arata, *Fictions of Loss*, for background on this late Victorian context.

6. For examples of such readings, see Claussen, "Degeneration, 'Fin-de-Siècle' Gothic, and the Science of Detection," and Wynne, *Colonial Conan Doyle*, ch. 2.
7. On Doyle's Boer War activities, see Krebs, *Gender, Race, and the Writing of Empire*, ch. 4.
8. Wynne, for example, bases her claim for Doyle's nationalism in part on his public defense of Roger Casement, who was found guilty of conspiring to aid the 1916 Easter Rising in Dublin by recruiting Irish POWs captured by Germany in World War I to the cause. However, as Doyle biographer Daniel Stashower records, Doyle's defense consisted of the plea that Casement's actions indicated obvious mental derangement (324–25).
9. See the essay "Cave Canem Nocte" by Lloyd Rose on the "folkloric origins" of the hound.
10. For discussion of the "woman as land metaphor," see Hutner, *Colonial Women*.
11. See Curtis, *The Cause of Ireland*, ch. 5, for a thorough account of the Land Wars.
12. On Lord Leitrim, see Clark, *Social Origins of the Irish Land War*, 163.
13. Terry Eagleton provides a wide-ranging chronicle of British difficulties with achieving hegemony in Ireland in the eighteenth and nineteenth centuries in *Heathcliff and the Great Hunger* 27–103.
14. Coextensive with recent anthropological reassessments of the Doyle oeuvre, recent years have also brought a reassessment of Holmes, who has transformed from a staunchly rational, law-abiding public guardian to an exoticized and hybridized figure who mingles in his personal features and investigative activities the Manichean elements of the British geopolitical interface. See, for example, McLaughlin, *Writing the Urban Jungle*, ch. 3, and Taylor-Ide, "Ritual and the Liminality of Sherlock Holmes."
15. See Ó Cadhla, *Civilizing Ireland*, and also Andrews, *A Paper Landscape*, on the Ordnance Survey of Ireland.
16. Caroline Reitz's *Detecting the Nation* is of interest on the question of the larger convergences between Doyle and Kipling. As she argues, the two are allied not only in terms of their imperialist political leanings but also through molding their staple genres, detective and adventure/romance fiction, to reflect those leanings.
17. Among the studies that advance some version of this reading are McBratney, *Imperial Subjects, Imperial Space*; Nagai, *Empire of Analogies*; Tim Watson, "Indian and Irish Unrest"; and Wegner, "'Life as He Would Have It.'"
18. Two exemplary texts are Boehmer, *Empire, the National, and the Postcolonial*, and the collection of essays *Ireland and India*, edited by Foley and O'Connor.
19. For a fascinating account of the Massacre and the Irish role in it, see Kenny, "The Irish in the Empire," 90–95.
20. I refer here to Nessa Cronin's essay "Monstrous Hybridity: Kim of the 'Eye-rishti' and the Survey of India" and Julia Wright's brief reading of the novel in *Ireland, India, and Nationalism in Nineteenth-Century Literature*.
21. On Broca, see Stocking, *Race*, 56–58. Broca's work utilized what was known as "the cephalic index," a metric of skull measurement devised, according to

L.P. Curtis Jr., by the German Anders Adolf Retzius at midcentury. See *Apes and Angels*, ch. 2. Stocking notes the role played by the index in several major anthropological texts of the late 1800s, for example Paul Topinard's *Éléments d'anthropologie générale* (1885). Broca's formative influence in generating the stereotype of the "round-headed Celt" is noted in two anthropological studies of the early twentieth century: *The Phoenician Origin of Britons, Scots, & Anglo-Saxons* (1924) by L.A. Waddell (134) and Henri Hubert, *The Rise of the Celts* (1934), which states, "Since Broca wrote, the name of the Celts has been attached to the type of dark round-heads of Western Europe and the Alpine regions" (29).

22. See David Alan Richards, "Early Editions of Kim," on these illustrations.
23. See John Lockwood Kipling, "Kim and the Lama," on *The Victorian Web*, for an image of this bas-relief.
24. Cronin's reading exemplifies the tendency to see Kim's hybridity as untenable, as do Ian Baucom's in chapter 2 of *Out of Place* and Sailaja Krishnamurth's in "Reading Between the Lines: Geography and Hybridity in Rudyard Kipling's *Kim*." Neither Baucom nor Krishnamurth relates Kim's hybridity to his Irishness.
25. See Abdul JanMohamed, "The Economy of Manichean Allegory," and Edward Said's introduction to the Penguin Classics edition of *Kim*, for analysis of the novel's binary racial elements.
26. These quotations are of course from "The Ballad of East and West" and "The White Man's Burden," respectively.
27. The Indian Rebellion or "Sepoy Mutiny" was precipitated by the spread among the native ranks of the army of the British Raj of a rumor that its leaders had used animal fat to grease the cartridges of the infantry's rifles. Native soldiers forced to bite these cartridges in order to load their weapons turned on their British superiors upon hearing that the animals used were cows, sacred to Hindus, and pigs, sacred to Muslims. See *Raj*, by Lawrence James, 233–53, for an account of these events.
28. On the origins of the concept and its foundational role in the first wave of British imperial expansion in the seventeenth century, see Wood, *Empire of Capital*, ch. 5; Armitage, *The Ideological Origins of the British Empire*; and the *locus classicus* of the doctrine of "improvement," Locke's *Second Treatise of Government*.

## CHAPTER 3

1. In addition to the critical studies of modernist "primitivism" discussed in the introduction, this outline of the transition from an imperial romantic to a modernist Celticism also bears out the findings of Nicholas Daly's *Modernism, Romance and the Fin de Siècle*, which identifies in British modernism a basic inversion of the ideological and aesthetic priorities of its predecessor.
2. As Tim Christensen has noted, readings of *The Nigger of the "Narcissus"* that emphasize race are surprisingly scarce. Perhaps this peculiarity results in part from Conrad's own proclamation—in the prefatory note that accompanied the text's first American printing—that the novel's title figure "is merely the center

of the ship's collective psychology," rather than a substantial character whose individual traits, racial or otherwise, bear any deeper significance ("To My Readers" 168). For whatever reason, *"Narcissus"* does not seem to have inspired much racial exegesis. In addition to Christensen, "Racial Fantasy,'" the more noteworthy analyses of race in the novel are North, *The Dialect* 37–58; Redmond, "Racism, or Realism?"; Parry, *Conrad and Imperialism*; Messenger, "'We did not want to lose him'"; Livingston, "Seeing Through Reading"; and Goonetilleke, "Racism and *The Nigger of the 'Narcissus'*." Also relevant to the analysis of Conrad's racial views are Patrick Brantlinger's and Chinua Achebe's denunciatory readings of *Heart of Darkness*. See Brantlinger, "*Heart of Darkness*: Anti-Imperialism, Racism, or Impressionism?" and Achebe, "An Image of Africa."

3. See Frost, "Racism, Work, and Unemployment," and the volume from which the essay comes more generally, Frost, *Ethnic Labour and British Imperial Trade*, on this aspect of the history of British capital. Also of note are Frost, "Colonial Labour and Work Palaver"; Lunn, "A Racialized Hierarchy of Labour?"; and Tabili, *"We Ask for British Justice."*
4. Regarding this stereotype in nineteenth-century Britain, see Stocking, *Victorian*, in particular chapter 6. This stereotype plays a major role not only in *"Narcissus"* but in *Heart of Darkness*, where Marlow marvels at the "restraint" of Congolese natives participating in the Belgian imperial enterprise.
5. Christensen's Lacanian reading offers a persuasive theoretical means for grasping this dynamic. As he describes, because of his blackness, "Wait is encountered as the inassimilable outside of the symbolic order to which he gives birth, holding forth the possibility of its destruction, emphasizing its fragility and incompleteness" (35).
6. See Roediger, *The Wages of Whiteness.*
7. The *locus classicus* for the analysis of the generic and period hodgepodge of which *Lord Jim* consists is of course Fredric Jameson's essay "Romance and Reification" in *The Political Unconscious*, 206–80.
8. See Watt, *Conrad in the Nineteenth Century*, 169–79, and Jameson, 210–42, for discussions of the "impressionist" affiliations of Conrad's early style. The original description of his "impressionism" is Ford Madox Ford's. Also of interest on this point are Matz, *Literary Impressionism and Modernist Aesthetics*, 138–54; Peters, *Conrad and Impressionism*; and Levenson, *A Genealogy of Modernism*, 1–10.
9. I take the term "sympathetic magic," which denotes an epistemological modality in which "like produces like" by a primitive mimetic faculty, from James Frazer's compendium of Victorian anthropology, *The Golden Bough*. See 13–57 for a full definition of this faculty, of which I read "sentimentality" as a specimen.
10. Cedric Watts questions the "inconsistency of narratorial identity" in his introduction to the Penguin edition, and points to no fewer than seven different narrative perspectives as controlling it at various moments. See xix–xx for this analysis. Also of note on the question of the novel's narrative shiftiness are Foulke, "Postures of Belief in *The Nigger of the 'Narcissus'*," and Ross, "*The Nigger of the 'Narcissus'* and Modernist Haunting."

11. Among the racial readings of the novel cited above, Goonetilleke in particular argues for a coherent—and conservative—political perspective on Conrad's part vis-à-vis both race and the novel's depiction of maritime labor. The classic study of Conrad's personal ideology is Avrom Fleishman's *Conrad's Politics*. Also of interest on this question is the essay "Bound in 'Blackwood's,'" by William Atkinson, which addresses Conrad's history of publishing in politically conservative periodicals.
12. See Torgovnick, *Gone Primitive*, chapter 8; Gasiorek, "War, 'Primitivism,' and the Rise of 'The West'"; Booth, "Lawrence in Doubt"; Bell, *Literature, Modernism and Myth*, 93–119; and Bell, *D.H. Lawrence: Language and Being*.
13. On the controversy surrounding McPherson's fraudulent Celticism, see Garrigan Mattar, *Primitivism*, ch. 1.
14. See Sherry, "T.S. Eliot, Late Empire, and Decadence," on Sweeney as one of Eliot's "caricature primitives" (111). Sherry cites Marshall McLuhan as reporting that "Eliot had said to him that the original for Sweeney was an Irish-Canadian airman, billeted in London during the war" (118). For a more comprehensive account of the origins of the Sweeney figure, see the editorial commentary to the title of "Sweeney Erect" in the recent *The Poems of T.S. Eliot, Volume I*, 497–99.
15. On the Irish-American basis of these excised materials, see Chinitz, *T.S. Eliot and the Cultural Divide*, 42–44, as well as the editorial notes to "He Do the Police in Different Voices," in *The Poems of T.S. Eliot*, 595–600.
16. There are suggestive connections, both ideological and real-historical, between this trans-colonial facet of British modernist Celticism and what Elleke Boehmer has called "anti-imperial interactions across the colonial borderline." See the introduction to her *Empire, the National, and the Postcolonial, 1890–1920*.

## CHAPTER 4

1. Thus Thomas Richards, in *The Commodity Culture of Victorian England*, is able to treat Ireland as but a regional site within the title "culture," rather than as distinct through its colonial difference. For general histories of the rapid modernization of the Irish economy after the Famine, see Lee, *The Modernisation of Irish Society 1848–1918*, and O'Grada, *Ireland: A New Economic History 1780–1939*, ch. 9–14.
2. This narrative is pervasive in Irish Studies, so much so that quoting specific passages is barely necessary. Among the most prominent texts are Deane, *Celtic Revivals* and *Strange Country*; Cairns and Richards, *Writing Ireland*; Lloyd, *Anomalous States* and *Irish Times*; Gibbons, *Transformations in Irish Culture*; Eagleton, *Heathcliff and the Great Hunger*; Kiberd, *Inventing Ireland*; and Cleary, *Outrageous Fortune*.
3. For a comprehensive history of the League, see McMahon, *Grand Opportunity*.
4. For reasons of space, I have avoided engaging directly with the heated Revivalist debate over whether the admission of "cosmopolitan" influences exerted a denationalizing influence on Irish culture. For an overview of this debate, see Kiberd, *Inventing Ireland*, ch. 9.

5. For the imperialist argument against which Hyde writes, see Gladstone's *The Irish Question*: "What is there in Separation that would make it advantageous for Ireland? . . . Why should she be supposed desirous to forego the advantage of an absolute community of trade with the greatest among all commercial countries, to become an alien to the market which consumes (say) nine-tenths of her produce, and instead of using the broad and universal paths of enterprise now open to her, to carve out for herself new and narrow ways as a third-rate State? Why, when her children have now, man by man, the free run of the vast British Empire, upon terms of absolute equality with every native of Great Britain, should she be deemed so blind as to intend cutting away from the greatest of all the marts in the world for human enterprise, energy, and talent, and to doom them to be strangers among nearly three hundred million men, with whom they have now a common citizenship?" (23).
6. See *Douglas Hyde: A Maker of Modern Ireland* by J.E. and G.W. Dunleavy for further biographical information.
7. See the end of Hyde's "Plea," p. 80, and Moran's "Future of the Irish Nation," p. 26, on this point.
8. See Matthews, *Revival*, 100–103, on Moran's consent for the continuation of Ireland's imperial subordination.
9. David Lloyd's essay "Counterparts" reads the Revival in similar, Nietzschean terms. See pp. 130–33 for Lloyd's contextualization of Irish nationalism's "transvaluation of values," and see sections 61–62 of *The Antichrist* for Nietzsche's presentation of this revolutionary imperative.
10. I have also omitted from direct discussion here such texts as T.W. Rolleston's *Imagination and Art and Gaelic Literature* and John R. Whelan's "Literature and Nationality," both of which, like Yeats's early folklore, deploy an openly Arnoldian ethnological framework but without its capitalist aspects.
11. In the chapter of his *Irish Classics* devoted to *The Aran Islands*, Kiberd provides background information on the Revivalist fetishization of the islands, and argues that such texts as Arthur Symons's essay "The Isles of Aran," published in *The Savoy* in 1896, lend Synge's work an "intertextuality" that undercuts its seeming essentialist agenda. See chapter 24.
12. In the same chapter, Kiberd argues convincingly that Synge's writing displays feelings of guilt about his own responsibility for bringing modernity to the islands through such media as his Kodak camera. See 422–24.
13. Gramsci, *The Prison Notebooks*, 12.
14. See chapter 3 of Lyons's *Culture and Anarchy in Ireland 1890–1939* for his overview of this factional split.
15. This account emerges in works such as P.J. Matthews's *Revival* and Joe Cleary's *Outrageous Fortune*, where, to quote the former, Catholic nationalism tries "to refute the imperial conception of Irish culture by idealizing it and exaggerating its inherent morality" (45). Cleary's analysis is more complex, but like Matthews, he accepts the premise that Catholic nationalism "absorbed" much of its identity from

England, from its "Victorian mass-culture sentimentalism" to its "philistine anti-intellectualism and the assiduous pursuit of bourgeois respectability" (65). Also of interest on this point is Katherine Mullin's account of the "social purity" movement in *James Joyce, Sexuality and Social Purity*, which argues that while Irish Catholic mores controlled private sexual standards during the period, a United Kingdom–wide, Protestant-led campaign for "social purity" controlled public ones.

16. See pp. 59–60 of *Writing Ireland* for Cairns and Richards's account of the cultural roots of this "deployment of sexuality" by Catholic nationalism. Also of interest is chapter 1 of Alexander J. Humphreys' book *New Dubliners*.
17. See pages 35–45 of Matthews's *Revival* for an account of the "Mahaffey/Atkinson Affair."
18. This phrase is taken from Duffy's essay "What Irishmen May Do for Irish Literature," where he opposes these virtues to what he calls "the dram-drinking of sensational literature" (13).
19. The *locus classicus* for this aesthetic humanism is Schiller's *On the Aesthetic Education of Man*.
20. See Lloyd, "Counterparts," for a specifically Irish analysis of this postcolonial dynamic.
21. See Lyons, *Ireland Since the Famine* 252–53, on this point. It is also noteworthy, within the context of the Revival's commodity critique, that Griffith draws further parallels between the popular culture of Austria and that of England based on their common dissemination of "stage" caricatures of Magyar and Irish identity: "Nor were the potent weapons of calumny any more neglected by Austria than by England. Austria, like England, had the ear of the world. . . . In her Press, in her theatre, in her society, the Magyar was ever held up to ridicule. . . . In the Austrian beer-gardens—the equivalent of the English music-halls—vulgar beings, clad in grotesque imitation of the Hungarian costume, who sang vile songs reflecting on the Hungarian character, were the popular buffoons. The Austrians called them 'Magyar Miska,' or 'Hungarian Michaels'—Michael being the popular peasant-name in Hungary—as the English call their music-hall Irishmen 'Irish Micks' or 'Irish Paddies.'" (79).
22. In *Ireland: The Union and Its Aftermath,* Oliver MacDonagh records, "the pages of *An Claidheamh Soluis* were frequently used to drum up support for 'native manufactures' and to advance the argument that there was a link between the decline of the language and the loss of industry in rural Ireland in the nineteenth century. At times the campaign for Irish industry was pursued to the point of absurdity: in 1901 a directive was passed ordering that no prize be awarded to a competitor in the Oireachtas unless they were dressed in clothes of Irish manufacture" (28). For the *Homestead*'s efforts on behalf of "Irish manufactures," see the special edition devoted to the Irish Textile Exhibition in Dublin in 1897, titled "Some Irish Industries."
23. See chapter 4 of part II of *Ireland Since the Famine* for Lyons on "Constructive Unionism."

24. On Connolly's involvement in these organizations, see Milotte, *Communism in Modern Ireland*, ch. 1.

## CHAPTER 5

1. This question has preoccupied a number of critics in Irish Studies over the last several decades, with a sizable contingent arguing that on the whole, the Revival did not produce a properly modernist aesthetic. Seamus Deane's account of Yeats as merely a "late Romantic" in *Celtic Revivals* (40), Terry Eagleton's labeling of the Revival as an "archaic avante-garde" in *Heathcliff and the Great Hunger*, and, most recently, Gregory Dobbins's claim, in *Lazy Idle Schemers*, that "in the Irish case, the more experimental formal qualities of modernist writing" as exemplified by Joyce, O'Brien, and Beckett, "signal an important break from the stylistic patterns of the Revival" (16), provide representative examples. For counterarguments, see the introductions to Gregory Castle, *Modernism and the Celtic Revival*, and Paige Reynolds, *Modernism, Drama, and the Audience for Irish Spectacle*.
2. Describing Yeats's efforts to make the theater a "magical" organ of social transformation, Howes argues that Yeats's stage management during the 1890s and early 1900s—instructing actors in the use of "slow, formalized gestures" and to utter dialogue in "a melodious, chant-like incantation," and arranging his sets by "spatial relations and contrasting color schemes" evocative of poetic rhythm and seasonal cycles—was intended to generate a "great racial gathering" through primitivist ritual (71). Hogan and Kilroy detail Synge's efforts to insure that the "caoine," the ritual wail of mourning uttered by the mother in *Riders*, be transmitted in all its estranging power, by hiring a Galway woman to instruct the play's actors in its performance. See *Laying the Foundations* 115 for this account.
3. Valente concurs with Foster on the play's dual authorship. See *The Myth* 94.
4. Frank Fay, clearly, underwent something of a change of heart regarding the Literary Revival's aims between his criticism of Yeats's and Synge's early efforts and his participation in the Abbey.
5. Many readings neglect this dimension of the text: Cairns and Richards, *Writing Ireland* 84–88; Castle, *Modernism*, ch. 4; Deane, *Celtic* 51–62; Devlin, "J.M. Synge's *The Playboy of the Western World*"; Fleming, *A Man Who Does Not Exist*; Garrigan Mattar, *Primitivism*, ch. 4; Gibbons, *Transformations* 23–36; Kiberd, *Inventing*, 166–88; and Shaun Richards, "The Playboy of the Western World." Noteworthy exceptions occur in Paige Reynolds, *Modernism*, ch. 2, and in Valente, *The Myth*, ch. 4.
6. See Nicholas Daly, *Sensation and Modernity in the 1860s*, as well as the essays in Maunder and Moore, *Victorian Crime, Madness and Sensation*, and Harrison and Fantina, *Victorian Sensations*, on the genre's characteristics and social impact.
7. Devlin's reading is particularly noteworthy for its insistence on the premodernity of the play's setting. He defines *Playboy* as depicting "a western world with its own

idyllic pre-industrialized culture, owing little to Dublin or London" (374). Gibbons, who describes the play as "reverting to an image of pre-Famine Ireland," also tends in this direction (*Transformations* 34).

8. Reynolds provides a compelling analysis of the celebrity status Christy achieves, but does so without reference to the The Police Intelligence as a popular-cultural context. See 51–56.
9. See Mairead Reynolds, *A History of the Irish Post Office*, regarding this aspect of the Office's activities.
10. Frank Sweeney's account of newspapers in County Donegal during the 1890s in *The Murder of Connell Boyle* helps contextualize the influence of The Police Intelligence in Mayo. As he describes, "in the 1890s there was a gradual falling away from traditional storytelling to hear the newspaper reading of national and international events," among which he lists "exciting scandals and court cases from Ireland and abroad" (18–19).
11. See Kilroy's *The "Playboy" Riots*, in particular 7–20, for an account of the audience's "riotous" response. Regarding the Lynchehaun case, see Patricia Byrne, *The Veiled Woman of Achill*.
12. See, for example, the story "Capital Punishments" in Leonard De Vries,*'Orrible Murder*, 137–39.
13. For example, the story "Execution in Galway," from *The Connaught Telegraph* on 26 April, 1902, relates that "a large crowd witnessed the hoisting of the black flag" upon the death of one Thomas Keeley, convicted of murdering a Mary Clasby with "a painter's hammer." The Cavan report "Arrival of the Executioner" similarly states that upon his arrival at Armagh "a considerable number were at the station to get a glance at Scott" and that a second "large number collected in jail square to see" him "pass . . . into the prison" ("The Cavan Parricide: Arrival").
14. On the commercial industry surrounding Jack the Ripper, see Wilson, *A History of British Serial Killing* 26–27. For an equally remarkable account of the commercial phenomena to which the Simpson murder trial gave rise, see George Lipsitz's essay "White Fear." Information regarding the sensations surrounding the Anthony and Knox trials is available in the *Seattle Times* article "Courthouse Crowd Anguished by Casey Anthony Verdict," by Audra Birch, and the *Guardian* article "Amanda Knox freed after four years in case that has no winners," by John Hooper and Tom Kington.
15. David Schmid's account of the American fascination with serial killers such as Manson, Ted Bundy, and Richard Ramirez ("The Night Stalker") in *Natural Born Celebrities: Serial Killers in American Culture* persuasively characterizes such fanaticism as a kind of celebrity worship. For a fascinating and disturbing illustration of the practice of collecting serial killer–related memorabilia, see the website *Supernaught.com*.
16. *The Aran Islands* provides the touchstone for Synge's ideals here. Secondary texts exploring these ideals include Fleming, *A Man*; G.J. Watson, *Irish Identity and the*

*Literary Revival*, ch. 2; Kiberd, *Irish Classics*, ch. 24; and Kiberd, *Synge and the Irish Language*.

17. See Valente, "The Novel and the Police (Gazette)," regarding the ambivalence of tabloid reporting. Valente explores the presence of the US-based *National Police Gazette* in the "Cyclops" chapter of *Ulysses* and argues that such coverage as the *Gazette* featured "not only traffics in transgressive pleasures, but maintains its own rhetorical force that marks them as such," thus evoking contradictory yet mutually reinforcing impulses to voyeuristic enjoyment and moral disapproval (17).
18. Kiberd's *Inventing Ireland* is the foremost example of the trend of reading Christy's performance as an instance of the tendency of colonial nationalism to be "derivative" of imperial conceptual categories, in Chatterjee's formulation. See chapter 10 on the manner in which "the tripartite structure of [the] play . . . corresponds . . . with Frantz Fanon's dialectic of decolonization, from occupation, through nationalism, to liberation" (184).
19. I draw here on Andreus Huyssen's distinction between a "high modernist" and an "avant-garde" aesthetic in *After the Great Divide*, which is defined by their respective "autonomous" detachment from and engagement with popular-cultural forms. See vii–xii.
20. The best-known formulations of the "alienation effect" of Brecht's "epic theater" are his essays "A Short Organum for the Theater" and "Alienation Effects in Chinese Acting."
21. Michel Foucault's *The History of Sexuality* considers the repressive dictates of "respectability" as a form of "biopower." See, in particular, *Volume I*, which begins with the introductory essay, "We 'Other Victorians,'" for his analysis of this code's biopolitical implications.
22. For a discussion of this gendered figuration of the colonial relationship, see the introduction to Valente's *James Joyce and the Problem of Justice*.
23. See Valente, *The Myth* 129, for his analysis of the policeman's embodiment of "shoneenism."
24. It is difficult to find definitive reference points for Moran's "Guy and Belinda," which seems to pair the two characters as a kind of template for romantic courtship. Though it seems likely these are just stock characters in "penny novelettes" whose ephemerality and cheapness predisposed them for the dustbin of history, it is possible that Moran has in mind Maria Edgeworth's canonical novel of respectability, *Belinda*, and a symmetrical text of chivalric manliness such as George Alfred Wallace's *Guy Livingstone*, both of which might have been available in this cheap format in Ireland at the fin de siècle.
25. The original reference occurs in Wilde's Socratic dialogue "The Decay of Lying," in which Cyril, paraphrasing the thesis of his counterpart, "Vivian," that "Life imitates art far more than Art imitates life," states, "I can quite understand your objection to art being treated as a mirror. You think it would reduce genius to the position of a cracked looking-glass" (307).

26. The phenomenon of the colonial spectacle bears some implications for the model of postcolonial nationalism offered in Benedict Anderson's canonical *Imagined Communities*. Synge's handling of "The Police Intelligence" in particular—itself merely an advanced version of the Revival's critique of the print culture of the metropole—aligns in significant ways with Anderson's notions of modern nationalism as the product of a linguistic homogenization consolidated by print capitalism and of a later, postcolonial nationalism that is the product of such homogenization colliding with extant, indigenous cultural attachments. What the Irish colonial spectacle reveals is a decolonizing "intelligentsia" (in Anderson's terms) recognizing the pivotal role played by print capitalism in the consolidation of the imperial order and devising an aesthetic technology for short-circuiting that consolidation. See especially chapters 6 and 7 of Anderson's study regarding the dynamics of postcolonial nationalisms.
27. I refer of course to *Simulacra and Simulation*. In its words, under the aegis of the simulacrum, there is no longer a division between signification and reality; rather, "It is a question of substituting signs of the real for the real" (1–2). For a general discussion of the "precession of simulacra" as well as a number of fascinating examples of how, through this "precession," human activities become converted into "hyperreal events" (21), see 1–42.

## CHAPTER 6

1. This definition is taken from the *Modern Catholic Dictionary*, compiled by Father John Hardon.
2. Over the last several years, the notion of an Irish Late Modernism has become increasingly popular. See Quigley, *Empire's Wake*, and Keane, *Ireland and the Problem of Information*. Many of the essays of *Yeats and Afterwords*, edited by Howes and Valente, implicitly propound such a view as well.
3. In addition to Cheng and Castle, the following texts are of major interest regarding the relationship of *Ulysses* to Arnoldian ideas, in particular Celticism: Deane, "Masked with Matthew Arnold's Face"; Gibson, *Joyce's Revenge* 66–67 and 171–72; and Barlow, *The Celtic Unconscious*.
4. See Hyde, *The Love Songs of Connacht* 29–31.
5. See Orem, "Corpse-Chewers: The Vampire in *Ulysses*," on the novel's vampire theme, including his reading of Mulligan and Stephen as vampiric "persons who malign the departed" (66).
6. See Arata, *Fictions of Loss*, ch. 5, on Dracula's Anglophilic acculturation.
7. The notion that this Meredith quotation sits awkwardly amid the scene is supported by the fact that Joyce published a scathing response to an appreciative review of Meredith's work in the *Daily Express* on 11 December, 1902. Joyce calls Meredith a mere "man of letters" whose novels have "no value as epical art" (*Occasional* 64).

8. For alternative readings of this scene's dynamics, see Gibson, chapter 3, and Platt, *Joyce and the Anglo-Irish* 73–86.
9. See Gifford 217 regarding Arnold's original sonnet.
10. Eglinton would later repeat this gesture through a critical commentary in his *Irish Literary Portraits* (1935), in which he "demur[red]" against the suggestion that Joyce "is of the company of the Greeks" on the basis that the novel lacks the "simplicity and synthesis" of those "inventors of science and logic" (158).
11. As Mark Gaipa, Sean Latham, and Robert Scholes have recently underscored in *The Little Review Ulysses*, the earliest surviving notebook for Ulysses, from October 1917, emphasized "Irish, Jews, and Art" as among its select list of projected "key topics" (346). Ellman's biography describes Joyce as "insisting" on "the similarity of the Jews and the Irish," which he viewed as "alike . . . in being impulsive, given to fantasy, addicted to associative thinking, wanting in rational discipline" (395). For a more extended examination of the novel's Irish-Jewish connections, see Bender, *Israelites in Erin*.
12. In *James Joyce, Ulysses, and the Construction of Jewish Identity*, Bruce Davison argues that while Joyce draws on Arnoldian definitions of the Jew, those notions were "revised through his reading of Friedrich Nietzsche," who in texts such as *Beyond Good and Evil* proffered a distinct view of Greek and Jewish influences (14). Davison further argues that "Arnold's ideas . . . are positioned as the centrifugal target of Joyce's sabotage of Victorian liberal culture" (14). My reading above agrees in spirit with Davison's claims, but it suggests that Joyce's "sabotage" of Arnoldianism first, extends to Arnold's Revivalist legacies; and, second, motivates the embrace of the figure of the Jew as the antithesis of Arnoldian thinking. In this sense, Joyce's Jew appears more, not less, indebted to Arnold, at the same time as his portrait of Bloom complicates prevailing stereotypes.
13. On *Ulysses*'s engagement with newspapers and an account of its larger place within prevailing, modernist perceptions and uses of the medium, see Collier, *Modernism on Fleet Street*, ch. 4. Collier reads the novel as highlighting newspapers' intrusions on privacy, while I view Joyce's aim as more neutral and documentary.
14. See Feinstein, "Usurers and Usurpers" 39–41, and Valente, "Neither Fish Nor Flesh" 116, on the role of Bloom's Jewishness in "Cyclops" specifically.
15. Dobbins's *Lazy Idle Schemers* relates the flux of commodification to Walter Benjamin's concept of *Erlebnis* in *The Arcades Project*, arguing that the "phantasmagoria" of the "immediate experience" of consumption in which Joycean modernism revels offers a critique of the progressive historical narratives of both British colonialism and Irish nationalism (19–25). If we understand Revivalist nationalism, however, as devoted to a critical interrogation of consumption as a vehicle of colonial retrenchment, the predominance of such fulsome commodification in Joyce instead stages a postcolonial Irishness that has failed to transcend these narratives.
16. Keane finds the perennial trotting-out of this "single paragraph of a single broadcast" by de Valera as an illustration of Irish postcolonial realities "almost

touching," and he complicates its seeming portrayal of an insular, antimodern '40s Ireland by recovering the responsiveness of the remainder of the speech to both World War II and the "field of mediation" produced by midcentury radio technology (3–5). Though I am guilty of relying on de Valera's "single paragraph," my reading of postcolonial Ireland as caught up in an increasingly globalized network of economic forces accords with the spirit of Keane's critique.

17. Helen Vendler argues that the phrase "wherever green is worn" shows Yeats "humbl[ing] himself by gesturing to a piece of popular poetry . . . "The Wearing of the Green," thus departing from his "unremitting hatred of green as a political symbol" (*Our Secret Discipline* 24).
18. Regarding Yeats's ambivalent view of the event, see Kiberd, *Inventing Ireland* 213–18, and Perloff, "'Easter, 1916': Yeats's First World War Poem."
19. Among the volume's many compelling contributions, Howes's "Yeats's Graves" and Jed Esty's "'All that consequence'" offer the most "late"-oriented considerations of the Yeats oeuvre.
20. The essay offers a late example of Yeats's "humbling" embrace of popular symbols. He writes, "I walked along the south side of the Dublin quays a couple of years ago; looked at the funnels of certain Dublin steamers and found that something incredible had happened; I had not shuddered with disgust through they were painted green on patriotic grounds; that deep olive green seemed beautiful. I hurried to the Parnell monument and looked at the harp. Yes, that too was transfigured; it was a most beautiful symbol; it had ascended out of sentimentality, out of insincere rhetoric, out of mob emotion" (486–87). On the divorce bill, see R.F. Foster, *W.B. Yeats: A Life*, 2:293–300.
21. On Yeats's eugenic turn, see North, *The Political Aesthetic of Yeats, Eliot, and Pound*; Bradshaw, "The Eugenics Movement in the 1930s and the Emergence of *On the Boiler*"; Howes, *Yeats's Nations*, ch. 6; and Childs, *Modernism and Eugenics*, ch. 7.
22. As Marjorie Howes has argued, the high modernist phase of Yeats's career, which aligns with his increasing commitment to "Big House" culture, increasingly positions female sexual desire as the linchpin of his ideals. See Howes, *Yeats's Nations*, ch. 4 and 5, regarding the centrality of female desire to Yeats's "Big House" ideology.
23. See "The Poetics of Politics" in Lloyd's *Anomalous States* for his analysis of Yeats's syntactical indeterminacy.
24. Paige Reynolds similarly reads the old man's remarks as repudiating the more engaged modernist practices she identifies as central to Revival-era theatrical productions, and which she distinguishes from the anti-popular tendencies of "international modernism" (*Modernism* 1–2).
25. In "The Controversy over The Playboy of the Western World," Yeats had attributed the popular backlash against Synge's play to "a demand born of Puritan conviction and shopkeeping timidity and insincerity" (192)
26. The texts referred to here as defining O'Brien's work as "postmodernist," "absurdist" and "carnivalesque" are, respectively, Hopper, *Flann O'Brien*; Declan

Kiberd's essay "Gaelic Absurdism" in *Irish Classics*; and Booker, *Flann O'Brien, Bakhtin, and Menippean Satire.*

27. On the centrality, both material and symbolic, of the watch in capitalist modernity's consolidation, see E.P. Thompson's canonical Marxist essay "Time, Work-Discipline and Industrial Capitalism." My reading of the novel's temporal dynamics also intersects with Dobbins's consideration of the novel's depiction of its protagonist's "heroic indolence" as marking a uniquely "Irish time" derived from the nation's uneven, colonial development and critically posed against the normative, developmental temporality of Éire and the 1937 Constitution (181–84).
28. Among the works that have conducted this recent shift toward Irish readings of Beckett are Morin, *Samuel Beckett and the Problem of Irishness*; McKee, "Breaking the Habit: Samuel Beckett's Critique of Irish Ireland"; the collected essay volume *Beckett and Ireland*, edited by Sean Kennedy; Bixby, *Samuel Beckett and the Postcolonial Novel*; Hansen, *Terror and Irish Modernism*, ch. 5; Quigley, *Empire's Wake*, ch. 3; and Dobbins, *Lazy Idle Schemers*, ch. 6. Harrington's *The Irish Beckett* is an early forerunner of this turn.
29. Tyrus Miller's reading of the novel, which is central to his definition of Late Modernism as a period, similarly emphasizes the manner in which Murphy's "pursuit of total autonomy from any shared, socially determined world, destroys the aesthetic life and subordinates it in the most brutal way to economic necessity" (186).
30. For an example of the resistance to identifying such a meaning, see the introduction to Ackerley, *Demented Particulars: The Annotated* Murphy.
31. On the complex Asian affiliations and sources for Revival-era Celticism, see Lennon, *Irish Orientalism*. See esp. 205–324 on the "syncretic," Orientalist-Celticist nature of the discourse.

## CONCLUSION

1. See Dobbins's reading, which rests upon his very different view of the Revival itself.
2. I refer here to Declan Kiberd, who sees Murphy's wish as affirming an allegiance to the "ancient idealism" of the Theatre Movement. See *Inventing Ireland*, 533.
3. For an economically minded literary history of post-independence Ireland, see Joe Cleary's *Outrageous Fortune*, in particular the chapter "Modernization and Aesthetic Ideology," 203–32. Quigley provides an equally illuminating account of the ways in which Irish literature in this period reflects what he calls "the slow synchronization of Irish postcoloniality with global capitalism," one that places particular emphasis on the work of Beckett, in *Empire's Wake* (171). See chapter 3 for his reading of Beckett.
4. See the "O'Brien Coin Guide" regarding the "Irish Ten Shilling Commemorative Coin." Yeats had, of course, earlier served on the committee to create a new Irish coinage for the Free State in 1926–27. The committee issued designs that

accorded with Yeats's urging that "certain simple symbols that all can understand as expressions of national products" adorn one side of each coin, with a harp adorning the other (quoted in the second volume of Foster, *W.B. Yeats*, 333). The critical light in which the Cuchulain statue is depicted by the play, however, suggests an equally critical view of iconography like the later coin exemplifies.

5. On the history of "The Academy" and its 2007 reopening, see "Academy to Reopen as Offices" in *The Irish Times* of 17 September 2007. On the building's use by Twitter, see Justin Comiskey, "Former Twitter Headquarters on Pearse Street to Let," in *The Irish Times* of 5 October, 2016.

# WORKS CITED


"Academy to Reopen as Offices." *Irish Times*, 17 Sept. 2007

Achebe, Chinua. "An Image of Africa: Racism in Conrad's *Heart of Darkness*." *Massachusetts Review*, vol. 18, 1977, pp. 782–94.

Ackerley, C.J. *Demented Particulars: The Annotated* Murphy. Edinburgh UP, 2004.

Adorno, Theodor W. *Aesthetic Theory*. Edited by Robert Hullot-Kentor, U of Minnesota P, 1997.

Adorno, Theodor W., and Max Horkheimer. *Dialectic of Enlightenment*. Translated by John Cumming, Continuum, 1972.

AE (George Russell). *Co-Operation and Nationality: A Guide for Rural Reformers from this to the Next Generation*. Maunsel and Co., 1912.

———. *The National Being: Some Thoughts on an Irish Polity*. Macmillan, 1930.

———. "Nationality and Imperialism." *Ideals in Ireland*, edited by Lady Gregory, Unicorn, 1901, pp. 15–24.

Anderson, Amanda. *The Powers of Distance: Cosmopolitanism and the Cultivation of Detachment*. Princeton UP, 2001.

Anderson, Benedict. *Imagined Communities: Reflections on the Origin and Spread of Nationalism*. Verso, 1991.

Andrews, J.H. *A Paper Landscape: The Ordnance Survey in Nineteenth-Century Ireland*. Four Courts P, 1993.

Appadurai, Arjun. *The Future as Cultural Fact: Essays on the Global Condition*. Verso: 2013.

———. *Modernity at Large: Cultural Dimensions of Globalization*. U of Minnesota P, 1996.

———, editor. *Globalization*. Duke UP, 2001.

Appiah, Kwame Anthony, and Amy Guttman. *Color Conscious: The Political Morality of Race*. Princeton UP, 1996.

Arata, Stephen. *Fictions of Loss in the Victorian Fin de Siècle*. Cambridge UP, 1996.

Armitage, David. *The Ideological Origins of the British Empire*. Cambridge UP, 2000.

Armstrong, Nancy. *Desire and Domestic Fiction: A Political History of the Novel*. Oxford UP, 1987.

Arnold, Matthew. *Culture and Anarchy*. *Arnold:* Culture and Anarchy *and Other Writings*, edited by Stefan Collini, Cambridge UP, 1993, pp. 53–211.

———. *England and the Italian Question*. Duke UP, 1953.

———. "The Function of Criticism at the Present Time." *Arnold:* Culture and Anarchy *and Other Writings*, edited by Stefan Collini, Cambridge UP, 1993, pp. 26–51.

———. "The Incompatibles." *Irish Essays*, Smith, Elder & Co., 1882, pp. 1–81.

———. *The Study of Celtic Literature*. Smith, Elder & Co., 1891.

Atkinson, William. "Bound in 'Blackwood's': The Imperialism of 'The Heart of Darkness and Its Immediate Context." *Twentieth-Century Literature*, vol. 50, no. 4, Winter 2004, pp. 368–93.

"The Attempted Murder of a Sweetheart in Cork." *Freeman's Journal and Daily Commercial Advertiser* [Dublin], 6 Jan. 1899. *British Library Newspapers*, Gale Group.

Attridge, Derek, and Marjorie Howes. *Semicolonial Joyce*. Cambridge UP, 2000.

Barkan, Elazar, and Ronald Bush, editors. *Prehistories of the Future: The Primitivist Project and the Culture of Modernism*. Stanford UP, 1995.

Barlow, Richard. *The Celtic Unconscious: Joyce and Scottish Culture*. U of Notre Dame P, 2017.

Baucom, Ian. *Out of Place: Englishness, Empire and the Location of Identity*. Princeton UP, 1999.

Baudrillard, Jean. *Simulacra and Simulation*. Translated by Sheila Glaser, U of Michigan P, 1995.

Beckett, Samuel. "Censorship in the Saorstat." *Disjecta: Miscellaneous Writings and a Dramatic Fragment*, John Calder, 1983, pp. 84–88.

———. *Murphy*. Grove, 1957.

———. "Recent Irish Poetry." *Disjecta: Miscellaneous Writings and a Dramatic Fragment*, John Calder, 1983, pp. 70–76.

Beddoe, John. *The Races of Britain: A Contribution to the Anthropology of Western Europe*. Trubner and Co., 1885.

Begam, Richard, and Michael Valdez Moses. "Introduction." *Modernism and Colonialism: British and Irish Literature, 1899–1939*. Duke UP, 2007, pp. 1–19.

Bell, Michael. *Literature, Modernism and Myth: Belief and Responsibility in the Twentieth Century*. Cambridge UP, 1997.

——. *D.H. Lawrence: Language and Being*. Cambridge UP, 1991.

Bender, Abby. *Israelites in Erin: Exodus, Revolution, and the Irish Revival*. Syracuse UP, 2015.

Berman, Jessica. *Modernist Commitments: Ethics, Politics, and Transnational Modernism*. Columbia UP, 2012.

Bhabha, Homi. *The Location of Culture*. Routledge, 1994.

Birch, Audra D.S. "Courthouse crowd anguished by Casey Anthony verdict." *Seattle Times*, 5 July 2011.

Bixby, Patrick. *Samuel Beckett and the Postcolonial Novel*. Cambridge UP, 2009.

Boehmer, Elleke. *Empire, the National, and the Postcolonial, 1890–1920: Resistance in Interaction*. Oxford UP, 2005.

Booker, M. Keith. *Flann O'Brien, Bakhtin, and Menippean Satire*. Syracuse UP, 1995.

Booth, Howard. "Lawrence in Doubt: A Theory of the 'Other' and Its Collapse." *Modernism and Empire*, edited by Howard J. Booth and Nigel Rigby, Manchester UP, 2000, pp. 197–223.

Booth, Howard, and Nigel Rigby. "Introduction." *Modernism and Empire*, edited by Howard J. Booth and Nigel Rigby, Manchester UP, 2000, pp. 1–10.

Boylan, Thomas A., and Timothy P. Foley. *Political Economy and Colonial Ireland: The Propagation and Ideological Function of Economic Discourse in the Nineteenth Century*. Routledge, 1992.

Bradshaw, David. "The Eugenics Movement in the 1930s and the Emergence of *On the Boiler*." *Yeats Annual*, vol. 9, 1992, pp. 189–215.

Brantlinger, Patrick. "*Heart of Darkness*: Anti-Imperialism, Racism, or Impressionism?" *Criticism*, vol. 27, 1985, pp. 363–85.

Brecht, Bertolt. "A Short Organum for the Theater." *Marxist Literary Theory*, edited by Drew Milne and Terry Eagleton, Blackwell, 1996, pp. 107–35.

———. "Alienation Effects in Chinese Acting." *Brecht on Theater: The Development of an Aesthetic*, edited and translated by John Willett, Hill and Wang, 1992, pp. 91–99.

Brennan, Timothy. "From Development to Globalization: Postcolonial Studies and Globalization Theory." *The Cambridge Companion to Postcolonial Literary Studies*, edited by Neil Lazarus, Cambridge UP, 2004, pp. 120–38.

———. "Postcolonial Studies between the European Wars: An Intellectual History." *Marxism, Modernity, and Postcolonial Studies*, edited by Crystal Bartolovich and Neil Lazarus, Cambridge UP, 2002, pp. 185–203.

Brown, Terence. *Ireland: A Social and Cultural History, 1922–2001*. Cornell UP, 1985.

———, editor. *Celticism*. Rodopi, 1996.

Buck-Morss, Susan. *The Origin of Negative Dialectics*. The Free Press, 1979.

Byrne, Patricia. *The Veiled Woman of Achill: Island Outrage and a Playboy Drama*. Collins P, 2012.

Cairns, David, and Shaun Richards. *Writing Ireland: Colonialism, Nationalism and Culture*. Manchester UP, 1988.

Cascardi, Anthony J. *The Subject of Modernity*. Cambridge UP, 1992.

Castle, Gregory. *Modernism and the Celtic Revival*. Cambridge UP, 2001.

Castle, Gregory, and Patrick Bixby, editors. *A History of Irish Modernism*. Cambridge UP, 2019.

"The Cavan Murders." *Freeman's Journal and Daily Commercial Advertiser* [Dublin], 6 Jan. 1899. *British Library Newspapers*, Gale Group.

"The Cavan Parricide: Arrival of the Executioner in Armagh." *Freeman's Journal and Daily Commercial Advertiser* [Dublin], 10 Jan. 1899. *British Library Newspapers*, Gale Group.

"The Cavan Parricide: The Execution of Thomas Kelly." *Freeman's Journal and Daily Commercial Advertiser* [Dublin], 11 Jan. 1899. *British Library Newspapers*, Gale Group.

Césaire, Aimé. *Discourse on Colonialism*. Translated by Joan Pinkham, Monthly Review P, 2001.

Chakrabarty, Dipesh. *Provincializing Europe: Postcolonial Thought and Historical Difference*. Princeton UP, 2000.

Chatterjee, Partha. *The Nation and Its Fragments*. Princeton UP, 1993.

———. *Nationalist Thought and the Colonial World: A Derivative Discourse*. U of Minnesota P, 1993.

Cheng, Vincent. *Joyce, Race and Empire*. Cambridge UP, 1995.

Chesney, Duncan McColl. "Beckett, Minimalism, and the Question of Postmodernism." *Modernism/Modernity*, vol. 19, no. 4, 2013, pp. 637–55.

Chibber, Vivek. *Postcolonial Theory and the Specter of Capital*. Verso, 2013.

Childs, Donald. *Modernism and Eugenics*. Cambridge UP, 2001.

Chinitz, David. *T.S. Eliot and the Cultural Divide*. U of Chicago P, 2005.

Chrisman, Laura. "Nationalism and Postcolonial Studies." *The Cambridge Companion to Postcolonial Literary Studies*, edited by Neil Lazarus, Cambridge UP, 2004, pp. 183–98.

Christensen, Tim. "Racial Fantasy in Joseph Conrad's *Nigger of the 'Narcissus'*." *ARIEL*, vol. 37, no. 1, Winter 2006, pp. 27–43.

Clark, Samuel. *Social Origins of the Irish Land War*. Princeton UP, 1979.

Claussen, Nils. "Degeneration, 'Fin-de-Siècle' Gothic, and the Science of Detection: Arthur Conan Doyle's 'The Hound of the Baskervilles' and the Emergence of the Modern Detective Story." *Journal of Narrative Theory*, vol. 35, no. 1, 2005, pp. 60–87.

Cleary, Joe. "Misplaced Ideas: Locating and Dislocating Ireland in Colonial and Postcolonial Studies." *Marxism, Modernity and Postcolonial Studies*, edited by Crystal Bartolovich and Neil Lazarus, Cambridge UP, 2002, pp. 101–24.

———. *Outrageous Fortune: Capital and Culture in Modern Ireland*. Field Day, 2007.

Collier, Patrick. *Modernism on Fleet Street*. Routledge, 2006.

Collini, Stefan. *Arnold*. Oxford UP, 1988.

Comiskey, Justin. "Former Twitter Headquarters on Pearse Street to Let." *Irish Times*, 5 Oct. 2016.

Conrad, Joseph. *The Nigger of the "Narcissus."* Edited by Richard Kimbrough, W.W. Norton & Co., 1979.

———. "Preface." *The Nigger of the "Narcissus,"* edited by Richard Kimbrough, W.W. Norton & Co., 1979, pp. 145–48.

———. "To My Readers in America." *The Nigger of the "Narcissus,"* edited by Richard Kimbrough, W.W. Norton & Co., 1979, pp. 167–69.

Connolly, James. *Erin's Hope: The End and the Means*. New Books Publications, 1972.

———. "Socialism and Nationalism." *James Connolly: Selected Writings*, edited by P. Beresford Ellis, Pluto P, 1988, pp. 121–24.

Corbett, Mary Jean. *Allegories of Union in Irish and English Writing, 1790–1870*. Cambridge UP, 2000.

Cronin, Nessa. "Monstrous Hybridity: Kim of the 'Eye-rishti' and the Survey of India." *Ireland and India: Colonies, Culture and Empire*, edited by Tadhg Foley and Maureen O'Connor, Irish Academic P, 2006.

Culleton, Claire, and Maria McGarrity, editors. *Irish Modernism and the Global Primitive*. Palgrave MacMillan, 2009.

Curtis, L.P. Jr. *Anglo-Saxons and Celts: A Study of Anti-Irish Prejudice in Victorian England*. U of Bridgeport, 1968.

———. *Apes and Angels: The Irishman in Victorian Caricature*. Smithsonian Institution P, 1971.

Curtis, Liz. *The Cause of Ireland: From the United Irishmen to Partition*. Colour Books, 1994.

———. *Nothing but the Same Old Story: The Roots of Anti-Irish Racism*. Information on Ireland, 1984.

Daly, Mary. *Industrial Development and Irish National Identity, 1922–1939*. Syracuse UP, 1992.

Daly, Nicholas. *Modernism, Romance and the Fin de Siècle: Popular Fiction and British Culture 1880–1914*. Cambridge UP, 1999.

———. *Sensation and Modernity in the 1860s*. Cambridge UP, 2009.

Davison, Bruce. *James Joyce, Ulysses, and the Construction of Jewish Identity*. Cambridge UP, 1996.

Deane, Seamus. *Celtic Revivals: Essays in Modern Irish Literature*. Wake Forest UP, 1985.

———. "Masked with Matthew Arnold's Face': Joyce and Liberalism." *Canadian Journal of Irish Studies*, vol. 12, no. 1, 1986, pp. 11–22.

———. *Strange Country: Modernity and Nationhood in Irish Writing Since 1790*. Clarendon P, 1997.

Debord, Guy. *The Society of the Spectacle*. Black & Red, 1983.

Deckard, Sharae, and Nicholas Lawrence, editors. *Combined and Uneven Development: Towards a New Theory of World Literature*. Liverpool UP, 2015.

Devlin, Joseph. "J.M. Synge's *The Playboy of the Western World* and the Culture of Western Ireland under Late Colonial Rule." *Modern Drama*, vol. 41, 1998, p. 371.

De Vries, Leonard. *'Orrible Murder: An Anthology of Victorian Crime and Passion*. Taplinger, 1971.

Dobbins, Gregory. *Lazy Idle Schemers: Irish Modernism and the Cultural Politics of Idleness*. Field Day, 2010.

Doyle, Arthur Conan. "The Adventure of the Empty House." *The Classic Illustrated Sherlock Holmes*, Longmeadow P, 1987, pp. 449–63.

———. *The Hound of the Baskervilles*. *The Complete Sherlock Holmes, Volume I*, Barnes and Noble Classics, 2003, pp. 571–695.

Doyle, Laura, and Laura Winkiel, editors. *Geomodernisms: Race, Modernism, Modernity*. Indiana UP, 2005.

Duffy, Enda. *The Speed Handbook: Velocity, Pleasure, Modernism*. Duke UP, 2009.

Duffy, Sir Charles Gavin. "What Irishmen May Do for Irish Literature." *The Revival of Irish Literature*, edited by Sir Charles Gavin Duffy, George Sigerson, and Douglas Hyde, T. Fisher Unwin, 1894, pp. 9–33.

Dunleavy, J.E., and G.W. Dunleavy. *Douglas Hyde: A Maker of Modern Ireland*. U of California P, 1991.

Eagleton, Terry. *Heathcliff and the Great Hunger: Studies in Irish Culture*. Verso, 1995.

———. *The Ideology of the Aesthetic*. Verso, 1992.

Eglinton, John. *Irish Literary Portraits*. MacMillan, 1935.

Eliot. T.S. *The Poems of T.S. Eliot: Volume 1: Collected and Uncollected Poems*. Edited by Christopher Ricks and Jim McCue, Johns Hopkins UP, 2015.

Ellman, Richard. *James Joyce*. Oxford UP, 1983.

Esty, Jed. *Unseasonable Youth: Modernism, Colonialism, and the Fiction of Development*. Oxford UP, 2013.

"Execution in Galway." *Connaught Telegraph* [Castlebar, Ireland], 26 Apr. 1902. *Irish Newspaper Archives*, irishnewsarchive.com.

Fallon, Brian. *An Age of Innocence: Irish Culture 1930–1960*. Palgrave Macmillan, 1998.

Fanon, Franz. *Black Skin, White Masks*. Grove P, 1967.

———. *The Wretched of the Earth*. Grove P, 1963.

Faverty, Fredric E. *Matthew Arnold the Ethnologist*. Northwestern UP, 1951.

Feinstein, Amy. "Usurers and Usurpers: Race, Nation, and the Performance of Jewish Mercantilism in *Ulysses*." *James Joyce Quarterly*, vol. 44, no. 1, 2006, pp. 39–58.

Felski, Rita. *The Gender of Modernity*. Harvard UP, 1995.

Felski, Rita, and Susan Stanford Friedman. *Comparison: Theories, Approaches, Uses*. Johns Hopkins UP, 2013.

Fleishman, Avrom. *Conrad's Politics: Community and Anarchy in the Fiction of Joseph Conrad*. Johns Hopkins UP, 1967.

Fleming, Deborah. *A Man Who Does Not Exist: The Irish Peasant in the Work of W.B. Yeats and J.M. Synge*. U of Michigan P, 1995.

Foley, Tadhg, and Maureen O'Connor, editors. *Ireland and India: Colonies, Culture and Empire*. Irish Academic P, 2006.

Foster, R.F. *W.B. Yeats: A Life*. 2 vols. Oxford UP, 1997.

Foucault, Michel. *The History of Sexuality, Volume 1: An Introduction*. Vintage, 1990.

Foulke, Robert. "Postures of Belief in *The Nigger of the 'Narcissus'*." *The Nigger of the "Narcissus,"* edited by Richard Kimbrough, W.W. Norton & Co., 1979, pp. 308–21.

Frazer, James. *The Golden Bough: A Study in Magic and Religion*. Penguin, 1996.

Friedman, Susan Stanford. *Planetary Modernisms: Provocations on Modernity across Time*. Columbia UP, 2016.

Frost, Diane. "Colonial Labour and Work Palaver: Labour Conflict in Britain and West Africa." *Racializing Class, Classifying Race: Labour and Difference in Britain, the USA and Africa*, edited by Peter Alexander and Rick Halpern, St. Martin's P, 2010, pp. 150–67.

———. "Racism, Work, and Unemployment: West African Seamen in Liverpool 1880s–1960s." *Ethnic Labour and British Imperial Trade: A History of Ethnic Seafarers in the UK*, edited by Diane Frost, Frank Cass, 1995, pp. 22–33.

Gaipa, Mark, Sean Latham, and Robert Scholes, editors. *The Little Review Ulysses*. Yale UP, 2015.

Gaonkar, Dilip, editor. *Alternative Modernities*. Duke UP, 2001.

———. "Introduction." *Alternative Modernities*, edited by Dilip Gaonkar, Duke UP, 2001, pp. 1–23.

Garrigan Mattar, Sinéad. *Primitivism, Science, and the Irish Revival*. Clarendon P, 2004.

Garvin, Tom. *Preventing the Future: Why Was Ireland So Poor for So Long?* Gill and Macmillan, 2005.

Gasiorek, Andrzej. "War, 'Primitivism,' and the Rise of 'The West': Reflections on D.H. Lawrence and Wyndham Lewis." *Modernism and Colonialism: British and Irish Literature, 1899–1939*, edited by Richard Begam and Michael Valdez Moses, Duke UP, 2007, pp. 91–110.

Gibbons, Luke. *Transformations in Irish Culture*. U of Notre Dame P, 1996.

———. *Edmund Burke and Ireland: Aesthetics, Politics, and the Colonial Sublime*. Cambridge UP, 2003.

Gibson, Andrew. *Joyce's Revenge: History, Politics, and Aesthetics in Ulysses*. Oxford UP, 2002.

Gifford, Don. *Ulysses Annotated: Notes for James Joyce's* Ulysses. U of California P, 2008.

Gilbert, Sandra, and Susan Gubar. *The Madwoman in the Attic: The Woman Writer in the Nineteenth-Century Literary Imagination*. Yale UP, 1979.

Gladstone, W.E. *The Irish Question*. John Murray, 1886.

"The Glosheens Tragedy." *Connaught Telegraph* [Castlebar, Ireland], 19 Mar. 1904. *Irish Newspaper Archives*, irishnewsarchive.com.

Goonetilleke, D.C.R.A. "Racism and *The Nigger of the 'Narcissus.'*" *Conradiana*, vol. 43, no. 2, 2011, pp. 51–66.

Gramsci, Antonio. *Selections from the Prison Notebooks*. Edited by Quinton Hoare and Geoffrey Nowell Smith, International Publishers, 1971.

Griffith, Arthur. *The Resurrection of Hungary: A Parallel for Ireland*. James Duffy & Co., M.H. Gill & Son, Sealy, Bryers & Walker, 1904.

Guha, Ranajit. *Elementary Aspects of Peasant Insurgency in Colonial India*. Duke UP, 1999.

———. *Dominance without Hegemony: History and Power in Colonial India*. Harvard UP, 1998.

Guha, Ranajit, and Gayatri Spivak, editors. *Selected Subaltern Studies*. Oxford UP, 1988.

Guillory, John. *Cultural Capital: The Problem of Literary Canon Formation*. U of Chicago P, 1993.

Habermas, Jurgen. "Modernity: An Incomplete Project." *The Norton Anthology of Theory and Critcism*, edited by Vincent Lietch et al., W.W. Norton, 2001, pp. 1748–58.

Hansen, Jim. *Terror and Irish Modernism: The Gothic Tradition from Burke to Beckett*. State U of New York P, 2009.

Hardon, John. *The Modern Catholic Dictionary*. Doubleday, 1980.

Harrington, John P. *The Irish Beckett*. Syracuse UP, 1991.

———, editor. *Modern Irish Drama*. W.W. Norton & Co., 1991.

Harris, Susan Canon. *Gender and Modern Irish Drama*. Indiana UP, 2002.

Harrison, Kimberly, and Richard Fantina. *Victorian Sensations: Essays on a Scandalous Genre*. Ohio State UP, 2006.

Hart, Matthew. *Nations of Nothing but Poetry: Modernism, Transnationalism, and Synthetic Vernacular Writing*. Oxford UP, 2010.

Hayden, Mary. "Women Citizens: Their Duties and Training." *Handbook of the Irish Revival: An Anthology of Irish Cultural and Political Writings 1891–1922*, edited by Declan Kiberd and P.J. Matthews, U of Notre Dame P, 2015, pp. 342–46.

Hechter, Michael. *Internal Colonialism: The Celtic Fringe in British National Development, 1536–1966*. U of California P, 1975.

Hegglund, Jon. *World Views: Metageographies of Modernist Fiction*. Oxford UP, 2012.

Hogan, Robert, and James Kilroy. *Laying the Foundations, 1902–1904*. The Dolman P, 1976.

———. *The Abbey Theater: The Years of Synge 1905–1909*. The Dolman P, 1978.

Hooper, John, and Tom Kington. "Amanda Knox freed after four years in case that has no winners." *Guardian*, 3 Oct. 2011.

Hopper, Keith. *Flann O'Brien: A Portrait of the Artist as a Young Post-Modernist*. Cork UP, 1995.

Howes, Marjorie. *Yeats's Nations: Gender, Class, and Irishness*. Cambridge UP, 2010.

Howes, Marjorie, and Joseph Valente. *Yeats and Afterwords*. U of Notre Dame P, 2014.

Hubert, Henri. *The Rise of the Celts*. Routledge, 1996.

Humphreys, Alexander J. *New Dubliners: Urbanization and the Irish Family*. Routledge & Kegan Paul, 1966.

Hutner, Heidi. *Colonial Women: Race and Culture in Stuart Drama*. Oxford UP, 2001.

Huyssen, Andreus. *After the Great Divide: Modernism, Mass Culture, Postmodernism*. Indiana UP, 1986.

Hyde, Douglas. *The Love Songs of Connacht*. T. Fisher Unwin, 1893.

———. "The Necessity for De-Anglicizing Ireland." *The Revival of Irish Literature*, edited by Sir Charles Gavin Duffy, George Sigerson, and Douglas Hyde, T. Fisher Unwin, 1894, pp. 117–61.

———. "A Plea for the Irish Language." *Language, Lore and Lyrics*, edited by Breandán Ó Conaire, Irish Academic P, 1986, pp. 74–80.

Jackson, Alvin. "Ireland, the Union, and the Empire, 1800–1960." *Ireland and the British Empire*, edited by Kevin Kenny, Oxford UP, 2004, pp. 123–53.

James, Lawrence. *Raj: The Making and Unmaking of British India*. St. Martin's P, 1997.

Jameson, Fredric. *Late Marxism: Adorno, or, the Persistence of the Dialectic*. Verso, 2007.

———. *The Political Unconscious: Narrative as a Socially Symbolic Act*. Cornell UP, 1981.

———. *Postmodernism, or, the Cultural Logic of Late Capitalism*. Duke UP, 1992.

JanMohamed, Abdul. "The Economy of Manichean Allegory: The Function of Racial Difference in Colonialist Literature." *"Race," Writing and Difference*, edited by Henry Louis Gates Jr., U of Chicago P, 1986.

Jay, Martin. *The Dialectical Imagination: A History of the Frankfurt School and the Institute of Social Research, 1923–1950*. U of California P, 1996.

Jay, Paul. *Global Matters: The Transnational Turn in Literary Studies*. Cornell UP, 2010.

Jeffery, Keith. "The Irish Military Tradition and the British Empire." *"An Irish Empire"?: Aspects of Ireland and the British Empire*, Manchester UP, 1996, pp. 94–122.

Johnston, Dillon. "Cross-Currencies in the Culture Market: Arnold, Yeats, Joyce." *The South Atlantic Quarterly* vol. 95, no. 1 (1996), pp. 45–78.

Joyce, James. "Araby." *Dubliners*, edited by Terence Brown, Penguin, 1992.

———. *Occasional, Critical, and Political Writings*. Oxford UP, 2000.

———. *A Portrait of the Artist as a Young Man*. Edited by Seamus Deane, Penguin, 1992.

———. *Ulysses*. Edited by Hans Walter Gabler, Vintage, 1986.

Kalliney, Peter. *Commonwealth of Letters: British Literary Culture and the Emergence of Postcolonial Aesthetics*. Oxford UP, 2013.

Kant, Immanuel. *Critique of the Power of Judgment*. Translated by Paul Guyer and Eric Matthews, Cambridge UP, 2001.

Keane, Damien. *Ireland and the Problem of Information: Irish Writing, Radio, Late Modernist Communication*. Penn State UP, 2014.

Kennedy, Sean, editor. *Beckett and Ireland*. Cambridge UP, 2010.

Kenny, Kevin. "The Irish in the Empire." *Ireland and the British Empire*, edited by Kevin Kenny, Oxford UP, 2004, pp. 90–122.

Kiberd, Declan. *Inventing Ireland: The Literature of the Modern Nation*. Vintage, 1996.

———. *Irish Classics*. Harvard UP, 2001.

———. *The Irish Writer and the World*. Cambridge UP, 2005.

———. *Synge and the Irish Language*. Rowman and Littlefield, 1979.

Kilroy, James. *The "Playboy" Riots*. The Dolman P, 1971.

Kingsley, Charles. *Charles Kingsley: His Letters and Memories of His Life*. Macmillan and Co., 1890.

Kipling, John Lockwood. "Kim and the Lama." *The Victorian Web: Literature, History, & Culture in the Age of Victoria*, scanned image and text by Jacqueline Banerjee, 23 Jan. 2017, www.victorianweb.org/victorian/art/illustration/kiplingjl/19.html.

"Kipling's Kim." *Academy*, vol. 61, July/December 1901, p. 289.

Kipling, Rudyard. "The Ballad of East and West." *Collected Verse of Rudyard Kipling*. Doubleday, Doran and Company, 1935, pp. 136–40.

———. *Kim*. Penguin, 1989.

———. "The White Man's Burden." *Collected Verse of Rudyard Kipling*. Doubleday, Doran and Company, 1935, pp. 215–16.

Kirby, Peadar, Luke Gibbons, and Michael Cronin, editors. *Reinventing Ireland: Culture, Society and the Global Economy*. Pluto P, 2002.

Krebs, Paula M. *Gender, Race, and the Writing of Empire: Public Discourse and the Boer War*. Cambridge UP, 1999.

Krishnamurth, Sailaja. "Reading Between the Lines: Geography and Hybridity in Rudyard Kipling's *Kim*." *Victorian Review*, vol. 28, no. 1, 2002, pp. 47–65.

Krishnan, Sanjay. *Reading the Global: Troubling Perspectives on Britain's Empire in Asia*. Columbia UP, 2007.

Larkin, Emmet. "Socialism and Catholicism in Ireland." *Studies: An Irish Quarterly Review*, vol. 74, no. 293, Spring 1985, pp. 66–92.

Lash, Scott, and Celia Curry. *Global Culture Industry: The Mediation of Things*. Polity, 2007.

Lawrence, D.H. *Fantasia of the Unconscious*. *Fantasia of the Unconscious and Psychoanalysis of the Unconscious*, Penguin, 1971.

———. *The Plumed Serpent*. Vintage, 1992.

———. "The Princess." *The Woman Who Rode Away/St. Mawr/The Princess*, Penguin, 2006, pp. 177–216.

———. *St. Mawr*. *The Woman Who Rode Away/St. Mawr/The Princess*, Penguin, 2006, pp. 39–176.

Lazarus, Neil. "The Fetish of 'the West' in Postcolonial Theory." *Marxism, Modernity, and Postcolonial Studies*, edited by Crystal Bartolovich and Neil Lazarus, Cambridge UP, 2002, pp. 43–65.

———. *The Postcolonial Unconscious*. Cambridge UP, 2011.

Lebow, Richard. *White Britain and Black Ireland: The Influence of Stereotypes on Colonial Policy*. Institute for the Study of Human Issues, 1976.

Lee, Joseph. *The Modernisation of Irish Society 1848–1918*. Gill and Macmillan, 1973.

Lenin, V.I. *Imperialism: the Highest Stage of Capitalism*. International Publishers, 1939.

Lennon, Joseph. *Irish Orientalism: A Literary and Intellectual History*. Syracuse UP, 2008.

Levenson, Michael. *A Genealogy of Modernism: A Study of English Literary Doctrine, 1908–1922*. Cambridge UP, 1986.

Lipsitz, George. "White Fear: O.J. Simpson and the Greatest Story Ever Sold." *The Possessive Investment in Whiteness*, Temple UP, 1998, pp. 99–117.

Livingston, Robert Eric. "Seeing Through Reading: Class, Race, and Literary Authority in Joseph Conrad's *The Nigger of the 'Narcissus'*." *NOVEL*, vol. 26, no. 2, Winter 1993, pp. 133–52.

Lloyd, David. *Anomalous States: Irish Writing and the Post-Colonial Moment*. Duke UP, 1993.

———. "Counterparts: Dubliners, Masculinity and Temperance Nationalism." *Semicolonial Joyce*, edited by Derek Attridge and Marjorie Howes, Cambridge UP, 2000, pp. 128–49.

———. *Ireland after History*. U of Notre Dame P, 1999.

———. *Irish Times: Temporalities of Modernity*. Field Day, 2008.

———. *Nationalism and Minor Literature*. U of California P, 1987.

Locke, John. *The Second Treatise of Civil Government*. Edited by Thomas Peardon, Bobbs-Merrill, 1952.

Loomba, Ania, Suvir Kaul, Matti Bunzl, Antoinette Burton, and Jed Esty, editors. *Postcolonial Studies and Beyond*. Duke UP, 2005.

Lukács, György. *History and Class Consciousness: Studies in Marxist Dialectics*. Translated by Rodney Livingstone, MIT P, 1971.

Lunn, Kenneth. "A Racialized Hierarchy of Labour? Race, Immigration, and the British Labour Movement, 1880–1950." *Racializing Class, Classifying Race: Labour and Difference in Britain, the USA and Africa*, edited by Peter Alexander and Rick Halpern, St. Martin's P, 2010, pp. 150–67.

"Lynchehaun at Large Again." *Connaught Telegraph* [Castlebar, Ireland], 13 Sept. 1902. *Irish Newspaper Archives*, irishnewsarchive.com.

Lyons, F.S.L. *Culture and Anarchy in Ireland 1890–1939*. Clarendon P, 1979.

———. *Ireland Since the Famine*. Weidenfeld and Nicolson, 1971.

MacDonagh, Oliver. *Ireland: The Union and Its Aftermath*. George Allan & Unwin, 1977.

Mandler, Peter. *The English National Character: The History of an Idea from Edmund Burke to Tony Blair*. Yale UP, 2006.

Manganero, Marc. *Culture, 1922: The Emergence of a Concept*. Princeton UP, 2002.

———. *Modernist Anthropology: From Fieldwork to Text*. Princeton UP, 1990.

Marshik, Celia, editor. *The Cambridge Companion to Modernist Culture*. Cambridge UP, 2014.

Martyn, Edward. "A Comparison Between English and Irish Theatrical Audiences." *Beltaine*, no. 2, 1900, pp. 11–13.

———. *Maeve. Selected Plays of George Moore and Edward Martyn*, edited by David B. Eakin and Michael Case, Colin Smythe, 1995, pp. 269–98.

Marx, Karl. *Capital: Volume I.* Penguin, 1990.

———. *Economic and Philosophic Manuscripts of 1844. The Marx-Engels Reader*, edited by Robert C. Tucker, W.W. Norton, 1978, pp. 66–125.

Matthews, P.J. *Revival: The Abbey Theatre, Sinn Fein, The Gaelic League and the Co-Operative Movement.* U of Notre Dame P, 2003.

Matz, Jesse. *Literary Impressionism and Modernist Aesthetics.* Cambridge UP, 2001.

Maunder, Andrew and Grace Moore, editors. *Victorian Crime, Madness and Sensation.* Ashgate, 2004.

McBratney, John. *Imperial Subjects, Imperial Space: Rudyard Kipling's Fiction of the Native Born.* Ohio State UP, 2004.

McCormack, W.J. *Ascendancy and Tradition in Anglo-Irish Literary History from 1789 to 1939.* Clarendon P, 1985.

McDiarmid, Lucy. *The Irish Art of Controversy.* Cornell UP, 2005.

McKee, Alexander. "Breaking the Habit: Samuel Beckett's Critique of Irish Ireland." *New Hibernia Review*, vol. 14, no. 1, 2010, pp. 42–58.

McLauchlin, Joseph. *Writing the Urban Jungle: Reading Empire in London from Doyle to Eliot.* UP of Virginia, 2000.

McMahon, Timothy G. *Grand Opportunity: The Gaelic Revival and Irish Society, 1893–1910.* Syracuse UP, 2008.

Memmi, Alberto. *The Colonizer and the Colonized.* Beacon P, 1965.

Messenger, Nigel. "'We did not want to lose him': Jimmy Wait as a Figure of Abjection in Conrad's *The Nigger of the 'Narcissus'*." *Critical Survey*, vol. 13, no. 1, 2001, pp. 62–80.

Miller, Tyrus. *Late Modernism: Politics, Fiction, and the Arts Between the World Wars.* U of California P, 1999.

Milligan, Alice. "Industrial Ireland." *Shan Van Vocht*, vol. 3, no. 2, 7 Nov. 1898.

Millotte, Mike. *Communism in Modern Ireland: The Pursuit of the Worker's Republic since 1916.* Gill and Macmillan, 1984.

Moore, George. "Is the Theatre a Place of Amusement?" *Beltaine*, no. 2, 1900, pp. 7–10.

———. "Literature and the Irish Language." *Ideals in Ireland*, edited by Lady Gregory, Unicorn, 1901, pp. 45–54.

Moran, D.P. "The Battle of Two Civilizations." *The Philosophy of Irish Ireland*, edited by Patrick Maume, University College Dublin P, 2006, pp. 94–114.

———. "The Future of the Irish Nation." *The Philosophy of Irish Ireland*, edited by Patrick Maume, University College Dublin P, 2006, pp. 11–31.

———. "The Gaelic Revival." *The Philosophy of Irish Ireland*, edited by Patrick Maume, University College Dublin P, 2006, pp. 73–93.

———. "Is the Irish Nation Dying?" *The Philosophy of Irish Ireland*, edited by Patrick Maume, University College Dublin P, 2006, pp. 1–10.

———. "The Pale and the Gael." *The Philosophy of Irish Ireland*, edited by Patrick Maume, University College Dublin P, 2006, pp. 32–51.

———. "Statement of Principles." *The Philosophy of Irish Ireland*, edited by Patrick Maume, University College Dublin P, 2006, pp. 115–20.

Moretti, Franco. *Signs Taken for Wonders: On the Sociology of Literary Forms*. New Left Books, 1983.

Morin, Emilie. *Samuel Beckett and the Problem of Irishness*. Palgrave MacMillan, 2009.

Mullin, Katherine. *James Joyce, Sexuality and Social Purity*. Cambridge UP, 2003.

Nagai, Kaori. *Empire of Analogies: Kipling, India and Ireland*. Cork UP, 2006.

Nelson, Bruce. *Irish Nationalists and the Making of the Irish Race*. Princeton UP, 2012.

Nietzsche, Friedrich. *The Birth of Tragedy*. Dover, 1995.

———. *The Antichrist*. Translated by H.L. Mencken, Alfred A. Knopf, 1920.

Nilsen, Alf Gunvald. "Passages from Marxism to Postcolonialism: A Comment on Vivek Chibber's *Postcolonial Theory and the Specter of Capital*." *Critical Sociology*, vol. 34, no. 4–5, 2015, pp. 559–71.

Nolan, Emer. *James Joyce and Nationalism*. Routledge: 1995.

North, Michael. *Camera Works: Photography and the Twentieth-Century Word*. Oxford UP, 2007.

———. *The Dialect of Modernism: Race, Language and Twentieth-Century Literature*. Oxford UP, 1994.

———. *Machine-Age Comedy*. Oxford UP, 2008.

———. *The Political Aesthetic of Yeats, Eliot, and Pound*. Cambridge UP, 2010.

———. *Reading 1922: A Return to the Scene of the Modern*. Oxford UP, 2001.

"Objects of Inghinidhe na hÉireann (Daughters of Ireland)." *Handbook of the Irish Revival: An Anthology of Irish Cultural and Political Writings 1891–1922*, edited by Declan Kiberd and P.J. Matthews, U of Notre Dame P, 2015, pp. 92–93.

O'Brien, Flann. *At Swim-Two-Birds*. Dalkey Archive P, 1951.

"O'Brien Coin Guide: Irish Pre-Decimal Ten Shillings." *The Old Currency Exchange*, 27 June 2017, oldcurrencyexchange.com/2016/03/27/obrien-coin-guide-irish-pre-decimal-ten-shillings/.

Ó Cadhla, Stiofán. *Civilizing Ireland: Ordnance Survey 1824–1842*. Irish Academic P, 2007.

O'Connor, Laura. *Haunted English: The Celtic Fringe, the British Empire, and De-Anglicization*. Johns Hopkins UP, 2006.

O'Donnell, F. Hugh. "Souls for Gold: A Pseudo-Celtic Drama in Dublin." *Our Irish Theatre: A Chapter of Autobiography*, Lady Gregory, Colin Smythe, 1972, Appendix VIII.

———. *The Stage Irishman of the Pseudo-Celtic Drama*. John Long, 1904.

O'Grada, Cormac. *Ireland: A New Economic History 1780–1939*. Clarendon P, 1994.

Oram, Hugh. *The Advertising Book: The History of Advertising in Ireland*. MO Books, 1986.

Orem, William. "Corpse-Chewers: The Vampire in *Ulysses*." *James Joyce Quarterly*, vol. 49, no. 1, 2011, pp. 57–72.

Osteen, Mark. *The Economy of Ulysses: Making Both Ends Meet*. Syracuse UP, 1995.

Parry, Benita. *Conrad and Imperialism*. The MacMillan P, 1983.

———. "Liberation Theory: Variations on the Themes of Marxism and Modernity." *Marxism, Modernity, and Postcolonial Studies*, edited by Crystal Bartolovich and Neil Lazarus, Cambridge UP, 2002, pp. 125–49.

———. *Postcolonial Studies: A Materialist Critique*. Routledge, 2004.

Pearson, Nels. *Irish Cosmopolitanism: Location and Dislocation in James Joyce, Elizabeth Bowen, and Samuel Beckett*. UP of Florida, 2015.

Peart, Sandra J. and Donald M. Levy. "Not an Average Human Being: How Economics Succumbed to Racial Accounts of Economic Man." *Race, Liberalism and Economics*, edited by David Colander, Robert E. Prasch, and Falguni A. Sheth, U of Michigan P, 2004, pp. 123–44.

Pecora, Vincent P. "Arnoldian Ethnology." *Victorian Studies*, vol. 41, no. 3, 1998, pp. 355–79.

Perloff, Marjorie. "'Easter, 1916': Yeats's First World War Poem." *The Oxford Handbook of British and Irish War Poetry*, Oxford UP, 2007, pp. 227–45.

Peters, John G. *Conrad and Impressionism*. Cambridge UP, 2001.

Pittock, Murray. *Celtic Identity and the British Image*. Manchester UP, 1999.

Platt, Len. *Joyce and the Anglo-Irish: A Study of Joyce and the Literary Revival*. Rodopi, 1998.

———, editor. *Modernism and Race*. Cambridge: Cambridge UP, 2011.

Plunkett, Sir Horace. *Ireland in the New Century*. Kennikat P, 1904.

Poovey, Mary. *Making a Social Body: British Cultural Formation, 1830–1864*. U of Chicago P, 1995.

———. *Uneven Developments: The Ideological Work of Gender in Mid-Victorian England*. U of Chicago P, 1988.

Postone, Moishe. *Time, Labor and Social Domination: A Reinterpretation of Marx's Critical Theory*. Cambridge UP, 1993.

Quigley, Mark. *Empire's Wake: Postcolonial Irish Writing and the Politics of Modern Literary Form*. Fordham UP, 2013.

Ragussis, Michael. *Figures of Conversion: "The Jewish Question" and English National Identity*. Duke UP, 1995.

Ramazani, Jahan. *A Transnational Poetics*. U of Chicago P, 2015.

Redmond, Eugene. "Racism, or Realism? Literary Apartheid, or Poetic License? Conrad's Burden in *The Nigger of the 'Narcissus'*." *The Nigger of the "Narcissus,"* edited by Richard Kimbrough, W.W. Norton & Co., 1979, pp. 358–69.

Reitz, Caroline. *Detecting the Nation: Fictions of Detection and Imperial Venture*. Ohio State UP, 2004.

Renan, Ernest. *The Poetry of the Celtic Races and other Studies*. Translated by William G. Hutchison, W. Scott, 1896.

Reynolds, Mairead. *A History of the Irish Post Office*. MacDonnell Whyte, 1983.

Reynolds, Paige. *Modernism, Drama, and the Audience for Irish Spectacle*. Cambridge UP, 2008.

Richards, David Alan. "Early Editions of Kim." *The Kipling Society*. www.kiplingsociety.co.uk/members/paper_richardskim.htm. Accessed 22 June 2020.

Richards, Shaun. "The Playboy of the Western World." *The Cambridge Companion to J.M. Synge*, edited by P.J. Matthews, Cambridge UP, 2009, pp. 28–40.

Richards, Thomas. *The Commodity Culture of Victorian England*. U of Virginia P, 1998.

———. *The Imperial Archive: Knowledge and the Fantasy of Empire*. Verso, 1993.

Ricketts, Harry. *Rudyard Kipling: A Life*. Carroll & Graff, 1999.

Robinson, Tim. "Place, Person, Book: Synge's *The Aran Islands*." *The Aran Islands*, J.M. Synge, Penguin, 1992, pp. vii–l.

Roediger, David. *The Wages of Whiteness: Race and the Making of the American Working Class*. Verso, 1991.

Rose, Lloyd. "Cave Canem Nocte: The Folkloric Origins of *The Hound of the Baskervilles*." *Baker Street Journal: An Irregular Quarterly of Sherlockania*, vol. 26, no. 3, 1976, pp. 154–56.

Roughead, William. *Enjoyment of Murder*. Sheridan House, 1938.

Rolleston, T.W. *Imagination and Art in Gaelic Literature*. Dublin: Kilkenny, 1900.

Ross, Stephen. "*The Nigger of the 'Narcissus'* and Modernist Haunting." *Novel*, vol. 44, no. 2, 2011, pp. 268–91.

Rubenstein, Michael. *Public Works: Infrastructure, Irish Modernism, and the Postcolonial*. U of Notre Dame P, 2010.

Said, Edward. *Culture and Imperialism*. Vintage, 1993.

———. "Introduction." *Kim*. Rudyard Kipling. Penguin, 1989, pp. 7–46.

———. *Orientalism*. Vintage, 1978.

Saint-Amour, Paul K. "Weak Theory, Weak Modernism." *Modernism/Modernity*, vol. 25, no. 3, 2018, pp. 437–59.

San Juan, E. Jr. "Postcolonialism and the Problematic of Uneven Development." *Marxism, Modernity, and Postcolonial Studies*, edited by Crystal Bartolovich and Neil Lazarus, Cambridge UP, 2002, pp. 221–39.

Schiller, Arthur. *On the Aesthetic Education of Man*. Edited and translated by Elizabeth M. Wilkinson and L.A. Willoughby, Clarendon P, 1967.

Schmid, David. *Natural Born Celebrities: Serial Killers in American Culture*. U of Chicago P, 2005.

Seshagiri, Urmila. *Race and the Modernist Imagination*. Cornell UP, 2010.

Shaw, George Bernard. *John Bull's Other Island*. *Modern Irish Drama*. Edited by John P. Harrington, W.W. Norton & Co., 1991, pp. 119–203.

———. "Preface for Politicians." *Modern Irish Drama*, edited by John P. Harrington, W.W. Norton & Co., 1991.

Sherry, Vincent. "T.S. Eliot, Late Empire, and Decadence." *Modernism and Colonialism: British and Irish Literature, 1899–1939*. Duke UP, 2007, pp. 111–35.

Shih, Shu-mei, and Françoise Lionnet, editors. *Minor Transnationalism*. Duke UP, 2005.

Sinha, Subir, and Rashmi Varma, "Marxism and Postcolonial Theory: What's Left of the Debate." *Critical Sociology*, vol. 34, no. 4–5, 2015, pp. 545–58.

Smith, Neil. *Uneven Development: Nature, Capital, and the Production of Space*. U of Georgia P, 2008.

"Some Irish Industries." *Irish Homestead Special*. Dublin: 1897.

Spivak, Gayatri Chakravorty. *An Aesthetic Education in the Era of Globalization*. Harvard UP, 2013.

———. "Can the Subaltern Speak?" *Marxism and the Interpretation of Culture*, edited by Cary Nelson and Lawrence Grossberg, U of Illinois P, 1988.

———. *A Critique of Postcolonial Reason: Toward a History of the Vanishing Present*. Harvard UP, 1999.

———. "Postcolonial Theory and the Specter of Capital." *Cambridge Review of International Affairs*, vol. 27, no. 1, 2014, pp. 184–98.

Stashower, Daniel. *Teller of Tales: The Life of Arthur Conan Doyle*. Henry Holt and Company, 1999.

Stephens, James. *The Charwoman's Daughter*. Dodo P, 2009.

Stocking, George. *Race, Culture, and Evolution: Essays in the History of Anthropology*. U of Chicago P, 1982.

———. *Victorian Anthropology*. The Free Press, 1987.

Sullivan, Zohreh. *Narratives of Empire: The Fictions of Rudyard Kipling*. Cambridge UP, 1993.

*Supernaught.com*. n.p. 1 April 2012.

Sweeney, Frank. *The Murder of Connell Boyle, County Donegal, 1898*. Four Courts P, 2002.

Synge, J.M. *The Aran Islands*. Penguin, 1992.

———. *The Playboy of the Western World. The Complete Plays of John M. Synge*, Vintage Books, 1935, pp. 1–80.

Tabili, Laura. *"We Ask for British Justice": Workers and Racial Difference in Late Imperial Britain*. Cornell UP, 1994.

Taylor, Charles. "Two Theories of Modernity." *Alternative Modernities*. Duke UP, 2001, pp. 172–96.

Taylor-Ide, Jesse Oak. "Ritual and the Liminality of Sherlock Holmes in *The Sign of Four* and *The Hound of the Baskervilles*." *English Literature in Transition*, vol. 48, no. 1, 2005, pp. 55–70.

Thompson, E.P. "Time, Work-Discipline and Industrial Capitalism." *Past and Present*, vol. 38, no. 1, 1967, pp. 56–97.

Torgovnick, Marianna. *Gone Primitive: Savage Intellects, Modern Lives*. U of Chicago P, 1990.

Trotsky, Leon. *The History of the Russian Revolution*. Translated by Max Eastman, U of Michigan P, 1957.

Valdez Moses, Michael. "Disorientalism: Conrad and the Imperial Origins of Modernist Aesthetics." *Modernism and Colonialism: British and Irish Literature, 1899–1939*, Duke UP, 2007, pp. 43–70.

Valente, Joseph. *James Joyce and the Problem of Justice*. Cambridge UP, 1995.

———. *The Myth of Manliness in Irish National Culture*. U of Illinois P, 2011.

———. "Neither Fish nor Flesh: How 'Cyclops' Stages the Double Bind of Irish Manhood." *Semicolonial Joyce*, Cambridge UP, 2000, pp. 96–127.

———. "The Novel and the Police (Gazette)." *NOVEL: A Forum on Fiction*, vol. 21, no. 1, 1995, pp. 8–18.

Vendler, Helen. *Our Secret Discipline: Yeats and Lyric Form*. Harvard UP: 2007.

Waddell, L.A. *The Phoenician Origin of Britons, Scots, & Anglo-Saxons*. Williams and Norgate, 1924.

Walkowitz, Rebecca. *Cosmopolitan Style: Modernism Beyond the Nation*. Columbia UP, 2006.

Walkowitz, Rebecca, and Douglas Mao. *Bad Modernisms*. Duke UP, 2006.

Watson, G.J. *Irish Identity and the Literary Revival: Synge, Yeats, Joyce and O'Casey*. Catholic U of America P, 1994.

Watson, Tim. "Indian and Irish Unrest in Kipling's *Kim*." *Postcolonial Theory and Criticism*, edited by Laura Chrisman and Benita Parry, D.S. Brewer, 2000, pp. 95–113.

Watt, Ian. *Conrad in the Nineteenth Century*. U of California P, 1979.

Watts, Cedric. "Introduction." *The Nigger of the "Narcissus,"* edited by Cedric Watts, Penguin, 1988, pp. xi–xxx.

Weber, Max. *The Protestant Ethic and the Spirit of Capitalism*. Translated by Talcott Parsons, Charles Scriber's Sons, 1958.

Wegner, Phillip. "'Life as He Would Have It': The Invention of India in Kipling's *Kim*." *Cultural Critique*, vol. 26, Winter 1993–94, pp. 129–59.

Weygandt, Cornelius. *Irish Plays and Playwrights*. Houghton Mifflin Company, 1913.

Whelan, John R. "Literature and Irish Nationality." *Shan Van Vocht*, vol. 2, no. 13, 8 Jan. 1897, pp. 10–12.

Wicke, Jennifer A. *Advertising Fictions: Literature, Advertisement, and Social Reading*. Columbia UP, 1988.

Wilde, Oscar. "The Decay of Lying." *The Artist as Critic: Critical Writings of Oscar Wilde*, edited by Richard Ellmann, Random House, 1968.

———. "Preface." *The Picture of Dorian Gray*, Norton Critical Edition, 2003.

Williams, Daniel. *Ethnicity and Cultural Authority from Arnold to Du Bois*. Edinburgh UP, 2006.

Williams, Raymond. *Culture and Society: 1780–1950*. Columbia UP, 1983.

Wilson, David. *A History of British Serial Killing: The Shocking Account of Jack the Ripper, Harold Shipman and Beyond*. Sphere, 2009.

Winkiel, Laura. *Modernism, Race, and Manifestos*. Cambridge UP, 2008.

Wood, Ellen Meiksens. *Empire of Capital*. Verso, 2003.

Wright, Julia M. *Ireland, India and Nationalism in Nineteenth-Century Literature*. Cambridge UP, 2007.

Wynne, Catherine. *Colonial Conan Doyle: British Imperialism, Irish Nationalism and the Gothic*. Greenwood P, 2002.

Yeats, W.B. *Cathleen ni Houlihan. The Collected Plays of W.B. Yeats*, Macmillan, 1953, pp. 49–58.

———. "The Celtic Element in Literature." *Essays and Introductions*, Collier Books, 1961, pp. 173–88.

———. *The Celtic Twilight. Mythologies*. Collier Books, 1959, pp. 1–144.

———. "The Controversy over the Playboy." *Uncollected Prose, Vol. 2: Reviews, Articles, and Other Miscellaneous Prose, 1897–1939*, edited by John P. Frayne and Colton Johnson, Columbia UP, 1976, pp. 348–52.

———. *The Death of Cuchulain. The Collected Plays of W.B. Yeats*, Macmillan, 1934, pp. 437–46.

———. "The Dramatic Movement." *Samhain 1904. Explorations*, MacMillan & Co., 1962, pp. 124–40.

———. "Easter, 1916." *The Collected Poems of W.B. Yeats*, edited by Richard J. Finneran, Simon & Schuster, 1996, pp. 180–82.

———. "Edmund Spenser." *Essays and Introductions*, Collier Books, 1961, pp. 356–86.

———. "First Principles." *Samhain 1908. Explorations*, MacMillan, 1962, pp. 231–43.

———. "Ireland, 1921–1931." *Uncollected Prose, Volume 2: Reviews, Articles and Other Miscellaneous Prose, 1897–1939*, edited by J.P. Frayne and C. Johnson, pp. 486–90.

———. *The Land of Heart's Desire. The Collected Plays of W.B. Yeats*, Macmillan, 1953, pp. 33–48.

———. "Literature and the Living Voice." *Samhain 1906. Explorations*, MacMillan, 1962, pp. 202–21.

———. *Memoirs*. Edited by Denis Donaghue, Macmillan, 1972.

———. "Moral and Immoral Plays." *Samhain 1903. Explorations*, MacMillan, 1962, pp. 111–13.

———. "Nationality and Literature." *Uncollected Prose. 1: First Reviews and Articles, 1886–1896*, Columbia UP, pp. 266–75.

———. *Purgatory. The Collected Plays of W.B. Yeats*, Macmillan, 1934.

———. *Samhain 1901. Explorations*, MacMillan & Co., 1962, pp. 73–84.

———, editor. *Fairy and Folk Tales of Ireland*. Gerrards Cross and Colin Smythe, 1988.

Young, Robert J.C. *Colonial Desire: Hybridity in Theory, Culture and Race*. Routledge, 1995.

# INDEX

CPSIA information can be obtained
at www.ICGtesting.com
Printed in the USA
LVHW020111090721
692195LV00004B/339